PROTECTING THE WORLD'S CHILDREN

Protecting the World's Children: Impact of the Convention on the Rights of the Child in Diverse Legal Systems is a review of the ways in which the Convention on the Rights of the Child (CRC) has been incorporated into national legislation around the world. It comprises four studies that compare experiences from countries with different types of legal traditions, highlighting common characteristics, developments and trends as a basis for the work of practitioners in this area. The book provides examples of ways in which the CRC has been successfully incorporated into diverse legal systems and derives from that experience a framework for improved alignment of national legislation with human rights instruments and with the CRC in particular, taking into account not only the provisions of the CRC but also its underlying principles, such as indivisibility of rights and the importance of partnership in realizing children's rights. As such it provides practitioners with a tool for supporting the legal aspects of implementation of the CRC as a foundation for implementation overall.

UNICEF has brought together leading jurists with expertise in different legal systems to produce *Protecting the World's Children: Impact of the Convention on the Rights of the Child in Diverse Legal Systems*. UNICEF works in 191 countries through country programmes and national committees to uphold the Convention on the Rights of the Child and the achievement of the Millennium Development Goals.

Protecting the World's Children

IMPACT OF THE
CONVENTION ON THE RIGHTS OF THE CHILD
IN DIVERSE LEGAL SYSTEMS

UNICEF

CAMBRIDGE UNIVERSITY PRESS
Cambridge, New York, Melbourne, Madrid, Cape Town, Singapore, São Paulo, Delhi

Cambridge University Press
32 Avenue of the Americas, New York, NY 10013-2473, USA

www.cambridge.org
Information on this title: www.cambridge.org/9780521875134

UNICEF
3 UN Plaza, New York, NY 10017
www.unicef.org

First published 2007

Printed in the United States of America

A catalog record for this publication is available from the British Library.

Library of Congress Cataloging in Publication Data

Protecting the world's children : impact of the Convention on the Rights
of the Child in diverse legal systems / UNICEF.
   p. cm.
Includes bibliographical references and index.
ISBN-13: 978-0-521-87513-4 (hardback)
ISBN-10: 0-521-87513-7 (hardback)
1. Children – Legal status, laws, etc. 2. Children (International law)
3. Convention on the Rights of the Child (1989) I. UNICEF. II. Title.
K639.P75   2007
342.08'772 – dc22   2006035204

ISBN   978-0-521-87513-4 hardback

The views and opinions expressed in this book are those of the author
of the relevant chapter and do not necessarily reflect the positions and
policies of UNICEF.

Contents

v

Acknowledgements

This initiative would not have been possible without the remarkable drive of Savitri Goonesekere, Emilio García Méndez, Rebeca Rios-Kohn, and Shaheen Sardar Ali, the contributors to this book, as well as the commitment of Elizabeth Gibbons, Chief of the Global Policy Section in UNICEF, Division of Policy and Planning.

Warm words of appreciation are addressed to Saad Houry, Director of the Division of Policy and Planning, for supporting this endeavour.

Special thanks go to the following UNICEF country offices, which enthusiastically embraced and participated in this initiative: Armenia, Azerbaijan, Barbados, Benin, Botswana, Burkina Faso, Dominican Republic, Ghana, Jamaica, Jordan, Mauritania, Morocco and Zimbabwe. In particular, we would like to express our gratitude to Jean Gough, UNICEF Deputy Regional Director in Latin America and the Caribbean (TACRO), and UNICEF Representatives Bertrand Bainvel, Souleymane Diallo, Philippe Duamelle, Joan French, Festo Kavishe, Maie Ayoub von Kohl, Ruth Leano, Gordon Jonathan Lewis, Tad Palac, Dorothy Rozga, Hanaa Singer and Anne Skatvedt whose support of the process has been outstanding.

Preparation of this book was aided by a series of country case studies prepared by experts on children's rights from various parts of the world. These are Humay Afandunjeva, Mohammad Al-Quda, Mary Bellof, Myriam Claudine, Fortune Dako, Candis Hamilton, Leighton Jackson, Garton Kamchedzera, Hayk Khemchyan, Yabiyuré Konsimbo, Ana Gena Martinez, Rihab Qaddoumi, Kofi Quashigah, Tracy Robinson, Abderrahmane Yessa and Michelle Zerrari. We would like to express our special thanks to these experts.

Many UNICEF staff members and experts provided extremely useful comments and suggestions and generously reviewed the different drafts. In particular, we would like to thank Maria Asuad, Veronica Avati, Naira Avetisyan, Rajae Berrada, Tewabech Bishaw, Susan Bissell, Monica Canafoglia, Candie Cassabalian, Jay Chaubey, Enrique Delamonica, Beatrice Duncan, Radhika Gore, Maha Homsi, Brahim Ould Isselmou, Noreen Khan, Fode Konde, Geoffrey Ljumba, Muriel Mafico, Siraj Mahmudov, Nada Marasovic, Rhea Saab, Saudamini Siegrist, and Heather Stewart.

This initiative also benefited greatly from the invaluable counsel and support of Marta Santos Pais, Director of UNICEF, Innocenti Research Centre and of Peter Mason and Patricia Moccia from UNICEF Headquarters.

Our sincere appreciation to Akila Belembaogo, then Head of the Gender Equality and Human Rights Unit in UNICEF's Global Policy Section, for her able and full support to this project.

Many thanks are due to the management team for this project, particularly to Nadine Perrault and Vanessa Sedletzki, whose commitment and dedication have contributed to making this project a reality.

We also gratefully acknowledge the financial support provided by DFID.

Foreword

In 2000, with the adoption of the Millennium Declaration, nearly 200 nations pledged to promote respect for human rights and to endeavour to protect and promote the full spectrum of rights in their territories.

As then Secretary-General Kofi Annan notes in a foreword to UNICEF's *State of the World's Children Report 2005*, "Only as we move closer to realizing the rights of all children will countries move closer to their goals of development and peace."

The Millennium Development Goals (MDGs) – which include eradicating extreme poverty and hunger, achieving universal primary education, promoting gender equality and reducing child mortality – provide a solid foundation upon which countries can build an environment that stimulates social justice, equity, liberty, development and good governance. Among those committed to advancing the best interests of children in the context of the MDGs, legislative reforms have been of particular interest.

Legislative reform not only advances progress toward the MDGs, but it is also needed to support their achievement. Both the adoption and the effective implementation of laws and policies to protect children; promote their survival, education and development; eliminate inequalities and promote gender equality and the empowerment of women are critical to help meet the MDGs.

Indeed, there are clear signs in many parts of the world that governments are paying serious attention to the structural and legal barriers that threaten children's well-being. Laws and regulations are being reviewed and amended; constitutions are being changed. Evidence has confirmed that legislative reform is critical to addressing discrimination and alleviating poverty. Improved legal and policy frameworks are improving education rates and maternal health, reducing child mortality, combating diseases and promoting environmental sustainability. Legislative reform is helping to establish the accessible, competent and effective institutions necessary for achieving good governance and results for children.

This is not to say that there is not still work to be done. In order for legislative change to pass from rhetoric into practice, we must significantly change our approach for children. Otherwise, we will not fully realize measurable improvements in their lives. For example, as we lead the fight against under-five mortality and HIV/AIDS, or ensure access to education, we also must support the establishment of appropriate legal frameworks. At the same time, we should be advocating for the institutions, budget allocations and economic and social policies that also are needed.

All of these elements work together to advance the survival, development and protection of the world's children. And all of them are necessary to achieve meaningful results and move closer to reaching our shared ambition of a world that is truly fit for children.

Ann M. Veneman
Executive Director of UNICEF

Contributors

Savitri Goonesekere, a national of Sri Lanka, is Professor of Law Emeritus at the University of Colombo, Sri Lanka. Professor Goonesekere was previously Professor of Law and Vice Chancellor of the university. She also was a member of Sri Lanka's University Grants Commission, National Education Commission, the National Committee on Women, and the National Committee on the Rights of the Child. She has held Visiting Fellowships at the School of Oriental and African Studies, University of London UK, UNICEF International Child Development Centre (now Innocenti Research Centre) Italy, and also in the Human Rights Programme at Harvard Law School. Professor Goonesekere is currently a member of the boards of several international and regional non-governmental organizations. She has written several books and published articles and chapters in books in the areas of comparative family law, human rights, law and development with a focus on women's and children's rights, and legal history. Her major publications include the *Sri Lankan Law on Parent and Child* (1987), *Child Labour in Sri Lanka: Learning from the Past* (ILO, 1993), *Children Law and Justice: A South Asian Perspective* (1998), and *Muslim Personal Law in Sri Lanka* (2000). She also has edited and contributed as author to the book *Violence, Law and Women's Rights in South Asia* (2004).

Professor Goonesekere acts regularly as a consultant for a range of international bodies and as an advisor to several UN agencies and to the Commonwealth Secretariat in London on areas of human rights, including women's and children's rights, and law and development. Professor Goonesekere has represented Sri Lanka at a number of international forums. She was a member of the UN Committee on the Elimination of All Forms of Discrimination against Women (1999–2001) and Chairperson of the Asian Development Bank External Forum on Gender (2003–2005).

Rebeca Rios-Kohn, a national of Uruguay, was educated in the United States, where she received a Juris Doctor from T.C. Williams Law School, University of Richmond, Virginia (1981). Admitted to practice law in Virginia and New York, she began her career as an attorney. In light of her deep interest in human development, in 1983 she joined International Planned Parenthood Federation (WHR), concentrating on population policy issues in the Latin American and Caribbean region. Beginning in 1989, she worked for

UNICEF, where she held several positions that focused on promoting the implementation of the Convention on the Rights of the Child and providing policy advice on human rights. Ms. Rios-Kohn joined UNDP in 1998 as Principal Adviser on Human Rights, where she engaged in a wide range of activities that aimed to integrate human rights with human development. She has written a number of articles on the rights of the child that were published in US law journals.

More recently, she has carried out a number of case studies for UNICEF and UNDP, including *Peru Case Study: A Human Rights Approach* (UNICEF, 2002), *Human Rights-Based Programming in Mali* (UNICEF, 2002), and *Human Rights-Based Programming in Jordan* (UNICEF, 2003). Ms. Rios-Kohn currently works as an international consultant on human rights and human development for a range of organizations.

Emilio García Méndez, a national of Argentina, is the Chair of Criminology University of Buenos Aires. He has a law degree from the University of Buenos Aires (1974). Professor García Méndez obtained his Ph.D. in law at the University of Saarland, Germany (1984). He was a researcher in the field of criminology and juvenile delinquency at the United Nations Interregional Crime and Justice Research Institute (UNSDRI) in Rome (1985–1990), and worked for UNICEF in Brazil (1990–1993). Professor García Méndez was UNICEF's Regional Advisor on Child Rights for Latin American and the Caribbean from 1993 to 1999. His main field of work is child rights with special reference to juvenile justice. His main publications include *Infancia, Ley y Democracia en América Latina, Derecho de la Infancia Adolescencia en América Latina,* and *Adolescents and Penal Responsibility* (Ad-Hoc, 2001).

Professor García Méndez is a Guest Professor at the Faculty of Law, University of Buenos Aires. Professor García Méndez consults, independently, for different national and international organizations, namely, UNICEF, ILO, the Inter-American Institute for Human Rights, San Jose de Costa Rica, the Inter-American Institute for Children, and the Organization of Inter-American States – Montevideo, Uruguay. He is currently the President of the Sur-Argentina Foundation – Child Rights and Human Rights.

Shaheen Sardar Ali, Ph.D., is a Professor of Law at the University of Warwick and Professor II, Department of Public Law, University of Oslo. She was formerly Professor of Law, University of Peshawar, Pakistan. Her teaching and research interests include Islamic law and jurisprudence, international law of human rights and in particular women's human rights, children's rights, public international law, gender and the law, constitutional theory and alternate dispute resolution. She has written a number of articles on human rights and Islamic law. Some of her more recent publications include two monographs: *Gender and Human Rights in Islam and International Law: Equal Before Allah, Unequal Before Man?* (Kluwer Law International, 2000) and *Indigenous Peoples and Ethnic Minorities of Pakistan* (NIAS/Curzon Press, 2002, with J. Rehman).

Professor Ali regularly acts as a consultant for a range of international bodies and has represented Pakistan at a number of international forums. She was a member of the National Commission of Inquiry on Women as well as the Prime Minister's Consultative Committee on Women in Pakistan. Professor Ali also has served as Minister for Health, Population Welfare and Women's Development in the Government of the North West Frontier Province (Pakistan), and chaired the National Commission on the Status of Women of Pakistan. She is one of the founding members and coordinator of the South Asian Research Network on Gender, Law and Governance (ARG).

Protecting the World's Children

IMPACT OF THE CONVENTION ON THE RIGHTS OF THE CHILD IN DIVERSE LEGAL SYSTEMS

Savitri Goonesekere

The Convention on the Rights of the Child (CRC) was adopted by the United Nations in 1989. It was the only international human rights Convention that came into force (on 2 September 1990) just one year after adoption. It is also the only Convention whose entry into force was accompanied by a major world conference that focused on implementation of the rights guaranteed by the treaty. A World Summit for Children of Heads of State gathered in New York at the end of September 1990, and adopted a Summit Declaration with specific goals and targets on implementation. Children, up to then the most invisible segment of society in the area of international human rights law, now had a Convention that was actually combined with a 'World Plan of Action', with goals and targets on implementation to be achieved within the next decade. One commitment in the Summit Declaration was universal ratification of the Convention by the beginning of a new millennium in 2000.

The United Nations Children's Fund (UNICEF) played a major role in the Summit meeting, and initiated a process that helped to ensure that the CRC was ratified by all countries, except Somalia and the United States of America, by 2000. Both Somalia and the United States have signed the treaty and thus indicated their intention to ratify. However, to date Somalia does not have an established government, and the United States has, up to now, failed to ratify the Convention. This near-universal ratification within just a decade is unique in the history of a human rights treaty. The Convention on the Elimination of All Forms of Discrimination against Women (CEDAW), for instance, was adopted by the United Nations in 1979. It took a decade and a half, up to the time of the World Conference on Women (1995), for wide ratification of the treaty. It has almost achieved near universal ratification only as recently as in 2005.

The CRC is sometimes perceived in Asian and African countries, and even by some scholars in the West, as a Convention that originated in the West and articulated the legal norms and values on children that had evolved in the West.[1] This is a correct perception, as there was a noticeable absence of participation from other regions in the early stages of the drafting of the Convention, although participation was broadened later. Some articles such as those on adoption (Article 20) and on the role of the extended family (Article 5) thus reflect some of the concerns of the Asian and African regions. In addition, the Convention benefited from the developments that had taken place in international human rights law and integrated core concepts on the universality and indivisibility of human rights. The CRC therefore does not adopt a completely culturally relativist approach but sets out, in general, universal standards and norms of achievements. Civil and political rights and socio-economic rights are included as equally important rights. Significantly, the Convention focuses on implementation and monitoring of children's rights through adequate allocation of national resources and cooperation and solidarity among the State, families and communities, civil society, and the international community. The concept of 'evolving capacity' as a child grows from childhood to adolescence, and the definition of childhood in terms of an upper limit of 18 years, also focus on children's participation in implementing these norms and on monitoring performance.

The CRC describes a range of interventions to implement rights and sets out the core obligation "to take appropriate legislative, administrative and other measures" to implement the rights guaranteed by the Convention.[2] Using law and the legal systems is therefore basic to implementation.

Although UNICEF played a less significant role than many other child rights organizations in the actual drafting of the Convention, UNICEF is referred to specifically as a key agency in implementation and monitoring, in Article 43 of the CRC. UNICEF's traditional focus has been on those areas of the Convention that cover health, nutrition and education, or development rights. Even the Summit Declaration and World Plan of Action focused almost exclusively on the development rights of children in the Convention. Apart from contributing to the near-universal ratification of the Convention, UNICEF in the post-CRC period worked with new partners at the national and international levels on politically sensitive controversial issues. Child labour, sexual exploitation and abuse, female infanticide, genital mutilation, forced marriage and discrimination against the girl child became the focus of many programmes. Legislation and the legal system, the traditional strategies used to prevent violation of rights, received attention in campaigns on these

---

[1] P. Alston, ed., *The Best Interests of the Child* (Oxford: Clarendon Press, 1994); N. Lewis, 'Human Rights, Law and Democracy in an Unfree World', in *Human Rights Fifty Years On: A Re-appraisal*, ed. T. Evans (Manchester: Manchester University Press, 1998), p. 77.

[2] Convention on the Rights of the Child, G.A. res. 44/25, annex, *adopted* 20 Nov. 1989, 44 U.N. GAOR Supp. (No. 49) at 167, Article 4. U.N. Doc. A/44/49 (1989), *entered into force* 2 Sept. 1990.

issues. Law reform came to be perceived as relevant to implementing protection rights or a child's right to protection from abuse and exploitation under the CRC. Yet, increasingly, both UNICEF and partner organizations have realized that a programme of legislative reform 'to put the law in place' on protection issues is inadequate to achieve effective implementation, without a more complex understanding of the interconnected nature of the rights guaranteed by the Convention. It seemed important to examine the country experience of harmonizing the CRC through legislative reform more closely and ascertain the connected measures referred to in Article 4 that are necessary to support effective implementation of the rights guaranteed by the CRC.

A Legislative Reform Initiative was thus launched by UNICEF as part of its continuing efforts to fulfil its mandate under the Convention, support CRC implementation within countries, and a human rights–based approach to development.

Legislative reform and the work of the courts, although relevant, were considered only limited dimensions of CRC implementation. Institutional reform and law enforcement through effective budget allocations, social policies, and wider partnerships among concerned actors were considered important aspects of a law reform initiative. Understanding the dynamics of legislative reform in a holistic sense was considered important to using law reform effectively in implementing children's rights and integrating them into development efforts. The Initiative thus initially focused on the need to understand both the scope and limitations of using law reform in implementing children's rights in developing countries. UNICEF is an agency that has programmes in these countries, which share similar social and economic conditions and face both specific and greater challenges in implementing the CRC. In addition, the largest proportions of children whose rights are guaranteed under the CRC come from developing countries that confront problems of poverty and low economic growth.

Rather than engage in a developing country-based review of law reform in the post-CRC decades, the project focused on analyzing the experience of developing countries linked to a particular legal tradition or system. The common law and civil law traditions of the Western world and Islamic law were identified as major traditions or systems that applied in these countries and could impact on the law reform process. All countries have plural sources of law such as the constitution, religious and/or customary law, and legislation. However, countries colonised by Western powers inherited legal systems that incorporated a variety of legal traditions. They evolved as countries with a dominant common law, civil law or Islamic law, or with plural or mixed legal systems. In the latter, both Western colonial law and indigenous customary or religious laws applied as distinct legal traditions but with the colonial law as the dominant system. One of the studies, therefore, considers law reform in harmonization with the CRC in countries with a mixed or plural legal system. Mauritania, Morocco, and Jordan, with plural sources, are discussed with the Islamic jurisdictions because the dominant system in these countries is Islamic law.

Choice of countries for each of these studies had necessarily to be limited in terms of the time frame and resources. UNICEF country offices identified for the project were asked to prepare desk studies on legal reform in their countries, using consultants and all available materials. These were shared with the authors of the studies on law reform in the different legal traditions. Certain countries were selected for inclusion in each of the legal tradition studies by UNICEF in consultation with the authors. The selection was based on an assessment of the interest and relevance of those country experiences for the particular legal tradition and the broad objectives of the project. These UNICEF country studies have been used by the authors, who also have used other materials including court cases and statutes wherever these sources were accessible. Because a broad rights-based development approach has been adopted, the studies do not focus primarily on statutes and case law in their analysis.

The selected country experiences are discussed in the studies in relation to a particular system, but comparative materials on a legal tradition also have been used. This means that some court cases of comparative interest have been discussed in several studies. This also reflects the potential for cross-fertilization of ideas in legal reforms. The significance of the same provisions of the CRC as well as some of the jurisprudence of the Committee on the Rights of the Child has inevitably been discussed in several of the studies.

The studies consider the challenges of implementing the CRC in different legal traditions or systems, identified in this overview as common law system, civil law system, Islamic law system, and plural legal systems. They have adopted somewhat different approaches. The studies on plural legal systems, common law, and Islamic law discuss in detail the background and experience on legislative reform and implementation in the selected countries. The study on plural legal systems draws on the country experiences to highlight the general issues of concern on child rights in plural legal systems. The studies on the common law, civil law, and Islamic law, by contrast, focus on key features of these particular legal systems, and draw on the experience of selected countries to describe some post-CRC legislative reforms and their implementation. The studies on the common law and plural legal systems both discuss jurisprudence in the courts, which is an important source in developing children's rights in these systems. The study on the civil law is an overview that comments on the special issues that arise in regard to law reform and implementation in this legal system. Country experiences and jurisprudence are not focused upon in detail in this study. The Islamic law study recognizes that comparative jurisprudence in Islamic law can be useful, but it does not deal with this aspect. Despite these contrasting approaches, the four studies offer comparative insights in regard to the problems and challenges, as well as spaces that can be created for strengthening a legal system's contribution to realizing children's rights.

I. INTEGRATING THE CRC AND INTERNATIONAL HUMAN RIGHTS LAW INTO NATIONAL LEGAL SYSTEMS: THE CHALLENGES

Because all the countries selected for the legal system studies as well as those that are cited for comparative analysis have ratified the CRC, law reform initiatives have been analyzed according to international treaty law and the CRC framework on the human rights of children. The studies also discuss dimensions of women's human rights under CEDAW and the interface with the human rights of children, including girl children. They have highlighted that all four legal systems have evolved from a context of discrimination against women and varying degrees of limitations on the legal status of children.

The study on civil law systems demonstrates how its evolution was based on common 'protective' approaches to women and children. The four studies indicate that, historically, both women and children were denied legal rights in all four systems because of this protective value system. Emilio García Méndez demonstrates how, in what he describes as an 'exclusion pact', the protection of women and children gave legitimacy to their legal incapacity. Protection of their persons was not interpreted as a protection of their rights. Realizing women's rights is thus highlighted in all the studies as an interlinked dimension of realizing children's rights. The plural legal systems study and the study on Islamic law address the interface in more specific terms, as religious and customary laws often reflect values that are different from generally applicable national laws, the CRC, and CEDAW.

The universality and indivisibility of human rights reflected in the CRC pose special challenges for law reform in all systems. All the studies indicate that the CRC's rights agenda is not simply about using internally consistent value-based laws to protect children from violations. What were perceived prior to the CRC as supportive social policies and measures on matters such as health and education now become an indivisible dimension of children's rights that must be incorporated into law. Yet all studies reflect the neglect of socio-economic rights, and the over-focus on using law in traditional areas that concern protecting children from exploitation and abuse. Socio-economic rights in regard to basic needs such as health, food, security, education and shelter continue to be perceived as discretionary and distinct administrative initiatives that fall into the realm of social policy rather than enforceable law. All studies highlight the fact that continued perceptions in this regard prevent legislative reform that is holistic, and ultimately result in the contravention of the core human rights norms of the CRC. Specific problems and challenges in this regard will be considered later.

The studies highlight the fact that civil law and common law systems adopt different approaches to reception of treaties in national law. Civil law countries in general adopt a monist approach, which means that a treaty once ratified by Parliament and promulgated by a public procedure becomes an intrinsic part of national law. The civil law study demonstrates that in this legal system, treaties have been ratified without reservations. The monist approach is occasionally followed in plural legal systems, which generally do not adopt this view on the application of treaties. Benin, with a French civil law influence, follows the monist approach on promulgation of treaties even though it has a plural system.

A dualist approach to treaties is usually adopted in common law systems. This means that treaties apply in a domestic legal system only if they have been incorporated and received by a national legal procedure. Constitutions and/or legislation or executive decisions or judicial interpretation facilitate the process of national reception within the Commonwealth Caribbean countries discussed in the common law study. Where common law is a strong influence in plural legal systems, as in Ghana and Zimbabwe, a dualist approach to treaties is followed.

A dualist approach to treaties seems to dictate the approach to reception of the CRC, even when constitutions and the national legal systems sometimes adopt the rhetoric of monism. An inevitable process of national law-making and policy formulation determine in practice the aspects of the CRC that are integrated into legal systems. Thus, in an Islamic jurisdiction such as Jordan or in a civil law jurisdiction such as Guatemala, a monist approach to treaties is reflected, and treaties become part of national law, even superseding domestic law. However, there is in fact no procedure for invoking treaty provisions in the courts, and harmonization of treaties is a slow and difficult process, both for the legislative and other organs of government. Often there is a failure of the judiciary to apply treaties as a result of a lack of information on treaties, or the low priority given to treaty law. This aspect is discussed in some depth in the civil law study, which describes the phenomenon of token or 'hypocritical monism' and demonstrates the different ways in which the legal system perceives treaties within the perspective of monism. Treaties are a supra-constitutional norm that ranks above domestic law, or are norms integrated through the constitution. The civil law study also shows how legislative assimilation or incorporation can be vital in integrating treaties in domestic law, even in civil law jurisdictions when monism is in reality not followed within the country, especially by courts of law. Implementing child rights after CRC ratification becomes problematic in all legal systems when the pre-existing laws continue until they are repealed by the legislature. Monist theory would suggest that these laws cease to apply, but the civil law study indicates that this does not happen in practice even in these legal systems.

It has been noted that the Committee on the Rights of the Child, which monitors the Convention, has in its General Comment No. 5 and Concluding Observations on States parties' reports stressed that incorporation of the treaty is the most suitable method to bring national law in harmony with the Convention. The Committee has constantly emphasized that, in any case, there must be a consistent effort to initiate law reform and harmonize domestic law with the CRC. All studies reveal that this is easier said than done.

The countries reviewed in all four legal traditions adopt processes of national incorporation that take the form of general children's acts and/or ad hoc legislation in regard to specified topics. Belize is the only country in the Caribbean that has incorporated the whole CRC into domestic law. Not even countries that follow the monist civil law tradition of direct application of treaties have incorporated the CRC wholesale. Children's acts or children's codes incorporate some of the main provisions of the treaty. The latter represents a practical response, as it is easier to set down the core norms in a general children's act and regulate specific topics through legislation. Experience from all four legal systems suggests that given the scope of the CRC, a wholesale incorporation is unrealistic and would create even more complex problems of implementation.

It is clear from all the studies that adoption of regional human rights instruments and standards represents an important method of incorporating children's rights. The plural legal systems study refers to the African Charters on Human Rights,[3] and the untapped potential for using them in strengthening domestic law. The African Charters have introduced higher standards relating to law reform and interventions to repeal customary laws that deny child rights. They reinforce the CEDAW standards and also elaborate on them. Shaheen Ali describes regional standard setting in Islamic law–based legal systems, and suggests that regionalization is an assertion of identity in an environment where Islamic law systems must interact with the international human rights system through the reporting process of treaty bodies.

Regional standard setting in Africa and in Islamic jurisdictions reflects the desire to regionalize what are perceived as 'Western' human rights so

---

[3] The African Charter on Human and People's Rights (*adopted* 27 June 1981, OAU Doc. CAB/LEG/67/3 rev. 5, 21 I.L.M. 58 (1982), *entered into force* 21 October 1986) and the Protocol on the Establishment of an African Court on Human and Peoples' Rights, *adopted* 10 June 1998 and *entered into force* 2004. The African Charter on the Rights and Welfare of the Child (OAU Doc. CAB/LEG/24.9/49, Art. (1990), *entered into force* 29 Nov. 1999).) was followed by the Protocol to the African Charter on Human and Peoples' Rights on the Rights of Women in Africa, *adopted* 11 July 2003.

that they resonate as meaningful norms in their own social, economic, and cultural contexts. Yet the studies on the Islamic and plural legal systems indicate that the regional standards have not significantly impacted on law reform initiatives within countries. The common law study, however, notes the impact of the European Convention on Human Rights in the United Kingdom, through the incorporation of that instrument by the Human Rights Act 1998. The common law study also shows how a complaints mechanism in a regional instrument can help to strengthen implementation of the CRC in domestic law. Rebeca Rios-Khon refers to a case in the Inter-American Court of Human Rights under the American Convention on Human Rights. The case considered the legality of judicially sanctioned corporal punishment in Trinidad and Tobago. A complaints mechanism in a regional instrument can foster the development of a regional consensus on child rights norms when countries respect the decisions of the regional court.

Constitutions may refer to the application of treaties or contain a Bill of Fundamental Rights that applies generally or specifically to children. Common law countries in the Caribbean, for example, Jamaica and Barbados, and the African countries considered in the plural legal systems study incorporated a general bill of rights, rather than children's rights, when they gained independence from colonial rule. These general rights are not as comprehensive as the CRC or CEDAW. Yet South Africa and Uganda, which have plural legal systems, have both incorporated specific children's rights derived from the CRC and its core principles, in their post-independence constitutions. Where such rights are articulated either as part of a bill of rights or as specific children's rights as in some common law countries and in plural legal systems, there is space for the courts to enforce those rights. However, a method of enforcement that is accessible must, as in South Africa or in Caribbean countries such as Barbados and Jamaica, be incorporated into the constitution. The absence of an effective enforcement procedure makes the rights declared in the constitution merely aspirations or declaratory statements that use the rhetoric of rights, without providing practical relief and remedies. We shall note later the impact of constitutional provisions on children's rights when remedies are incorporated as part of a bill of rights.

The study on the Islamic law jurisdictions discusses in depth the problems faced in incorporating the CRC into Islam-based legal systems. Shaheen Ali notes the origins of the CRC in a Western legal tradition, and the reality of a political environment that demands assertion of an Islamic identity. The balance appears to have been achieved in the early years of ratification of the CRC by the entry of reservations to the treaty at the time of ratification. Some reservations specifically refer to the need to conform to Islamic law. Others are broader and refer to the national legal environment in general terms. Reservations appear to be a precautionary measure to protect an Islamic legal tradition.

Shaheen Ali demonstrates that in the rush to enter reservations, States parties ignored the fact that the reservations were in conflict rather than in harmony with Islam. She refers in this context to the reservation entered by Islamic countries to the article on nationality, despite the fact that the CRC provisions are in harmony with Islamic law. Her discussion of the sources of Islamic law and the varied interpretations of these sources, particularly in areas such as nationality adoption and fosterage and parental authority, indicates that there are opportunities for harmonization with the CRC. She suggests that these reservations can and should be reviewed and withdrawn. She demonstrates how these reservations inhibit the capacity of the State and the community to realize the core standards of the CRC in harmony with Islamic law. She notes that only a few countries such as Pakistan, Egypt, and Bangladesh have withdrawn reservations entered at the time of ratification.

Developing national legislation and jurisprudence in the courts that link the regional charters and the CRC and CEDAW do not, in general, pose a problem. Shaheen Ali's study indicates that initiatives on regionalization of human rights in the Muslim world through Islamic declarations, developed specifically for an Islamic context, can present a risk of diluting CRC and CEDAW standards ratified by countries. However, regional declarations on Muslim women's human rights[4] show that, as in Africa, creative efforts can be made to strengthen and reinforce the commitment of Islamic countries that have ratified human rights treaties, in fulfilling their commitments under international law. Shaheen Ali points out that the norm of international human rights law *pacta sunt servanda* is recognized in Islamic law. She endorses the view that treaties, once ratified, bind Islamic States to respect, promote and fulfil those rights.

II. CATALYSTS FOR LEGISLATIVE REFORM

The studies of the four legal traditions indicate that different models of governance are adopted. The common law jurisdictions of the Caribbean countries in general have systems of parliamentary democracy, based on the British or Westminster model. Unlike in Britain, where a Human Rights Act was introduced in 1998, post-independence constitutions are written documents with bills of rights. These constitutions do not refer specifically to the broad sweep of children's rights in the CRC and recognize only civil and political rights. Rebeca Rios-Kohn describes in some detail the limitations in the constitutional guarantees on fundamental rights in Barbados and Jamaica. Countries with plural legal traditions are sometimes modelled on

---

[4] Cairo Declaration on Human Rights in Islam, 5 Aug. 1990, U.N. GAOR, World Conf. on Hum. Rts., 4th Sess., Agenda Item 5, U.N. Doc. A/CONF.157/PC/62/Add.18 (1993); Universal Islamic Declaration of Human Rights, *21 Dhul Qaidah 1401* (19 Sept. 1981).

the Westminster system of parliamentary governance but with constitutional guarantees on fundamental rights. The plural legal systems study suggests that constitutions in some of these countries, too, have not addressed children's rights and are limited in scope. The Islamic jurisdictions discussed have different systems of parliamentary governance. The king or sovereign Head of State has wide executive powers. Nevertheless, Parliament or the legislative body has a major voice in law reform. These countries have not incorporated constitutional guarantees on fundamental rights.

In classic common law constitutional theory on parliamentary governance, there is a clear separation of powers between the three arms of government. The legislature is supreme and enacts laws and controls budgets. The executive branch of government is responsible for the administration, whereas the judiciary interprets the laws. However, the separation of powers does not in fact operate in this clear-cut manner. The Executive plays an important role in initiating policy and translating it into legislation. The Executive can therefore be either apathetic or a major force in pushing forward an agenda of law reform. The judiciary has always modified common law and legislation through a process of interpretation, and identifying the perceived legislative intent of the legislature. As Rebeca Rios-Kohn points out in the common law study on the Caribbean Commonwealth, the separation of powers is respected mostly through the concept of the independence of the judiciary from legislative and executive control. An effective legislative agenda therefore requires the cooperation of the legislative branch and the active involvement of the executive. The judiciary can make a contribution through its positive interpretations of the legislation.

In countries with plural legal systems, too, legislative reform requires the active interest of the Executive in proposing reform, and the support of the legislature to enact the laws. Courts have the same role in interpreting law, as the system of courts and judicial administration is derived from the common law legal tradition with its emphasis on case law and precedent. This is clarified in the studies on Zimbabwe and Ghana.

The study on the civil law jurisdictions indicates the same importance of cooperation between the legislative and executive branches of government in initiating law reform, even though the legislature ratifies treaties and is the supreme authority. The study addresses in particular the importance of legislation in sustaining social policies and financial allocation to support them. It notes the limited role of the judiciary both in terms of the exercise of judicial discretion and their approach to interpretation. Civil law systems emphasize the importance of legal rules, and interpretations by the judiciary, according to Emilio García Méndez, tend to be legalistic rather than focused on interpreting the law in the social context. The contribution of the judiciary is therefore seen as less creative in carrying through the legislative reform agenda.

Shaheen Ali's discussion of Islamic jurisdictions suggests that the role of the judiciary can be interpretive and contextualized even within the framework of the accepted sources of *Shari'a* law. The executive authority assumes especial importance where monarchies have wide powers. In Jordan and Morocco, the royalty have influenced a process of progressive law reform on children's rights. The impact of the Executive is seen in all four studies. They reveal that the Executive has followed the ratification of the CRC by initiating projects on law review and reform, and has been the major influence in efforts to integrate the CRC, giving leadership to the legislature. Ratification has therefore inspired reform initiatives that have often coincided, in African countries, with the submission of an initial report to the Committee on the Rights of the Child. By contrast, the regional charters on human rights in Africa have not had this impact on the Executive. In any event, initiatives of the Executives have not always received the support of the legislature. Laws are sometimes proposed by the Executive but not enacted.

The Committee on the Rights of the Child has pronounced 'General Comments' interpreting the Convention, and made specific Concluding Observations on law reform, when reviewing country reports. Although the Executive has responded to reporting by initiating some reforms, their approach has not been guided closely by the specific Concluding Observations. All studies suggest that country performance has not been effectively monitored, whether nationally, regionally, or internationally, in terms of the Committee on the Rights of the Child's work. The Committee's concerns have only reinforced reform agendas on child rights issues that have already been raised by international and national non-governmental organizations (NGOs) working on this agenda. The integration of the Committee's Concluding Observations in a systematic manner has yet to be achieved.

The ad hoc nature of the legislative reform processes is noticed in all jurisdictions. The studies reveal that child protection issues have been prioritized in all four systems, and they have been influenced by international rather than regional or local concerns. Thus, protection issues such as juvenile justice, child labour, and child sexual exploitation have received special attention in the law reform agenda, largely because of the international focus. Socioeconomic rights have been ignored in all four systems, although poverty reduction, education and health policies have received attention as a dimension of delivery of welfare and social services. Wholesale incorporation of the CRC has not been considered an option. Yet even when comprehensive children's codes have been enacted or children's fundamental rights are guaranteed in constitutions, there is an absence of holistic legislative, executive, and judicial efforts to integrate the CRC. This is partly because there has been very little advocacy with legislators or training for judges on human rights, including children's rights, even though both are key groups in implementing a child rights agenda.

Only isolated programmes in some countries such as Zimbabwe, Ghana and Benin have tried to address the need for consistent training and advocacy on human rights, including child rights, through workshops. The impact of this lack of awareness and training is seen in the lack of consistency in judicial decision making in important areas that concern children and women's human rights. It is also rarely, as seen in Botswana and Burkina Faso, that the support of traditional rulers has been obtained for legislative reform initiatives, even though they play an important role in dispute settlement in African countries with a plural legal system and customary law. Islamic court judges in these jurisdictions also have not been the focus of advocacy programmes on human rights and children's rights. The Islamic jurisdictions study and the plural legal systems study reveal that they need not necessarily be negative to human rights but, rather, a resource for harmonization of the CRC and CEDAW standards. The concept of shared access to resources and social responsibility for children in customary law and Islamic law are considered norms that can be used to promote accountability in governance, and especially socio-economic rights and exercise of parental authority.

Local authorities and the community seem to be rarely consulted or encouraged to become actively engaged in initiatives to realize children's rights. A rare instance of government-led initiatives to consult the community in reform of customary law is seen in both Burkina Faso and Botswana. The civil law study also draws attention to a similar example in the provisions for equal representation of civil society in local municipal councils, provided for by the Children and Adolescents Law of Brazil. However, government and civil society organizations operating at the national level, and international agencies, have not usually involved community-based organizations to encourage community support for law reform. The participation of civil society has not been ensured by institutionalizing it. Rarely has NGO participation been formalized or provided for in legislation on children's concerns, either by giving them membership of key statutory bodies dealing with children or by giving them an official monitoring role. The plural legal systems study cites examples from Ghana and Benin where some NGO participation or involvement is seen in the work of local human rights commissions. Consequently, reform initiatives are fragile and are not often sustained. Although these law reform programmes are in fact relevant to the problems facing children, the seeming 'alienness' of the child rights reform agenda and arguments based on local custom and culture are used by anti–child rights NGOs, as in Bermuda, to undermine reform efforts as a 'foreign' initiative.

The involvement of NGOs and civil society with government and international agencies in the reform scene is evident in Islamic jurisdictions. This is in harmony with what Shaheen Ali refers to as the Islamic ideology of childhood as a social responsibility. However, the nature and extent of this involvement are not clear. It is suggested that NGOs are sometimes perceived negatively as setting a donor-funded, foreign agenda. Shaheen Ali discusses the regional processes and the holding of major conferences in Tehran and Islamabad, which have produced conference declarations that focus on women's rights and connect with child rights. These regional initiatives seem to be a response to concern with interpreting international human rights in conformity with Islamic rather than 'Western' values. The pressure for an alternative discourse also has stimulated scholarship on Islamic law and human rights. Islamic scholars have contributed to the Tehran and Islamabad Declarations. Women's groups have been active in the NGO movement on child rights in the other legal systems. Women's contribution is implied in Islamic jurisdictions, but there is no clear indication of involvement of women's groups in regard to legislative reform on child rights.

Despite these limitations, all studies show that NGOs, including women's groups, have been working nationally and regionally as activists and advocates in promoting law reform on children's rights. There has been in general a favourable environment, and NGOs have worked in cooperation with the executive branch of government rather than the legislature. Their activism in this regard has in general not brought them into conflict with government – an interesting contrast to NGO–government relations when NGOs pursue other human rights agendas. The later discussion on the type of legislative reforms initiated will, however, clarify that despite the positive developments referred to earlier, there are striking similarities in regard to gaps in NGO activism in all four legal traditions.

It is clear from the studies that NGO participation on the child rights agenda has been fostered where there has been a return to civilian rule after a period of military dictatorship. NGOs are also active even when a regime has been considered in international fora as repressive and having a poor record on child rights. Thus, NGOs and civil society organizations continue to work with international agencies on child rights and law reform in Zimbabwe. Yet it is also evident from these studies that the scope of legislative reform is limited when there are reversals in the democratization process, and contradictions surface in the reform agenda pursued by NGOs. The civil law study documents the manner in which the democratization process in Latin American countries contributed to advancing the child rights agenda. The study also shows how a reversal and return to authoritarianism in some countries have undermined child rights, including children's participation rights. This is also reflected in the plural legal systems and Islamic jurisdictions study.

The common law and plural legal systems studies refer to the contribution of NGOs, both to the preparation of the government report to the Committee on the Rights of the Child, and 'shadow' reports that evaluate the performance of governments. The studies on Islamic jurisdictions and the civil law do not address the subject of shadow reporting. 'Shadow' reporting has gained acceptance in many countries as a legitimate rather than adversarial exercise. It is an important process in treaty monitoring. In general, the government consultation with NGOs in reporting to the Committee has not seen a vigorous engagement of interest, in any legal system. The Committee has had occasion to comment on this adversely, in considering country reports. NGOs have thus contributed to the legislative reform agenda but only in a limited manner. They have not used the CRC reporting process adequately to sustain their contribution to the legislative reform process. Shadow reporting is not yet a well-established procedure and needs strengthening in all legal systems.

In South Africa and India where NGO activism is vibrant, NGOs bring court cases on infringement of human rights in national courts. This is discussed in the plural legal systems study. Rebeca Rios-Kohn records a similar procedure in the submission of an amicus brief by an international NGO in the corporal punishment case concerning Trinidad and Tobago, before the Inter-American Court of Human Rights. The application of a complaints procedure can thus promote public interest litigation, through the activism of NGOs, which in turn can stimulate activism on the part of the judiciary in responding to infringements of child rights. An environment that encourages NGO activism and has an effective complaints procedure also enables NGOs to work on budget issues. In countries with plural legal systems such as South Africa and India, NGOs monitor budgets, an area that is normally considered the exclusive concern of the State.

It is perhaps a measure of the absence of a vibrant culture of democratic participation in the countries discussed in these studies that there is very little evidence of children's participation, or the participation of local authorities in realizing child rights. There are some examples of ad hoc token events, such as children's gatherings or children's 'parliaments'. In Jamaica, in the common law study, and Zimbabwe, Benin, and Burkina Faso that have plural legal systems, the voices of children have sometimes been heard on issues in 'children's parliaments'. Latin American countries appear to have sometimes held what are described by Emilio García Méndez as 'decorative and manipulated participation events', involving small children in particular. All studies reveal either token participation (as in the common law plural and civil law traditions), or no child participation at all, as in the Islamic jurisdictions. There are no examples of the engagement of older children or adolescents in policy consultations or law reform initiatives. Local authorities also do not feature in law reform initiatives or budgetary and financial allocation discussions.

UNICEF and other United Nations organizations such as the International Labour Organization (ILO) also have worked with government, NGOs, and local agencies on the legislative reform agenda, in countries representing all four legal systems. UNICEF in particular has often supported research and review of domestic law, with a view to promoting harmonization with the CRC. The United Nations Development Programme (UNDP), United Nations Development Fund for Women (UNIFEM), and UNICEF also have supported constitutional reform processes in plural jurisdictions, whereas UNICEF in particular has facilitated sharing of regional experiences in Zimbabwe. The organization has encouraged budget analysis in Latin American jurisdictions such as Ecuador. The plural legal systems study refers to UNICEF's programmes on advocacy and capacity building on child rights implementation in the government and non-governmental sectors. The same pattern of government and international agency cooperation is seen in the work of international child rights NGOs such as Save the Children. The 'solidarity' effort in realizing child rights that the CRC contemplates appears to have been realized in the countries discussed in all the studies. This seems a remarkable achievement, given the diversity of the four legal traditions.

III. THE SCOPE OF LEGISLATIVE REFORM

The consistent political will to initiate legislative reform in fulfilment of CRC commitments can be observed in all countries selected from each of the four legal systems, as well as in those countries discussed in each study for comparative analysis. The submission of an initial report to the Committee on the Rights of the Child often has been the occasion for a review of legislation and the enactment of new laws. National bodies such as commissions have, when set up, performed a useful role in this regard.

In the post–CRC period, the children's acts introduced in many countries and in all systems often focus on the protection areas, bringing all the laws into one enactment. Rarely does a children's act incorporate the general principles of the CRC. This type of general act has been introduced in Ghana in the post-independence period, and is under consideration in Botswana and Jordan. Such acts are particularly important in plural legal systems to set core norms applicable to all children. But even such acts are not comprehensive, and other areas of significance to children are dealt with in piecemeal reform.

Despite the diversity of legal traditions, similarities surface in regard to the areas that have been the focus of reform. As stated earlier, the 'internationalization' of certain child rights issues, and the work of international agencies and NGOs as well as local child rights groups on protection rights, has impacted on the reform process.

It is also possible that protection rights or protecting children from exploitation and abuse have been the traditional and familiar areas for legislative intervention. The areas of protection covered may not be identical but, in general, similar areas of protection rights have been addressed in legislative reform.

Thus, juvenile justice and problems of children in conflict with the law receive high priority. Legislative reform takes the form of reviewing old laws or enacting new ones. Participation rights are addressed incidentally in this context, as when laws of evidence and procedure are modified so as to facilitate children's access to justice and protect child witnesses and victims. These reforms also connect to the topic of child labour and sexual abuse of children, trafficking, and reforms to the criminal law on violence against children. Reforms to the penal codes and laws on sexual exploitation feature importantly in all countries. Domestic violence and HIV/AIDS laws have been introduced in some countries and can be considered an extension of the concern with protection from sexual violence. The age of majority is often addressed as a topic for reform because 'protection' requires identification of children by an appropriate age cohort. Law reforms do not in general adopt a holistic approach to definition of childhood in terms of the CRC's overarching concept of child rights. Inconsistencies in the definition of childhood for varying purposes remain untouched, even when legislation clarifies an age of majority.

Family law and personal status is also an area that has been addressed in law reform. Forced marriage is addressed in law reform in Islamic jurisdictions and plural legal systems with a component of customary law. Guardianship, parental rights, and custody feature as common areas for law reform.

There is in general a reluctance to address the issue of corporal punishment and citizenship as areas for law reform. A few countries in Islamic jurisdictions and mixed legal systems have reviewed the approach to passport laws, citizenship and visas from the perspective of women's and children's rights. The plural legal systems and Islamic law studies show how women's rights and issues of discrimination on the basis of gender have been addressed to only a limited extent in law reform. We have noted that both women and children were denied legal rights in all four legal traditions. Despite the changes in the law that have occurred over time, some reform on women's rights continues to interface with reforms on child law. This is seen in the area of criminal laws on sexual exploitation and trafficking, domestic violence, harmful customary practices, citizenship and immigration, HIV/AIDS, guardianship and custody and forced marriage.

The reform initiatives on women's rights and children's rights have been pursued invariably as parallel projects and not on the basis of connected approaches to realizing the standards of both CEDAW and the CRC. The studies do not suggest that reforms have been introduced in regard to areas such as harmful customary practices and forced marriage as a core concern with eliminating gender discrimination. The plural mixed legal system study shows that law reform has not touched a range of discriminatory colonial and customary laws.

Codification of Islamic family law, as in Maldives and Egypt, or the review of family law in Morocco and the enactment of family law codes in Benin, Botswana and Burkina Faso have provided opportunities to harmonize both Conventions in national law. Children's acts that set out general norms as in Ghana and Botswana have provided a similar opportunity to realize the rights of both groups.

Codification and consolidation are efforts to simplify the law and make it accessible. Codification seeks to bring laws relating to a particular area into one statute. Consolidation brings distinct laws pertaining to a topic into one compilation of distinct statutes so that all the laws on a topic can be accessed easily. The plural legal systems study reveals how codification in the colonial period transformed customary law. The civil law study reveals that codification, the traditional method of law-making in that system, nevertheless sets out specific rules in complex language. The law becomes inaccessible to the average person. 'Ignorance of the law' is then all pervasive, and people's knowledge of the law becomes in fact a myth.

Common law systems and plural legal systems with a component of common law and civil law introduce legislative reform through a codification process. Some Islamic countries also have codified principles of Islamic family law. Codification provides an opportunity for resolving conflicts in legal principles, and a review of colonial law or religion and customary law. It is an opportunity to integrate human rights. Consolidation, by contrast, is a limited exercise where all laws on children are brought together. Consolidation has been recorded as a strategy used in Burkina Faso in the post–CRC period.

A child rights agenda can be perceived as a 'foreign' imposition. The initiatives in Burkina Faso and Botswana to popularize child rights in a context of customary law are important endeavours. The plural legal systems and Islamic jurisdiction studies show how customary law and Islamic law were transformed in the colonial period. The interaction with superior colonial courts and new laws, codification and changing social and economic conditions transformed Islamic and customary law. A further reform process to transform customary law in harmony with international human rights is possible and necessary.

Because law reform has been piecemeal and ad hoc initiatives, certain aspects of the CRC are not covered at all. A range of earlier laws, including colonial laws that conflict with the CRC, continue to apply in all systems. Colonial laws have been repealed in countries with a heritage of English common law. Parliament's capacity to modify common law has always been recognized. Yet such legislative reform has been slow in the Commonwealth Caribbean discussed in the common law study and, in the countries influenced by common law, in the plural legal systems study. Automatic repeal of these laws has not taken place even in civil law jurisdictions influenced by the monist approach to treaties. In all four systems, participation rights and survival and development rights have not been addressed in legislative reform. It is very rarely that legislation introduces a compulsory age at which a child should be in school. As noted earlier, occasionally child participation has been facilitated by reforms in the criminal law on evidence and proce- dure. Sometimes, laws that seek to protect children, on the one hand, are combined with others that violate child rights, on the other hand. This is seen when child abuse is prohibited and use of corporal punishment is not prohibited or regulated by legislation. Similarly, the general human rights situation and legislation on maintenance of law and order, as in Zimbabwe, which restricts freedom of speech and expression, impacts negatively on children's rights to education and information. This law contradicts the many positive interventions taken to introduce law reform in harmony with the CRC.

Legislative reform in Islamic jurisdictions also indicates a focus on pro- tection, even when general children's acts are introduced as a response to ratification of the CRC. Reforms focus on family law and protection issues including child labour and juvenile justice. Some Islamic countries focus in particular on abandoned children and the disabled. Sexual abuse has not been addressed in general, although trafficking has been covered in some post-CRC reforms. Introduction of a legislative reform agenda becomes a very complex task when there is a movement to locate reform in Islamic law. Tensions emerge in regard to the scope of reform.

Some concepts of child care such as adoption are considered taboo under Islamic law, even though Shaheen Ali argues that other interpretations of Islamic law are possible. It is important to recall that the CRC does not suggest that adoption must be recognized as a system of alternative care. Article 20(3) refers to various forms of care, which include both adoption and foster care. *Kufala* or a particular type of foster familiar in North African Islamic countries is specifically referred to in Article 20(3). Reservations on the adoption article, and the perception of adoption as creating a problem in harmonizing law reform with the CRC in Islamic countries, fail to recognize the flexibility embedded in Article 20(3). The study on Islamic jurisdictions reveals that countries have not used Islamic principles on fosterage and social responsibility to children to enact child-friendly legislation in harmony with the CRC.

Defining minimum ages for marriage and participation rights poses dif- ficult problems because of Islamic law's focus on parental guardianship and control over a child's marriage and religious upbringing. Shaheen Ali's study examines the sources of Islamic law and suggests lines of interpretation that can be explored to harmonize human rights principles with the core norms of Islam in these areas. She refers in particular to the different interpretations adopted in the many schools of Islamic jurisprudence. She argues that this pluralism in views of jurists and the general concept of social responsibility for children provides space for child rights–focused interpretations. She does not, however, address the difficult issue of the status of non-marital children who are considered 'illegitimate' in a context in which Islam adopts a prohibitionist approach to sexual relations outside Islamic marriage. This remains a problematic area, despite the principles of law that Shaheen Ali discusses, which reflect Islamic law's humane approach to foundlings (*lakeet*) and abandoned children.

The study on Islamic jurisdiction highlights the recent efforts in the Islamic world to interpret women's rights in harmony with human rights norms and especially CEDAW. Some of the areas where there is an interface are noted. However, there is no evidence that there has been a connected or coordinated effort to link the CRC and CEDAW in legislative reform initiatives.

IV. SOME COMMON PROBLEMS IN INITIATING LEGISLATIVE REFORM

1. The Best Interests of the Child

The CRC requires that 'the best interests of the child' should provide a core foundation for legislative reform. The phrase is also used in CEDAW to reflect a balance between women's rights and children's rights.[5] This concept has found its way into the African Charter on the Rights and Welfare of the Child.[6]

The common law study has an in-depth discussion on the evolution of the concept, but its impact is revealed in all four legal systems.

Traditionally, the concept of the child's 'best interests' has roots in the English common law on guardianship and custody. The experience of plural legal systems and civil law jurisdictions clarifies that the English common law concept was incorporated by judges into the law of guardianship and custody by interpreting civil law. In the case of plural jurisdiction with Roman Dutch law such as Zimbabwe, Botswana and South Africa, the common law 'best interests' concept reinforced the concept of the courts as the *parens patriae* or 'superior' 'Upper Guardians of Children', acting on behalf of the State to protect children's interests. Both the common law and plural legal systems chapters show how the legislature and courts have also used the concept of the child's best interests in other ways. The concept is incorporated in national constitutions, children's acts, family law codes and juvenile justice

---

[5] CEDAW, op. cit., Art. 5(b).
[6] African Charter on the Rights and Welfare of the Child, op. cit., Art. 4.

laws as a core norm. It is applied in areas like immigration by the courts, to pronounce child-friendly decisions.

When personal laws based on ethnicity and religion apply in plural jurisdictions, there is flexibility and also lack of clarity in regard to the meaning of the phrase. On the one hand, 'the best interests' concept provides a uniform norm that courts can use to make child-centred decisions on legal aspects of custody and guardianship. Shaheen Ali, for instance, expresses the view that "the best interests of the child concept are the very foundation of the pro-child provisions of Islamic law." The concept has thus facilitated the development of a core of common legal values in respect of children governed by a variety of legal systems. On the other hand, the 'best interests' concept is sometimes interpreted in both civil law and plural legal systems in a culturally relativist manner so as to become contextualized in a particular socio-cultural environment.[7] Customs and practices that may be considered contrary to the international law on child rights and the CRC and CEDAW are justified from a socio-cultural perspective that is relevant to a particular situation. The civil law study shows how the principle is applied in more limited areas than in the common law, and the wide judicial discretion in interpreting the best interests of the child creates a situation where the rights guaranteed by the CRC may be undermined. The study points to the dangers of the 'best interests' concept being interpreted so as to legitimize arbitrary decision making. Participation rights in particular may be perceived as contrary to the best interests of children.

All the studies reinforce the critical importance of interpreting the best interest's concept so as to guarantee what Emilio García Méndez refers to as "the best satisfaction of rights and the best interests of the CRC". This means that the concept can no longer be interpreted in a relativist or arbitrary manner in countries that have ratified the Convention so as to infringe the CRC standards on a child's survival, development, protection and participation rights.[8]

2. Social Policies, Institutions, and Resources

All four studies clarify that the range of holistic and important measures needed to realize rights, according to CRC Article 4, have not been introduced. This has led to a pattern of law reform and legislation to harmonize the CRC in domestic law, without the accompanying combination of social policies, institutions and resources.

---

[7] See Alston, op. cit.

[8] S. Goonesekere, *Children Law and Justice: A South Asian Perspective* (New Delhi: Sage Publications, 1998) and Alston, ibid., p. 117.

a. Social policies versus socio-economic rights

All studies comment on the interconnectedness of social policies and the rights of a child under the CRC. They all demonstrate how legislation prohibiting child labour and seeking to protect a child is meaningless without realizing his or her development rights of access to adequate health and education.

Such social policies also must be implemented at the local level rather than through a centralized process that leaves no room for local level participation. The civil law study refers to the empowerment of municipal councils in this regard through the Brazil Children's and Adolescent's Law. Such an approach does not seem to have been followed in general in any of the systems.

The plural legal systems study and the Islamic jurisdiction study describe the concept of social responsibility for children and 'social trust' and access to national resources. Yet even in these systems in which 'culture' and 'identity' are emphasized in political rhetoric, these concepts have not been used to stimulate reform and recognize important socio-economic rights. The studies highlight the manner in which constitutions and legislation focus on protection rights and civil and political rights. We have noted that legislation has been enacted in areas such as child labour, juvenile justice trafficking and sexual exploitation without focusing on a child's development and participation rights. The legislative reform projects in all jurisdictions rarely reflect the indivisibility of human rights as highlighted in the CRC and CEDAW. There are rare exceptions, such as in the South African Constitution.

All studies indicate the importance of moving away from the idea that fulfilment of socio-economic needs and poverty reduction are a matter of discretionary social policy, rather than indivisible human rights. They suggest that it is the incorporation of socio-economic rights in domestic constitutions and/or legislation that can make governments accountable to use national resources in the interest of all citizens. The civil law study discusses the issue of social policy in depth and describes trends that are also common to the other jurisdictions. The study notes that CRC ratification has not promoted universal policies on health and education, and this period has even seen a reduction of such policies and, in the context of economic transformation, a shift towards discretionary welfare policies. The development of national plans of action has not arrested these trends. The civil law study reiterates the findings in other studies that sustainable social policies must be backed by constitutional or legislative provisions. Incorporation of socio-economic rights into law can prevent successive governments cutting back on social expenditure. The shift from discretionary policies to rights can thus contribute to sustainable initiatives on development.

b. Institutions and budgets

All studies demonstrate that the failure to recognize the indivisibility of rights also contributes to inadequate resource allocation and establishment of appropriate institutional arrangements to realize children's rights. Courts and law enforcement agencies, which are the traditional agencies responsible for realizing civil and political rights, receive some, but not necessarily adequate, resources. The studies reveal that child laws are codified and legislation introduced, but implementation is weak. There is a plurality of institutions such as human rights commissions, ombudspersons offices, children's law commissions, children's departments of government and police units, all of which receive very little human and material resources. Resources are often spread thin. There is a duplication of institutions without proper coordination and parallel layers of bureaucracy. This undermines the capacity for efficiency and strong holistic and focused interventions to realize the complex range of rights under the CRC. The Ghana Human Rights Commission has been recognized as an exceptional example of a successful human rights institutional arrangement. However, child rights have not received special priority yet as an important dimension of the Commission's work.

The CRC calls for optimum use of resources. It is implied that this refers to economic resources. The study on Islamic jurisdictions describes the Islamic concept of child care as a social responsibility, reflected in provisions such as limitations on the disposition of one's property by will. The study suggests that access to education and resources for social policies must be considered rights. However, none of the studies indicate that Islamic or other countries are optimizing both human and economic resources to realize child rights. This accounts for the weakness in implementing legislation and constitutional provisions, when they are put in place to harmonize with the CRC and CEDAW. The civil law study addresses the issue of non-sustainability of social policies, lack of transparency and corruption when executive decisions rather than legislative acts of Parliament carry through a child rights reform agenda, under the CRC. The failure to introduce new institutions or reform old ones presents a major obstacle to effective implementation.

The human development indicators for the common law countries considered, and budget allocation for education in the Caribbean countries and some of the Islamic countries, suggest that larger percentages of the budget are spent on the social sector. However, the relevant percentages are not given. The civil law study and the plural legal systems study discussing African countries suggest that budgetary allocations for the social sector are low. The failure to allocate resources in these countries is often traced to the burden of debt servicing and pressure from international financial institutions to introduce market economic policies in a context of globalization. All the studies indicate that good governance, controlling corruption and maximizing the available human resources could make a difference to children. The plural legal systems study argues that the international cooperation in responding to the 2004 Asian tsunami disaster offers insights into the potential for acting on the CRC concept of realizing children's rights through debt relief and development cooperation. The cost of not allocating resources and giving priority to realize rights is clearly seen in all the studies as imposing a much greater human and material cost.

There is a clear need for proper use of a range of human and material resources. Yet all four studies reveal the lack of transparency in allocating even material resources, formulating budgets and monitoring resource utilization. Civil society and groups interested in child rights, including children, do not have access to information on budgets. The studies reinforce the comments of the Committee on the Rights of the Child on inadequate budgetary allocations in most countries. Although gender budgetary analysis and child rights budgets have been discussed, none of the studies reveal that there are data in this regard or budget assessments. However, the plural legal systems study shows how in some countries, where civil society is free to scrutinize government performance, NGO think tanks are now monitoring budgets. The plural legal systems study also refers to budget analysis projects in Ecuador and the experience of South Africa in costing its juvenile justice legislation. The civil law study refers to the example of Brazil where municipalities are regulated by a federal law that requires them to spend 25 per cent of their budget on education. The concept of specifying percentages of budget allocation to support implementation of laws on children may be one way of ensuring and sustaining required financial allocations. These are experiences that should be shared and stimulate attention to this critical area of child rights implementation. The studies point to the fact that resource allocation must be treated as an intrinsic and accompanying aspect of a legislative reform project in any legal tradition.

Capacity building and strengthening human resources and leadership are considered an important institutional support in realizing rights. The plural legal systems study discusses civil service reform in this context in some African countries.

3. Addressing Disparities and Discrimination

Gender discrimination and its impact are referred to in all the studies and discussed in greater detail in the studies on plural and Islamic legal systems. The lack of support for female heads of households, inadequate investment in health and education, women's lack of equal access to land and protection from violence and abuse are common problems that impact on women and girls. In plural legal systems, not enough has been done to change a range of customary and colonial laws that reflect and entrench discrimination against women. The failure to allocate institutional, financial and human resources in a concerted effort to eliminate gender-based discrimination continues to make both women and children disadvantaged citizens in their countries. Studies clarify that the elimination of this discrimination must be at the core of realizing children's rights under the CRC. The studies show that a de-linked agenda of reform cannot address the reality or impact on gender discrimination. The issue of ethnic discrimination is not discussed in the studies. The civil law study refers to a negative practice of some countries restricting social policies in their application to non-nationals. Ethnic discrimination clearly must be of concern in a legislative reform project in any system.

V. LAW ENFORCEMENT AND THE CONTRIBUTION OF THE COURTS

Law enforcement and the contribution of the judicial system are addressed in varying detail in the studies. They all address the importance of human rights awareness programmes, and judicial and professional legal training on child rights as an essential dimension of effective enforcement. Ignorance of the law, as Emilio García Méndez points out in the civil law study, is not excused. Yet the beneficiaries of the legal system and judges and lawyers lack awareness of human rights laws and cannot either assert rights or contribute to effective domestic law reform or CRC implementation. The Islamic legal systems study refers to the creative role of the judiciary and its importance in harmonising Islamic law with international human rights norms. The study addresses the particular dimension of knowledge of Islamic jurisprudence and human rights so as to be able to harmonize both ideologies. The potential for doing so is described through a detailed discussion of Islamic texts and the work of scholars in recent decades.

The plural legal systems study also discusses the role of traditional rulers and alternative systems of dispute resolution in mixed legal traditions with customary law. The experience of Botswana and Burkina Faso affords useful insights in making linkages between human rights approaches and the CRC and customary law enforcement systems through traditional tribunals. The need to strengthen alternative dispute resolution systems and yet harmonize their work with the CRC standards and human rights is as much a challenge for countries with customary law as it is for Islamic jurisdictions. The lack of clarity in the content of the law, and the transformation of values as a result of emerging social and economic conditions, in some ways represent an opportunity for human rights–focused interpretation and law reform in countries with customary law. The study on Islamic legal systems points out that the Islamic identity was sustained in family law through decades of colonialism, when secular courts and legislation transformed criminal and civil law. However, Shaheen Ali shows how juristic interpretation has been embedded in Islamic jurisprudence, and also shows that these techniques of human agency can be used to prevent distortion of the texts that undermine children's and women's rights.

The earlier discussion on 'best interests' refers to the contribution of the courts. The existence of written constitutions in common law jurisdictions and mixed legal systems provides an important opportunity to interpret and integrate international human rights law, including the CRC and CEDAW, in domestic legal systems. This leads to harmonization between international law and domestic law and undermines the dichotomy in norms.

The plural legal systems study and the common law study discuss in detail the jurisprudence developed in courts, and the judicial interpretation of international human rights norms. The civil law study refers to the importance of written codes of law in this system and points to the growing importance of case law, while highlighting the reluctance of judges to give up the wide discretion they had in applying written codes of early law. The exercise of this discretion is perceived by Emilio García Méndez as arbitrary and in conflict with CRC values.

A bill of rights in constitutions can impact on state action and promote state commitments on treaty obligations. However, the Inter-American Court and the European Court have recognized the capacity to challenge violation of rights by private non-state actors through the concept of state inaction in preventing these violations.[9] This is an important development for realizing both women's rights and children's rights, as the CRC and CEDAW contemplate the responsibility of private non-state actors.

Some countries have bills of rights without a procedure for enforcement. Both the common law and plural legal systems studies emphasize the importance of remedies to enforce rights. They point out that the power of judicial review and widened standing to permit public interest legislation are crucial to enforcement of the rights guaranteed in constitutions. They discuss developments that have taken place in this regard in several jurisdictions. Both studies emphasize the importance of judicial colloquia, judicial training, and sharing of comparative experiences as a catalyst for judicial activism. The plural legal systems study reveals the easy manner in which jurisprudence from different courts is shared and fertilizes the law in countries such as South Africa, India and Sri Lanka. In common law countries, too, there is a shared legal heritage and a cross-fertilization of jurisprudence. The common law study suggests that there might be greater judicial conservatism in this regard. However, both studies recognize the enriching impact of comparative jurisprudence and the need to facilitate it in integrating the CRC and CEDAW.

---

[9] *Velásquez Rodríguez v. Honduras*, 29 July 1988, Inter American CHR (1988) OAS/Ser 1/L/V/III 19 Doc 13; *X and Y v. Netherlands*, 91 Eur Ct H.R. Ser A (1985).

Both studies clarify that the declarations from judicial colloquia in Bangalore and Victoria Falls represent important initiatives in this regard. Both studies also refer to the significance of regional instruments and the work of regional tribunals when a regional charter has a complaints procedure. The Inter-American Court, the Committee on the Elimination of Discrimination against Women under the Optional Protocol and the proposed African court can be a catalyst for creating harmony in the jurisprudence on children's rights and women's rights that emerges from these agencies and domestic courts.

The problems faced in interpreting provisions on equality and non-discrimination in constitutions and harmonizing them with conflicting provisions in local legislation, customary and colonial law are discussed in the plural legal systems and common law studies. It is also noted that these bills of rights often do not address socio-economic rights or refer to only one aspect such as education, undermining the capacity to use these rights to initiate changes in customary law. Some constitutions, for example, those in Benin and Ghana, give precedence to constitutional provisions over customary law. Others, such as the Zimbabwe Constitution, support non-intervention with customary law, thus creating a source of conflict between customary law, the CRC and CEDAW, and other international human rights.

The plural legal systems study demonstrates how customary laws have been transformed in the colonial period and that there is a constant process of growth and change. This dimension is also highlighted in the study of Islamic law. All three studies demonstrate the importance of consistency in judicial interpretation in harmonizing the norms and eliminating a conflict of legal standards. The common law study and the plural legal systems study discuss cases that resolved the conflict. They demonstrate how constitutional guarantees of fundamental rights can be used to challenge colonial and customary law and so promote legislative reform. These studies also refer to the importance of creating a single appellate court system, fostering the independence of the judiciary, and creating broad-based awareness of human rights, including the CRC and CEDAW. A system of law reporting and advocacy on rights is crucial to this information and communication project.

The Islamic law, plural legal systems and common law studies conclude that international human rights reinforced in constitutions affords a basis for rejecting the 'foreignness' of a human rights agenda. The plural legal systems study shows how the 'repugnancy clauses' in legislation and the legal concepts in common law were used to reject customary laws of importance and relevance to the community. It is also pointed out that this process and the choice to opt out of customary law created core norms applicable to all citizens. The sensitivity to diversity and assertion of local sovereignty in the post-colonial period encourages the rejection of international standards as an alien imposition. It is suggested that the incorporation of these standards in a constitution can legitimize them as relevant and meaningful standards in the domestic context.

VI. CONCLUSIONS AND REFLECTIONS ON THE NEED FOR NEW APPROACHES IN GENERAL

1. The Convention on the Rights of the Child originated in the West and articulates in general the legal norms of the common law and civil law. Yet it does reflect concerns relevant to other regions and has received near-universal ratification. It has evolved as an instrument that reflects the universality and indivisibility of children's human rights. The internationalization of issues in areas such as protection rights and the solidarity effort in promoting child rights among governments, international agencies and civil society have been a factor in promoting the CRC. The current selective and limited agenda needs to be widened to incorporate other aspects highlighted in these studies.

2. The different legal systems adopt either a monist or dualist approach to the application of treaties and the CRC and CEDAW. The CRC, in fact, has not been applied directly even when a monist approach is accepted. Ratification has, however, catalysed a process of domestication by legislative reform in all systems.

3. Sometimes, post-independence constitutions have incorporated fundamental rights, and specifically children's rights. This is critical in plural legal systems. Constitutional incorporation of children's rights becomes a strategy for developing uniformity in child rights standards in place of diversity. This also legitimizes the reality that customary law has been and is capable of transformation and change. Customary law can thus be assessed according to a local standard that harmonizes with international law. Consistency in judicial interpretations also can be promoted by highlighting provisions that recognize the universality and indivisibility inherent in the CRC and human rights norms.

The constitutions thus emerge as both an important method of incorporating child rights and harmonizing local laws with international treaties such as the CRC and CEDAW. Constitutional provisions are sometimes purely aspirational or declaratory and limited in scope. To be effective, constitutions must incorporate a broad sweep of rights and an enforcement procedure and recognize the power of the courts to review laws against the constitutional standards. Constitutional provisions and norms also should permit scrutiny of both state and private actions by the courts. The studies indicate the importance of incorporating the concept of indivisibility and economic and social rights in constitutions and making them enforceable.

4. The introduction of reservations is used most in Islamic legal systems. Reservations are an effort to localize the CRC and also combine ratification with an assertion of religious identity. However, reservations turn out to be based on premises that are not relevant to local contexts and even contravene local norms such as those of Islamic law. The practice of reviewing reservations should be continued, and this will eventually strengthen the internalization of CRC standards in legal systems as locally relevant, universally applicable norms.

5. Regional instruments and declarations on children's and women's rights are also an effort to address locally relevant cultural and religious concerns in interpreting rights. Such efforts are seen as especially relevant in Islamic and mixed legal systems. However, regionalization should not undermine CRC standards but rather strengthen them. The African Charters and the Protocol on African Women's Rights introduce higher standards and also reinforce international standards. They represent a useful model in this regard. Regional instruments can be used but have not yet had an impact in the domestic legal systems. The introduction of a complaints procedure and the establishment of a court are important for effective implementation at the domestic level.

6. Although the Committee on the Rights of the Child recommends the wholesale incorporation of the CRC in domestic legislative reform as the best method of incorporation, this has prove to be impractical. All legal systems adopt a method of codification and reflect an approach in which some norms are incorporated in general children's acts and/or in piecemeal ad hoc reforms. The former method of a general codified children's act combined with area-specific legislation seems the most practical and appropriate. Such legislation provides an opportunity to review outdated colonial laws derived from English common law and civil law. The best examples come from the mixed legal system countries such as Ghana. Compilation of children's laws is very rarely adopted and seems superfluous, unless combined with a process of review and codification.

7. The protection focus in legislative reform has led to contradiction in norms and concepts and limited coverage in the reform agenda. Participation and development rights have been neglected in all systems. It is unsatisfactory in failing to recognize the need for a holistic approach to integration of child rights and the CRC in domestic legal systems. It is particularly inadequate when the limitations of Islamic law and customary law remain untouched, and they themselves have been transformed negatively by interaction with colonial law. In these systems, scholarship and consultation with the community and internal discussion and review can reveal the manner in which customary law and Islamic law have been transformed. Consultation and

dialogue with the community and traditional rulers can be used, as in Burkina Faso and Botswana, to promote the need for transforming customary law in harmony with the CRC and CEDAW. Yet such initiatives are rare, and need to be introduced to support legislative reform.

8. Legislative and legal incorporation of child rights is in general critical for giving initiatives continuity and ensuring that they are permanent and sustained by successive governments. However, legislative reform alone is inadequate. Article 4 of the CRC on implementation requires harmonization of local legislation and a holistic approach that requires legislative reform to be supported by a range of other measures including institutional reform and allocation of resources. This type of holistic policy planning and implementation and law reform is not evident in any of the studies. Introducing this approach poses both common and different challenges in countries with common law, civil law, Islamic law, or plural mixed legal systems derived from these different sources as well as indigenous customary law.

9. Although the CRC requires a State to respect, promote and fulfil all rights, there has been a lack of political will in giving priority to all child rights. Concluding Observations of the Committee on the Rights of the Child have not been implemented with consistency. There has been an over-focus in all systems on legislative reform to protect children and prevent infringement of their right to protection from violence and exploitation. Juvenile justice, child labour, trafficking and sexual exploitation have been prioritized in legislative reform. Citizenship and passport laws have occasionally received attention. Legislative reform has rarely been combined with institutional reform and resource allocation to realize the universal social policies envisaged by Article 4 and children's development and participation rights under the CRC. The obligation to fulfil these socio-economic rights by positive measures has not been considered as important. The studies show that legislative reform to protect children has not been effective in an environment where the other rights of development and participation have been neglected. A holistic and balanced approach that focuses on the full range of rights, therefore, seems critical for an effective legislative reform initiative, and a shift from the discretionary 'child-welfare' to a 'child-rights' approach. The aspect of children's access to justice and implementing agencies, including the courts, through the development of legal assistance programmes, accessible complaints mechanisms and child-friendly court procedures has not received adequate attention.

10. The process of legislative reform to harmonize the CRC is closely connected with harmonization of CEDAW through legislative reform, as all legal systems continue to be linked to a historical legal tradition that is intended to protect, but in fact discriminates and imposes disadvantages on

both women and children. Gender-based discrimination impacts on girls as well as the capacity to realize children's rights, as the life situations of women and children are closely connected. The interface must be addressed in legislative reform to harmonize the CRC in national legal systems. Yet issues of discrimination, including the need to promulgate uniform legal values based on human rights in plural legal systems, have not received priority. Where gender discrimination has been addressed, it has been dealt with in reforms to family law in areas such as forced marriage. Reforms based on CEDAW and the CRC have been pursued as parallel rather than interfacing strategies. This means that discriminatory provisions continue to remain in the legal system. A holistic review and reform of all laws from a gender perspective is the only method of eliminating discriminatory provisions and harmonizing domestic law, including customary law, with both the CRC and CEDAW.

SPECIFIC AREAS

Catalysts for Legislative Reform

Despite the differences in legal systems in the structures of governance, the Executive plays an important role in initiating legislative reform. However, the support of the legislature is required to carry through the reform agenda. Both the legislature and the Executive must therefore be addressed in advocacy programmes on children's right using in particular the Concluding Observations and Comments of the Committee on the Rights of the Child and the Committee on the Elimination of Discrimination against Women.

The judiciary has an important role in interpretation of the law and legislation, which has not been maximized in any system, and is largely ignored in the civil law systems surveyed. The regional charter complaints procedures can but have not been effectively used to promote the child rights agenda in harmony with the CRC.

NGOs and government and international agencies have cooperated in legislative reform projects in all legal systems surveyed. This cooperation is striking but also inherent in the CRC ideology of human rights, and the Islamic law concept of 'social responsibility' to children. This cooperation should be further strengthened to sustain and develop the legislative reform efforts. Women's groups and community-based organizations need to be more involved in these efforts. The corporate sector is a new partner whose interest should be harnessed through the evolving ideology of corporate social responsibility and support for good governance. The corporate sector has already become engaged in issues of child abuse and elimination of child labour in South Asian countries and is a resource that can be used to support reform initiatives.

NGOs have not played a monitoring role nor effectively used the reporting procedures under the CRC. The gap is most evident in Islamic countries. Consequently, the Concluding Observations of the Committee on the Rights of the Child have not been used effectively to monitor sustained progress on legislative reform. NGO monitoring of the CRC through use of Concluding Observations and Comments of the Committee on the Rights of the Child and the Committee on the Elimination of Discrimination against Women and some formalized procedure will fill a gap in all systems.

Traditional rulers and tribunals are involved in dispute settlement in mixed and Islamic legal systems. Alternative methods of dispute settlement including mediation are relevant for all systems, but are most in harmony with Islamic and mixed legal systems. They should be used to support law reform in harmony with the CRC.

The Concept of the Best Interests of the Child

In all legal systems, this core norm has been incorporated in a variety of legal enactments such as constitutions, children's acts, or piecemeal legislation in the familiar protection areas, and in codification of family law. It is also used by the courts in judicial interpretation. It has provided a way of connecting children's rights and women's rights, as when judges make decisions on immigration issues connected with passports and visas.

In plural legal systems and Islamic jurisdictions, the concept has been used in guardianship and custody laws to promote internal consistency among diverse systems and arrive at child-centred judicial decisions. However, the flexibility of the concept and its discretionary interpretation by judges in all systems also have encouraged relativist interpretations that justify the introduction of principles that undermine the rights guaranteed by the CRC. It is critical that the 'best interests of the child' concept is interpreted in legal systems according to specified guidelines as a norm that enables the domestic incorporation of the full range of rights guaranteed by the CRC, and its core norm of non-discrimination.

Social Policies, Institutions and Resources

The CRC contemplates a 'solidarity effort' to realize child rights. This includes development cooperation and commitment to universal social policies rather than discretionary welfare measures. The concept of 'social responsibility' for children in Islam and the concept of social trust and community access to resources reinforce this approach to child rights implementation in the CRC.

All studies clarify that the legislative reform agenda has not been effectively implemented because of inadequate political will, resource allocation, institutional support and the non-recognition of the CRC's approach to basic child development needs as child rights. Poverty reduction and service delivery in key areas such as health and education are considered discretionary social policies. Lack of financial resources is often used to justify the failure to realize the CRC's concept of development and participation rights. This is a gap that must be addressed if a legislative reform agenda, and 'putting the law in place', is to be combined with effective enforcement. Accountability for good governance and resource allocation is promoted by the CRC, and this is denied when socio-economic rights are described as 'needs and policies'. Poverty reduction initiatives must therefore integrate a rights approach so that economic transformation initiatives do not further marginalize women and children. The State's role in the delivery of basic services in health and education must not be eliminated, and an appropriate balance between public and private sector participation must be developed.

All chapters in this book reflect the need for budget scrutiny and accountability in the allocation of financial resources to be linked with a legislative reform agenda. This has to be combined with the development of effective institutions and human resources. Although a range of child rights institutions have been established, they lack adequate human and financial resources and often replicate responsibilities. Institutional reform and capacity building are shown to be a necessary part of legislative reform, and review of this aspect must be integrated into law reform initiatives.

Devolution of authority and resources to local institutions is also highlighted in the studies as an important dimension of successful legislative reform. An over-centralized system places limitations on the capacity for enforcement and implementation.

Law Enforcement and the Contribution of the Courts

All legal systems recognize the important contribution of the courts and civil society, and general public awareness of rights, in effective implementation of a legislative reform agenda. NGO activism and involvement in public interest litigation, presenting amicus briefs and monitoring child rights, must be considered a dimension of effective implementation. Judicial training programmes and advocacy and public awareness-raising on child rights are clearly a critical support for effective implementation of legislation. The need for human rights awareness and training in alternative systems of dispute resolution, and traditional customary tribunals, emerges from the plural legal systems study.

The plural legal systems study and the common law study indicate that there should be a method of law reporting and case law to domesticate the CRC, CEDAW and international human rights at the national level. There is also an urgent need for legal education and continuing legal education to incorporate courses on international human rights, including child rights, to strengthen the capacity of lawyers and judges to integrate these norms in domestic law.

The common law, plural legal system and Islamic jurisprudence studies reinforce the importance of comparative jurisprudence in facilitating the harmonization of domestic law with the CRC, CEDAW and international human rights. The influence of received colonial law and similar transformations of the legal regimes through this interaction are seen in all these studies. There is already an environment for cross-fertilization of ideas. Judicial colloquia and conferences that bring together judges belonging to different regions as well as those in a particular legal tradition can be a useful strategy for both promoting awareness and the capacity for harmonizing international norms in local law. Exposure to these colloquia can undermine the judicial tendency to pronounce judgements that conflict with CRC standards.

Constitutional jurisprudence and other judicial interpretations emerge as the traditional method of developing the laws on child rights and implementing them. Judicial interpretations are also important for developing Islamic jurisprudence. Scholarship on child rights, comparative sharing of experiences and advocacy on the potential for harmonizing Islamic jurisprudence with international human rights law including the CRC and CEDAW seem vital in Islamic jurisdictions. Failure to explore the potential for interpretation and harmonization can lead to the entrenchment of legal concepts that are contrary to both Islamic law and the CRC and CEDAW.

CHAPTER ONE

A Comparative Study of the Impact of the Convention on the Rights of the Child

LAW REFORM IN SELECTED COMMON LAW COUNTRIES

Rebeca Rios-Kohn

INTRODUCTION

The Convention on the Rights of the Child (CRC) was adopted by the United Nations in 1989 and entered into force in 1990. The aim of this chapter is to assess the impact of this treaty on law review and reform in selected countries of the Commonwealth Caribbean[1] that apply the common law tradition, to compare the progress achieved to date and to identify ways to further encourage its implementation. To understand the meaning and significance of the CRC under common law, which is the basis of the legal systems in numerous Commonwealth countries, it is useful to review how the common law developed originally, its main characteristics and its virtues. In those countries with a history as British territories or former colonies, such as the ones of the Caribbean region, the common law tradition still prevails. Many statutes continue to reflect English common law or were enacted with the intention of restating the common law through codification.[2]

Some of the finest legal minds in England, such as Sir William Blackstone, have written extensively about the many virtues of the common law.[3] The scope of this chapter is more limited because it focuses primarily on those specific characteristics that influence directly or indirectly the implementation of the CRC, one of the most widely ratified international human rights treaties. It touches on the principle of 'the best interests of the child' by exploring briefly its historical roots in the common law tradition and comparing the way in which it is being applied today in some Commonwealth

---

[1] The Commonwealth Caribbean region includes countries located in the West Indies, which is composed of both dependent and independent States.

[2] See Wikipedia, the Free Encyclopedia, 'History of the Common Law', www.en.wikipedia. org/wiki/Common_Law (accessed 14 Dec. 2005).

[3] See W. Blackstone, *Commentaries on the Laws of England* (Oxford: Clarendon Press, originally published 1765–1769, 4 vols.). See also facsimile edition, Intro. S. N. Katz (Chicago: Univ. Chicago, 1979). Overview available at www.en.wikipedia.org/wiki/Commentaries_ on_the_Laws_of_England (accessed 14 Dec. 2005).

countries. The origin of the best interests principle is linked to the status of the child under common law and the notion of childhood in Victorian England, where children were treated like property or chattel, did not have any rights within the family or society and corporal punishment was both the norm and frequently severe. Many of the common law attitudes towards the child were reflected in the laws and policies that were subsequently adopted in former British colonies. This historical perspective helps to understand the current context and to appreciate the significance of the United Kingdom's Children Act 1989 and Human Rights Act 1998, which may influence similar developments in other countries that follow the common law.

The chapter also examines the duties of the Commonwealth Caribbean States since becoming States parties to the CRC and the nature of their obligations under the common law and international law. The wide range of measures that have been undertaken by States to implement the CRC domestically are highlighted in order to ascertain the progress achieved and the remaining challenges. A review of the legislative reform in recent years demonstrates that there is a need to place more effort on encouraging States parties to fulfil their obligations by harmonizing their national laws with the provisions of the CRC. The status of international human rights treaties in domestic law is identified as an important issue in need of increased attention in the future by all those interested in promoting the CRC and the realization of children's rights.

The chapter discusses also the role of the judiciary under the common law, recognizing the critical role it plays in deciding disputes and taking into account the reality that individuals most frequently seek remedies for human rights violations through domestic courts. The role of the judiciary is changing in a globalized world, with courts becoming interdependent and reaching across cultural boundaries. There is evidence of a growing willingness to apply international human rights norms in domestic cases. It is apparent that this trend, although still in its infancy, will have a significant impact on the implementation of the CRC and on the treaty's application, as shown by some of the emerging case law.

In preparing this chapter, national studies previously commissioned by the United Nations Children's Fund (UNICEF) as part of its Legislative Reform Initiative were a primary source of reference, in addition to the wide range of sources cited in the footnotes. The countries considered in the research were *primarily* the larger countries in the Commonwealth Caribbean region. These are Barbados and Jamaica, and, to some extent, Trinidad and Tobago. A number of independent countries, members of the Organization of Eastern Caribbean States (OECS), namely, Antigua and Barbuda, Dominica, Grenada, St. Kitts and Nevis, St. Lucia and St. Vincent and the Grenadines, also were included in the research but resulted in few significant findings. (Some developments from other countries that form part of the Commonwealth Caribbean such as Belize and Guyana also were included.) Most of the material on the United Kingdom is intended to provide a historical perspective and a general reference for understanding the evolution of the common law and to identify recent pertinent developments. Given that the information available for the national studies and therefore this chapter varied in content and quality, a thorough account of the impact of the CRC in each Caribbean country has not been possible. The objective of the review and analysis has been to highlight key developments, identify the trends and draw some general conclusions that would provide some insights into the common law legal tradition for future advocacy in promoting the implementation of the CRC. The chapter was prepared for a multidisciplinary audience, keeping in mind UNICEF's mission in developing countries. In these countries, UNICEF plays an important role in assisting countries to fulfil their obligations to improve the lives of children by protecting and realizing their rights through the implementation of the CRC and by reaching the Goals adopted by the United Nations in the Millennium Declaration and those of the 2002 UN Special Session on Children.

I. THE CONTEXT FOR LEGAL REFORM UNDER COMMON LAW: PAST AND PRESENT

The common law is rooted in historical England, whereby judicial decisions were based on tradition, custom and precedent. The common law reflected the religious beliefs and values of the community, and it evolved in light of the changing social and economic conditions under what is known as the adversarial system. It was devised as an efficient legal method for dispute resolution based on fairness and objectivity, which intended to compensate the wronged party and applied to civil and criminal cases. This method requires a form of reasoning that reflects social values as they have evolved over time and have been accepted as legal standards through judicial interpretation and application.[4] In *Commentaries on the Laws of England,* Blackstone maintained that "the common law consists of rules properly called *leges non scriptæ,* because their original institution and authority were not set down in writing as Acts of Parliament are, but they receive their binding power and the force of laws by long immemorial usage and by their universal reception throughout the kingdom."[5]

In deciding individual disputes, courts using the common law draw from previous legal reasoning or past judicial decisions, known as precedent. Legal

---

[4] See M. Cooray, *The Australian Achievement: From Bondage to Freedom,* excerpt found under 'Common Law Statute and the Rule of Law', www.ourcivilisation.com/cooray/btof/index18.htm (accessed 14 Dec. 2005) [Cooray, *Australian Achievement*].

[5] See 'Common Law' in the Catholic Encyclopedia, www.newadvent.org/cathen/09068a.htm (accessed 14 Dec. 2005).

reasoning is applied to the first case ultimately culminating in a statement of the rule of law, which must be applied to the facts of a subsequent case, if they are similar in principle, or rejected if they are not. It is the obligation of the judge to determine whether the facts are similar or different, and if it is the former, then he or she is bound by the statement of the rule of law issued by the prior court. The doctrine of *stare decisis*, which in Latin means 'stand by the decided matter', is what gives judicial precedents their strength. In the practice of law, decisions of the highest court in a given jurisdiction are binding on all other lower courts. Many legal scholars are of the view that the doctrine of *stare decisis* tends to result in more impartial adjudication because courts are obligated to base their judicial reasoning on past decisions, allowing less room for arbitrary rulings.[6]

Like other legal traditions such as the civil law tradition, the common law recognizes the rights and duties of individuals and that the principal aim of society is to protect individuals in the enjoyment of those rights.[7] One of the strongest virtues of the common law tradition, which is relevant to the application of international human rights treaties, is that, under this system, individual rights and duties are claimed and evaluated and, at the same time, the interests and concerns of the community are taken into account in an attempt to reconcile the competing interests. In other words, common law judges must balance the competing interests of the parties and draw from the norms of conduct and prevalent values respected by the community in reaching a decision.

This legal system is also based on the doctrine of the supremacy of the law. "Originally, supremacy of the law meant that not even the king was above the law, today it means that acts of governmental agencies are subject to scrutiny in ordinary legal proceedings."[8] Other essential features of the common law include the importance granted to personal liberties such as freedom of speech and expression and the right to own property. Many national constitutions embody personal liberties derived from the common law principles that evolved in England.

Under the common law, the courts play a leading role in interpreting statutes. As a rule, those statutes that reflect English common law are interpreted in light of this legal tradition, whereas those that create a new cause of action and were not recognized under the common law are interpreted more narrowly. At the same time, the courts recognize and respect the separation of powers and the predominant role of the legislature in drafting and

---

[6] M. Cooray, 'Human Rights in Australia' (1985), www.ourcivilisation.com/cooray/rights/chap3.htm (accessed 14 Dec. 2005).

[7] Blackstone, op. cit.

[8] High-Beam Encyclopedia, 'common law', http://www.encyclopedia.com/doc/1E1-commonla.html. (From *The Columbia Encyclopedia* (New York: Columbia University Press, 6th edn., 2006)).

passing statutes, as well as the judiciary's more limited role in interpreting the meaning of the law. The respect for this division of labour, which serves as restraint on the judiciary, has led to strengthening the image of many courts functioning under the common law system. For these reasons, courts in many jurisdictions enjoy the reputation of being impartial and of ensuring a greater degree of fairness. Legal scholars have noted "unlike political institutions, the common law courts have no licence to arbitrary action. Judicial discretions, unlike political discretions, are strictly limited to the application or adjustment of already established norms and standards."[9] The jurisprudence shows that under this legal system there is a greater tendency by judges to be concerned about reassuring the public that their judicial decisions are not arbitrary and in maintaining the public's confidence in the judiciary.[10]

From the main characteristics and virtues of the common law, a number of conclusions can be drawn that are relevant to understanding the way in which an international human rights treaty should be promoted to the courts, legislators and legal practitioners working under this legal system:

- *Identify the legal trends* – Because common law is rooted in the English legal system, the emerging jurisprudence developing in a number of Commonwealth countries should be reviewed and analyzed in order to identify the trends of the judiciary and legislature.
- *Examine relevant case law* – Because all common law jurisdictions are bound by precedent and judges are obligated to follow the decisions of previous cases, prior relevant case law should be examined and new cases followed closely in order to identify positive and negative trends. Related to this is the fact that, under the common law system, judges play a critical role in deciding a wide range of disputes, and, therefore, closer attention must be paid to their legal reasoning.
- *Learn what factors influence legal decisions* – It is essential to become familiar with the processes by which judges in a particular jurisdiction decide cases. In addition to the available sources of law that include case law, statutes and the national constitution, the outcome also can be influenced by tradition, custom, conception of social needs and the community's standards of justice and morals.
- *Distinguish whether it is a common law or statutory law* – It should be taken into account that large areas of the law today are found in a statutory framework and judges will be called upon to interpret the meaning of the statute. Judges prefer to interpret statutes that are clearly drafted; some texts can be difficult and questions arise that lead to the

---

[9] Ibid.

[10] C. McCrudden, 'Common Law of Human Rights?: Transnational Judicial Conversations on Constitutional Rights', *Oxford J. of Legal Stud.* 23(4) (2000): p. 514.

application of different rules of interpretation. The court also may decide that it is a matter best left for the legislature.

- *Recognize the important role of the judiciary* – It is critical to recognize the authority vested under the common law system in the courts and judges having the power to determine controversies, as well as to protect the rights and interests of persons and of property.
- *Recognize differences between the weight of common law and statutory law in the jurisdiction* – In some countries, the common law has been diminished by the statutes passed by Parliament. For example, in both England and Australia the common law is increasingly regarded as subservient to the laws adopted by Parliament.[11] Robinson points out that there has been a strong influence of the English common law in Barbados; however, it is perceived today as a "rapidly diminishing source of law." This is because Parliament nowadays has the power to enact laws that overrule the common law. Nevertheless, there remain a number of common law principles received during the colonial period that continue to apply, including the inherent jurisdiction of the court to act in the interests of the child by making a child a ward of the court.[12]

II. THE STATUS OF THE CHILD UNDER COMMON LAW

According to historians, the concept of childhood did not emerge until the seventeenth century and before that time, in most of Europe "the special nature of children was ignored and children were treated as miniature adults."[13] The historical roots of the British common law system also reveal a "brutal indifference to a child's fate."[14] It is well documented that until approximately the nineteenth century, children were treated like property or chattel but were valued by their families for their contributions through their work. As Blackstone pointed out, the father "may indeed have the benefit of his children's labour while they live with him, and are maintained by him: but this is no more than he is entitled to from his apprentices or servants."[15] Although the principle of the best interests of the child has deep Anglo-Saxon roots, a review of the historical development of parenthood and childhood under early common law shows indeed that the notion of children's rights did not exist whatsoever. Children had a low status within

[11] Cooray, *Australian Achievement*, op. cit.

[12] T. Robinson, 'Legislative Reform Initiative, National Study of Barbados' (unpublished study for Legislative Reform Initiative, UNICEF, 2004), p. 10.

[13] M. Flekkoy and N. Hevener Kaufman, *Rights and Responsibilities in Family and Society* (London: Jessica Kingsley Publishers, 1997), p. 15.

[14] J. C. Hall, 'The Waning of Parental Rights', *Cambridge LJ* 31 (1972): p. 265.

[15] Blackstone, op. cit., Book 1, Ch. 16.

society and within the family. The law, which usually reflects the values and traditions of a society, treated them accordingly.

At common law, a child was one who had not attained the age of 14 years.[16] As in most developing countries today, many children were forced to work as a result of their level of poverty. Child labour was not only acceptable, but it also was promoted at the highest levels; for example, by Parliament, which stated that a working child was more useful to his family. It was further justified by society's perception that for those children of the lower classes, education was not necessary as child labourers were deemed essential to the country's economy. Thus, the vast majority of working children had very little schooling. In 1840, only 20 per cent of children had gone to school and, finally, in 1870, the Education Act was passed in England, requiring all children between the ages of five and ten to attend school.[17]

Early common law did not provide any special treatment for children who committed crimes; thus, they were liable for their actions the same as adults. The minimum age of criminal responsibility was set as young as seven, and children guilty of crimes were imprisoned. The harshness of the laws at that time is illustrated by the Stubborn Child Statute enacted by the State of Massachusetts in 1646, which provided that a stubborn or rebellious son above 15 years of age could be put to death pursuant to a complaint submitted by the child's parents.[18] According to historical records, children were hanged as late as 1708 and the notion of a juvenile court for juvenile offenders only emerged in the early twentieth century.[19]

To a large extent, the law treated children as if they were invisible. The 'Mary Ellen Affair' is often cited to illustrate the fact that in nineteenth-century England and in the United States, some jurisdictions had enacted laws protecting animals from cruelty before they would enact legislation to protect children from abuse. In this 1874 case that occurred in New York City, a child's parents were prosecuted for keeping their daughter chained to a bed and fed only bread and water. Because of the absence of legal protection for children at the time, the prosecutors were forced to draw an analogy with a law for the prevention of cruelty against animals.[20]

It was not until the early twentieth century that the principle of the best interests, also understood as 'the child's welfare', came to be recognized by the English courts as the paramount consideration in custody battles. English

---

[16] See 'Child', *Black's Law Dictionary* (St. Paul, MN: West Publishing Co., 6th edn., 1990).

[17] See 'Child Labour in Victorian England', www.freeessays.cc/db/18/ehc33.shtml (accessed 14 Dec. 2005).

[18] G. Van Bueren, *The International Law on the Rights of the Child* (The Hague: Martinus Nijhoff Publishers for Save the Children, 1995), p. 72.

[19] Encyclopedia Britannica, 'Human Rights', www.britannica.com/eb/article-9106289/human-rights (accessed 14 Dec. 2005).

[20] R. Rios-Kohn, 'The Convention on the Rights of the Child: Progress and Challenges', *Georgetown J on Fighting Poverty* (Summer 1998): p. 140.

common law did not recognize a legal relationship between parent and child, only those between parents and their legitimate children. At common law, a child born to a woman outside of marriage was regarded as a *filius nullius*, or bastard, and had few rights. As Blackstone noted, "he can inherit nothing, being looked upon as the son of nobody." The mother had no parental rights but had a duty to support the child. At the same time, the father of a child born outside of marriage could not acquire parental rights nor had any legal duties in relation to the child's upbringing and well-being.[21] Under the English common law, all children born before matrimony were deemed bastards by the law. Blackstone's reasoning aims to justify the common law's refusal to grant children born outside of marriage legitimate status even if subsequent to their birth the parents became legally married. This view reflects the way the laws were drafted at the time, to protect certain societal interests but not necessarily those of the child's.

Goonesekere has explained that the common law system recognized "the superior parental right of a man in a family unit created within a marriage, and was more concerned with safeguarding his parental rights than the interests of children." Legal authority over legitimate children was vested in the father, thereby excluding the mother, and the welfare of the child was not considered.[22] Fathers were recognized as the legal head of the family, children were under their authority, and they made all the decisions concerning them. Giving the father absolute authority was considered essential for maintaining stability and protecting the family within the society. In regard to the low status of the wife in a marriage, Blackstone further reasoned, but not without some degree of irony, that the legal disabilities of married women were "for the most part intended for her protection and benefit. So great a favourite is the female sex of the laws of England."[23]

According to Goonesekere, although courts were reluctant to protect children's interests and preferred instead to protect those concerns they regarded as greater for the society as a whole, some positive developments took place gradually through the intervention of the Court of Chancery using equity as opposed to common law.[24] Equity was a system of rules and principles that originated in England as an alternative to the harsh rules of common law and under which justice was administered according to fairness.[25] The Court

---

[21] G. Douglas and N. Lowe, 'Becoming a Parent in English Law', in *Parenthood in Modern Society: Legal and Social Issues For the Twenty-First Century*, ed. J. Eekelaar and P. Šarčević (Dordrecht: Martinus Nijhoff Publishers, 1993), p. 145.

[22] S. Goonesekere, 'The Best Interests of the Child: A South Asian Perspective', in *The Best Interests of the Child: Reconciling Culture and Human Rights*, ed. P. Alston (Oxford: Clarendon Press, 1994), p. 117 [Alston, *Best Interests of the Child*].

[23] As noted by J. Eekelaar, 'Interests of the Child and the Child's Wishes', in Alston, *Best Interests of the Child*, op. cit., p. 44.

[24] Goonesekere, op. cit., p. 119.

[25] See definition in *Black's Law Dictionary*, op. cit.

of Chancery could intervene between parent and child by making a child a
'ward of the court', which allowed the court to enforce orders concerning
the child's welfare and education. Eventually, as a result of the successful
administration of equity, English courts finally recognized the best interests
of the child as the first and paramount consideration in all custody disputes.
This acceptance of the principle by English law led to the adoption of more
child-focused legislation during the nineteenth century. In a series of statutes,
the father's virtual absolute custodial right was modified and the courts had
the power to grant custody of a legitimate child to the mother. The Guardianship Act of 1925 required courts to regard the "child's welfare as the first
and paramount consideration."[26]

The 1989 Children's Act and Human Rights Act of 1998
in the United Kingdom

The law has made considerable progress to protect children in the United
Kingdom since the Victorian period. Most significant are the Children's Act
passed in 1989, the ratification of the CRC in 1991 and the Human Rights
Act adopted in 1998. The Children's Act seeks to provide greater protection
to children and is based on the belief that children are generally best looked
after within the family, with both parents playing a full part and without
resort to legal proceedings. The Act provides that the welfare of the children
"is the paramount consideration." The Act further recognizes that children
should always be *consulted* (subject to age and understanding) and kept
informed and should *participate* about decisions that concern them. Thus,
its provisions are aimed to:

i. make children's welfare a priority;
ii. recognize that children are best brought up within their families wherever
possible;
iii. ensure the local authority can provide services for children and families
in need;
iv. promote partnership between children, parents and local authorities; and
v. improve the way courts deal with children and families with rights of
appeal against court decisions.[27]

The CRC came into force in the United Kingdom in 1992, but because
it has not been incorporated into domestic law, it is regarded as not giving

---

[26] Goonesekere, op. cit., p. 120.
[27] See The Children Act 1989, National Teaching Advisory Service, www.ntas.org.uk/
resources/childrenact.htm (accessed 15 Dec. 2005); The Children's Act (1989) (UK), available at www.opsi.gov.uk/acts/acts1989/Ukpga_19890041_en_1.htm.

"enforceable rights directly to individual children, but imposing obligations on the State to bring those rights into national law."[28]

In 1951, the United Kingdom signed and ratified the European Convention on Human Rights (ECHR), which enshrines fundamental civil and political rights (but not economic, social and cultural rights) and is a treaty agreement of the Council of Europe. Since coming into force on 2 October 2000, the Human Rights Act of 1998 has made rights from the ECHR, the original source of the Act, enforceable in British courts because it incorporates the ECHR into the law of England and Wales. It should be noted that the ECHR had not been incorporated previously into domestic law because it was perceived that the common law already protected human rights. According to the Department for Constitutional Affairs of the United Kingdom, the Human Rights Act incorporates the rights and freedoms of the European Convention on Human Rights as follows:

i. It makes it unlawful for a *public authority* to violate Convention rights, unless, because of an Act of Parliament, it had no choice (a public authority includes local authorities, government departments, police, prison and immigration officers, public prosecutors, courts and tribunals and any other individual exercising a public function).
ii. It states that all UK legislation should be given a meaning that fits with the rights, if that is possible. If a Court says it is not possible, it will be up to Parliament to decide what to do.
iii. Cases can be dealt with in a UK court or tribunal and it is not necessary to bring a case before the European Court of Human Rights in Strasbourg.
iv. Cases under the Human Rights Act can only be brought by 'victims' of a breach of one or more Convention rights by a public authority.[29]

The Act facilitates the role of judges in the United Kingdom when an individual's rights are violated. However, the Human Rights Act was intended to preserve the primacy of Parliament. In other words, a judge's decision cannot overrule Parliament. "If a judge finds that a piece of primary legislation is incompatible with the Act, (s)he can make a 'declaration of incompatibility', but it remains for Parliament to decide what, if any, action to take."[30]

The Human Rights Act was passed in light of the numerous cases emerging from England and Wales that provoked a growing awareness that the common law did not adequately protect human rights and therefore

---

[28] See Children and Young People's Unit (CYPU), Young People and Families Directorate UK, www.allchildrenni.gov.uk (accessed 14 Dec. 2005).
[29] Department for Constitutional Affairs of the United Kingdom, Frequently Asked Questions, www.dca.gov.uk/peoples-rights/human-rights (accessed 14 Dec. 2005).
[30] Ibid.

incorporation of the ECHR was necessary.[31] According to legal commentators, the Act is expected to have an enormous impact on the common law system in the United Kingdom or "revolutionise the practice of law in Britain":

> The role of the judiciary will be immensely important and examinations this year will almost certainly include questions considering the effect which the Act will have on English law and the judicial interpretation of statutory provisions in the light of the European Convention, i.e. the effect which the Act will have on the common law.[32]

It also has been pointed out that the interpretation of the Act will raise the issue of the extent to which British courts will be willing to use jurisprudence from other countries in order to help in interpreting the new law.[33]

III. THE PRINCIPLE OF THE 'BEST INTERESTS OF THE CHILD' UNDER COMMON LAW

The principle of the 'best interests of the child' has an established history under the common law tradition, particularly in the area of family law in England, countries of the Commonwealth, the United States, and in the English-speaking Caribbean. The 'best interests of the child' is a legal standard that is used today by courts of the common law system in deciding cases of child custody and guardianship, child support, and other issues of family law. The standard is frequently applied to determine legal obligations and entitlements in situations in which a child is born outside of marriage. In Australia, the court applies the standard in relation to custody, guardianship, or welfare of a child, where it must consider the 'welfare of the child' as the paramount consideration.[34] In the 1976 English Adoption Act, the court "shall have regard to all the circumstances, first consideration being given to the need to safeguard and promote the welfare of the child throughout her or his childhood."[35] In order to ascertain what is in the best interests of the child, courts turn to a wide range of sources and order investigations through social workers, teachers, psychologists and other professionals.

The standard is recognized as one of the overarching or umbrella principles of the CRC, which provides that the best interests of the child shall be

---

[31] J. Wadham and H. Mountfield, 'Rights Brought Home' (White Paper, 1997), p. 187. Also see J. Wadham, H. Mountfield, and A. Edmundson, *Blackstone's Guide to the Human Rights Act of 1998* (Oxford: Oxford Univ. Press, 2003).

[32] C. Bobb-Semple, 'The Common Law and Human Rights', *Concilio (the daily online magazine for law students)*, www.spr-consilio.com/humanrights.html.

[33] McCrudden, op. cit., p. 499.

[34] S. Parker, 'The Best Interests of the Child – Principles and Problems', in Alston, *Best Interests of the Child*, op. cit., p. 27.

[35] Ibid.

"a primary consideration in all actions concerning children."[36] The principle is also applied to other rights enshrined in the CRC:

- Article 9, in relation to the separation of the child from his or her parents;
- Article 18, regarding the responsibility of both parents for the upbringing and development of the child;
- Articles 20 and 21, regarding a child temporarily or permanently deprived of a family environment and concerning national and intercountry adoption; and
- Articles 37 and 40, regarding a child deprived of liberty or arrested and accused of having infringed the penal law and therefore subject to the justice system.

The principle is further relevant as an aid to construction when there is a need for clarification of a provision in the CRC or when there are competing rights that must be resolved in order to ensure the most favourable outcome in all actions that concern the child.[37] As the CRC has been adopted and has reached virtual universal ratification (with the exception of Somalia and the United States), the principle of the best interests of the child has gained international status and has been examined by a number of prominent jurists from different cultural perspectives. The principle is included in two provisions of the Convention on the Elimination of All Forms of Discrimination against Women (CEDAW), addressing the common responsibility of men and women in the upbringing of their children and the placement of a child outside the care of the child's own parents.[38] The African Charter on the Rights and Welfare of the Child also provides that "in all actions concerning the child undertaken by any person or authority the best interests of the child shall be the primary consideration."[39] The use of the principle, including with variations, is also found in other international human rights instruments.[40] Alston notes that the complexity of the principle and the lack of a precise meaning pose challenges in its application. Despite these factors

---

[36] Ibid.; Convention on the Rights of the Child, Convention on the Rights of the Child, G.A. res. 44/25, annex, *adopted* 20 Nov. 1989, 44 U.N. GAOR Supp. (No. 49) at 167, Art. 3, U.N. Doc. A/44/49 (1989), *entered into force* 2 Sept. 1990. Reprinted in 28 *ILM* (1989): p. 1448 [CRC].

[37] P. Alston, 'The Best Interests Principle: Towards a Reconciliation of Culture and Human Rights', in Alston, *Best Interests of the Child*, op. cit., p. 16.

[38] Convention on the Elimination of All Forms of Discrimination against Women, G.A. res. 34/180, *adopted* 18 Dec. 1979, 34 U.N. GAOR Supp. (No. 46) at 193, Arts. 5(b) and 16(1)(d), U.N. Doc. A/34/46, *entered into force* 3 Sept. 1981.

[39] African Charter on the Rights and Welfare of the Child, Art. 4(1), OAU Doc. CAB/LEG/ 24.9/49, *adopted* July 1990, *entered into force* 29 Nov. 1999.

[40] See, for example, the 1924 Declaration of the Rights of the Child adopted by the League of Nations and United Nations Declaration of the Rights of the Child (G.A. res. 1386 (XIV), 14 U.N. GAOR Supp. (No. 16) at 19, U.N. Doc. A/4354 (1959)).

and the diverse interpretations that may be given, "the principle has come to be known in one form or another to many national legal systems and has important analogues in diverse cultural, religious and other traditions."[41] The best interests principle has been incorporated in national constitutions, children's acts, family law codes and a wide range of juvenile justice laws.

Alston further points out that, in the past, the drafters of international human rights instruments have drawn upon principles and standards that have been widely accepted within domestic legal systems. He further observes that "those domestic courts which seek to apply the Convention may seek to adopt a rather different approach from that which they themselves have hitherto developed, primarily within the limited context of custody decisions."[42] However, it is also possible that because domestic courts functioning under the common law system are more familiar with the standard, they may be more willing to apply it in other cases outside of family law. The CRC requires its application "in all actions concerning children whether undertaken by public or private social welfare institutions, courts of law, administrative authorities or legislative bodies."[43] Clearly, actual implementation of the principle may raise problems when it is interpreted in a culturally relativist manner to justify customs and practices that are contrary to CRC and CEDAW. It is therefore most critical to stress the importance of interpreting the best interests principle so as to guarantee the rights as per the CRC, as well as CEDAW.

McDowell reports that in the Commonwealth Caribbean region the welfare of the child is of paramount importance in custody cases, and in all "cases of disputes concerning children", the best interests of the child, also applied in Article 9 of the CRC, is "the overriding criteria."[44] The Family Law (Guardianship of Minors, Domicile and Maintenance) Act of Trinidad and Tobago, for example, provides in Section 3 that the court in deciding questions concerning the legal custody or upbringing of a minor, or the administration of any property belonging to or held in trust for a minor or the application of the income thereof, shall regard the welfare of the minor as the first and paramount consideration.[45] McDowell cites a number of cases in the Commonwealth Caribbean in which "the interest and welfare of the child in question were given priority."[46]

---

[41] Alston, *Best Interests of the Child*, op. cit., p. 5.

[42] Ibid., p. 17.   [43] CRC, op. cit., Art. 3.

[44] Z. McDowell, *Elements of Child Law in the Commonwealth Caribbean* (Kingston, Jamaica: University of the West Indies Press, 2000), p. 237.

[45] Laws of the Republic of Trinidad and Tobago, Chap. 46:08, as reported McDowell, in ibid.

[46] Ibid. See, for example, *Durity v Benjamin* (unreported) 30 July 1993 (High Ct., Trin. & Tobago) (No. 1596 of 1993); *Sounders v Sounders* (unreported) 26 Feb. 1993 (S. Ct., Bahamas) (No. 307 of 1990); *Clement v Graham* (unreported) 2 Apr. 1993 (High Ct., Trin. & Tobago) (No. 2441 of 1991); *Campbell v Campbell* et al. (unreported) 3 July 1993 (High Ct., Trin. & Tobago) (No. 719 of 1982); *Balraj v Dewar* (unreported) 30 June 1994,

In Barbados, the principle of the best interests of the child is recognized by law. Thus, the welfare of the child must be of paramount consideration and this is reflected in diverse legislation. Under "the Family Law Act (chap. 214, sect. 43 (1)) in matters relating to guardianship, custody, or access to children, the court must regard the welfare of the children as the first and paramount consideration." In accordance with this law, the court must not issue an order that "is contrary to the wishes of a child who has attained the age of 16 years, unless the court feels that in the circumstances it is necessary to do so." Similar to the English common law, in Barbados the common law provides that "the court also has an inherent jurisdiction to act in the interests of a child by making the child a ward of court, the Crown offering protection as *parens patrae*. In addition, the concept of the best interests of the child is stated in the Juvenile Offenders Act (chap. 138), the Adoption Act (chap. 212) and the Child Care Board Act (chap. 381)."[47]

Recognizing the complexity and multidimensional character of the CRC, Alston maintains that the principle is perhaps the most important of all in the treaty because all the other provisions derive their inspiration and force from it.[48] The wide acceptance of the principle of the best interests of the child provides many entry points in connection with the promotion of the CRC within the legal community. As noted, judges and lawyers, as well as the legislature, will already be familiar with the principle, which provides a window of opportunity to introduce it in other areas such as health and education, as well as in relation to some civil and political rights. Accordingly, here are some points to consider in the promotion of this principle:

- *Introduce the principle of the best interests of the child to a multi-disciplinary audience* – Courts look to a wide range of professionals to assess what is in the best interests of the child, which has important socio-economic and cultural considerations. It would be opportune to introduce the principle to a multidisciplinary audience that includes teachers, social workers, psychologists, law enforcement officers and other professionals.

- *Provide an entry point for CRC* – With so many legal systems in different cultures having accepted the principle of the best interests, it provides an important entry point for promoting other articles of the CRC that include it (i.e, Articles 9, 18, 20, 21, 37 and 40), particularly in countries where the CRC has not been incorporated into domestic law.

(High Ct., Trin. & Tobago) (No. 5–878 of 1993); *Nicholls v Goulding* et al. (unreported) 1 Sept. 1994, (High Ct., Barb.) (No. 352 of 1993); *Garcia v Garcia* (unreported) 30 June 1997 (High Ct., Trin. & Tobago) (No. 795/95).

[47] Committee on the Rights of the Child, 'Initial Reports of States Parties due in 1992: Barbados', U.N. Doc. CRC/C/3/Add.45, 11 Feb. 1997, paras. 45–47 ['Initial State Party Report: Barbados'].

[48] P. Alston, *Best Interests of the Child*, op. cit., p. 3.

- *Target family law lawyers* – Because the best interests principle is more widely used in family law matters, it is important to promote the whole of the CRC with lawyers practicing family law who may be more willing to use its provisions in their legal arguments before the courts.

- *Identify judicial precedents and trends* – In the application of the best interests principle, it is important to identify judicial precedents and trends, particularly in light of the weight that judicial interpretation may have on the rest of society in a specific jurisdiction.

- *Raise awareness of interpretations contrary to CRC* – Implementation of the principle may raise problems when it is interpreted in a culturally relativist manner to justify customs and practices that are contrary to the CRC and CEDAW.

- *Encourage all relevant actors to apply the best interests principle in all pertinent legislation, policies and programmes* – that should also be in accordance with the norms and standards of the CRC.

IV. THE GOVERNMENT SYSTEM AND LEGAL TRADITION IN
SELECTED COMMON LAW COUNTRIES OF THE
COMMONWEALTH CARIBBEAN

Barbados was first settled by the British in 1627 and slaves worked the sugar plantations established on the island until 1834, when slavery was abolished. Gradually there were social and political reforms during the 1940s and 1950s that led to independence in 1966. Jamaica shares a similar heritage. The British began their full colonization of Jamaica as early as 1661, and the country only gained full independence within the British Commonwealth in 1962. The islands of Trinidad and Tobago came under British control in the eighteenth century and were granted independence also in 1962.[49] Today, a majority of the OECS countries are independent states (Antigua and Barbuda, Dominica, Grenada, St. Kitts and Nevis, St. Lucia, St. Vincent and the Grenadines) and a small minority (Anguilla, British Virgin Islands and Montserrat) remain as British territories.

Most of the Caribbean countries considered in the study are Commonwealth realms, in which the Head of State is the Queen of England, represented by a Governor General. They use the parliamentary system in which the head of government depends upon the support of the Parliament.[50] Seven

---

[49] Information provided by UNICEF Caribbean Area Office, which, at the time of writing, had overall responsibility for Antigua and Barbuda, Barbados, the British Virgin Islands, Dominica, Grenada, Montserrat, St. Kitts and Nevis, St. Lucia, St. Vincent and the Grenadines, Suriname, Trinidad and Tobago, Turks and Caicos Islands – with an aggregate population of 2.5 million. Information also was provided by UNICEF Jamaica.

[50] See Central Intelligence Agency (US), *The World Factbook*, www.cia.gov/cia/publications/factbook/geos/jm.html (accessed 14 Dec. 2005).

of the independent States considered have the Queen of England as their Head of State who is represented by the Governor General. The exceptions are Dominica, Guyana and Trinidad and Tobago. Dominica is a parliamentary democracy within the Commonwealth of Nations with a president as Head of State. It was never a Commonwealth realm with the British monarch as Head of State, as it became a republic when it was granted independence by the United Kingdom in 1978. Trinidad and Tobago is also a parliamentary democracy but with a president elected by an electoral college that consists of members of the Senate and House of Representatives. Guyana also is a republic and is the only country belonging to the Commonwealth that is located on the mainland of South America.

Under the parliamentary system of government, there is not a defined separation of powers between the legislative and executive branches of government. There are, however, clear separate roles between the head of government and Head of State. The head of government is normally the prime minister, whereas, the Head of State is primarily a ceremonial position. In these countries, the principal sources of law are the constitution – the supreme law of the land – followed by statutory law and common law.

The most popular and widespread parliamentary system is the 'Westminster model'. With origins in the United Kingdom, it was adopted in many of the Commonwealth countries including those of the English-speaking Caribbean. In the United Kingdom, Parliament is the supreme legislative authority and is composed of three bodies – the Queen and the two Houses of Parliament (the House of Lords and House of Commons), which function and operate separately. The Parliament in the United Kingdom has broad legislative powers; however, it does not exercise its supremacy without taking into account the common law and public opinion. Although the United Kingdom does not have a formal written constitution containing a bill of rights, the possession of rights and freedoms is an inherent part of being a member of society and can only be restricted by an Act of Parliament.[51]

With few exceptions, therefore, the Commonwealth-Caribbean governments have adopted the Westminster model. After gaining its independence, Barbados adopted the Westminster parliamentary system of government. Under the Barbados Constitution of 1966, Parliament is composed of the British monarch, the Senate and the House of Assembly. The Governor General, the prime minister and his cabinet have executive authority, but the prime minister is the most powerful figure both in the Executive and in the cabinet, with the latter being the principal vehicle for policy. Similarly, in most of the other selected countries, the executive power is primarily vested in the prime minister and cabinet.

---

[51] See Wikipedia Encyclopedia, 'Parliamentary system', www.en.wikipedia.org/wiki/Parliamentary_system (accessed 14 Dec. 2005).

The majority of the English-speaking Caribbean States selected for the study (Antigua and Barbuda, Barbados, Grenada, Jamaica, St. Lucia and Trinidad and Tobago) have bicameral parliaments, whereas three have single chambers (Dominica, St. Kitts and Nevis, and St. Vincent and the Grenadines). In Barbados, legislative bills may be submitted to either the Senate or the House of Assembly and become law after they are passed by both houses and signed by the Governor General.

An important feature of the Westminster system of government is that the "most significant transfer of power occurs between the legislature and the executive, by the former vesting in the latter substantial powers to make delegated legislation principally in the form of regulations. The separation of powers doctrine is most strongly epitomized in relation to the independence of the judiciary from the other branches of government, and is protected from encroachment by the constitution."[52] It should be noted that in the Caribbean context there is a higher concentration of power within the executive branch, granted by the constitutions. It has been pointed out that despite the separation of powers doctrine being a feature of the Westminster model, in practice there is no strict separation (i.e., of powers as between the executive branch and legislative branch of the government). In the case of Barbados, for example, the prime minister has extensive power to dissolve Parliament and control over the appointment and removal of the Ministers of Cabinet.[53]

Historically, the legal system of all the countries of the Commonwealth Caribbean is based primarily on the British common law, a legacy of the colonial period, with the exception of Guyana and St. Lucia. Guyana has the influence of the Roman-Dutch tradition and St. Lucia of the French civil law. In addition, there were minor influences arising from other legal traditions such as Hindu/Indian and Islamic law that were incorporated into the legislation of some of these countries.[54] The legal system in Jamaica resembles closely the system of the United Kingdom, of which it was a colony until achieving independence in 1962.

Subsequent to gaining their independence from the United Kingdom, most of the countries of the Commonwealth Caribbean continued to depend upon its legal system. The Judicial Committee of the Privy Council was maintained by each State as its highest court of appeal, in addition to the local trial and appellate courts. The Privy Council based in London acted as the court of last resort for most of the English Caribbean States until

---

[52] L. Jackson, 'Report on Law Reform Initiatives Relating to the Convention on the Rights of the Child in the OECS' (unpublished study for Legislative Reform Initiative, UNICEF, 2004), p. 5.

[53] Robinson, op cit.

[54] See Y. Dina, 'Guide to Caribbean Research', www.llrx.com/features/Caribbean.htm (accessed 14 Feb. 2006).

very recently, when the Caribbean Court of Justice was inaugurated in 2005. Although there had been considerable interest since the 1970s in establishing a higher court in the region, it did not materialize until 2001, when some 11 countries agreed to replace the British Court with a new Caribbean Court of Justice, which would become the region's highest court of appeal. Presently, the Court sits in Trinidad and Tobago.[55] According to the 'Guide for Caribbean Research' by a law librarian at the College of the Bahamas Law Library, all the countries in the region have published their own legislation since their independence.[56] In addition, Barbados, Jamaica and Trinidad and Tobago currently publish Law Reports. The OECS also produces its own Law Reports.[57]

V. THE STATUS OF INTERNATIONAL HUMAN RIGHTS TREATIES IN DOMESTIC LAW IN SELECTED COMMON LAW COUNTRIES

Most of the countries in the study were prompt to ratify the CRC soon after it entered into force in 1990, with Barbados that same year, Jamaica in 1991 and the members of the OECS more than 10 years ago. According to international monitoring treaty bodies such as the Committee on the Rights of the Child, for the most part, the duties and obligations of the State primarily reported on are those that involve the executive and legislative branches of government – those branches that are central to the ratification/accession process, for withdrawing reservations, establishing national monitoring mechanisms and for legislative and constitutional reform, among other things. It should be noted that the executive and legislative branches will again play a leading role in the ratification of the additional protocols to the CRC, in those countries that have not yet done so.[58] Thus far, only Jamaica has ratified the Optional Protocol concerning children in armed conflict. Other Caribbean States signatories to the CRC wishing to take such a step will be required to carry out another ratification process.

These countries also have committed themselves to respecting and protecting human rights by ratifying other major international and regional treaties, which reinforce a number of human rights that are embodied in

---

[55] See CARICOM, 'Caribbean Court of Justice', www.jis.gov.jm/special_sections/ CARICOMNew/ccj.html (accessed 15 Feb. 2006).

[56] Dina, op. cit.

[57] See ibid. Based on information from UNICEF Barbados, the Cayman Islands, the Bahamas and Belize also have Law Reports.

[58] Neither the Optional Protocol to the Convention on the Rights of the Child on the involvement of children in armed conflict nor the Optional Protocol on the sale of children, child prostitution and child pornography have been ratified by Barbados or by most of the countries of the OECS including Grenada, St. Kitts and Nevis, St. Lucia, or by Zimbabwe (as of November 2006). Antigua and St. Vincent and the Grenadines have only ratified the latter.

the CRC.[59] Some of the countries are further bound through their voluntary ratification to implement the American Convention on Human Rights, and may participate in the activities of the Inter-American Commission on Human Rights. Signatories to the American Convention currently include Barbados, Dominica, Grenada and Jamaica.[60] The Convention provides: "Any State Party may, when it deposits its instrument of ratification of or adherence to this Convention, or at any later time, declare that it recognizes the competence of the Commission to receive and examine communications in which a State Party alleges that another State Party has committed a violation of a human right set forth in this Convention."[61] Furthermore, a State party "may upon depositing its instrument of ratification or adherence to the Convention declare that it recognizes as binding the jurisdiction of the Court on all matters relating to the interpretation of application of this Convention."[62] To date, only two of the countries in the study have accepted the jurisdiction of the Inter-American Court of Human Rights. Barbados accepted competence of the Court in June 2000, and Trinidad and Tobago accepted jurisdiction in 1991 but later denounced the Convention in 1999.

A number of factors influence the extent to which international human rights standards are implemented at the national level. These include the political commitment to human rights, the social and cultural conditions and the existence of a human rights culture within the society, as well as the overall economy of the country. The common law requires yet another important factor, which is the incorporation of a treaty into domestic law. In other words, under what is known as the 'dualist model', as a general rule, in nearly all common law countries international treaties cannot be enforced and have no legal effect in domestic courts unless they have been incorporated into domestic law through legislation. The exception to the rule is that an international treaty can influence the interpretation and application of a law when it is ambiguous.[63]

---

[59] These include the International Covenant on Civil and Political Rights; the International Covenant on Economic, Social and Cultural Rights; the Convention on the Elimination on All Forms of Discrimination against Women and the Convention on the Elimination of all Forms of Racial Discrimination.

[60] Inter-American Commission on Human Rights, Basic Documents: 'Signatures and Current Status of Ratifications, American Convention on Human Rights', www.cidh.org/ Basicos/basic4.htm.

[61] American Convention on Human Rights, adopted at the Inter-American Specialized Conference on Human Rights, San José, Costa Rica (22 Nov. 1969), Art. 45.

[62] Ibid., Art. 62(1).

[63] For more information on the dualist theory under common law, see Office of the High Commissioner for Human Rights (OHCHR) and the International Bar Association, *Human Rights in the Administration of Justice* (Geneva: United Nations, 2003), Ch. 1 (International Human Rights Law and the Role of the Legal Professions: A General Introduction), https:// webmcdev.ucc.fsu.edu/human-rights/ch1/ch1.html (accessed 14 Dec. 2005). Also see 'Is the Dualist-Monist Controversy in International Law' Simply a Fiction? at http://mezinarodni2. juristic.cz/51001/clanek/mpv1 (accessed 14 Dec. 2005).

Following this reasoning, unless there is incorporation, in the event of a conflict between a provision of an international human rights treaty and national legislation, the latter will prevail. This is all based on the premise that the legislature did not intend to legislate in a manner that is contrary to international law. In other words, although in common law systems the dualist theory predominates, nevertheless under international law, national laws are expected to be in conformity with the international treaties that have entered into force in the country. Otherwise, the State is supposed to take steps to modify domestic law in keeping with the treaties ratified.

Through the act of 'incorporation' an international human rights treaty can become part of domestic law, but this requires an Act of Parliament. Moreover, through incorporation, the treaty itself remains in its original form. An alternative to incorporation is to repeal the relevant rules of law and to propose new laws, which requires drafting them in accordance with the provisions of the CRC. In General Comment No. 5, the Committee on the Rights of the Child has indicated that incorporation is the preferred approach.[64] Although the General Comments of the Committee are not binding on States parties to the CRC, they are nevertheless useful references and can be used as persuasive authority in advocacy aimed at promoting the implementation of the treaty. Given the comprehensive nature of the CRC, ideally the Convention should be incorporated through a consolidated children's rights statute that should be supplemented through sectoral law reform in order to ensure harmony and consistency and avoid contradictions.

In this context, it is important to distinguish between treaties that are signed and ratified by States and thus become binding on them and customary international law, which consists of principles and norms that have been widely accepted as a result of practices by States. In the United Kingdom, customary international law forms part of the common law, whereas international treaties are regarded as purely executive, rather than legislative acts. Thus, a treaty under British law only becomes part of domestic law if the corresponding legislation is adopted. These principles likewise apply in those countries where English common law has been established as the legal tradition. Some common law countries that have a written constitution take a different approach in the incorporation of international law into the domestic law. Ireland provides an example in which the Constitution stipulates that the country will not be bound by any treaty involving public funds without first seeking the approval of the legislature.[65]

Law reform is further necessary in the different sectors such as health, education, welfare, family law, justice and in those areas of the law that

---

[64] Committee on the Rights of the Child, General Comment No. 5: 'General measures of implementation for the Convention on the Rights of the Child', para. 20, U.N. Doc. CRC/GC/2003/5, 3 Oct. 2003 [General Comment No. 5].

[65] See Encyclopedia Britannica, 'Human Rights', op cit.

address particular protection issues, such as sexual exploitation and abuse. The purpose of the reform is to ensure that, for example, laws and regulations regarding health are in accordance with Article 24 and other relevant provisions of the CRC including the principle of non-discrimination, the principle of the best interests of the child and the principle of the right of the child to participate in decisions that concern him or her in accordance with his or her evolving capacities.[66] None of the countries of the Commonwealth Caribbean (with one exception) have initiated an 'act of incorporation' of the CRC or of any other international human rights instrument. The exception is Belize, which is the only example of a country in the region that has incorporated the entire CRC through a legislative act, The 1998 Families and Children Act, First Schedule.[67] For the most part, the legislative reform undertaken has not been uniform and rather piecemeal in the different sectors, primarily in the area of family law, juvenile justice and in regard to protection issues.

A review of the current legal journals and studies that refer to the application of international law in the domestic legal system without incorporation demonstrates that for many common law jurists and judges, it is deemed a controversial issue. The usual arguments are raised, such as the issue of the independence of state sovereignty and the fact that international obligations will be respected so long as there is not a conflict with domestic laws. One writer reiterated that "in Jamaica, international treaties will only have domestic effect when they are adopted into Jamaican law by domestic legislation."[68] It was further noted that in regard to customary international law, although in theory Jamaican courts can take judicial notice of this source of law, to date there were no cases in which such a law had been applied by the judiciary.[69]

In light of the fact that the CRC has not been incorporated in these countries, as required by the common law system, it merits advocacy to encourage enabling legislation. In this context, some States have argued that their national constitutions provide adequate safeguards for the protection of the rights of the child within the jurisdiction. Many constitutions do guarantee fundamental rights and freedoms, but they have been deemed inadequate for the CRC to have the full force of the law in the particular country, as well as to guarantee all the rights set forth in the treaty.[70] One

---

[66] CRC, op. cit., Arts. 2, 3, 5 and 12, respectively.

[67] Z. McDowell, *Elements of Child Law in the Commonwealth Caribbean* (Kingston, Jamaica: University of the West Indies Press, 2000), p. 246.

[68] S. Vascianne, 'International Law and Selected Human Rights in Jamaica', *West Indian LJ* (2002): p. 1.

[69] C. M. Hamilton, 'National Study of Legislative Reform Initiative, Jamaica' (unpublished study for Legislative Reform Initiative, UNICEF, 2004).

[70] See General Comment No. 5, op. cit.

way to correct this would be to accord the CRC constitutional status through constitutional reform.

The constitutions of the independent countries of the Commonwealth Caribbean all contain provisions guaranteeing protection of human rights closely modelled on the Universal Declaration of Human Rights.[71] The Constitution of Barbados of 1966, for example, contains a bill of rights that is comparatively similar to the Universal Declaration of Human Rights and that guarantees a number of fundamental rights such as: the rights to life and personal liberty; protection from slavery and forced labour; protection from inhuman treatment; the rights to freedom of conscience, assembly and association; protection from discrimination on grounds of race, place of origin, political opinions and colour or creed.[72] The Constitution also provides that a person may apply to the High Court for redress, thus granting the High Court the important role of enforcing the protection provisions on human rights. Nevertheless, the Constitution of Barbados does not recognize all the human rights contained in the CRC, which includes economic, social and cultural rights, as well as civil and political rights. Moreover, the Constitution of Barbados, which is the supreme law of the land, further stipulates that if any other law is inconsistent with the Constitution, the latter shall prevail and any other law to the extent of the inconsistency will be declared void.[73]

The prevailing view that constitutional provisions are normally inadequate to ensure that all the provisions of the CRC are guaranteed at the national level is also a result of the comprehensive nature of the CRC, which recognizes a number of human rights that go beyond those of most national constitutions. Jamaica's Constitution provides a good example of such limitations, as was pointed out by the Committee on the Rights of the Child in its Concluding Observations issued to the State after it submitted its second periodic report.[74] It pointed out the lack of constitutional provisions prohibiting *all* forms of discrimination and recommended that the State amend its Constitution and legislation to ensure that they fully correspond to the provisions of Article 2 of the CRC. It further noted that this would ensure the full implementation of non-discrimination provisions, giving special attention to children living with HIV/AIDS, children with disabilities, equality

---

[71] A. R. Carnegie, 'Using the Available Remedies – 1. Caribbean Constitutional Remedies', in *International Human Rights Law in the Commonwealth Caribbean* (The Hague: Martinus Nijhoff Publishers, 1991), p. 1.

[72] Barbados Const. (The Barbados Independence Order 1966) Ch. III (Protection of Fundamental Rights and Freedoms of the Individual). See University of Richmond, 'Consitutional Finder', http://confinder.richmond.edu/country.php.

[73] 'Core Document Forming Part of the Reports of States Parties: Barbados', U.N. Doc. HRI/CORE/1/Add.64/Rev.1, 25 June 1998.

[74] Jamaican Const. (The Jamaica (Constitution) Order in Council, 1962), Ch. III (Fundamental Rights and Freedoms), http://pdba.georgetown.edu/Constitutions/Jamaica/jam62.html (Jamaican Constitution of 1962 with Reforms through 1999).

between boys and girls and racial discrimination.[75] A similar recommendation was issued by the Committee to St. Vincent and the Grenadines.[76]

Finally, efforts to enact legislation in order for the provisions of the CRC to be incorporated into domestic law also entail ensuring that all relevant legislation reflects the 'overarching principles' of the CRC contained in: Articles 2, regarding the principle of non-discrimination; Article 3, regarding the principle of the best interests of the child; Article 6, regarding the child's inherent right to life and to survival and development and Article 12, regarding the child's right to express his or her views freely in "all matters affecting the child."[77]

In view of the foregoing, a number of conclusions can be drawn:

- *Direct advocacy efforts at legislative and executive branches* – Advocacy on child rights should be directed at both the Executive and legislature, the two branches of government that are central in the ratification/accession process, withdrawing reservations, establishing national monitoring mechanisms and legislative reform.
- *Assess the knowledge of Members of Parliament (MPs) of the CRC* – Given the years that have passed since ratification/accession to the CRC, it would be useful to assess to what extent MPs became familiar with the content of the CRC at the time of ratification/accession, as well as their current knowledge and awareness of the treaty.
- *Promote incorporation of the CRC into domestic law* – In the selected common law countries, international treaties do not have the force of law and have no legal effect in domestic courts unless they have been incorporated into domestic law through legislation enacted by Parliament.
- *Advocate incorporation of the CRC supplemented by sectoral law reform* – The CRC may be incorporated through a consolidated children's rights statute, which should be supplemented through law reform in all the different sectors such as health, education, justice, welfare, family law and so on that should reflect the principles and standards of the CRC.
- *Promote the General Comments of the international treaty body* – The General Comments of the Committee on the Rights of the Child are not binding on States parties to the CRC but are useful references that can serve as persuasive authority in advocacy aimed at promoting the implementation of the CRC.

[75] Committee on the Rights of the Child, 'Concluding Observations: Jamaica', U.N. Doc. CRC/C/15/Add.210, 4 July 2003 ['Concluding Observations: Jamaica, Second Report'].
[76] Committee on the Rights of the Child, 'Concluding Observations of the Committee on the Rights of the Child: St. Vincent and the Grenadines, UN Doc. CRC/C/15/Add.184, 13 June 2002 ['Concluding Observations: St. Vincent and the Grenadines'].
[77] General Comment No. 5, op. cit.

- *Distinguish between treaties and customary international law* – It is necessary to distinguish between treaties that are signed and ratified by States and thus become binding on them and customary international law, which consists of principles and norms that have been widely accepted as a result of practices by States.
- *Assess the extent of constitutional guarantees in relation to the CRC* – Many national constitutions do guarantee fundamental rights and freedoms, but they have been deemed inadequate for the CRC to have the full force of the law at the national level, as well as to guarantee all the human rights set forth in the treaty. Ideally, a national constitution also should provide a method of redress, as does the one of Barbados.
- *Advocate to accord the CRC constitutional status* – In order to provide constitutional guarantees to provisions of the CRC, it is necessary for the treaty to be accorded constitutional status through constitutional reform.
- *Advocate for legislative reform to be in accordance with CRC's overarching principles* – This involves ensuring that all relevant proposed legislation reflects the principles of the CRC found in Articles 2, 3, 6, and 12.
- *Follow the work of the Inter-American Commission on Human Rights and of the Inter-American Court* – Given the voluntary ratification by some Caribbean countries of the American Convention on Human Rights, which allows them to declare the competence of the Inter-American Commission on Human Rights and to accept the jurisdiction of the Inter-American Court of Human Rights (as per Articles 45 and 62 of the treaty), it is important to follow all relevant jurisprudence and activities of these regional bodies.

The Status of the Child in the Commonwealth Caribbean

This section provides a brief snapshot of the numerous development challenges and a few of the legal obstacles that impede the realization of children's rights in the countries selected for this study. As mentioned, Barbados, Jamaica, and most of the countries that are primarily addressed in this study belong to the OECS, were former English colonies and have strong British ties. Although there are many cultural, political, and economic similarities among the countries of the Commonwealth Caribbean, there are also wide variations. Barbados, Jamaica and all OECS Member States (which include both independent States and territories of the United Kingdom) have made progress in human development in the past decade, from expanding knowledge, to improving survival, to raising standards of living. Behind this picture of progress, nevertheless, most of the countries have reported difficult socio-economic conditions, characterized by poverty and unemployment, which have placed limitations on the State's financial and human resources. The incidence of hurricanes and natural disasters further exacerbates the difficult socio-economic conditions of these countries.

In all the countries selected for this study, the lives of children are being shaped by the numerous development challenges. A quick review of some of the human development indicators in Barbados and Jamaica provides a good picture of the socio-economic conditions facing children in the Caribbean region. For example, in Barbados, 8 per cent of the population of 279,254 lives in poverty and about 25 per cent of households are headed by women.[78] Children account for 39 per cent of Jamaica's population of 2.6 million and, although the overall poverty rate declined from 26 per cent in 1996 to 16.9 per cent in 1999, children represent 43 per cent of all poor, with the majority living in rural areas.[79] Also in Jamaica, more than 45 per cent of households are headed by women. Most of the countries have made good progress in reducing under-five mortality and infant mortality. In Barbados, it is currently about 13 and 12, respectively, for every 1,000 live births, but these figures vary in the region. Maternal mortality ratios are below 100 per 100,000 live births in all countries.[80]

Although universal, free and compulsory primary education has been nearly achieved in all countries, unfortunately, drop-out and repetition rates are increasing, and a marked gender performance gap in favour of girls has been recorded. According to UNICEF, although near-universal primary enrolment exists in Jamaica, the quality and efficacy of learning and teaching are regarded as an important development challenge. For example, estimates indicate that 30 per cent of students, mostly boys, are functionally illiterate at the end of the primary cycle. In addition, there is a tendency for low attendance and dropout rates to increase by age.

HIV/AIDS in Jamaica is transmitted mainly through heterosexual relations and has emerged as another major development challenge in the region, with the general infection rate estimated at around 2 per cent and growing rapidly. Adolescents and young adults, especially girls between 15 and 19 years old, are particularly vulnerable, in part because of early sexual initiation. As compared to other countries in the region, Jamaica has a high HIV/AIDS prevalence (1.6 per 1,000 persons) and nearly 8 per cent of those infected are children under 10 years of age, with mother-to-child transmission a major contributing factor.[81]

---

[78] See *World Factbook*, op. cit., Barbados entry, www.cia.gov/cia/publications/factbook/geos/bb.html.

[79] Committee on the Rights of the Child, 'Initial Reports of States Parties due in 1993: Jamaica', U.N. Doc. CRC/C/8/Add.12, 17 Mar. 1994 [Initial State Party Report of Jamaica].

[80] Information provided by UNICEF Caribbean Area Office.

[81] United Nations Children's Fund, *The State of the World's Children 2001* (New York: UNICEF, 2000), p. 25.

Among the major social problems in the region are juvenile delinquency and children in conflict with the law. With regard to adolescents in Jamaica, the main concerns are high levels of suicides, alcohol abuse and acts of violence, accidents and criminal offences. Added to this is the fact that the juvenile justice and correctional systems have inadequate standards of detention, placement and training, as well as insufficient resources.

In the Concluding Observations issued by the Committee on the Rights of the Child to Jamaica in 2003, the international treaty body urged the State to strengthen its efforts to address and condemn violence in the Jamaican society, including against women and children, particularly within the family, schools and community.[82] It further recommended the need to take legislative measures to prohibit all forms of physical and mental violence, including corporal punishment and sexual abuse. Similar recommendations were issued by the Committee to other Caribbean countries such as Antigua and Barbuda and St. Vincent and the Grenadines.[83] In addition to assessing the situation of children by looking at human development indicators, it is also essential to determine from a legal perspective the extent to which the rights of the child are being enjoyed in the country. Some insights of how the law treats the child in the Caribbean region are provided by the national studies commissioned by UNICEF as part of the Legislative Reform Initiative mentioned earlier in the introduction. For example, in the national study of Barbados, the author concludes that despite some important legislative reform undertaken, there are remaining issues such as: "residual discrimination on the basis of birth status, the juvenile justice laws are antiquated, there are inadequate and under-utilized child protection laws and aspects of the law relating to the punishment of children that are not only inconsistent with the CRC but also with the Constitution."[84]

In a comprehensive study addressing child law in the Commonwealth Caribbean, the author explains that in the past, when much of the law depended upon the common law structure and before it was supplemented by local legislation, there were numerous forms of discrimination. For example, legal and racial discrimination against children was common on sugar plantations, legitimate children were granted advantages that were denied to illegitimate children and legitimate male children were favoured over legitimate female children.[85] McDowell's study maintains that, generally, in the region, the law as it regards the child is in various stages of development with some laws deriving either from the common law alone or older legislation from the United Kingdom, and newer legislation emerging which has improved the rights of children that is also based on more recent laws of

[82] See 'Concluding Observations: Jamaica, Second Report', op cit.
[83] See, e.g., 'Concluding Observations: St. Vincent and the Grenadines', op. cit.
[84] Robinson, op cit., p. 18.   [85] McDowell, op. cit., p. 1.

the United Kingdom.[86] The larger countries of Barbados, Guyana, Jamaica and Trinidad and Tobago are considered to be taking the lead in legislative reform, which is at the same time being influenced by global trends.[87] McDowell concludes that the Convention on the Rights of the Child is having a positive impact on the way laws regarding children are being developed in the region.[88] Thus far, Belize is the only country that has taken a major step towards implementation by incorporating the entire CRC into domestic law through the adoption of the The 1998 Families and Children Act, First Schedule, which reads as follows: "A child shall have the right to . . . all the rights set out in the UN Convention on the Rights of the Child with appropriate modifications to suit the circumstances of Belize."[89]

Although viewed as a significant achievement in terms of the impact the CRC is having in the Caribbean region, unfortunately this new piece of legislation also contains discriminatory provisions based on birth status regarding children born outside of marriage. As McDowell rightly concludes, this results in a major contradiction because "since there is a direct conflict between the convention and domestic law, then the domestic law supporting discrimination prevails."[90] The present study earlier addressed fully the issue of incorporating the CRC through a legislative act, such as the one taken in Belize, which evidently poses challenges when it is not undertaken pursuant to a comprehensive review of existing legislation to ensure harmony and consistency with the provisions of the treaty.

VI. THE DUTIES AND RESPONSIBILITIES OF COMMON LAW STATES TO IMPLEMENT THE CRC ACCORDING TO INTERNATIONAL HUMAN RIGHTS LAW

In order to be able to compare the progress achieved through law review and law reform in the selected countries of the Commonwealth Caribbean region, first it is necessary to establish the duties and responsibilities of the State to implement the CRC. All three branches of government have a duty to implement the rights in the CRC. Through ratification or accession, a State becomes party to an international human rights treaty and is bound to implement its provisions. It should be noted that the countries in this study became States parties to the CRC without reservations, which implies that its principles and standards were fully accepted by each State.

The previous section focused on the status of a human rights treaty under the common law legal system once it has been ratified. It was pointed out that

---

[86] Ibid., p. 2.
[87] Ibid. Guyana, under its constitutional reforms, now automatically elevates the CRC and other major human rights treaties as part of higher law, critical in interpreting the Constitution. (Information provided by UNICEF Barbados.)
[88] Ibid. p. 10.   [89] Ibid. p. 245.
[90] Ibid. p. 246.

as a rule under the common law tradition a treaty is not part of domestic law unless it has been incorporated through an Act of Parliament. This is different from the civil law system in which, in many countries, the ratification of a treaty is a legislative act and, as a general rule, upon ratification the treaty becomes part of domestic law, is accorded constitutional status and may be invoked in court. Moreover, in most of the civil law countries the status of an international human rights treaty within the domestic legal framework is established by the national constitutions.

At the same time, the Vienna Convention on the Law of Treaties, which is binding on all States, stipulates: "Every treaty in force is binding upon the parties to it and must be performed by them in good faith."[91] It follows then that in accordance with international law, States parties to the CRC have consented to be bound by the treaty and have a duty to ensure that national legislation is compatible with the treaty. In other words, as was noted previously, although in the countries that are primarily the focus of the study there has not been any act of 'incorporation', the obligations of the State are also subject to the rules established under international human rights law.

The rules established by international human rights law necessitates understanding the legal language commonly used in the treaties. Like other international human rights treaties, the CRC was drafted with terms that have a particular legal definition. As a point of departure in interpreting the duties of the State, the nature of the obligation undertaken through ratification/accession must be assessed and whether it represents a negative or an affirmative obligation. Under the CRC, each State party is committed to "respect and ensure" the rights set forth in the treaty.[92] The words 'respect and ensure' have important legal connotations. The word 'respect' means that the State is under an obligation to refrain from any actions that may violate the rights of the child under the CRC. It is therefore regarded as a negative obligation. The word 'ensure' implies an affirmative obligation because the State must adopt measures that are necessary to create conditions for the effective enjoyment of the rights in the Convention.[93] In both instances, action is required by the State in order to give the rights in the CRC their full effect.

As stated in the CRC, States parties "shall respect and ensure" the rights set forth in the CRC "without discrimination of any kind." They also undertake to adopt all *appropriate* legislative, administrative and other measures "to ensure that the child is protected against all forms of discrimination."[94] Santos Pais explains that although the State may decide "on the opportune

---

[91] Art. 26, 1155 U.N.T.S. 331, *adopted* 23 May 1969 and *entered into force* 27 Jan. 1980.
[92] CRC, op. cit., Art. 2.
[93] P. Alston, 'The Legal Framework of the Convention on the Rights of the Child', in *Bulletin of Human Rights* (Geneva: United Nations, 1991) [Alston, 'Legal Framework'].
[94] CRC, op. cit., Art. 2.

time and on the nature of the measures to be implemented, its freedom of choice is not unlimited."[95] Moreover, the State is bound to adopt *all measures* that may be necessary for the implementation of the CRC and, in doing so, the State must be guided by 'the best interests of the child' as a primary consideration in accordance with its Article 3.[96] It is for the State to determine, however, which measures are 'appropriate'.

Alston further clarifies that the obligation to 'undertake' measures does not depend upon the availability of resources; it is of immediate application.[97] In other words, as a general rule, the State must take immediate steps to implement the provisions of the CRC and not give, as a general excuse for inaction, the lack of resources. Furthermore, with regard to economic, social and cultural rights, States undertake to adopt such measures "to the maximum extent of their available resources" and, where needed, within the framework of international cooperation.[98] This means the exception to the rule is in regard to economic, social and cultural rights, which the CRC recognizes will be implemented in a progressive manner and double "subject to available resources". But even in regard to these rights, the State must take steps towards implementation and show it is acting in good faith.

Following are the specific measures that were foreseen by the international treaty bodies and that are points for discussion during the reporting process and on-going dialogue between the State and the treaty body, including the Committee on the Rights of the Child, which monitors the implementation of the CRC. Accordingly, the State is expected to undertake measures to:

- Harmonize national laws and policy with the provisions of the Convention;
- Create mechanisms or strengthen existing ones at the national or local level for coordinating policies that concern children and for monitoring the implementation of the CRC;
- Make the principles and provisions of the CRC widely known to adults and children;
- Provide adequate remedies in the case of non-compliance;
- Allocate budgets to programmes that benefit children;
- Submit periodic reports to the Committee on the Rights of the Child on the progress achieved and obstacles encountered in the implementation of the CRC.[99]

With regard to legislative measures, although it is for the State to decide what is 'appropriate', nevertheless, ensuring full conformity between

---

[95] M. Santos Pais, 'The Convention on the Rights of the Child', in *Manual on Human Rights Reporting* (Geneva: United Nations, 1997), p. 394.
[96] Ibid.   [97] Alston, 'Legal Framework', op. cit.
[98] CRC, op. cit., Art. 4.   [99] Santos Pais, op. cit., p. 400.

national law and the CRC is a critical step towards implementation. This requires reviewing existing legislation and enacting changes as necessary. The Committee on the Rights of the Child has emphasized this requirement when it issued General Comment No. 5, which provides that "a comprehensive review of all domestic legislation and related administrative guidance to ensure full compliance with the Convention is an obligation" of the State.[100] Other essential steps toward meaningful implementation include the incorporation of the CRC into domestic legislation and according the rights of the treaty constitutional status or recognition.

It should be pointed out, however, that although the CRC does not require constitutional measures to be undertaken, they are regarded as highly effective and therefore desirable by common law jurists that take part in the international human rights discourse on the implementation of international human rights treaties. It is argued that according the CRC constitutional recognition or constitutional status would have enormous impact in the countries using the common law system. This is because the national constitution as supreme law of the land carries enormous weight because it is the basis for measuring other domestic laws. Finally, the reference in Article 2 to undertaking 'other measures' means it also can include administrative, budgetary or judicial measures.

Measures Undertaken by the State to Implement the CRC in Selected Countries

This section highlights some of the steps towards implementation of the CRC that have been undertaken in the selected countries using the six specific measures that have been established by Committee on the Rights of the Child, pursuant to international human rights law. The purpose is to draw conclusions by identifying any trends and to ascertain the role played by the different branches of the State, namely, the Executive, legislature, and judiciary.

1. *Measures to harmonize national laws and policy with the provisions of the Convention*

To date, in most countries a government-led comprehensive review of the domestic laws has not been undertaken in order to determine whether there is compliance or to 'harmonize' national laws with the provisions of the CRC. In 1994 in Jamaica, important steps were taken to conduct analytical reviews of legislation related to children's and women's rights. A decade later, The Child Care and Protection Act was finally passed into law on 16 March 2004, which is intended to "bring national legislation in line with the provisions

---

[100] General Comment No. 5, op. cit., para. 18.

of the Convention on the Rights of the Child."[101] Although there has been significant legislative reform since Barbados ratified the CRC, it has been piecemeal and ad hoc. Interestingly, the Initial State Party Report of Barbados submitted to the Committee on the Rights of the Child makes the following observation:

> At the date of its ratification of the Convention, the Government of Barbados found itself in a fortunate position in that it had enacted much of the legislation required to implement the Convention. Since ratification of the Convention, two areas were specifically addressed, namely: (a) The non-imposition of capital punishment in respect of convicted offenders under the age of 18 years; (b) The provision of legal aid services to and for the benefit of minors.[102]

This important legislative development was the result of the mobilization efforts initiated by non-governmental organizations (NGOs) that promoted the rights of the child and the CRC itself, leading up to the ratification of the treaty in Barbados. However, the statement implies that the laws of Barbados were virtually in compliance with the provisions of the CRC, which was not the case. The fact is that a comprehensive review of the legislation had not been conducted, either before or after ratification, to assess to what extent domestic laws were in harmony with the CRC.

In the OECS countries, most of the legislative changes that have taken place have been brought about by piecemeal reform concerning primarily issues of domestic violence, sexual offences, child protection and the age of majority. These legislative changes have been interpreted by UNICEF and jurists as a positive development indicating that OECS governments are willing to bring national laws in conformity with the standards of the CRC. There is a Family Law and Domestic Violence Reform Project underway that, when completed, will represent the most comprehensive review of the law and social policy in relation to children of the OECS.[103] According to Jackson's study, the areas of law covered under this project include: the status of children, custody of children, maintenance of children of parties to a marriage, maintenance of children born outside of marriage (or as is usually referred to under the antiquated common law phrase 'out of wedlock'), the adoption of children, family court, juvenile justice, domestic violence, child protection and the social service implications of family law reform.

Except for Jamaica, none of the countries considered in this study have undertaken a comprehensive and 'rigorous' review of the legislation as required by General Comment No. 5 issued by the Committee on the

---

[101] Hamilton, op. cit., p. 4, citing The Honourable House of Representatives, Item No. 7 under Public Business, 2 Mar. 2004.
[102] 'Initial State Party Report: Barbados', op. cit., para. 7.
[103] Jackson, op. cit.

Rights of the Child. One can therefore conclude that it is an important area that needs to be addressed and encouraged by organizations and institutions that are promoting the rights of the child. UNICEF has a key role to play in supporting such initiatives. Keeping in mind that, upon ratification of a treaty, it is the duty of the legislature to undertake a full review of national legislation, parliaments need to be reminded of their obligations under international human rights law. Parliaments have a duty to undertake a comprehensive review to ascertain the need for legislative reform. As mentioned, in common law jurisdictions, an Act of Parliament for the purpose of incorporating the CRC in domestic law is fundamental and necessary and should be encouraged.

The difficulty States are having in harmonizing legislation with the CRC was pointed out by the Inter-American Court of Human Rights in an Advisory Opinion that was requested by the Inter-American Commission on Human Rights. The Court stated:

> Even though the Convention on the Rights of the Child is one of the international instruments that has the greatest number of ratifications, not all countries of this continent have harmonized their domestic legislation with the principles set forth in that Convention, and those that have done so face difficulties applying them.[104]

Why the legislatures are having difficulty in complying with the duty to conduct a comprehensive review, which is a fundamental step to initiate legal reform in a more holistic manner, merits further study. McDowell suggests that serving as an obstacle to the implementation of the CRC is the controversy over the fact that the CRC does not adequately indicate what are the 'duties of children', and the criticism that the treaty contains 'cultural biases' has been also raised in the Caribbean context.

> From a Commonwealth Caribbean perspective, the convention ignores certain cultural values in terms of the mutuality of the parent-child relationship. In the African and Indian cultures of the Commonwealth Caribbean, for example, children are brought up to respect their parents, and in some instances, the law stipulates that children are even obligated to maintain parents. If for example a seventeen-year-old male child, who is not academically inclined, gives up his right to an education because he prefers to find work and invests his time in a career, then it is assumed in our culture that that child will financially assist his weak and ailing mother who is unable to fend for herself. Section 4 of the *Jamaica Maintenance Act* for example, creates obligations to maintain parents and grandparents.[105]

---

[104] Inter-American Court of Human Rights, Advisory Opinion OC-17/2002, 'Juridical Condition and Human Rights of the Child' (28 Aug. 2002), p. 19, www.corteidh.or.cr/seriea_ing/index.html.

[105] McDowell, op. cit., p. 243.

Given the unprecedented success of the CRC worldwide, such controversies should be further examined in the context of harmonization of domestic laws and policies with the CRC. Given the vagueness and ambiguity of some of the provisions of the CRC, there are bound to be many instances in which there will be conflicts between the provisions of the CRC and either domestic laws or cultural and traditional practices. This is where the overarching principles of the CRC can be applied, such as the best interests principle, in order to find a suitable outcome that is in keeping with the spirit of the treaty.

2. *Measures to create national mechanisms to coordinate policies for children and to monitor the implementation of the CRC*

In all the countries included in the study, the State has taken steps to create national mechanisms for the purpose of coordinating policies and activities, and monitoring implementation of the CRC. Barbados counts on a number of national entities that are concerned with a wide range of issues related to children and the family. They include, for example: the Child Care Board that provides guidance to the Ministry of Social Transformation regarding laws addressing the care and protection of children; the Family Council that makes recommendations regarding the implementation of the Family Law Act and other legislation related to family law; the Constitution Review Commission that makes recommendations regarding the Independence Constitution of 1966 and those that may have implications for children's rights to nationality and citizenship and a National Committee for Monitoring the Rights of the Child established in 1998 that includes a legal subcommittee.

Although the establishment of a monitoring committee is a step in the right direction, a number of obstacles and factors have prevented this mechanism from carrying out its work effectively. These include primarily leadership and management constraints such as the lack of defined terms of reference with a clear demarcation of responsibilities for monitoring the CRC vis-à-vis other bodies, the lack of professional capacity to carry out a comprehensive review of the laws and weak civil society representation and leadership.

In the case of Jamaica, in the Concluding Observations issued by the Committee on the Rights of the Child in response to the Initial State Party Report, the monitoring body was most critical in its observation that Jamaica lacked "an overall integrated mechanism to monitor the activities designed to promote and protect children's rights," leading to "insufficient coordination between the various governmental departments, as well as between central and regional authorities, in the implementation of the policies to promote and protect the rights of the child."[106]

---

[106] Committee on the Rights of the Child, 'Concluding Observations of the Committee on the Rights of the Child: Jamaica', para. 8, U.N. Doc. CRC/C/15/Add.32, 15 Feb. 1995.

Although there have been good-faith efforts in the selected countries to establish suitable mechanisms at the national level to coordinate policies and monitor implementation of the CRC, most of these bodies are facing a number of constraints. There is a great need for capacity development and for human and financial resources to strengthen these mechanisms so that they can function more effectively. They also need the authority and credibility to interface regularly with NGOs and to have more access to civil society. Ideally, there should be a mix of governmental and non-governmental monitoring mechanisms in place at national and local levels, to coordinate policies and monitor implementation, including an Office of the Ombudsperson.

3. Measures to make the principles and provisions of the CRC widely known

The Government of Barbados stated in its Initial State Party Report that it was committed to publicizing the CRC following the signing and subsequent ratification of the Convention. A wide range of activities were held to assist with promoting the Convention that involved the media, radio programmes and newspapers, all aimed at educating the public.[107] Although the Government of Jamaica fully recognized its responsibility as a signatory of the Convention to make its principles and provisions known to adults and children alike, the most active were the Jamaican Coalition on the Rights of the Child, a combination of non-governmental organizations and UNICEF.[108] In its Initial State Party Report, the goals of the Coalition are set forth as follows:

8. The Coalition was formed in 1989 with the following objectives:

(a) To lobby the Government of Jamaica to include the Convention on the Rights of the Child in all Government of Jamaica plans, policies and programmes;

(b) To contribute to the process of legal reform which impacts on the rights of children;

(c) To educate the general public about the rights of children;

(d) To assist social service organizations to understand and prepare for the implementation of the Convention.

9. The member agencies of the Coalition have been tireless in their efforts to educate the public on the Convention as they have been unflagging in their efforts to "lobby the Government of Jamaica to include the Convention on the Rights of the Child in all Government of Jamaica plans, policies and programmes". Their activities have included the formation of groups islandwide operating with the Mission Statement: To provide a vehicle for

---

[107] See 'Initial State Party Report: Barbados', op. cit., paras. 13–21.
[108] See 'Initial State Party Report of Jamaica', op. cit., para. 7.

educating the public on the Convention and to promote the Rights of the
Child in Jamaica.[109]

A review of the measures undertaken to promote the CRC shows that
this task frequently becomes the responsibility of NGOs interested in promoting the rights of the child. In general, thanks to the support provided by
international organizations such as UNICEF, NGOs working for children
and human rights groups promoting the rights of the child, the task of promoting the CRC has been carried out through a wide range of activities. In
the future, to encourage further legislative review and reform, there should
be more efforts designed for and directed at members of Parliament, judges
and other members of the legal community. This is particularly important in
common law countries where:

- parliamentarians are responsible for passing the law that 'incorporates'
  the CRC into domestic law;
- judges have the duty to interpret legislation and apply it in individual
  cases; and
- lawyers are responsible for bringing cases before the courts and can use
  the principles and standards of the CRC in their arguments, at the minimum as persuasive authority.

4. Measures to provide adequate remedies in the case of non-compliance
The Universal Declaration of Human Rights provides that "Everyone has
the right to an effective remedy by the competent national tribunals for acts
violating the fundamental rights granted him by the Constitution or law."[110]
The International Covenant on Civil and Political Rights further provides
that each State party undertakes to ensure that the legal system and competent authorities shall enforce such remedies.[111] In its General Comment
No. 5, the Committee on the Rights of the Child has underscored that "for
rights to have meaning, effective remedies must be available to redress violations."[112] Although the General Comments of the Committee are not binding
on States, they nevertheless represent the treaty body's critical role as persuasive authority. The Committee has emphasized that this requirement is
implicit in the CRC and is consistently referred to in the other major international human rights treaties. To date, there is little evidence that States
in the selected countries are taking steps to ensure this requirement is met.

---

[109] Ibid., para. 8.
[110] Universal Declaration of Human Rights, GA Res. 217A (III), Art. 8, U.N. Doc. A/810
(1948), p. 71, *adopted* 10 Dec. 1948. Reprinted in *Am. J. Int'l L.* 43 (Supp. 1949): p. 127.
[111] International Covenant on Civil and Political Rights, G.A. res. 2200A (XXI), 21 U.N.
GAOR Supp. (No. 16) at 52, Article 2(3)(a), (b), (c), U.N. Doc. A/6316 (1966), 999 UNTS
171, *adopted* 16 Dec. 1966 and *entered into force* 23 Mar. 23, 1976. Reprinted in *ILM* 6
(1967): p.368.
[112] General Comment No. 5, op. cit.

Part of the problem is the perception shared by some members of the legal community who regard the CRC as representing rights that are merely aspirations and not judicially enforceable.

Under the common law, if there is a right, then there is a specific claim and a remedy that is enforceable through judicial means or other competent bodies. Domestic laws normally provide entitlements with sufficient detail, which enables remedies for non-compliance. Because many of the provisions of the CRC are written in a language that is often vague, this poses a problem for those practicing common law lawyers that are in pursuit of legal remedies for redressing violations. For example, Article 24 of the CRC, which recognizes the right of the child to the "enjoyment of the highest attainable standard of health," mainly provides guidance for the State in the area of health delivery, but it does not identify the specific claim for individuals exercising the right.[113] Related to this are the constraints faced by children themselves to pursue legal remedies when their rights are violated. In the countries selected for this study, there have been few actions taken to ensure that effective remedies are available to redress child's rights violations.

One study carried out by the UNICEF Innocenti Research Centre for the purpose of reviewing all State party reports and that examined the extent that States were addressing this obligation concluded:

> Very few states appear to have confronted this challenge directly or indirectly and held an inquiry into the extent to which the Convention rights are truly exercisable in domestic law; the extent to which children themselves believe they have appropriate access to the necessary advice, advocacy and complaints procedures and ultimately to the courts. It is in this spirit that the child should have an opportunity to be heard in any administrative or judicial proceedings affecting him or her.[114]

The Committee on the Rights of the Child has further recognized that children have a 'special and dependent status' that makes it difficult for them to pursue legal remedies when their rights are denied or violated. Its General Comment No. 5 reads:

> States need to give particular attention to ensuring that there are effective, child-sensitive procedures available to children and their representatives. These should include the provision of child-friendly information, advice, including support for self advocacy, and access to independent complaints procedures and to the courts with necessary legal and other assistance. Where rights are found to have been breached, there should be appropriate reparation, including compensation and where needed measures to promote

---

[113] CRC, op. cit., Art. 24.

[114] UNICEF, 'Law Reform to Implement the Convention on the Rights of the Child' (unpublished study, UNICEF Innocenti Research Centre, Florence, January 2004).

physical and psychological recovery, rehabilitation and reintegration (as required by Article 39 of the CRC).[115]

One of the obstacles facing children in many jurisdictions is the general profile of the courts, including the family courts, which provide a number of services for families and children. Many individuals and families feel alienated from the courts. As was pointed out, "there is still the general fear of courts and judges by adults and children alike."[116] In light of this, in Jamaica, although children are permitted to voice their concerns and speak with judges in chambers, the establishment of children's courts has been proposed.[117] According to the State party report submitted by Jamaica to the Committee on the Rights of the Child, legal assistance is being provided to children who come into conflict with the law along with other assistance such as counselling, reunion with parents, as well as other services provided by children's officers and correctional officers.[118] Under the common law system, the courts play a leading role in ensuring effective remedies and in restoring rights that have been violated. (The role of the courts in protecting the rights of children and adolescents is addressed in a later section in this chapter.) There also are other effective mechanisms that have been established in some countries, such as a national human rights institution for the promotion and protection of human rights, an ombudsperson for human rights or a children's commissioner who focuses exclusively on children's rights. These mechanisms can help to ensure that children have access to legal representation and to bring their complaints before the proper administrative or judicial body. The ombudsperson also can work with legal aid services available to the poorer and more disadvantaged sectors of society, or with lawyers that undertake pro bono work. Although many of these institutions are often attached to the executive branch of government, they can be established to enjoy a certain level of independence and to carry out an impartial investigatory function. They also can be authorized by law to receive complaints from individuals.[119]

To date, out of the countries selected for this study, few have established such mechanisms. Trinidad and Tobago has had a constitutionally established Ombudsman since about 1984. According to official documents submitted to the international human rights treaty bodies, Barbados and Jamaica have established an Office of Ombudsman. Barbados enacted the Ombudsman Act (1981) and thus established the Office of Ombudsman,

---

[115] General Comment No. 5, op. cit., para. 24.
[116] Hamilton, op. cit., p. 24.   [117] Ibid.
[118] Committee on the Rights of the Child, 'Second Periodic Reports of States Parties due in 1998: Jamaica', U.N. Doc. CRC/C/70/Add.15, 12 Feb. 2003.
[119] United Nations, *National Human Rights Institutions* (Geneva: United Nations, Professional Training Series No. 4, 1995).

whose function is to investigate and report on administrative conduct. Jamaica indicates that in addition to the courts, the authorities with jurisdiction affecting human rights include the "Ombudsman and the institutions which are generally responsible for dealing with the public."[120] The Committee on the Rights of the Child nevertheless recommended to Jamaica the need to establish an independent and effective mechanism, for example, an Office of a Children's Advocate, on the basis of international standards regarding national human rights institutions. Thus, to ascertain the current status of the ombudsman in these countries, the extent of their competence and whether they are accessible to children requires further study.[121]

Individuals also can submit complaints concerning violations of their human rights to international treaty bodies within the United Nations. Regional bodies such as the Inter-American Court of Human Rights also receive individual petitions regarding human rights violations from individuals residing in countries that have ratified the American Convention on Human Rights. Several countries of the English-speaking Caribbean have ratified the American Convention, but only two have accepted the jurisdiction of the Inter-American Court. To bring a case before this court, an individual must first exhaust domestic remedies, which means that every reasonable opportunity for redress under national law must have been tried. Only after the exhaustion of national remedies is it possible to bring a case before an international body. However, it is also difficult for children to bring such complaints before the treaty monitoring bodies for the same reasons that were mentioned earlier regarding their 'special and dependent status' that hinders them from pursuing legal remedies.

The International Centre for the Legal Protection of Human Rights (INTERIGHTS), an international NGO with its headquarters in the United Kingdom, submitted an *amicus curiae* brief to the Inter-American Court of Human Rights in the case of *Winston Caesar v Republic of Trinidad and Tobago*.[122] The Court considered, for the first time, at its session held in November 2004, the lawfulness of judicially sanctioned corporal punishment. In its legal brief, INTERIGHTS presents international and comparative legal material, including jurisprudence from a broad range of human rights bodies and national courts. The NGO's principal argument is that

---

[120] See 'Core Document Forming Part of the Reports of States Parties: Jamaica', para. 39, U.N. Doc. HRI/CORE/1/Add.82, 23 June 1997.

[121] For further information regarding national human rights institutions related to children, see General Comment 2 of the Committee on the Rights of the Child ('The Role of Independent Human Rights Institutions in the Protection and Promotion of the Rights of the Child', U.N. Doc. CRC/GC/2002/2, 15 Nov. 2002).

[122] See *Winston Caesar v. Republic of Trinidad and Tobago,* Inter-American Court of Human Rights judgement of 11 Mar. 2005, Series C. No. 123, J. Jackman (concurring judgement) (Organization of American States, InterAmerican Court of Human Rights jurisprudence, www.oas.org/OASpage/humanrights.htm).

corporal punishment has been rejected as inconsistent with international human rights standards. It further maintains that judicially sanctioned corporal punishment is, by its very nature, cruel, inhuman and degrading punishment in violation of Article 5 of the American Convention on Human Rights and other international legal obligations. The Court's judgement issued on 11 March 2005 explains in detail the extent to which international human rights jurisprudence has prohibited cruel, inhuman and degrading punishment. Whether the outcome of this legal proceeding will influence future case law and policies on corporal punishment in the Caribbean region, where it is still a common practice within the family, in schools, juvenile detentions centers and prisons, remains to be seen. It should be noted that Trinidad and Tobago did not appear or participate in the proceedings because, as the Inter-American Court noted, it had "exercised its sovereign right to denounce and withdraw from the Convention."[123]

A number of points raised in the concurring judgement of Judge Oliver Jackman of Barbados, one of the seven judges who sits on the Inter-American Court, are of particular relevance to this study. First, he points out that the practice of corporal punishment by States parties to the American Convention is in flagrant breach of the treaty, and further refers to the Constitution of Trinidad and Tobago, which also provides that, "Parliament may not . . . impose or authorize the imposition of cruel and unusual treatment or punishment." Second is the Court's "insistence of the absolute necessity that the States should respect their treaty obligations." He also observes that there is no evidence that any of the States parties to the Convention have taken any action to meet their obligation set forth in Article 2 to give 'domestic legal effect' to the rights or fundamental freedoms in the Convention either through legislative or other measures as may be necessary to give effect to those rights and freedoms. In regard to Trinidad and Tobago's denunciation of the Convention and non-appearance in the case, Judge Jackman concludes that it was "profoundly regrettable for the cause of a universal regime of human rights protection, but the State was fully within its rights to take that unprecedented step." Finally, Judge Jackman concludes that judging from its failure to participate in the hearing of the case, it is unlikely that Trinidad and Tobago will comply with the decision of the court.[124]

5. *Measures to allocate budgets that benefit children*
The national studies conducted in Barbados, Jamaica and the countries of the OECS all indicated that no policy, law, or administrative rule had been adopted requiring that a portion of the budget shall be dedicated to social expenditure for children. In all the countries concerned obtaining information on budget allocation is difficult and not easily accessible. In most

---

[123] Ibid., p. 3.   [124] Ibid., p. 2.

cases, it is the Ministry of Finance that prepares the national budget after consulting with the relevant ministries and presents the budget to Parliament for adoption. In the countries of the OECS, the prime minister prepares the national budget along with the Minister of Finance and a report is prepared that is subsequently presented to Parliament, debated and adopted by a vote.[125]

In some of the countries of the OECS it was reported that priority has been given to budget allocations for health and education services. In St. Lucia a significant sum was allocated to the Ministry of Education, Youth, and Sports in 2004, which represents 54.9 per cent of the total amount allocated for social services. Another substantial amount was dedicated to the rehabilitation of schools.[126]

Some information regarding the allocation of budgets to social programmes related to children can be found in the State party reports to the Committee on the Rights of the Child; however, the specific amounts that benefit children are not indicated. In some of these reports, there appears to be increased awareness of the State's duty to allocate resources to implement the CRC. For example, Jamaica reported a slight increase in its allocation to primary health care in its State party report of 2003, and also acknowledged that it had not yet achieved the 5 per cent of gross domestic product recommended by the World Health Organization (WHO) to be expended on health services. At the same time, it emphasized that official development assistance plays a vital role in maintaining health services. The Committee on the Rights of the Child has frequently expressed concern that budgetary allocation is insufficient for the implementation of the CRC and has recommended for States to prioritize resources for children to the maximum extent of available resources and within the framework of international cooperation.[127]

One of the major obstacles for the effective implementation of the CRC is the lack of available resources. Article 4 of the CRC requires governments to implement economic, social and cultural rights "to the maximum extent of their available resources." Under the CRC, although it is understood that some rights may be implemented progressively and with international cooperation, nevertheless the State has immediate obligations to give priority to children. It has been suggested in an Innocenti study that the concept of available resources needs to be interpreted more broadly to include human resources, economic resources and organizational resources.[128]

---

[125] Jackson, op. cit.   [126] Ibid.

[127] See Committee on the Rights of the Child, 'Concluding Observations: Dominica', U.N. Doc. CRC/C/15/Add.238, 30 June 2004.

[128] UNICEF, 'Implementing the Convention on the Rights of the Child – Resource Mobilization in Low-Income Countries' (Florence: UNICEF Innocenti Research Centre, 1996), p. 4.

Another important factor in determining the availability of resources is the need to recognize that "they are available at all points of society, public, and private, from the individual or household level to the national and international levels."[129] One of the constraints facing monitoring mechanisms at the national level is the lack of capacity to monitor the allocation of budgets. The lack of transparency in some countries regarding the availability of resources and of the expenditures incurred by the State is yet another major obstacle. Given that limited financial resources pose serious constraints for human development in most developing countries, the issue of availability of resources and the allocation of budgets in connection with the State's obligation to implement the CRC could be analyzed and assessed within a broader context at all different levels as suggested by the Innocenti study.

6. Measures to submit periodic reports to the Committee on the Rights of the Child

States parties to the CRC are required to submit periodic reports to the Committee on the Rights of the Child within two years after ratification and, thereafter, every five years. This is one obligation that most States parties are complying with regularly, although some reports are submitted late, and the quality of the reports may vary. All the countries selected for this study have been reporting to the Committee on the Rights of the Child. Many NGOs in these countries follow the ongoing dialogue that takes place between representatives of national governments and the monitoring treaty body. They also follow the discussions that are held between the treaty body and NGOs, as well as with UN agencies on the progress achieved and obstacles encountered in the implementation of the CRC.

It should be noted that in the Concluding Observations issued by the Committee upon reviewing the State party report, there are regularly recommendations on the need to conduct law review and law reform, as well as the need to enact new legislation on a wide range of specific issues. Unfortunately, these documents are rarely circulated at the national level, which could provide an opportunity to initiate public dialogue and increase advocacy on many important issues including on action for legislative reform.

There have been criticisms raised by some common law jurists in regard to the obligations of the State in instances in which there is tardy presentation of the periodic report or in cases where the report provides a misleading account of the status of human rights in a particular jurisdiction. They object to the fact that the State is not subject to any effective sanctions imposed by the international human rights treaty, even when it ignores the recommendations issued by the monitoring body. It was pointed out, for example, that Jamaica was 11 years late in submitting its periodic report to the Human

---

[129] Ibid., p. 7.

Rights Committee and that in response, the treaty body merely stated that it "deplored" Jamaica's tardiness.[130] It should be understood, however, that the value of the reporting system is in the continuous *constructive dialogue* that takes place between the international treaty body and government, the wealth of information that is generated in the process and in the recommendations that are issued by the treaty bodies after a comprehensive review of materials from a wide range of sources. The whole process is extremely useful for the purpose of law review and law reform in connection with the implementation of the CRC and for improving the situation of children.

A number of suggestions have been made in connection with the reporting process. The first and most common is that in many instances the State party reports are prepared by a 'ministry' in an isolated manner with little participation of the civil society. Ensuring wide participation of NGOs and other members of the civil society is critical to fully reflect the progress achieved and the obstacles that remain for the implementation of the CRC. Second, the discussions that are held and recorded in Geneva that involve the Committee on the Rights of the Child and the State party government delegation, after it has reviewed the report, along with the Concluding Observations and Recommendations issued by the treaty body, should be made available to the general public at the country level. Wide dissemination of all the relevant documents resulting from the reporting process should inform legislators and other policy makers in a timely manner. Finally, the participation of children in all aspects of the reporting process is essential and effective as a means to comply with the rights and full spirit of the CRC at the national level. Children's participation further promotes recognizing the child as a 'subject and holder of rights' and as an individual who can engage in active, free and meaningful participation in his or her own development rather than merely as a passive object in need of protection.

VII. LEGISLATIVE REFORM AND POLICY INITIATIVES IN SELECTED COMMON LAW COUNTRIES

A comprehensive regional study on laws regarding children in the Commonwealth Caribbean states that in addition to the constitutional provisions that protect the fundamental rights and freedoms of the child, there are already a number of specific pieces of legislation that safeguard the rights of children in conformity with the provisions of the CRC:

> Various pieces of legislation in the Commonwealth Caribbean give specific rights to children..., there is specific legislation providing for the maintenance of children, education, succession and property rights; legislation requiring the registration of their birth, immunization against disease;

[130] Vascianne, op. cit., pp. 54–83.

legislation imposing penalties for neglect, cruelty, physical abuse, sexual abuse and domestic violence. While the legislative provisions in the several states are not uniform, some having "old", others "newer", and others more "modern" legislation, nevertheless, the basic and more important rights are provided for. And, various laws of the region impose criminal penalties for neglect or refusal of the parents or guardians to fulfill the basic duties.[131]

The study does not indicate whether these laws were enacted prior to the ratification of the CRC by the countries in the region. It is assumed that they were already enacted at the time of ratification. In any case, the conclusion reached in the regional study is that most of the laws are already "consistent or not very far removed from the ideals reflected in the convention."[132]

It is evident, however, in reviewing the more recent national studies undertaken by UNICEF, the State party reports and Concluding Observations of the Committee on the Rights of the Child issued to the selected countries that the CRC has served as a catalyst for legislative reform and policy initiatives in a number of areas. The progress achieved may be considered relatively slow; however, it is fair to point out that in most countries the act of legislating is a time-consuming process that tends to take years. In any case, there are positive developments that are noteworthy in all the countries considered even if there is still much room for improvement. As noted earlier, what has occurred since the ratification of the CRC in the selected countries is the adoption of specific legislation in certain sectors, but mostly on a piecemeal basis and ad hoc. This section therefore examines more in depth the pieces of legislation and key policy initiatives that have been adopted, which are in accordance with the spirit of the CRC, and identifies as well some of the remaining obstacles for the treaty's full implementation.

The abolition of the death penalty for all persons below age 18 in St. Vincent and the Grenadines is one example of important progress achieved.[133] In Jamaica, the National Strategic Plan for HIV/AIDS/STI, the establishment of a special unit in the Ministry of Education for children with disabilities, and the creation of the Office of Children's Advocate are other such positive examples.[134] Activities that promote the participation of children and the child's right to be heard have been noted in a number of countries. A Street Children's Conference and a Children's Parliament, both held in 1996 in Jamaica, were good-faith attempts to ensure disadvantaged children a voice, as well as a chance to be heard in the policy-making process. The Children's Parliament provided children an opportunity to discuss the National Policy on Children.

---

[131] McDowell, op. cit., p. 236.   [132] Ibid.
[133] Concluding Observations: St. Vincent and the Grenadines, op. cit.
[134] The Office of Children's Advocate was established in Jamaica in 2006.

Despite progress, in many cases there is still a need to strengthen the State's policy and develop a national plan of action for the implementation of the CRC.[135] In this context, the Committee on the Rights of the Child urged Antigua and Barbuda to develop and implement a comprehensive national plan of action for the full implementation of the CRC and incorporation of the goals adopted by United Nations Member States during the UN Special Session on Children in May 2002, and contained in the document 'A World Fit for Children'.

The legislative reform in Barbados has concentrated mainly on laws regarding the care and protection of children that include: The Protection of Children Act, Sexual Offences Act, Domestic Violence Act (focusing on Protection Orders), Drug Abuse Prevention and Control Act and Bail Act. Significant reform has taken place in the area of juvenile justice with the Penal Reform Act adopted, which raised the age of criminal responsibility from seven to eleven.[136] Other legislative developments in Barbados since ratification of the CRC include amendments to the Education Act establishing every child's right to five years of secondary school and also giving teachers the authority to search children in school as a safety measure.

The recommendations issued by the Constitution Review Commission on the need to reform the Constitution by removing discriminatory provisions in regard to citizenship were also accepted by the Government of Barbados. As in most common law jurisdictions, the Constitution of Barbados is the supreme law of the land and any statute or common law that is found through judicial review to be inconsistent with its provisions is unconstitutional and cannot be enforced. An important aspect of the Constitution is its Bill of Rights, which recognizes fundamental rights and freedoms that help to safeguard human rights in the country. As noted earlier, despite the fact that many national constitutions have been drafted with important provisions safeguarding human rights, nevertheless they may need to be reviewed to ensure that they are fully in accordance with the CRC's norms and standards. The Constitution of Jamaica is one example because it fails to include sex among the prohibited grounds of discrimination.[137]

Robinson concludes that despite the legislative reform undertaken to date in Barbados, "there is residual discrimination on the basis of birth status, the juvenile justice laws are antiquated, there are inadequate and under-utilized child protection laws and aspects of the law relating to the punishment of children are not only inconsistent with the CRC but also with the Constitution."[138] Robinson further points out that the recommendations of the Committee on the Rights of the Child issued upon reviewing the Initial

---

[135] Ibid.
[137] See Jamaican Const., op. cit.

[136] T. Robinson, op. cit.
[138] T. Robinson, op. cit., p. 18.

State Party Report of Barbados regarding the need for law reform, remain valid today.[139]

In Jamaica, the most important legislative reform to date related to children is the Child Care and Protection Act that came into effect in March 2004. It was the product of 10 years of work involving both government and non-governmental organizations and is generally considered a positive development for the legal protection of children's rights in Jamaica. Some concerns have been raised, nevertheless, in regard to the possible discriminatory effect the law could have on the poor, and there is also criticism that it contains elements that are gender biased; both of which merit further study. The National Plan of Action of 2002 provides the framework for legislative reform for the protection of the best interests of the child and for establishing mechanisms and institutions for monitoring and supervision. The Plan is broad in scope and addresses the following: civil rights and freedoms, education, health, culture, personal safety and security of the child, family and community environment.

Despite these positive developments, there is much to be improved before all the rights of all children are respected and protected in Jamaica. For example, although the Age of Majority Act defines a child as any person under the age of 18 in accordance with the CRC, 17 year-olds accused of criminal offences were treated as adults. Jamaica's Initial State Party Report to the Committee on the Rights of the Child provides: "The Juveniles Act defines as a 'juvenile' a person under the age of 17 years and subdivides this group into 'child', meaning a person under the age of 14 years, and 'young person', meaning a person who has attained the age of 14 years and is under the age of 17 years. This Act provides for the minimum age at which a person has criminal liability, matters relating to the employment of children, giving testimony in court, and the consumption of alcohol by children."[140] Piecemeal legislative reform also has been the case for the countries of the OECS in the areas of domestic violence, sexual offences, child protection and the age of majority. Many of the old statutes, such as juvenile acts, have remained despite the fact that some provisions of these acts are not in compliance with provisions of the CRC. In addition, whereas some of the statutes have been amended several times, they have not actually improved the status of the rights of the child. A number of the laws of the OECS countries are deemed discriminatory and in violation of Article 2 of the CRC. For example, countries that are governed by the common law rules on the status of children (Anguilla, Dominica, Montserrat and St. Lucia) discriminate against children on the basis of birth status. The common law defines the status of the child based on whether the individual is

---

[139] Ibid., p. 13.
[140] See 'Initial State Party Report of Jamaica', op. cit., para 19.

legitimate or illegitimate. Consequently, an illegitimate child is not accorded rights of inheritance from or through the father and is also discriminated against in regard to other related rights.[141]

On a positive note, other countries in the Commonwealth Caribbean, such as Antigua and Barbuda, have abolished the common law distinction between legitimate and illegitimate children by statute. St. Kitts and Nevis has express constitutional provisions on the equal status of children, thus removing any discriminatory effects of other legislation.

As has been highlighted earlier, most of the legal reform that has been undertaken in the selected countries has emphasized mainly child welfare and juvenile justice. For the most part, the legislation that has emerged includes detailed provisions that focus on children who are characterized as 'in need of care and protection'. Otherwise, it has been in response to society's concern for juvenile delinquency. Legislative reform and national policies have not yet developed in a more *holistic manner* and by taking into account the child's civil and political rights, as well as his or her economic, social and cultural rights.

From the foregoing discussion, a number of conclusions can be drawn:

- *The CRC has been a catalyst for legislative reform* – The CRC has served as a catalyst for legislative reform and policy initiatives in a wide range of areas, but there is still room for further achievement.
- *States need to develop a national plan of action for implementation of the CRC* – Despite the progress, in most countries there is still a need to strengthen the State's child rights policy and to develop a national plan of action for the implementation of the CRC and to integrate a human rights perspective into all government policies, programmes and activities.
- *Awareness of important legislative reform achieved in certain sectors should be promoted* – Since the ratification of the CRC in the selected countries, progressive legislation has been adopted in certain sectors, which should be promoted to create awareness among the general public.
- *There is need for comprehensive review of legislation* – In most countries, a comprehensive review of the legislation has not yet been fully conducted either before or after ratification to assess to what extent domestic laws were in harmony with the CRC and which is necessary for legislative reform. Why legislatures are finding it difficult to conduct a comprehensive review merits further study.
- *National constitutions to be reviewed* – Although many national constitutions have been drafted with important provisions safeguarding human

[141] Jackson, op. cit., pp. 12, 13.

rights, they may need to be reviewed to ensure that they are fully in accordance with the CRC's principles, norms and standards.

*   *The need to review and monitor domestic laws continues* – Despite the legislative reform undertaken to date, there is still a need to continue to review and monitor domestic laws that contain, for example, residual discrimination on the basis of birth status, or juvenile justice laws and other child protection laws that may be inadequate and in need of updating, as well as to check for other evidence of laws that are inconsistent with the CRC.

*   *Holistic legislative reform and development of national policies are needed* – Legislative reform and the development of national policies should be encouraged in a more holistic manner and by taking into account the child's civil and political rights, as well as his or her economic, social and cultural rights.

VIII. IMPLEMENTATION AND ENFORCEMENT: THE GROWING ROLE OF THE JUDICIARY

The role of the judiciary is changing. There is a sense that in this increasingly globalized world even the courts are becoming interdependent and reaching across cultural boundaries. A review of the latest articles, publications and law journals that are popular within the common law legal community point to this growing trend, even if it also has its critics. McCrudden explains that it is becoming "commonplace in many jurisdictions for judges to refer to the decisions of foreign jurisdictions when interpreting domestic human rights guarantees."[142] This trend has been developing since the end of World War II when human rights protection started to flourish within the national legal systems; many national constitutions were adopted containing a Bill of Rights; there was a significant increase in the application of customary international human rights law; and the incorporation of international human rights treaties into domestic law began.[143]

In many jurisdictions, courts play a critical role in protecting human rights, depending upon the independence of the judiciary and the autonomy of human rights law. It has been widely recognized that "human rights can only be protected through an independent and impartial judiciary free from any form of pressure and supported by an autonomous and well-resourced justice system."[144] The autonomy of human rights law is also essential. If it is

---

[142] McGrudden, op cit., p. 499.   [143] Ibid. at 500.

[144] See Suva Statement of Principles on Judicial Independence and Access to Justice, adopted at the First International Judicial Colloquium on Human Rights held in Fiji, 6–8 August 2004. Reprinted in INTERIGHTS, *Access to Justice in a Changing World: Collection of Papers and Suva Statement on the Principles of Judicial Indpendence and Access to Justice,* (2004), pp. 10–11.

perceived that human rights law is separate from the political and economic powers in the particular jurisdiction, it allows judges and lawyers to consider human rights laws more freely, as if it were any other law.

In interpreting the law, common law judges must still abide by rules that serve as judicial guidance. In addition to providing a literal interpretation of the law as written, among other things, judges must look to different 'authority' such as the legislative history to ascertain the intention of the legislator, prior judicial reasoning and the country's own history and traditions. Moreover, judges distinguish between two kinds of authority, namely, 'binding authority' and 'persuasive authority'. Judges are obligated to apply binding authority, which is established by precedent and statutory law. They also can consider persuasive authority when other relevant material is introduced that can help them in reaching a decision, but they are not obligated to apply it. Thus, persuasive authority is optional for the judge to apply.[145]

For a number of reasons, some judges are more open than others to using persuasive authority freely in reaching their judicial decisions. The issue of the application of international human rights treaties has been the focus of a number of international judges' colloquia that have been organized in different parts of the Commonwealth. The first one was convened in 1988 in Bangalore, India as a high-level judicial colloquium on the Domestic Application of International Human Rights Norms organized by the Commonwealth Secretariat. Participants adopted the Bangalore Principles, which have been widely disseminated within judicial and human rights circles.[146] The Principles provide guidance for judges on judicial conduct in using international human rights law. Among other things, the Principles stipulate that judges can apply a treaty even if it has not been incorporated to remove an ambiguity in the law:

> It is within the proper nature of the judicial process and well-established judicial functions for national courts to have regard to international obligations which a country undertakes whether or not they have been incorporated into domestic law.... However, where national law is clear and inconsistent with the international obligations of the State are concerned, in 'common law' countries the national court is obliged to give effect to national law. In such cases the court should draw such inconsistencies to the attention of the appropriate authorities since the supremacy of national law in no way mitigates a breach of an international legal obligation which is undertaken by a country.... It is essential to redress a situation where, by reason of traditional

---

[145] McGrudden, op. cit., p. 502.
[146] The Bangalore Principles were released as a summary of issues discussed at a Judicial Colloquium on 'The Domestic Application of International Human Rights Norms', held in Bangalore, India from 24–26 February 1988. Reprinted in *Developing Human Rights Jurisprudence: Conclusions of Judicial Colloquia and other Meetings on the Domestic Application of International Human Rights Norms on Government under the Law 1988–92* (London: Commonwealth Secretariat, 1992), p. 1.

dimension, judges and practicing lawyers are often unaware of the remarkable and comprehensive developments of statements of international human rights norms.[147]

Thus, the Principles make it clear that judges have a duty to point out when there are conflicts between national laws and the provisions of the human rights treaties that have been ratified by the State.

Between 1994 and 1996, four judicial colloquia were organized by the Gender and Youth Affairs Division of the United Nations and the Commonwealth Secretariat focusing on the promotion of the human rights of women and the girl child through the judiciary. The first was held in Zimbabwe in 1994, followed by another in Beijing in 1995, Hong Kong in 1996, and the last one in the Caribbean region held in Guyana in 1997. Since then, there have been many more judicial colloquia addressing the domestic application of international human rights norms. In Zimbabwe participants adopted the Victoria Falls Declaration of Principles for Promoting the Human Rights of Women, which reaffirmed the principles stated in Bangalore and also recognized that they had been confirmed in a number of judicial gatherings.[148]

The Bangalore Principles are now widely accepted in many jurisdictions and, as a consequence, some national courts have developed liberal interpretations of constitutional standards, thus enabling more effective protection of human rights.[149] The Victoria Falls Declaration further provides specific guidance for the legal community. When formulating legal opinions, the Declaration encourages the application of human rights principles and particular scrutiny by the judiciary in cases of discrimination based on gender. It also proposes that judicial officers in the Commonwealth jurisdictions be guided by CEDAW when interpreting and applying the provisions of the national constitutions and laws, including the common law and customary law. The Victoria Falls Declaration recognizes the need to ensure that judges, lawyers, and litigants are made aware of applicable human rights norms as stated in international and regional instruments, national constitutions and laws.[150]

At a 1997 conference on implementing international human rights, the Hon. Justice Michael Kirby addressed the issue of judicial utilization of unincorporated norms. He stated that in the years since the Bangalore Principles had been adopted there has been a significant change in several common law countries in the approach adopted by the courts, including in Australia,

---

[147] Ibid.

[148] A. Byrnes, J. Connors, and L. Bik eds., *Advancing the Human Rights of Women: Using International Human Rights Standards in Domestic Litigation* (London: Commonwealth Secretariat, 1996), p. 3 [*Advancing the Human Rights of Women*].

[149] *Developing Human Rights Jurisprudence: The Eighth Judicial Colloquium on the Domestic Application of International Human Rights Norms* (London: INTERIGHTS and the Commonwealth Secretariat, 2001).

[150] *Advancing the Human Rights of Women*, op. cit., p. 5.

which had become increasingly receptive to the use of international human rights norms in deciding domestic cases.

> The expectations of the international community accord in this respect with the contemporary values of the Australian people. The opening up of the international remedies to individuals pursuant to Australia's accession to the Optional Protocol to the International Covenant on Civil and Political Rights brings to bear on the common law the powerful influence of the Covenant and the international standards it imports. The common law does not necessarily conform with international law, but international law is a legitimate and important influence on the development of the common law, especially when international law declares the existence of universal human rights. A common law doctrine founded on unjust discrimination in the enjoyment of civil and political rights demands reconsideration.[151]

In his speech, Justice Kirby highlights the many arguments raised by critics and members of the legal community that favour the dualist model and who caution the use of international human rights law in judicial law-making. Critics point out, for example, that the process of ratification is often defective because treaties are frequently negotiated by the executive branch and should require more careful scrutiny by Parliament before ratification. The introduction of international human rights norms by judges is further criticized for not having the democratic backing of the legislature, which could be interpreted as undermining the separation of powers. Some critics have questioned the credibility of international courts and committees that pronounce human rights that "are composed from legal regimes very different from our own." Another point of contention is the broad language and lack of precision used in the human rights instruments, which allegedly opens the door for excessively creative interpretation by the judiciary and thereby undermines the role of the legislature. There is also the view that it further undermines "the sovereignty of a country by *judicial fiat* without the authority of the country's democratically accountable law-makers."[152]

In response to the critics, Justice Kirby reiterates what the supporters of the Bangalore Principles stated regarding the evolving jurisprudence of international human rights norms that have been applied in domestic litigation as follows:

- The *Bangalore Principles* do not undermine the sovereignty of national law-making institutions. They acknowledge that if those institutions have made (by constitutional, statutory or common law decision) a rule which

---

[151] M. Kirby, 'Domestic Implementation of International Human Rights Norms' (address at the Conference on Implementing International Human Rights, Australian National University Faculty of Law, 6 Dec. 1997), www.hcourt.gov.au/speeches/kirbyj/kirbyj_inthrts.htm.

[152] Discussion following address by Hon. Justice Michael Kirby at the Conference on Implementing International Human Rights, Australian National University Faculty of Law, 6 Dec. 1997.

is unambiguous and binding, no international human rights principle can undermine or overrule the applicable domestic law. To introduce such a principle requires the opportunity of a gap in the common law or of an ambiguity of a local statute. Far from being a negation of sovereignty, this is an application of it.

- The process which the *Bangalore Principles* endorse is an inevitable one. As countries submit themselves to the external scrutiny and criticism of their laws by the United Nations Human Rights Committee, the results must be addressed. If a domestic law is measured and found wanting, a country must bring its law into conformity or be revealed as engaged in nothing but "window-dressing".

- The concept of democracy today is more sophisticated than was formerly the case. It involves not merely the reflection in law-making of the will of the majority, intermittently expressed at elections. The legitimacy of democratic governance is now seen as depending upon the respect by the majority for the fundamental rights of minorities.

- So far as federal states are concerned, their constitutions do not stand still. They operate in a world of increasing international interrelationships in matters of economics and of human rights. Judges, no more than legislatures and governments, can ignore this reality.

- The knowledge that the judicial use of international law in this way is now becoming more frequent may have the beneficial consequence of discouraging ratification by the Executive where there is no serious intention to accept, for the nation, the obligations contained in a treaty.[153]

Justice Kirby concludes his speech by declaring "the tradition of the common law has always been open to outside and international influences. It is appropriate that a *rapprochement* between domestic and international law should be developed. As we enter a new millennium there will be increasing international law of every kind. It is part of the genius of our legal system that the courts should find a way to take cognisance of international human rights jurisprudence in appropriate cases and do so by appropriate and familiar techniques of judicial reasoning."[154]

In light of the apparent willingness of some common law judges to look to international human rights principles and standards in their decision making, some conclusions can be drawn for use by child rights advocates:

- *Advocate for the need to include courses on child rights and women's rights in the schools and universities* – It is imperative for advocacy on child rights to focus on the need for formal legal education, through the law schools and continuing legal education with respect to the CRC and other relevant human rights treaties.

---

[153] Kirby, op. cit.   [154] Ibid.

- *Promote awareness of the growing jurisprudence on international human rights treaties* – There is a wealth of jurisprudence developing where unincorporated international human rights treaties have been used by judges under the common law tradition, which also indicates that many members of the judiciary are open to drawing on case law emerging from other jurisdictions. An important goal is to increase awareness about the developing jurisprudence in the legal communities to influence future court decisions and consequently legislative reform and policies that are in keeping with the CRC.
- *Assess the independence of the judiciary* – In developing a strategy for enlisting the support of the judiciary at the national level, it is essential to assess the degree of independence enjoyed by the judiciary and autonomy of human rights law to achieve optimal results in child rights advocacy.
- *Tailor materials specifically for the judiciary and legal community* – Information materials on the CRC and CEDAW should be tailored for the judiciary and legal community including pertinent legal analysis that may serve as binding or persuasive authority. For example, the Bangalore Principles, the Victoria Falls Declaration and other such documents should be made available to the judiciary and members of the legal community at the national level.
- *Increase awareness in the legal community of the CRC, CEDAW and other international human rights treaties* – There is a need to ensure that judges, lawyers and other members of the legal community are made aware of the applicable human rights norms and standards contained in the CRC and other international and regional instruments.

IX. EMERGING CASE LAW IN COMMON LAW JURISDICTIONS USING INTERNATIONAL HUMAN RIGHTS NORMS

Keeping in mind that domestic courts are where an individual normally seeks remedies from human rights violations, the status of international human rights treaties under domestic law is fundamental to the outcome of any case brought before the judiciary. In light of a growing judicial trend in some common law jurisdictions showing receptivity to international human rights norms, a number of examples in which courts have used unincorporated treaties in reaching their decisions are worth highlighting. At the same time, the decisions reached in these cases reflect the fact that there are mixed views in all the common law jurisdictions as shown by the degree of importance accorded by the courts to international human rights treaties.

The cases that are highlighted in this section are relevant for further consideration because they touch on some of the issues that have been previously identified in relation to the need for legislative reform. For example, several cases involved the need for judicial interpretation of constitutional provisions that contained human rights guarantees and questioned whether some national laws were discriminatory and therefore unconstitutional. Two landmark cases in different common law jurisdictions show that the principle of the best interests of the child provides a strong argument for protecting the rights of children, particularly when the CRC has not been incorporated into domestic law. Finally, there is evidence that many members of the judiciary are increasingly willing to look to the jurisprudence emerging in other common law jurisdictions in formulating their own legal opinions.

Mendes has indicated in a survey of international standards in constitutional litigation in the Commonwealth Caribbean that, in the past, courts in the region have on occasion referred to international treaties and covenants as aids to interpretation of the rights and freedoms enshrined in their constitutions. He cites as an example a case in Antigua, *Attorney General and another v Antigua Times Ltd.*[155] He also notes that the Privy Council has referred to the European Convention for the Protection of Human Rights and Fundamental Freedoms, as well as the Universal Declaration of Human Rights, to interpret the Antiguan human rights provisions and cites a similar outcome in a case in Trinidad and Tobago.[156] CEDAW has been cited in recent years in an increasing number of cases, particularly in Commonwealth countries such as Australia, Canada and New Zealand and those in Southern Africa. According to Byrnes, these cases include using CEDAW as "an authoritative national rule and determinative of the outcome of the case, as a relevant source to be taken into account in the interpretation of a constitutional or statutory provision, or a statement of values relevant to the decision-making process, as well as in cases in which it may be cited simply as background material without any significant impact in the decision."[157]

In a 1992 case before the Court of Appeals of Botswana, *Attorney General of Botswana v Unity Dow,* various international human rights instruments were considered "as an aid to constitutional or statutory interpretation," to decide whether the constitutional guarantee of equality prohibited gender discrimination regarding a nationality law.[158] Examples of Commonwealth courts in Southern Africa that have also looked to international human rights jurisprudence in the interpretation of national

---

[155] *Attorney General and another v Antigua Times Ltd.*, (1973) 20 WIR 537 (C.A. of the West Indies Assoc. States); (1976) AC 16 (PC).

[156] D. Mendes, 'The Relevance of International Standards to Constitutional Litigation in the Commonwealth Caribbean: A General Survey with Emphasis on Gender Equality', in *Gender Equality and the Judiciary* (London: Commonwealth Secretariat, 2000), p. 142.

[157] A. Byrnes, 'Using Gender-Specific Human Rights Instruments in Domestic Litigation: The Convention on the Elimination of all Forms of Discrimination Against Women', in *Gender Equality and the Judiciary* (London: Commonwealth Secretariat, 2000), p. 67.

[158] *Attorney General of Botswana v Unity Dow*, (1991) LRC Const. 574 (High Ct); (1992) LRC Const. 623 (C.A.).

constitutional guarantees, including treaties that have not been incorporated by the State, are two cases that came before the Supreme Court of Zimbabwe, *State v Ncube* and *Rattigan v Chief Immigration Officer of Zimbabwe*.[159]

As noted earlier, most Commonwealth Caribbean countries have constitutional provisions that contain important human rights guarantees, some including a bill of rights. The Jamaican Constitution contains provisions recognizing fundamental rights and freedoms that help to safeguard human rights in the country. Moreover, a distinguishing feature of this Constitution is its recognition of remedies that are enforceable in courts of law. Goonesekere has pointed out that "national constitutions represent a valuable framework that should be used to link with international standards on child rights," to further the implementation of the CRC.[160] She also reports that public interest or social action litigation in the Supreme Court of India has been based upon constitutional provisions to protect individual or collective rights. In light of this, Goonesekere proposes two approaches aimed at securing the protection of children's rights within domestic law. The first one is to invoke the fundamental rights and freedoms provided by national constitutions. The second one is to apply the principle of the best interests of the child, which is recognized in most domestic legal systems.[161]

In some prominent common law jurisdictions, a few cases pertaining to the rights of the child also have emerged that raised some international interest. Two particular cases are noteworthy because the principle of the best interests of the child was applied and the CRC was considered. An important one for Australia was the 1995 ruling in *Minister for Immigration and Ethnic Affairs v Teoh*.[162] In the Teoh case, a Malaysian who was living in Australia on a temporary permit was convicted of importing and using heroin and was ordered for deportation by the Minister of Immigration. Teoh appealed on the grounds that his wife (an Australian citizen) was a heroin addict and their six children depended on his care and support and invoked the CRC. Despite the father's criminal record, the High Court ruled he was permitted to remain in Australia, stating that it was in the best interests of the children. The High Court judges held that although the CRC had not become part of Australia's law, even though it had been ratified, it did not mean that its ratification had no significance for Australian law. The High Court affirmed that: "Australia's ratification of the Convention can give rise to a legitimate expectation that

---

[159] As cited in *Advancing the Human Rights of Women*, op cit., p. 49, *State v Ncube* (1990) 4 SA 151 (S. Ct. of Zimbabwe); *Rattigan and Others v Chief Immigration Officer*, (1994) 103 ILR 224, (1994) 1 LRC 343, (1995) 2 SA 182 (Zimb. S. Ct.).

[160] S. Goonesekere, 'The Rights of the Girl-Child in Commonwealth Jurisdictions', in *Advancing the Human Rights of Women*, op. cit., p. 126.

[161] Ibid.

[162] *Minister for Immigration and Ethnic Affairs v Teoh*, 7 April 1995, (1995) 183 CLR 273, (1995) ICHRL 22 (Aust. High Ct.), available at INTERIGHTS, 'Commonwealth Human Rights Law Database', www.interights.org/searchdatabases.php?dir=databases.

the decision-maker will exercise that discretion in conformity with the terms of the convention."[163]

Another case, *Baker v Canada,* which ended up before the Supreme Court of Canada and which considered the CRC and the principle of the best interests of the child, involved a Jamaican citizen and mother of four who was ordered for deportation. She appealed the deportation decision on grounds that she was the sole caregiver of her two Canadian-born children and requested an exemption from the requirement that she apply for permanent residence from abroad. She based her argument on an immigration act that recognized 'humanitarian and compassionate considerations'. Her application was denied by the Immigration Office, which stated that the interests of the children did not constitute humanitarian and compassionate grounds to warrant processing the application for permanent residence within Canada. The lower court dismissed the application for judicial review. On appeal the question before the Court was: Although the Immigration Act did not incorporate international obligations arising from the CRC, must federal immigration authorities treat the best interests of the child as a primary consideration in assessing an applicant under the Immigration Act in question? The Appeals Court denied the appeal stating that the CRC did not obligate the government to give primacy to the children's best interests in cases concerning deportation.

The Supreme Court of Canada disagreed and allowed the appeal by holding that the immigration authorities that had denied Ms. Baker's appeal had totally dismissed the interests of Ms. Baker's children under the humanitarian and compassionate exception. Although the Court recognized that the provisions of the CRC had no direct application under Canadian law, it nevertheless underscored that "the values reflected in international human rights law may help inform the contextual approach to statutory interpretation and judicial review." The Court further expanded on the important role international human rights law has played as an aid in the interpretation of domestic law in other common law jurisdictions. The Court cited the principles of the CRC and other international human rights instruments, such as the Universal Declaration of Human Rights and United Nations Declaration on the Rights of the Child, noting that they both recognized the protection of children's rights and the principle of the best interests of the child.[164]

Another factor that is influencing the extent to which the CRC and other international human rights norms will be applied in domestic courts is the increasing willingness to look to foreign jurisdictions for guidance in judicial reasoning. For example, even before the CRC entered into force, it was

---

[163] Ibid.

[164] See *Baker v Canada* (Minister of Citizenship and Immigration) No. 25823 (9 July 1999); (1999) 2 S.C.R.

pointed out that a decision of the English Court could be persuasive authority in Barbados courts. In *Gillick v West Norfolk and Wisbech Area Health Authority,* the English Court recognized that parental authority "yields to the child's right to make his own decisions when he reaches a sufficient understanding and intelligence to be capable to making up his own mind on the matter requiring decision."[165] Accordingly, the Family Division of the Barbados High Court considered the opinion and was influenced by the decision of the English Court. Thus, in *Haloute v Adamira,* the wishes of a 14 year-old boy were taken into account and it served to shape the decision of the Barbadian court. In the Initial State Party Report of Barbados, both of these cases are cited and it is further provided: "The age of 16 is generally considered to be the age of sufficient understanding and intelligence to permit individual decision in several areas including consent to medical treatment."[166]

In New Zealand, whether there was an obligation to have regard to international human rights norms was considered by the New Zealand Court of Appeal in *Tavita v Minister of Immigration,* concerning the expulsion of an illegal immigrant. Although the court did not rule that international obligations must be considered in the administrative decision-making process, it did review the jurisprudence under the European Convention on Human Rights of the European Court of Human Rights and stated that this was an area of the law which was "undergoing evolution." The position of the court also was influenced by the fact that New Zealand had enacted a Bill of Rights in 1990 and a Human Rights Act in 1993.[167]

It is clear that the cases invoking the CRC and other international human rights treaties are still in their infancy. In the Commonwealth Caribbean, some cases that could have offered opportunities for introducing provisions of the CRC and other treaties have been missed. In a 1999 case from St Vincent and the Grenadines, *Kevin Lucas 'by next friend' Virginia Mascoll v Jack & Anor,* a High Court held that corporal punishment by a school teacher did not constitute inhuman or degrading treatment or punishment. The case involved a student at school who was flogged six times by a teacher using a leather strap. The student alleged that flogging violated his constitutional right not to be subjected to inhuman or degrading treatment or punishment and therefore the use of corporal punishment was unlawful. The Court held that although the Corporal Punishment Abolition Act of 1966 prohibited corporal punishment except in the cases of caning juvenile offenders, the corporal punishment the student had received, and in light of the injuries

---

[165] *Gillick v West Norfolk and Wisbech Area Health Authority,* (1986) A.C. 112.

[166] See *Haloute v Adamira,* unreported, Judgement No. 233 of 1989 (Barb. High Ct.), as cited in 'Initial State Party Report: Barbados', op. cit. paras. 26, 60.

[167] *Tavita v Minister of Immigration,* (1994) 1 LRC 421; 2 NZLR 257; (1996).

inflicted, did not constitute ill treatment or degradation, and, furthermore, that corporal punishment per se was not unlawful.[168]

As discussed earlier, the 2005 decision of the Inter-American Court of Human Rights in the case of *Winston Caesar v Republic of Trinidad and Tobago* regarding corporal punishment may influence the outcome of similar cases brought before the Caribbean courts in the future. The Inter-American Court considered international and comparative legal material, including jurisprudence from a broad range of human rights bodies and national courts. It should be noted that although four Commonwealth Caribbean countries have ratified the treaty, only two have accepted the jurisdiction of the Inter-American Court, namely, Barbados and Trinidad and Tobago, with the latter subsequently denouncing the Convention. As a result, there have been very few cases brought before this regional body from the Commonwealth Caribbean region.

An additional important development that will influence the extent to which the CRC will be applied by common law courts is the changing attitude towards the participation of children in legal proceedings. Under the common law, the traditional view has been that although children are a concern of the law and regarded as subjects of the law, they have not been accorded the right to participate in the legal process. This is based on the assumption that children lack the capacity to participate in legal processes to claim or defend their rights. In recent years, throughout the common law world, important changes have been noted in attitudes towards the participation of children in the legal process. Nowadays, in many jurisdictions children participate in family law proceedings, as well as in criminal law proceedings. In addition, legal reforms have facilitated the participation of child witnesses in the adversarial system.

From this quick review of some of the case law emerging from common law courts in diverse jurisdictions, it can be concluded that the judiciary can provide an important avenue for advancing human rights, particularly when an individual is directly affected by a law that requires judicial scrutiny. However, this will only occur when there is a valid claim or action brought before the court. Access to the courts is still a major challenge for the more disadvantaged sectors of the population in many developing countries, particularly for children in view of their 'special and dependent status'. In other instances where specific legislation or provisions of the national constitution are inconsistent with the CRC, in light of the separation of powers doctrine, the issue may need to be addressed within the domain of the legislature rather than by the courts.

---

[168] *Kevin Lucas 'by next friend' Virginia Mascoll v Jack & Anor*, (1999) ICHRL 140 (11 Oct. 1999), (2000) 5 LRC 415, as reported at INTERIGHTS, 'Commonwealth Human Rights Law Database', op. cit.

In light of this discussion regarding the emerging case law in common law jurisdictions, a number of conclusions can be drawn for consideration by child rights advocates:

- *Know the status of international human rights treaties under domestic law* – The status of international human rights treaties under domestic law, in addition to the CRC, is fundamental to the outcome of the case, but increasingly courts are willing to consider unincorporated treaties in their legal reasoning.
- *Courts are more open to consider international human rights norms and standards in their legal reasoning* – Some common law courts have been receptive to consider international human rights treaties as an aid to constitutional or statutory interpretation, and there is a growing willingness to look to the emerging jurisprudence of other jurisdictions for guidance.
- *Become familiar with the national constitution and the extent of protection it provides* – Some courts are willing to overrule domestic laws when they are in conflict with provisions of national constitutions that recognize human rights principles and include a bill of rights.
- *National constitutions can provide an important vehicle to further the implementation of the CRC* – National constitutions represent a valuable framework that should be linked with international standards on child rights and skilfully presented in the legal arguments brought before the courts to protect the rights of the child.
- *Apply the principle of the best interests of the child* – The principle of the best interests of the child has been successfully argued before the courts and provides an entry point for protecting the rights of the child and to further the implementation of the CRC.
- *The participation of children in legal proceedings is growing* – The changing attitude of some common law courts towards the participation of children in legal proceedings strengthens their capacity to claim their rights through the courts.

X. THE ROLE OF CIVIL SOCIETY IN LEGISLATIVE REFORM

Nowadays there is a more limited view of the capacity of the State, with many States finding it necessary to depend on the growing important role of the NGOs and of the private sector in developing countries. Consequently, the influence and valuable contributions of NGOs has grown considerably in many countries.

Legislative reform to further the implementation of the CRC and to ensure the realization of children's rights normally involves a wide range of actors, particularly NGOs. There has been ample evidence documented of the critical role that international NGOs and civil society organizations have played in the past at the national and local levels to promote the ratification and implementation of the CRC. NGOs also have been essential to the State party reporting process through their contributions of pertinent and valuable information regarding the progress achieved and obstacles encountered in the implementation of the CRC, which they have provided to governments, as well as to the Committee on the Rights of the Child in the form of 'shadow reports'. NGOs are highly active in other activities including the dissemination of the CRC and documents related to the State party reporting process such as the Committee on the Rights of the Child's Concluding Observations, in monitoring and training initiatives, as well as in advocacy efforts related to constitutional and legislative reform. In many instances, NGOs have been at the forefront in promoting the participation of children by sponsoring a number of events such as children's parliaments.

In the selected countries, NGOs have been involved in a wide range of activities. In Barbados, it is reported that NGOs are playing "an influential role in shifting public attitudes to parenting and the rights of children,"[169] and they are working closely with government ministries and organizations such as UNICEF. They also provide a long list of services. At the same time, there is concern that because there are few children's rights organizations, some NGOs that oppose the rights of women and children, which also have emerged in recent years in Barbados, are placing constraints on the promotion of children's rights. This unfortunate development merits further analysis and attention by child rights advocates.

In Jamaica, many activities directed at promoting the principles of the CRC have involved both the government and NGOs. Among other things, NGOs were noted to be actively engaged in the preparation of Jamaica's Second Periodic Report to the Committee on the Rights of the Child. The process was characterized as being highly participatory, including children who had the opportunity to provide their views on a number of issues.

In a few cases, the Committee on the Rights of the Child has expressed concern to some States of insufficient efforts to involve civil society in the implementation of the CRC. For example, it recommended to Antigua and Barbuda the need to systematically involve communities and civil society, including children, throughout all stages of implementation. The need for closer partnerships between government and NGOs has been pointed out by the Committee on the Rights of the Child as well.

In sum, building partnerships with NGOs and civil society organizations for the purpose of encouraging legislative reform should be a major priority. In most cases, NGOs can be highly effective in terms of initiating advocacy activities, conducting legal research and reaching out to influential members of the community including members of Parliament, members of the legal community, church leaders and a wide range of policy makers. Among other

---

[169] FINT Robinson, op. cit., p. 25.

achievements, through such partnerships, proposed legislation and progressive social policies can be promoted for acceptance by the general public, as well as public support for the allocation of budgets for the fulfilment of the rights of the child.

CONCLUSIONS

The status of the child has come a long way in common law countries since Victorian England, largely because of the development of a body of international human rights law, which has sought to safeguard the rights of the child by imposing duties and obligations directly on the State and its governance institutions, as well as indirectly on the community and the family. This study has attempted to provide a different perspective on the impact of the CRC on law review and law reform at national level by addressing some of the traditions, principles, rules and practices that may influence the legislative process in those jurisdictions that follow the common law. It is evident that there are many issues and different approaches to consider to further legislative reform and to encourage other action aimed at promoting the realization of children's rights under this legal tradition. Within this context, the study has emphasized the important functions of the legislature and judiciary, in addition to the Executive, in ensuring that the rights of the child are respected and protected.

There are general considerations that could be taken into account by those key organizations interested in advocating for increased action by the legislature and the judiciary. The first is the great advantage of understanding the rules of common law and knowing how courts and judges operate under this legal system. Related to this is the increasing and likely controversial role of the judiciary in the common law legal systems in promoting human rights through their judicial reasoning and in helping to shape domestic laws on matters that concern children. The second is the benefit of working more closely and in partnership with the legislature at the national level including with individual members of Parliament who have a duty to review legislation, draft and adopt new laws, approve budgets and more. The third is to enlist the support of the judiciary and other members of the legal profession who provide leadership in their communities and are in a position to mobilize the courts, as was reflected in the study. In this regard, it should be kept in mind that many common law lawyers were engaged in the drafting of many of the international human rights instruments that have been widely ratified. The fourth point concerns parliamentarians and judges, both of whom have been approached in the past in a rather superficial way, usually by seeking their endorsement of declarations and resolutions in support of the CRC. As a rule, they have not been singled out for their full potential, in view of the functions that parliamentarians have in relation to legislative reform and of the weight of the courts and judges under the common law system. Thus, it merits more concentrated efforts to enlist their total support.

This study also has demonstrated that the selected countries of the Commonwealth Caribbean region have already taken some important steps towards implementation, as required mainly by international human rights law. However, much more needs to be done for these States to be in compliance with their duties and obligations according to international law and to realize the rights of the child in keeping with the provisions of the CRC. There is a need to encourage comprehensive reviews of legislation and promote law reform to ensure that national laws are in accordance with the treaty. Effective national monitoring mechanisms need to be established in some countries, and the capacity and quality of those already created are in need of strengthening and improvement. Only a few of the countries have allocated budgets that benefit children. This is an issue that could be raised more systematically with members of the legislature who are responsible for approving the budgets. None of the countries studied have attempted to ensure there are effective remedies available for when the human rights of children are violated. The need to ensure access to the courts by all sectors of the population represents yet another area for advocacy and public discussion. A related issue is the advantage of establishing national institutions for the protection and promotion of human rights, including an ombudsperson for children.

Since the Universal Declaration on Human Rights was proclaimed in 1948, more than 150 countries have incorporated human rights standards into their legal systems.[170] The research undertaken for this study shows clearly a growing jurisprudence in diverse cultures and legal traditions with a tendency to grant significant weight to international human rights treaties that is "adding new dimensions to the concepts first articulated in the Universal Declaration on Human Rights".[171] The significant impact of the CRC can be singled out particularly as a result of its having reached virtual universal ratification in a short period of time since it entered into force in 1990. As a rule, the process of implementation is a lengthy one that requires effort by the States to disseminate information on the Convention and to promote its understanding. On a positive note, States are generally complying with the duty to make the CRC widely known and they do report regularly to the Committee on the Rights of the Child on the progress achieved in making rights a reality for all children. This ongoing constructive dialogue in which government and international human rights treaty bodies are formally engaged is of great value for informing and helping to shape

---

[170] N. Jayawickrama, *The Judicial Application of Human Rights Law: National, Regional and International Jurisprudence* (Cambridge: Cambridge University Press, 2003), Preface.
[171] Ibid.

law review and reform in common law jurisdictions. In the years to come, what action is taken at the national level to further the implementation of the CRC will determine to what extent the treaty's historic success at the international level has helped to visibly improve the lives of children in their homes, schools and community.

BIBLIOGRAPHY

Alston, P. 'The Legal Framework of the Convention on the Rights of the Child'. *Bulletin of Human Rights*. Geneva: United Nations, 1991: 91–2.

Alston, P. 'The Best Interests Principle: Towards a Reconciliation of Culture and Human Rights'. In *The Best Interests of the Child – Reconciling Culture and Human Rights*, edited by P. Alston. Oxford: Clarendon Press, 1994: p. 5.

Attorney General and another v Antiqua Times Ltd. (1973) 20 WIR 537. C.A. of the West Indies Assoc. States; (1976) AC 16 (PC).

Attorney General of Botswana v Unity Dow, (1991) LRC Const. 574 (High Ct.); (1992) LRC Const. 623 (C.A.).

Baker v Canada (Minister of Citizenship and Immigration). No. 25823 (9 July 1999); (1999) 2 S.C.R.

Bangalore Principles. Reprinted in *Developing Human Rights Jurisprudence*: Conclusions of Judicial Colloquia and Other Meetings on the Domestic Application of International Human Rights Norms on Government under the Law 1988–92. London: Commonwealth Secretariat, 1992: vol 3. and in *Afr. J of Int'l and Comp. Law/RADIC* 1 (1989).

Black's Law Dictionary. St. Paul, MN: West Publishing Co., 6th edn., 1990.

Blackstone, W. *Commentaries on the Laws of England*. Oxford: Clarendon Press, originally published 1765–1769: Book 1, Chapter 16 (Parent and Child).

Bobb-Semple, C. 'The Common Law and Human Rights'. *Consilio* (undated). www.spr-consilio.com/humanrights.html.

Byrnes, A. 'Using Gender-Specific Human Rights Instruments in Domestic Litigation: The Convention on the Elimination of all Forms of Discrimination Against Women'. In *Gender Equality and the Judiciary*. London: Commonwealth Secretariat, 2000.

Byrnes, A., J. Connors and L. Bik, eds. *Advancing the Human Rights of Women: Using International Human Rights Standards in Domestic Litigation*. London: Commonwealth Secretariat, 1997: p. 3+.

Carnegie, A. R. 'Using the Available Remedies – 1. Caribbean Constitutional Remedies'. In *International Human Rights Law in the Commonwealth Caribbean*. The Hague: Martinus Nijhoff Publishers, 1991.

Catholic Encyclopedia online. 'Common Law' and 'Human Rights'. www.newadvent.org/cathen/.

Central Intelligence Agency (US). *World Factbook*. www.cia.gov/cia/publications/factbook/geos/jm.html.

'Child Labour in Victorian England'. www.freeessays.cc/db/18/ehc33.shtml.

Children and Young People's Unit (CYPU), Young People and Families Directorate UK. www.cypuk.corporate/childrights/index.cfm.

Committee on the Rights of the Child. 'Concluding Observations: Dominica'. U.N. Doc. CRC/C/15/Add.238. 30 June 2004.

Committee on the Rights of the Child. 'Concluding Observations: Jamaica' [Initial Report]. U.N. Doc. CRC/C/15/Add.32. 15 Feb. 1997.

Committee on the Rights of the Child. 'Concluding Observations: Jamaica' [Second Periodic Report]. U.N. Doc. CRC/C/15/Add.210. 4 July 2003.

Committee on the Rights of the Child. 'Concluding Observations: St. Vincent and the Grenadines'. U.N. Doc. CRC/C/15/Add. 184. 13 June 2002.

Committee on the Rights of the Child. General Comment No. 2, 'The Role of Independent National Human Rights Institutions in the Promotion and Protection of the Rights of the Child'. U.N. Doc. CRC/GC/2002/2. 15 Nov. 2002.

Committee on the Rights of the Child, General Comment No. 5: 'General measures of implementation for the Convention on the Rights of the Child'. U.N. Doc. CRC/GC/2003/5. 3 Oct. 2003.

Committee on the Rights of the Child. 'Initial Reports of State Parties Due in 1992: Barbados'. U.N. Doc. CRC/C3/Add 45. 11 Feb. 1997.

Committee on the Rights of the Child, Initial Reports of States Parties Due in 1993: Jamaica'. U.N. Doc. CRC/C/8/Add.12. 17 Mar. 1994.

Committee on the Rights of the Child, Second Periodic Reports of States Parties Due in 1998: Jamaica'. U.N. Doc. CRC/C/70/Add.15. 12 Feb. 2003.

Connors, J. 'An Analysis and Evaluation of the System of State Reporting'. In *The UN Human Rights Treaty System in the 21st Century*, edited by Anne F. Bayefsky. The Hague: Kluwer Law International, 2000: pp. 3–22.

Convention on the Elimination of All Forms of Discrimination against Women, G.A. res. 34/180. *Adopted* 18 Dec. 1979, 34 U.N. GAOR Supp. (No. 46) at 193. U.N. Doc. A/34/46. *Entered into force* 3 Sept. 1981.

Convention on the Elimination of All Forms of Racial Discrimination, G.A. res. 2106 (XX), Annex. 20 U.N. GAOR Supp. (No. 14) at 47. U.N. Doc. A/6014 (1966), 660 U.N.T.S. 195. *Entered into force* 4 Jan. 1969.

Convention on the Rights of the Child. G.A. res. 44/25, annex. *Adopted* 20 Nov. 1989, 44 U.N. GAOR Supp. (No. 49) at 167. U.N. Doc. A/44/49 (1989). *Entered into force* 2 Sept. 1990. Reprinted in 28 *ILM* (1989): p. 1448.

Cooray, M. 'Common Law Statute and the Rule of Law'. Excerpt from *The Australian Achievement: From Bondage to Freedom*. (Undated).

'Core Document Forming Part of the Reports of States Parties: Barbados'. U.N. Doc. HRI/CORE/Add.64/Rev.1. 25 June 1998.

'Core Document Forming Part of the Reports of States Parties: Jamaica'. U.N. Doc. HRI/CORE/1/Add.82. 23 June 1997.

Declaration of the Rights of the Child. Adopted by the League of Nations, 1924.

Declaration of the Rights of the Child. G.A. res. 1386 (XIV). 14 U.N. GAOR Supp. (No. 16) at 19. U.N. Doc. A/4354 (1959).

Department for Constitutional Affairs of the United Kingdom. 'Frequently Asked Questions'. www.dca.gsi.gov.uk/peoples-rights/human-rights.

Developing Human Rights Jurisprudence: The Eighth Judicial Colloquium on the Domestic Application of International Human Rights Norms. London: INTERIGHTS and the Commonwealth Secretariat, 2001.

Dina, Y. 'Guide to Caribbean Research', www.llrx.com/features/Caribbean.htm.

Donnelly, J. *Universal Human Rights – In Theory and Practice.* Ithaca, NY: Cornell University Press, 2003.

Douglas, G. and N. Lowe. 'Becoming a Parent in English Law'. In *Parenthood in Modern Society: Legal and Social Issues For the Twenty-First Century*, edited by

J. Eekelaar and P. Šarčević, p. 145+. Dordrecht: Martinus Nijhoff Publishers, 1993.

Eekelaar, J. 'Interests of the Child and the Child's Wishes'. In *The Best Interests of the Child – Reconciling Culture and Human Rights*, edited by P. Alston. Oxford: Clarendon Press, 1994: 44+ .

Encyclopedia Britannica online. 'Human Rights'. www.britannica.com/eb/article-9106289/human-rights.

Families Need Fathers (UK). www.fnf.org.uk.childact.htm.

Flekkoy, M. and N. Hevener Kaufman. *Rights and Responsibilities in Family and Society.* London: Jessica Kingsley Publishers, 1997: 15+.

Gillick v West Norfolk and Wisbech Area Health Authority. (1986) A.C. 112.

Goonesekere, S. 'The Best Interests of the Child: A South Asian Perspective'. In *The Best Interests of the Child – Reconciling Culture and Human Rights*, edited by P. Alston. Oxford: Clarendon Press, 1994: 117+.

Goonesekere, S. 'The Rights of the Girl-Child in Commonwealth Jurisdictions'. In *Advancing the Human Rights of Women – Using International Human Rights Standards in Domestic Litigation.* London: Commonwealth Secretariat, 1997: 126+.

Hall, J. C. 'The Waning of Parental Rights'. *Cambridge LJ.* 31 (1972): 248–65.

Haloute v Adamira. Unreported. Judgement No. 233 of 1989 (Barb. High Ct.).

Hamilton, C. M. 'National Study of Legislative Reform Initiative, Jamaica'. Unpublished study for the Legislative Reform Initiative, UNICEF, 2004.

Human Rights Committee. 'Concluding Observations: Zimbabwe'. U.N. Doc. CCPR/C/79/Add.89. 6 Apr. 1998.

International Covenant on Civil and Political Rights. G.A. res. 2200A (XXI). 21 U.N. GAOR Supp. (No. 16) at 52. U.N. Doc. A/6316 (1966), 999 UNTS.

International Covenant on Economic, Social and Cultural Rights. G.A. res. 2200A (XXI). 21 U.N. GAOR Supp. (No. 16) at 49. U.N. Doc. A/6316 (1966), 993 U.N.T.S. 3. *Adopted* 16 Dec. 1966 and *entered into force* 3 Jan. 1976. Reprinted in 6 *ILM* (1967): p. 360.

Inter-American Court of Human Rights. Advisory Opinion OC-17/2002, 'Juridical Condition and Human Rights of the Child'. 28 Aug. 2002. www.corteidh.or.cr/seriea_ing/index.html.

Jackson, L. M. 'Report on Law Reform Initiatives Relating to the Convention on the Rights of the Child in the OECS'. Unpublished study for the Legislative Reform Initiative, UNICEF, 2004.

Jayawickrama, N. *The Judicial Application of Human Rights Law: National, Regional and International Jurisprudence.* Cambridge: Cambridge University Press, 2003.

Kevin Lucas 'by next friend' Virginia Mascoll v Jack & Anor. (1999) ICHRL 140 (11 October 1999); (2000) 5 LRC 415. INTERIGHTS, 'Commonwealth Human Rights Law Database'. www.interrights.org/serachdatabases.php?dir=databases.

Martenson, J. 'The United Nations and Human Rights Today and Tomorrow'. In. *Human Rights in the Twenty-First Century: A Global Challenge*, edited by K. E. Mahoney and P. Mahoney. Dordrecht: Martinus Nijhoff Publishers, 1993.

McCrudden, C. 'A Common Law of Human Rights?: Transnational Judicial Conversations on Constitutional Rights'. *Oxford J of Legal Stud.* 23.4 (2000): 514+.

McDowell, Z. *Elements of Child Law in the Commonwealth Caribbean.* Kingston, Jamaica: University Press of the West Indies, 2000.

Mendes, D. 'The Relevance of International Standards to Constitutional Litigation in the Commonwealth Caribbean: A general Survey with Emphasis on Gender Equality'. In *Gender Equality and the Judiciary*. London: Commonwealth Secretariat, 2000.

Minister for Immigration and Ethnic Affairs v Teoh, (1995) 183 CLR 273, (1995) ICHRL 22 (Aust. High. Ct.). 7 April 1995. INTERIGHTS, 'Commonwealth Human Rights Law Database'. www.interrights.org/serachdatabases.php?dir= databases.

National Teaching Advisory Service (UK). 'The Children Act 1989'. www.ntas.org. uk.childrenact.htm.

Parker, S. 'The Best Interests of the Child. Principles and Problems'. In *The Best Interests of the Child – Reconciling Culture and Human Rights*, edited by P. Alston. Oxford: Clarendon Press, 1994: p. 27+.

Rios-Kohn, R. 'The Convention on the Rights of the Child: Progress and Challenges'. *Georgetown J on Fighting Poverty*. Summer 1998: 140+.

Robinson, T. 'Legislative Reform Initiative, National Study of Barbados'. Unpublished study for the Legislative Reform Initiative, UNICEF, 2004.

Santos Pais, M. 'The Convention on the Rights of the Child'. In *Manual on Human Rights Reporting*. Geneva, United Nations, 1997: 394+.

Steiner, H. J. and P. Alston. *International Human Rights in Context, Law, Politics, Morals*. Oxford: Oxford University Press, 2000.

Tavita v Minister of Immigration. (1994) 1 LRC 421; 2 NZLR 257; (1996).

UNICEF, 'Implementing the Convention on the Rights of the Child – Resource Mobilization in Low-Income Countries'. Florence: UNICEF Innocenti Research Centre, 1996: 4+.

UNICEF, 'Law Reform to Implement the Convention on the Rights of the Child'. Unpublished study, UNICEF Innocenti Research Centre, Florence, January 2004.

UNICEF. *The State of World's Children 2001*. New York: UNICEF, 2000.

UNICEF. *The State of World's Children 2004*. New York: UNICEF, 2003.

Human Rights for Children and Women – How UNICEF Helps Make Them a Reality. New York: UNICEF, 1999.

UNICEF Regional Office for Latin America and the Caribbean.

UNICEF Office in Jamaica.

United Nations, *National Human Rights Institutions*. Geneva: United Nations, Professional Training Series No. 4, 1995.

Universal Declaration of Human Rights. GA Res. 217A (III). U.N. Doc. A/810 (1948), p. 71. *Adopted* 10 Dec. 1948. Reprinted in *Am. J Int'l L* 43 (Supp. 1949): p. 127.

Van Bueren, G. *The International Law on the Rights of the Child*. The Hague: Martinus Nijhoff Publishers for Save the Children, 1995, 72+.

Vascianne, S. 'International Law and Selected Human Rights in Jamaica'. *West Indian LJ*. 2002: 1+.

Victoria Falls Declaration of Principles for the Promotion of the Human Rights of Women. In *The International Human Rights of Women – Instruments of Change*, edited by C. E. Lockwood, D. B. Magraw, M. F. Spring, S. I. Strong. Washington, D.C.: American Bar Association Section of International Law and Practice, 1998.

Wadham, J. and H. Mountfield. 'Rights Brought Home'. White paper, 1997: 187+.

Wikipedia Encyclopedia. 'History of the Common Law' and 'Parliamentary system'. www.wikipedia.org/wiki.

Winston Caesar v. Republic of Trinidad and Tobago. Inter-American Court of Human Rights. Judgement of 11 Mar. 2005, Series C. No. 123. J. Jackman (concurring judgement). Organization of American States, 'InterAmerican Court of Human Rights jurisprudence', www.oas.org/OASpage/humanrights.htm.

CHAPTER TWO

A Comparative Study of the Impact of the Convention on the Rights of the Child

LAW REFORM IN SELECTED CIVIL LAW COUNTRIES

Emilio García Méndez

INTRODUCTION

The main objective of this study is to provide all those involved in the promotion and defence of the rights of the child with arguments and instruments that will help them understand the value and importance of the processes aimed at bringing norms and policies at the national level into line with the spirit and terms of the United Nations Convention on the Rights of the Child (CRC). The approach adopted in this chapter is to synthesize specific examples, obtained through direct and indirect experience, coupled with the discussion and conceptual analysis of a number of key problems. This will help readers understand the different kinds of impediments and main obstacles that lie in the path of these reform processes. Particular effort is made to explain the strategic and inevitable characteristics required of legal reform processes in order to achieve extensive and sustainable development of social policies in favour of children. Avoiding the regulatory fallacy whereby legal reform is conceived as an end in itself, the aim of this chapter is to show the complex nature of such types of reform, as an essential condition yet one that is, at the same time, insufficient for the realization of children's rights because the latter goes beyond the horizon of programmes of limited scope and leads to the formulation of policies for all children.

Four national studies previously commissioned by the United Nations Children's Fund (UNICEF) and undertaken in countries belonging to the civil law tradition yet with fundamentally different histories – Azerbaijan, Armenia, Burkina Faso and the Dominican Republic – are referenced and examined in this chapter. Whenever pertinent and possible, reference has been made to other countries in different parts of the world, including those with common law legal systems. Serious information gaps have been encountered with regard to references – above all historical – to regions outside Latin America in relation to processes for the development of children's rights. This problem is probably not devoid of significance. Such a lack of information is often the result of an excessive pragmatism or the adoption of an emergency-based approach, under which any kind of historical analysis is regarded as superfluous. For this reason, the reader will note a significant emphasis placed on examples and historical references relating to the Latin American region. This emphasis results not only from the author's familiarity with the legal processes embarked upon in this region (which pertains in its entirety to the civil law tradition) but also from the existence of a large amount of documentation available on this region, including both information on current legal reform processes and historical studies on the evolution of the rights of the child. There is, for a number of reasons, a visible absence of studies of this kind in the non–Latin American countries analyzed. Such lack of information is highly characteristic of both African and the former Soviet Union countries in particular. Lacking are analyses of a historical nature that would offer information on both the processes of social construction of the concept of children as a category of persons distinct from that of adults and on processes relating to the development of children's rights.

Finally, a major issue should be highlighted, although at the same time we should be in no hurry to draw from it definitive conclusions. We refer to the outstanding similarities in the problems and impediments encountered in the process of developing a culture (including a legal culture) in which the child is regarded as a subject of rights, progressively acquiring the capability to express his or her needs with autonomy. Such distinctions stand irrespective of the accelerated globalization process underway. The persistence of arbitrary and discretionary ways in which adults and institutions relate to children appears to be a common feature in countries with marked historical differences and at different stages of development.

I. THE CONTEXT FOR LEGISLATIVE REFORM: PAST AND PRESENT

My true glory is not to have won forty battles. Waterloo will efface the memory of so many victories. What nothing can efface, what will endure forever, is my Civil Code.

Napoleon Bonaparte

The Origins of Codified Law: The Historical and Political Dimensions

The codified law tradition is long established. Its roots are to be found in the Roman law codified by Emperor Justinian. In Ancient Rome, the sources of law were numerous and were broadly dispersed in books, laws and declarations. To put an end to such confusion, Justinian ordered his legal advisers to put all the laws together in a single code. This task was performed over a relatively short period of time, between the years 529 and 533 AD, in

Constantinople. Subsequent to this era, codified law took on a form comparable to a 'civil code', containing almost all the rules of private law. Contrary to the procedure under the common law system, courts examining a case from the civil law perspective base their decision firstly on what is written in the code; it is only after this that they consult previous judicial decisions for the sake of consistency. The rich tradition of Roman law codification, however, was lost throughout practically the whole of the Middle Ages, during which time it was the so-called *Ius Commune* that prevailed. The fragmentation of the feudal system interrupted, in this context (as it has done subsequently in many other historical contexts), the process of codification. The study of Roman law was resurrected by the glossarists of the lower Middle Ages, a period between classical antiquity and the dawn of the modern age. It was then marked by the French Revolution and later on reached its zenith with the administrative centralization process implemented under Napoleon. Nevertheless, the introduction of Roman law in France, in view of its close association with the Germanic Empire, was not straightforward. The teaching of Roman law was banned in the University of Paris from 1219 to 1679. Its true resurrection and the most immediate antecedent to Napoleonic codification came with the work of the jurist Robert Joseph Pothier (1699–1772), whose 1761 *Traité des Obligations* embraced both Roman and common law without considering them contradictory.

Two observations are worth making at this point. In the first place, it is clear that France represents, in terms of adherence to Roman law, a midway point between its almost total acceptance by Germany and its total rejection in England. Second, it is clear that, from the outset, the frontiers between civil and common law were somewhat indistinct and pervious. The tendency towards convergence of the two legal systems is probably most evidently shown by the increasingly important role played by case law within the civil law tradition, and by a marked shift toward the compilation of laws in codified form within the common law system.

The ascent of Napoleon Bonaparte, and the confirmation of his absolute power through his coronation as emperor, paved the way for the true consolidation and institutionalization of the codification process. On 20 March 1804, the civil code was enacted in its entirety under the title *Code Civil des Français*; it was subsequently reprinted in 1807 under the official name *Code Napoleon* (or Napoleonic Code). The context within which this process took place was not, however, one of social neutrality. Profound changes – which were not always consistent – were taking place within the family and in the relationship between adults and children.

It is important, generally, that we bear in mind both the temporal and formal differences in the processes of implementation, establishment and expansion of the civil law juristic culture in Europe and in other (so-called 'peripheral') regions where we now find developing countries. In Europe, the civil law juristic culture was introduced slowly and endogenously through centres of knowledge such as universities (the famous glossarist of the University of Bologna, Bartolus da Saxoferrato, is an outstanding example of this form of incorporation). By contrast, in other 'peripheral' regions, of which African and Latin American countries are excellent examples, the process was amazingly rapid, resulting from the conquest and colonization processes. Introduced in this manner, European law proved totally impervious to the pre-existent rules of law pertaining to indigenous cultures, which were almost invariably unwritten and mostly lacking any form of systematization. European law was a foreign body of law within the social context in which it was established.

There are numerous examples in Africa and Latin America of fundamental laws that remained in force for considerable periods of time (with varying degrees of actual implementation, irrespective of their legal validity) in languages unknown to the vast majority of the respective populations. This difference is fundamental to understanding the profound dissociation and lack of consistency between legal reform and institutional reform processes. The following example is particularly representative of this general trend: Whereas in England the Children's Courts were instituted (in 1905) simultaneously with those laws that, for the first time, provided a specific regulation for legal conflicts involving minors, in Latin America long periods of time elapsed between such legal reform and the actual establishment of the new institutions envisaged by the law. Argentina and the city of Buenos Aires, in particular, provide a clear example of this. A children's law was enacted in Argentina in 1919, such law being the first of its kind in Latin America. It was only 70 years later that the children's courts – the specific institutions envisaged in the 1919 law – actually became operational.

An understanding of this historical process of institutional establishment and the examples cited above is fundamental to grasp the functional peculiarities of the relevant institutions and the broad divide between the validly and efficacy of law. This is particularly relevant in peripheral regions in which the civil law juristic culture prevails. It is this kind of historical and social processes that explain – as we see in the case of Burkina Faso, although the same could be said of all the peripheral countries – how the principle 'ignorance of the law cannot be accepted' (as justification for an offence) can, paradoxically, be quite unreal under the prevailing codified law, but not under common law.

II. CIVIL LAW AND THE EVOLUTION OF SOCIAL ORGANIZATION: THE FUNCTION OF THE FAMILY, THE POSITION OF WOMEN AND SOCIETY'S PERCEPTION OF THE CHILD

There are two main reasons for drawing attention to the nature of the juristic transformations that came about through the Napoleonic Code. First, we should be aware of the contradictory nature of many of such transformations. Second, we need to understand their extraordinary impact, in both spatial and temporal terms.

The French Revolution, on the one hand, which represents and synthesizes more than any other single event the origins of the modern age in Western civilization, proposed, in terms of rights, a new and revolutionary culture of equality in the eyes of the law. On the other hand, however, and in the area of intra-family relations, certain practices and customs that belonged to the past were consolidated and re-legitimized under the new legal regime. The Napoleonic Code, surprisingly, gave renewed validity to certain aspects of the *Ancien Regimé*. No better synthesis of these contradictions is to be found than in the words of Napoleon himself: "Under even the most absolute forms of government, the despotisms ends at the doors of the family home, where it gravitates exclusively towards the head of the household. And just as the head of the family is at the entire disposal of the government, the family is at the entire disposal of its own head."[1] Premises such as those expressed by Napoleon subsequently contributed to the restriction of the rights of women and to their becoming second-class citizens. Whereas the special rights of the clergy and nobility were eliminated, on the one hand, along with the right of primogeniture (whereby hereditary rights corresponded exclusively to the firstborn son), on the other hand, women's subordinate status was legally consolidated, and the father/husband was attributed exclusive and almost absolute authority over the children. It should be borne in mind that the institution of *patria potestas* has survived with very little alteration through the centuries until the present day. However, the supremacy of man over woman is a concept that is neither natural nor evident; it requires social construction. Law, and family law in particular (although we should not overlook the role played by natural sciences such as medicine), plays a fundamental role in this social construction process. To legitimize the subordinate position of women within the family, the incapacity of women needs to be 'naturalized'. What we find here is, in reality, a vicious circle, in which a fundamental part is played by the concept of 'protection'. The generally perceived or real physical weakness of women is interpreted as their requiring protection. The legal protection afforded is, for its part, the irrefutable evidence of their incapacity. This is a false syllogism: Woman is perceived as incapable because she requires protection, and that 'protection' becomes the irrefutable evidence of her incapacity. The French Revolution left us the Declaration of the Rights of Man and of the Citizen, and the specific provisions of the subsequent Napoleonic Code enable us to conclude that, for the purposes of this concept, 'men' means everyone. But although women, children, foreigners and non-owners may all be 'men', not all 'men' are citizens. The term citizen refers only to those who have the capacity to

---

[1] L. M. Farto, *Códigos y Concordatos Napoleónicos*. (Buenos Aires: Dunken, 1998), p. 27.

actually carry into effect the rights formally established in respect of all persons.

And it was in this way that the modern age commenced, with an exclusion pact. It was subsequently the long and drawn-out process of conquest and colonization that spread the influence of this juristic culture to practically all corners of the planet. This explains the validity – up until the present day – of legal provisions, such as those mentioned, in geographical areas and societies as diverse as those to which the case studies mentioned above refer (i.e., Armenia, Azerbaijan, Burkina Faso and the Dominican Republic). By contrast, behind the processes of codification at the national level we almost invariably encounter processes of marked political centralization and of creation and re-creation of artificial (i.e., forced) forms of authoritarian State, established 'from the top downward'. The tasks that such States face include, paradoxically, the process of artificial and forced construction of civil society.

Specific consideration should be given, separately, to the position of the child. In this connection, Philippe Aries's pioneering and revolutionary work in the field of the historical study of childhood, *Centuries of Childhood*, must be cited. The central hypothesis of Aries's work can be summarized by his well-known and controversial affirmation that "childhood did not exist before the seventeenth century."[2] In other words, that before the seventeenth century there was no categorical distinction, in terms of social perception, between the child and the adult: Once the child had passed through the essential period of total dependence on adults (generally on the mother), he or she became, for better or for worse, a fully-fledged member of the adult world. The plastic art of the era is decisive in confirming this hypothesis. Paintings depicting public forms of social organization before the seventeenth century (note, for example, the absence of the child in the paintings of Pieter Brueghel, who depicted squares and popular markets) indicate the indistinct existence of the child within society. In the eighteenth century, however, this trend was radically inverted. This change can be appreciated in family portraits, most notably perhaps those of the Spanish painter Velázquez. A new social subject, 'the child', appears in the centre of the portrait, with a distinct clothing style and aesthetic totally different from that of adults.

This process, which also implies a revolution in sentimental attitude, can be looked upon as a process of 'discovery' or 'invention' of childhood.

Such a process had profound social and cultural consequences that were later on reflected in the legal sphere: The discovery of the child as a category of persons distinct from that of adults can be viewed as the discovery of the child's incapacity. An implicit pact was thus established between the world of adults and the world of this recently 'discovered' social category, which might be summarized as follows: I acknowledge you for what you

---

[2] P. Aries, *Centuries of Childhood: A Social History of Family Life* (London: Jonathan Cape Ltd., 1962).

cannot do, for what you do not know, for what you are incapable of. The juristically constructed conception of the child's incapacity fitted perfectly into this socially constructed concept of inability. The child was not competent as a witness, was incapable of autonomous action and so on.

The creation toward the end of the nineteenth century of a new right, the 'right of the minor', helped to synthesize and consolidate this trend, as well as to 'protect/control' the child's incapacity, which was more contrived than natural. It therefore comes as no surprise that the new jurisdictions for children (of which the Children's Court in Chicago – formed in 1899 – was the first scheme) were to be founded on the fundamental principle of 'the best interests of the child'.

Despite the differences, there are many common features in the processes of social construction whereby the woman, on the one hand, and the child, on the other, have come to be perceived as subjects who are incapable, and therefore the object of protection. As we shall see in due course, the protection of persons, as opposed to the protection of the rights of persons, has proven to be the most efficient mechanism to legitimize and consolidate the 'incapacity' of both children and women. The understanding of the evils present in this concept of protection of persons requires no more than common sense. When the object of the protection is the person, the content of such protection is invariably dependent on the discretion of the person exercising the protective function. The challenge set by the CRC, by contrast, is that it represents a move away from the 'protection of persons' in favour of the 'protection of the rights of persons'. This is not a question of semantics; it is one of substance. The rights of persons are their needs expressed in objectivized form, and this reduces considerably the possibility of exercising the protective function in an arbitrary, discretionary and exploitative way. The rules designed in the past for the 'protection' of women are particularly eloquent in this respect.

III. THE PRINCIPLE OF 'THE BEST INTERESTS OF THE CHILD': BEFORE AND AFTER THE CONVENTION ON THE RIGHTS OF THE CHILD

From various perspectives, 'the best interests of the child' principle is the most interesting yet at the same time the most complex principle to be grasped in order to understand the profound rearrangement proposed by the CRC with regard to relations between adults, institutions, and children. This principle not only preceded the Convention by almost a century but, paradoxically, also contributed fundamentally to the consolidation of a juristic culture that the CRC itself has served to overcome by law, although this has yet to be achieved culturally. We refer to the culture of 'discretion', that is, arbitrary decision making as to what is best for the other party without any argument being required for the purposes of legitimizing the decision. This discretionary approach is to be found in both interpersonal relations, particularly between parents and children, and in the relations maintained by those institutions responsible for the control and protection of entire categories of children (or 'minors') regarded as vulnerable.

Originally conceived as a way to extricate minors from the legal system applicable to adults, particularly in the area of criminal law, 'the best interests of the child' principle constituted an efficient formula to legitimize the exercise of judicial discretion in matters involving children, including civil and family law matters. Under this arrangement, which naturally assumed the form of a markedly authoritarian paternalism, the best interests principle was implemented in accordance with the all-encompassing volition of a judge, perceived as an exemplary 'father figure', and no less within the family – implemented by the actual father, who could act with both the unlimited power and severity of a judge.

The introduction of this principle within a culture that could not, did not want to or did not know how to protect its more vulnerable citizens, other than through coercive forms of institutionalization (a euphemism for the deprivation of freedom), resulted in resort to the best interests principle to legitimize discretionary forms of 'protection' that infringed on the most fundamental rights of the person being protected. Mention should be made at this point of the considerable similarities between these practices towards children and the various forms of protection (now generally viewed as absurd, both juristically and culturally) practiced by men towards women on the grounds of their 'vulnerability'.

There are various points of connection (without overlooking the existing significant differences) between the historical processes of both oppression and emancipation involving women and children. In both cases, we find a significant paradox: The greatest acts of cruelty and violation of rights committed by men against women and by adults (men or women) against children have been committed far more frequently in the name of protection, love, piety and compassion than in the name of repression. Let us consider two examples. The Italian Commercial Code (which was not reviewed until the 1960s) included a provision whereby a married woman having attained the legal age of majority required the authorization of her husband to be able to perform any kind of remunerated work. The 'protection' of women was the only reason and the only justification for 'legitimizing' this absurd provision. A Spanish criminal law (not amended until the 1980s) stipulated that "injuries, including serious injuries inflicted by parents against their children shall only be regarded as excessive only when they exceed what may be regarded as legitimate means of correction."[3]

---

[3] Código Penal (1980s) (Sp.).

It is clear, explicitly in the case of children and with a slightly greater degree of dissimulation in the case of women, that the best interests principle has been frequently used solely to legitimize arbitrary and discretionary judicial and administrative decisions with the sole effective result of restricting and violating children's rights.

Curiously enough, from the formal perspective, the CRC maintains the best interests principle in exactly the same terms in which it was proposed towards the end of the nineteenth century. In the Convention, however, the original sense of the principle is fundamentally altered.

Firstly, it should be explained that the best interests principle established in the CRC, together with the principle of non-discrimination, the principle of implementation, and the principles of capacity and participation, constitute what have quite rightly been called the structuring or guiding principles of the Convention.[4] In other words, these are the principles that govern and determine the true meaning of the entire Convention and the manner in which it is to be interpreted and function. As is quite rightly reflected in the provisions of the Convention, in the context of a legal instrument that recognizes needs as rights (whereby the legitimate and essential needs of the child are objectivized and rendered demandable as legitimate claims), the best interests of the child cannot mean nowadays anything other than the full realization of the child's rights. Hence, the correct application of the best interests principle, vis-à-vis the courts in particular, requires a combined and simultaneous analysis of those rights at stake and those that may be affected by the decision of the authorities concerned (in this case, the judicial authority). In all cases, the measure that should be adopted is that one that ensures the maximum possible fulfilment of rights and their minimum restriction. Consideration should be given thus not only to the number of rights at stake in the 'best interests' determination but also to their relative importance. On this basis it can be argued, for example, that any decision to deprive a child of his or her freedom or family environment should constitute an exceptional measure applied only as a last resort.[5]

Particular mention should be made of how the best interests principle is applied in those countries in which the common law juristic culture prevails. This principle has been applied in these countries for longer and more extensively than in countries with a civil law tradition. The principle is unarguably a landmark reference for practically all family law cases involving matters of guardianship, custody and adoption. In many African and English-speaking

---

[4] Convention on the Rights of the Child, G.A. res. 44/25, annex, *adopted* 20 Nov. 1989, 44 U.N. GAOR Supp. (No. 49) at 167, Arts. 3, 2, 4, 5, and 12, respectively, U.N. Doc. A/44/49 (1989), *entered into force* 2 Sept. 1990. Reprinted in 28 *ILM* (1989): p. 1448 [CRC].

[5] M. Cillero, 'El interés superior del niño en el marco de la Convención Internacional sobre los Derechos del Niño', in *Infancia, Ley y Democracia en América Latina*. Compiled by García Méndez, ed. M. Beloff (Bogota-Buenos Aires: Temis-Depalma, 1998), pp. 69–85.

Caribbean countries (Zimbabwe and Barbados being two main examples), the best interests principle can be claimed to constitute the very foundation of children's rights' functioning. A number of studies, however, have pointed out the challenges, or rather the hazards, brought about by its vague definition and content. Indeed, the application of this principle, beyond the quasi-universal context of the CRC, may lead to the re-legitimization of arbitrary and discretionary decision making in matters involving children. According to the typical interpretation in civil law contexts, the principle is deemed above all to imply the full and invariable realization of all children's rights, whereas within the common law tradition the principle appears still to be lacking precise formulation and is not applied in an extensive and systematic manner.

There is no better example of such hazards and challenges than the following, taken from the Barbados Family Law Act. In reference to cases involving minors aged under 18 years but more than 16 years, the law in question establishes that the court should not reach decisions that are contrary to the minor's will. In the same formulation of the principle, however, this provision is to be applied unless the court, "in the best interests of the child, decides otherwise."[6] In conclusion, it can be said that beyond the differences in how explicitly this principle has been formulated and for how long it has been used, the hazards and challenges in its application do not differ essentially between the two legal traditions.

The fact that the CRC takes the form of an international human rights treaty raises an issue affecting both international norms in general and human rights treaties in particular, which is a key problem of our age: the incorporation and effectiveness of international law in internal legal systems. The various possibilities and interpretations in this respect are examined at length in Part VI of this chapter.

Let us take a closer look now at the varying levels of impact of the CRC on the various State powers, based on the division of powers under the republican democratic tradition.

IV. THE IMPACT OF THE CRC ON STATE POWERS: THE LEGISLATURE, THE EXECUTIVE AND THE JUDICIARY

The Legislature

Invariably, and with far greater intensity and logic in the case of countries pertaining to the civil law tradition, the foremost and most direct impact of the CRC is on the legislature. This is a direct consequence not only of the provisions of national constitutions with respect to international treaties in

---

[6] Family Law Act (ch. 214, § 43) (1981) (Barb.).

general, but of the provisions of Article 4 of the Convention in particular, which establishes the following obligation: "State parties shall undertake all appropriate legislative, administrative and other measures for the implementation of the rights recognized in the present Convention."[7] In other words, not only does the actual incorporation of the international treaty (the Convention in this case) to be achieved through a law emanating from the legislature call for priority and decisive action by the legislature at national level, but so also do all the difficulties relating to the invocation of international treaties before local courts as well as to those provisions that are not self-applicable.

In addition to this crucial legislative function, which in this context we could refer to as being of a constitutional nature, another aspect that is linked to the specific relation between the CRC and the efficiency of social policies emanating from it should be further examined. The importance of the type of law in this context is not always acknowledged and is not always clear. In a democratic context in which we find, moreover, the classic distribution of power as defined by Montesquieu, only those social policy provisions that derive from law can hope to achieve permanence and sustainability, these being the conditions generally deemed necessary (although not sufficient in themselves) for an effective social policy. This does not mean that we should overlook the revocability of law. In developing countries in which there exists a civil law tradition, legal provisions emanating from Parliament (because of their consensual nature) are generally of far greater stability than those decisions resulting from administrative acts of government. But apart from the question of sustainability, it is the general nature of law that makes it possible to reproduce on a broad scale, with greater possibilities of success, small and fragmentary experiences gained through actual work with children, or in other words, to convert programmes into actual social policy.

The particularly negative aspect of social policy emanating from law is its financing. The relationship between the legislature and social policy budgets is a complex issue, which is nevertheless present not only in the four countries studied herein, but also in most countries in general. The influence of the legislature when it comes to determining the financial resources to be allocated to social policy ranges from very little to none at all. As a general rule, the action of Parliament is limited to voting in favour or against the budget presented by the Executive. The latter generally has at its disposal various means, both de jure and de facto, to alter the intended application of budgetary items. Only social pressure and lobbying strategies to influence parliaments can bring about an increase in the decision-making capacity of legislative powers with respect to the amount of financial resources to

---

[7] CRC, op. cit., Art. 4.

be allocated to social policies. In this sense, there exists no evidence – as appears to be confirmed by the example of the Children's Parliament in Burkina Faso – that any child participation programme has ever succeeded in influencing budget allocations and thus the financing of social policy.

In conclusion, it is important to stress and insist once again on the importance of the legislative function (despite the budgetary difficulties mentioned above), as the processes of legislative reform in general, and of adaptation to the CRC in particular, are ongoing. It must be noted that social developments and political and economic changes make periodic legislative adjustment necessary. The legislature, in this sense, has a permanent role that is crucial.

The Executive

It is hard to overstate the importance of the executive branch of government in the process of implementation of the CRC. This is especially true in developing countries, where we find untempered, growing powers of the Executive, almost always to the detriment of other branches of the State's authority.

Apart from the fact that legal reform initiatives are very often instigated by the Executive, the impact of the Executive (at any of its levels, of which there are three in diverse federal systems – federal, provincial and municipal – such as in Germany, Nigeria, India and Brazil) is decisive both for the formulation and the implementation of social policy in favour of children. The processes of legal adaptation at the national level tend to take place over two distinct stages. First, the reform of relevant laws is (or should be) followed by the commencement of an institutional reform process. Second, institutional reforms, which include the establishment of new institutions to support the implementation and enforcement of the laws, are set in motion. Yet these new institutions are not always put in place as the result of a law designed by the legislature. Very often, they are established as a result of decrees actually issued by the Executive. This tendency (which is on the increase) should be considered in conjunction with the process mentioned earlier of amplifying the Executive's functions, which is almost always detrimental to the legislature's powers. This trend, frequently perceived and portrayed as favourable, as it often helps to accelerate social policy decisions favourable to children, involves certain risks and problems that should not be overlooked. Speed is often achieved to the detriment of consensus and the legitimacy required by policies in general and by social policies for children in particular. National programmes for children adopted by decree (as in the case of the two national plans in Burkina Faso) often produce apparently positive results in the short term, but are doomed to utter failure in the medium term, generally because of a lack of sustainability. But it is not only consensus and legitimacy that are under threat; transparency and sustainability are also usually among the first victims of the increasing overreaching decision making of the Executive in this area. In particular, a serious problem that should be neither ignored nor underestimated is the major impact of corruption in its various forms, particularly in developing countries. The absence of adequate control mechanisms favours impunity, in which corruption proliferates, reaching intolerable levels. In many developing countries, the relation between the amount of national resources available and the level of corruption suggests that corruption not only affects social policy from an ethical and moral perspective, but that it lies also at the very heart of its formulation and development.

Although this is not always the case, the greater transparency that exists in parliamentary decisions would appear to restrict the practices of corruption to some extent. In any event, no serious analysis of the implementation of the CRC can exclude systematically analyzing the phenomenon of corruption, in all its various forms.

The Judiciary

A significant part of the work of the judiciary in the implementation process for the CRC will be analyzed implicitly in Section VI, which focuses on the relations among international treaties, national constitutions and domestic laws.

Theoretically, the greater adherence to actual laws than to case law in countries with a civil law tradition should, in comparison with common law countries, leave less scope for freedom or discretion in the application of the law. Yet this is not always the case. The function of the judiciary, especially in civil law countries, is to apply to the specific case the relevant legal provisions, which should be abstract and general in nature. This task, the judges' task in general, implies a certain level of discretion, which is necessary when relating a particular case, through interpretation, to a general norm. Various restrictions are imposed in these cases on the discretionary powers of the judiciary, the most important being the legal and institutional mechanisms for judicial review of judgements at first and at second instance and the technical/legal defence by the public or private defence counsellor. These restrictions are not without their difficulties, particularly in countries that are institutionally weak, as is the case of most developing countries. The serious issue of judicial discretion should neither be dismissed nor underestimated, particularly in the case of courts dealing with children and adolescents.

The analysis of the role played by the judiciary, specifically in matters affecting the child in the legal and institutional reform processes to implement the CRC in Latin America, is particularly enriching and enlightening. Moreover, many of the critical issues encountered in Latin America can be quite easily extrapolated to most developing countries. Although there are some regional differences, there are also some clear and surprising similarities among comparable situations in developing countries. The impossibility of an appeal (despite the existence of a constitutional court), in the case of Azerbaijan, constitutes the best example of this trend.

The juristic tradition of having a special law that was paternalistic and repressive, arbitrary and discretionary, specifically dealing with minors' matters, goes back in time in Latin American almost as far as the existence of specific norms and judicial institutions (e.g., the children's judge) in the United States and in Europe. The first children's court was that created in Chicago, Illinois (United States) in 1899. The creation process of children's laws and courts in Europe was based on the experience in Chicago. Between 1905 and 1920 (England being the first country), all the European countries established their own specialized child laws and children's judges.

In Latin America, this process took place between 1919 (in Argentina) and 1939 (in Venezuela). At the root of the problems that this study sets out to highlight, we find the perception of specific child law, by its creators and promoters, as an 'autonomous' law. The CRC, which changes not only the future of children's rights but the perception of their past as well, has enabled us very simply and yet with great technical accuracy to comprehend that this 'autonomy' of the old child law was in reality the autonomy of constitutional law and, accordingly, of any international human rights treaty. In this way, the Convention changes the future of children's rights, in addition to changing, and precisely because of this change, the perception of their past.

In the specific case of Latin America, in what can be regarded as an initial cycle of post-Convention reforms, legal reform aimed at adapting national laws to the CRC has been undertaken in more than 80 per cent of the countries in the region. Not only were such reforms not applied with the support of the judiciary but all countries also found more or less explicit resistance by children's judges, who were and are often still unwilling to give up the large room for discretionary power afforded to them under the old child laws. The current legal reforms being introduced in some African countries reflect this same trend (Angola is a clear example).

Thus, the reforms to which the CRC has given rise have invariably involved a scaling down of the all-encompassing, discretionary power of judges. This explains not only the intensity but also the cultural roots of the reluctance towards the introduction of a new juristic culture in which the child is viewed as a true subject of rights rather than as a mere object of protection. Without wishing to disregard the technical/juristic aspects, it is clear that the areas of greatest difficulty in the implementation of the CRC are of a cultural nature. There is still a long way to go in understanding that the essence of justice for children and adolescents is the same essence of justice in general. The task of achieving cultural transformation is fundamental, bearing in mind that it is not only children's judges who have such a welfare-orientated perception of their own function, but also that this vision, so contrary to the spirit and terms of the Convention, is generally shared by most other judges.

There is a long road still to travel before we come to understand that the judiciary's and judges' function, most especially in child-related cases, is not that of resolving socio-economic problems (in this, no one can replace the role of the Executive and civil society). Rather, their function is to resolve social conflicts from a legal perspective. Under the CRC, the judges' specific function is mainly to decide on issues involving a more or less permanent alteration of the child's legal status (e.g., adoption, guardianship, custody or parental authority), rather than solving administrative problems that result from inadequate social policies (e.g., lack of schooling, of vaccines, etc.). The root cause of judges' unwillingness to accept this change lies precisely in their actual refusal to accept a loss of authority.

V. THE CRC: CIVIL AND POLITICAL RIGHTS AND ECONOMIC, SOCIAL AND CULTURAL RIGHTS

As if to confirm the complex, holistic nature of the CRC, its text encompasses a real synthesis of civil and political and economic and social rights. The classic distinction between these two categories of rights derives from the specific agreements adopted by the United Nations General Assembly in early 1976: the International Covenant on Civil and Political Rights (ICCPR) and the International Covenant on Economic, Social and Cultural Rights (ICESCR).[8] The literature generated in relation to these covenants in particular and on the above-mentioned two categories of rights in general is practically never-ending. For this reason, we would rather concentrate on those areas in which both types of rights – the dividing line between them being historically displaceable and somewhat blurred – are at stake when applying the CRC.

The importance of this distinction between civil and political rights on the one hand and economic and social rights on the other, in relation to legal reform processes, derives from the increasing trend to divide up legal reforms by areas. There is indeed an increasing tendency to consider criminal issues involving minors separately from all the other norms affecting the child, and in particular separately from the codes intended to provide comprehensive regulation of children's rights. Moreover, and as we will see later when we turn our attention to different policies somehow related to

---

[8] International Covenant on Civil and Political Rights, G.A. res. 2200A (XXI), 21 U.N. GAOR Supp. (No. 16) at 52, U.N. Doc. A/6316 (1966), 999 U.N.T.S. 171, *adopted* 16 Dec. 1966 and *entered into force* 23 Mar. 1976. Reprinted in 6 *ILM* (1967): p. 360 [ICCPR]; International Covenant on Economic, Social and Cultural Rights, G.A. res. 2200A (XXI), 21 U.N. GAOR Supp. (No. 16) at 49, U.N. Doc. A/6316 (1966), 993 U.N.T.S. 3, *adopted* 16 Dec. 1966 and *entered into force* 3 Jan. 1976. Reprinted in 6 *ILM* (1967): p. 360 [ICESCR].

the child, in practically all countries and particularly in Latin America, the impact of the CRC on basic social policies such as health and education policies has proven to be either very limited or non-existent. The area of social policy continues to be dominated by a technocratic perspective predominantly closed off not only to children's participation but also to any form of community participation.

Returning to the content of the Covenants, it is worth recalling that both treaties contain provisions referring specifically to children and adolescents. For example, the ICCPR prohibits imposition of the death penalty "for crimes committed by persons under the age of eighteen."[9] Other provisions deal respectively with the separation of children from adults when imprisoned, the special criminal procedures applicable to minors, the non-discrimination principle and the right to a name and a nationality.[10] In the case of the ICESCR, examples are to be found in articles that deal with special measures for minors and the right to education.[11]

At this stage, it is worth reflecting briefly on the significance of the above-mentioned distinction between the two categories of rights. On what basis is a right to be placed in one category or the other? There is in reality, strictly speaking, nothing in the 'essence' of a right that allows it to be placed in one or the other category, and the same could be said with respect to its position in the hierarchy of norms. In the case of Burkina Faso, for example, the 1997 constitutional reform included the right to exercise sports among social and cultural rights.[12] However, there is no more pertinent example of the cross-over of a right from one category to the other than in the case of the right to education.

Originally viewed as an economic, social and cultural right, in the current age of technological revolution and in today's society defined as one of knowledge, the right to education would appear to be closer to the field of civil and political rights. The right to education should be considered in these times as a prerequisite and enabling right in relation to the exercising of other rights.

It is important to reflect on the way in which these two categories of rights have developed and on the obstacles and impediments affecting their implementation processes. Such an analysis may be regarded as essential to any legislative reform strategy.

First, mention should be made of the enormous differences in the implementation of either category of rights. The origin of the difficulties hindering the implementation of economic, social and cultural rights appears to be fairly easy to understand. The difficulties in implementing civil and political

---

[9] ICCPR, op. cit., Art. 6(5).   [10] Ibid., Arts. 10, 14, and 20, respectively.
[11] ICESCR, op. cit., Arts. 10 and 13.
[12] Constitution du Burkina Faso, Loi N° 002/97/ADP (1997), Art. 18.

rights, however, are a lot more complex. In the case of economic, social and cultural rights, the deficient implementation of the CRC seems to result from the limited financing of social policy (which is a visible problem in the four case studies belonging to the civil law tradition). In the case of economic, social and cultural rights, the clause "to the maximum of its available resources"[13] often conspires against State efforts or civil society efforts to increase the financing of social policy. In this case, added to budgetary complexities, civil society faces tremendous difficulties when it comes to accessing information, which, despite being public, is politically sensitive from the government's viewpoint. The situation with respect to civil and political rights is, or at least should be, different. There is no clause of the kind mentioned above to explain or even legitimize insufficient compliance in this area. Nevertheless, the infringements and omissions of civil and political rights in the case of children have tremendous and recurrent effects. One hypothesis supported by a large amount of evidence is that, in the case of civil and political rights, the problems derive to a great extent from the cultural factors manifested in different ways, as is observed in the specific countries studied.

The full realization of children's rights requires not only taking such rights seriously; it is also requires taking children seriously (which is something apparently rather more difficult). All the case studies reveal explicitly the lower status or non-political prominence of child-related issues. The lack of prominence of child-related issues in the political agenda tends to be reflected most clearly in budgets and public spending. While public spending in social areas is endemically scarce in non-industrialized countries, public spending on social policies affecting children is even less. Moreover, apart from such financial deficiencies, there is also inadequate institutional capacity to deal with child-related issues. This situation not only explains the absolutely unjustifiable breaches of children's civil and political rights but also the low level of moral indignation provoked by such infringements.

The distinction between these two categories of rights is also reflected in the legal reform processes aimed at incorporating the CRC into domestic law. This is particularly clear in Latin America, where more than 80 per cent of the countries have completed what could be referred to as the initial cycle of reform processes subsequent to the Convention's entry into force. Of all the countries that have completed this initial cycle of reforms in Latin America, approximately 50 per cent have done so by means of comprehensive laws, that is, laws that regulate both issues relating to child protection and the establishment of social policies for a comprehensive protection, and, in separate laws, issues relating to juvenile justice. In Africa, on the contrary,

---

[13] ICESCR, op. cit., Art. 2. This concept is reiterated explicitly in Article 4 of the Convention on the Rights of the Child. CRC, op. cit.

the tendency appears to have been to draw up codes of a comprehensive nature that regulate all areas in a single instrument. There appears as yet to be no trend in Africa to establish a legislative distinction and thus draft separate laws specifically dealing with juvenile justice issues.

The implementation process of the two categories of rights leads us to the complex problem of social policy financing. In general terms, in developing countries and especially in those countries with a legal tradition of codified law, in practice the financial aspects – that is, the budgetary implications – of legal norms are not incorporated within the process of legal reform (for example, this is true of each of the four countries studied). As we see in the case of Azerbaijan, the complexity of national budgets (and the lack of political prominence of child-related issues) makes it even more difficult to distinguish, within social policy, the amount of resources actually devoted to children's issues. A possible regulatory solution to the question of having a special budget for children is the possibility of allocating certain percentages of total expenditure or of total social expenditure to specific child-related policies. For example, under a federal law in Brazil, municipalities are required to spend 25 per cent of their budget on education.

VI. THE LEGISLATIVE REFORM INITIATIVE FROM A HISTORICAL PERSPECTIVE

The Status of Treaties in Domestic Law, with Particular Reference to Human Rights Treaties

The ways in which international treaties are received into domestic law are known to differ, comparing the common law tradition and the civil law tradition. Even within the civil law tradition, however, there are a number of routes taken for the incorporation of international human rights into domestic law. In general terms, and within the civil law tradition, it is possible to identify at least four different routes, namely:

a) 'super-constitutionalization';
b) constitutionalization;
c) first degree of 'sub-constitutionalization'; and
d) legislative assimilation

Although these four routes can be found within the civil law tradition, legislative assimilation is the clearest route taken under the common law tradition. The distinction between them derives from the existence of two major theories in international law. According to the monist theory, international law forms part of the internal legal system. According to the dualist theory, domestic law and international law are regarded as two separate legal systems. It should be pointed out that behind these juristic distinctions there lie specific historical processes that basically relate to absolute or relative conceptions about the delicate political question of state sovereignty and its limits.

Let us take a closer look at the possible routes that can be taken for the incorporation of international law – in this case international human rights law – within national law.

'Super-Constitutionalization'

Under this route or procedure, the international legal instrument is afforded a privileged status and ranks above any provision of domestic law, even above the national constitution itself. In other words, the international treaty must prevail even if it contradicts a provision or norm in the constitution. What this means, indirectly, is that the human rights treaty can bring about a reform of the constitution. The best example of this position is found in the Guatemalan Constitution of 1984, which stipulates under the title 'Pre-eminence of International Law': "It is established by way of a general principle that in terms of human rights, Treaties and Conventions accepted and ratified by Guatemala shall prevail over internal law."[14] Not even the Constitution is excluded in this clause from the concept of 'internal law', meaning that the Constitution is ranked beneath the treaty or convention. An important antecedent to this positiony is the Netherlands Constitution, reformed in 1953, which establishes that international treaties may deviate from the Constitution "when so required for the development of the international legal system."[15] In this case, however, the treaties in question must be approved by Parliament with a two-thirds majority of votes.

Constitutionalization

Under this route to incorporation, the constitution itself affords constitutional rank to the international agreement in question, which naturally thus becomes part of the domestic law by volition of the national constituent power. Strictly speaking, the treaty does not become part of the constitution but it does acquire 'validity' comparable to that of the constitutional text. This kind of incorporation can, in turn, take place in a number of different ways, as shown here.

The constitution mentions explicitly the international instrument in question. This is what we find in the 1994 Argentinean Constitution, which specifically affords 'constitutional rank' to 10 treaties, including the CRC. The same status also may be afforded to other international treaties approved by

---

[14] Guatemalan Constitution (1984), Art. 46.
[15] Statuut voor het Koninkrijk der Nederlanded (1953) (Constit.), Art. 63 (Neth.).

Parliament in the future, although in this case the votes of two-thirds of the members of both parliamentary chambers are required.[16]

Another means of incorporation is the acknowledgement, in favour of the inhabitants of the country, of the 'full validity' of the rights established in certain treaties that are explicitly mentioned in the constitution. This is what we find in the Constitution of Nicaragua.[17] Under this procedure, the constitution does not expressly state that the treaties in question are of constitutional rank, but they are nevertheless afforded such rank as it is the constitutional text that declares them to be valid in the country. An ordinary law that contradicted such treaties also would be contradicting the constitutional rule that declares those treaties mandatory. In this manner, treaties are afforded immediate constitutional rank.

The constitutionalization of a human rights treaty generates links between the treaty and both the constitution and the rest of the national laws. This procedure clearly does not rule out the possibility of conflict between treaty provisions and constitutional provisions. The rule favoured by contemporary expert legal opinion and gaining ever wider acceptance is that, in cases of conflict of this kind, priority should be given to the legal provision (either of the treaty or of the constitution) that best protects the rights of the individual.

First Degree 'Sub-Constitutionalization'

This incorporation procedure consists of affording to the treaty a position of sub-constitutionality and yet at the same time super-legality. In this case, a treaty (either a human rights treaty or any other type of treaty) is ranked beneath the constitution but above national laws. In other words, it is placed in an intermediate position between the supreme law and ordinary laws. A specific example of this is provided in the 1992 Constitution of Paraguay, which provides that "The supreme law of the Republic is the Constitution. This Constitution, approved and ratified international treaties, conventions and agreements, laws laid down by Congress and other legal provisions of lower hierarchical rank, duly approved, shall make up the positive law of the nation, in the order of priority herein established."[18]

Within this position, there exists the possibility of violating two basic principles of international law, namely: (a) the principle that treaties should be observed (*pacta sum servanda*) and (b) the principle of good faith. In several countries, however, this means that the constitution needs to be amended before ratifying a treaty whose provisions contradict the constitution. This ensures coherence with the national legal system, and increases democratic

---

[16] Constitución Argentina (1994), Art. 75(22).
[17] Constitución Política de la República de Nicaragua (1987), Art. 46.
[18] Constitución de la República del Paraguay (1992), Art. 137.

control and national acknowledgement of treaty obligations by triggering a debate before its ratification.

Legislative Assimilation

Under this system, international treaties are ranked beneath the constitution and there is no reason why they should be granted higher rank than ordinary laws (unless this is explicitly envisaged in the constitution). The arguments in defence of this position are based on the understanding that the national and the international legal systems are different and independent (the 'dualist' position). The domestic validity of the international treaty is therefore conditional firstly upon the constitution and subsequently on the adoption of a national law that declares the treaty applicable, to the extent and within the scope established in such law. The more radical interpretations of this line of thinking argue that national courts actually do not deal with international treaties, only with those national laws that incorporate such treaties into the domestic legal system. Although less straightforward and slower, this conception, referred to here as 'legislative assimilation' between international treaties and national legislation, is more commonly found in countries with a common law tradition. The procedures discussed above, by contrast, which envisage various kinds of legal supremacy, are more characteristic of countries with a civil law tradition.

Returning to the dualist position, under this system the treaty has the same legal status as the law. The following conclusions can therefore be drawn:

- Treaties rank beneath the constitution and may be viewed as unconstitutional if they are in conflict with the latter;
- A treaty approved by a law serves to repeal an earlier law that is in conflict with the treaty;
- A law subsequent to the treaty can repeal or amend the treaty; and
- The treaty should function in conformity with the prevailing juristic ideology of the local law.

As we have seen, the frontiers between the common law and the civil law juristic traditions are highly pervious. Based on actual practice, it can be affirmed that the application of treaties that are in accordance with the local juristic ideology is far more explicit and accepted under the common law tradition. Rather, under the civil law tradition, treaty application is formally denied yet implicitly accepted.

In this latter case and from the perspective of the civil law tradition, it can be clearly presumed – as noted above, in the hypothesis of legal assimilation that a subsequent law can repeal or amend a treaty – that there is infringement of the principle according to which treaties are required to be complied with (*pacta sum servanda*) and of the principle of good faith.[19]

Problems and Solutions in Relation to the Effective Validity of International Human Rights Treaties

The outline provided above of the four main routes within the civil law tradition vis-à-vis the relationship between domestic and international law certainly does not deal exhaustively with the problem of domestic validity and applicability of international treaties. It barely even serves to introduce it. As highlighted earlier, there are two main lines of expert legal opinion that explain and structure the relationship between domestic and international law: the dualist theory and the monist theory. On the one hand, the view taken under the dualist theory is that there are two coexistent and independent legal systems. Accordingly, both international law and domestic law have their own scope of validity and application. Under this theory, in short, there are two different legal systems with no possible conflict between them. This theory of radical separation has as its main exponent the work *Volkerrecht und Landesrecht* by the German jurist Triepel.[20]

On the other hand, monism is based on the interpretation that there exists a single legal system, and envisages two hierarchically related legal sub-systems. Such perceived legal unity implies that certain rules are ranked beneath others, forming a sole juristic system. International law thus simply incorporates the system of domestic law. The renowned Austrian jurist Hans Kelsen is undoubtedly the most representative exponent of this theory.[21]

A position such as this, and we refer specifically to the case of Guatemala, should not, however, lead us into what has been referred to as a regulatory fallacy, that is, the notion that the mere translation of the monist principle into a valid legal rule resolves the problem in reality. Guatemala is what we could call a textbook example, displaying the complex relationship between legal norms and social reality – also, for the historical reasons in peripheral regions of the world, explaining the enormous divide between law and reality. In this case, not only was the CRC not applied automatically by the local courts but it also took over a decade to get a national law adopted that explicitly incorporated the principles of the Convention.

There is no simple explanation of the way in which international treaties really function within local judicial practices, particularly in the case of the

---

[19] These principles are established and regulated in the Vienna Convention on the Law of Treaties, 1155 U.N.T.S. 331, *adopted* 23 May 1969 and *entered into force* 27 Jan. 1980.

[20] H. Triepel, *Volkerrecht und Landesrecht* (Leipzig: Hirschreid, 1899; reprint Aalen: Scientia Antiquariat, 1958).

[21] See, e.g., H. Kelsen, *Das Problem der Souveränität und die Theorie des Völkerrechts* (Tübingen: J. C. B. Mohr, 1920); H. Kelsen, *Reine Rechtslehre* ('Pure Theory') (Vienna: F. Deuticke, 1960).

rights of the child. We should recall – as mentioned in all the case studies – that both from the juristic viewpoint and the political viewpoint, the rights of the child suffer from what we might refer to as a 'lack of political prominence'. This lack of prominence helps to explain two specific problems affecting, first, any process of legal reform, and, second, its subsequent implementation.

The first problem relates to a resistance strategy against the application of the human rights provisions in the CRC. This derives, paradoxically, from tooth-and-nail adherence to a legal interpretation that we might call 'hypocritical monism'. This interpretation is based on the argument that no legislative reform is required at the national level to incorporate the provisions of an international treaty that, as such, automatically form part of the domestic legal system. Actual practice, however, shows that local courts do not apply directly the provisions of international treaties, as we can see explicitly in Azerbaijan, Burkina Faso and in practically all the Latin American countries. A second problem relates to the possibility of private individuals invoking the provisions of international treaties directly before local courts. In all the Latin American countries and other countries studied herein, private parties can invoke the CRC provisions in court. On most occasions, however, and for a variety of reasons, such citation proves fruitless.

The citation by private parties of the provisions of the CRC, particularly in countries in which there is a constitutional court, should at least generate gradual and fragmentary incorporation of the Convention. Because of the low status or lack of political prominence of children's issues, however, it is very rare for children's rights-related cases to get as far as the high courts. This is precisely the case of Azerbaijan, where although there is a constitutional court, cases involving children's rights do not even reach the courts of appeal.

As we have tried to show, and as clearly illustrated by the Azerbaijan case, the difficulties relating to the effective legal force of international human rights treaties mainly result from a juristic culture that underestimates the rights of the child. This explains, in particular, the poor functioning of institutions related to children's issues – rather than the absence of regulation through constitutional provisions. In this sense, current practice on the ground is showing that legal action in courts at all levels, undertaken by lawyers specializing in children's rights, is perhaps the best strategy for ensuring effective compliance with fundamental guarantees that constitutions, in general terms, recognize all human beings, without discrimination of any kind, not only on grounds of sex, race or religion, but also on grounds of age.

We shall examine these issues in greater depth later, taking as our starting point the various problems encountered in the actual application of the CRC within legal systems following the civil law tradition.

The Actual Position of the CRC in Domestic Legislation:
Legal Reform in Action

In general terms, in all the countries pertaining to the civil law tradition there are certain key common problems affecting the national ratification of the CRC that are worth analyzing. Ratification of the CRC is almost invariably followed by a process of incorporation – complete or incomplete, technically successful or unsuccessful – of the Convention into national law. Such is the case, for example, in Latin American countries, where after ratification of the CRC almost all the countries in the region undertook what we might refer to as an initial cycle of legislative reforms. The expression 'initial cycle' implies awareness of the ongoing – and therefore always unfinished – nature of the legal reform process. The pre-existence of earlier laws on 'minors', directly inherited from the colonial era (as in Burkina Faso) or adopted at around the same time as the European countries (for example in Latin America), has given rise to serious problems, as follows.

We find situations of profound legal contradiction, in particular the simultaneous validity of multiple laws that regulate the same thematic areas and that are, however, antagonistic in their content. Thus, there was not one Latin American country in which the ratification of the Convention brought about the automatic repeal of the old 'child laws'.

This legal contradiction can be summarized, in general terms, as the conflict between a first kind of laws specifically dealing with children's issues (such as the laws on minors approved in Latin America between 1919 and 1939), under which only a limited number of children, those most socially disadvantaged, were viewed as mere objects of protection, and a new type of laws based on the CRC, under which all children are regarded as subjects of rights. We should recall that the creation of special laws dealing specifically with children's issues began in Chicago towards the end of the nineteenth century (when the first children's court was set up). This process was exported from the United States to Europe, where the first children's courts were created between 1905 and 1920.

This juristic and institutional culture was exported then from Europe to Latin America. In this region, the adoption of specific norms and establishment of a specific jurisdiction for children's matters, based on the European model, was completed between the years 1919 (in Argentina) and 1939 (in Venezuela). In African countries, this juristic and institutional implementation took place a lot later and coexisted with a strong tradition of customary law resulting in the actual institutional incorporation becoming even more deficient than in Latin America.

Curiously enough, none of the independence processes taking place in Africa from the 1960s gave rise to any reform of child-related legal statutes inherited from the colonial era. The real cultural conflict occurred with the CRC because the Convention was aimed at becoming a legal framework of reference, not only for all countries and all rights but also – what is far more important in this context – *for all children*. It is precisely this dissension between laws targeting only certain children and a new legal framework encompassing rights for *all* children that lies at the root of the difficulties affecting all legal reform processes taking place after the entry into force of the CRC in 1990.

The possibilities and strategies for the incorporation of the CRC principles into national legal systems constitute a major issue. It is precisely at this point that the legal reform processes come up against the diverse, and even antagonistic, interpretations of human rights treaties. Apart from what has already been said with respect to the relations between international treaties and domestic law, a commonly drawn distinction between treaties – whether human rights treaties or any other kind of treaty – is between those that are *self-applicable* and those that are *not self-applicable*. As the term itself indicates, self-applicable rights do not require another norm to make the human right that they enunciate immediately applicable. For example, the American Convention on Human Rights (the San José de Costa Rica Convention) stipulates that "the death penalty shall not be re-established in those states in which it has been abolished."[22] This provision requires no regulation to be complied with; however, another provision establishes "All persons shall be entitled to compensation in accordance with the law in the event of being definitively convicted by judicial error."[23] A national law is clearly required to regulate the realization of this right. In this latter case, the actual operational force of an international human rights norm can be hindered if no domestic norm is issued to regulate its application. The cultural developments in relation to the implementation of human rights treaties has nevertheless been such that it can occur (and in fact it tends to occur) that the right in question becomes operational even when the corresponding national law has not yet been issued. One paradigmatic case is that of the provision of the San José de Costa Rica Convention concerning the exercising of the right of reply (or right of response).[24] The view taken by the Inter-American Court of Human Rights was that this right is enforceable even in the absence of a national regulatory rule.[25]

---

[22] American Convention on Human Rights, adopted at the Inter-American Specialized Conference on Human Rights, San José, Costa Rica (22 Nov. 1969), Art. 4(3).

[23] Ibid., Art. 10.   [24] Ibid., Art. 14(1).

[25] M. Ventura and D. Zovatto., *La función consultiva de la Corte Interamericana de Derechos Humanos* (Madrid: Civitas, for Instituto Interamericano de Derechos Humanos, 1989), p. 393 et seq.

The specific application of the CRC in civil law countries generally, and in the four countries studied above in particular (Azerbaijan, Armenia, Burkina Faso and the Dominican Republic), is characterized by certain peculiarities worth examining.

Let us begin by considering certain features common to the four countries, despite the considerable political and cultural differences between them.

None of the four countries in question raised any reservations to the CRC, and in each of them the status of international treaties corresponds to the process referred to above as 'constitutionalization'. In theory, this means that no subsequent national laws should be required for the direct applicability of international treaties. This is nevertheless far from what occurs in real practice. As mentioned, the theory is practically dissociated from the actual integration of international treaties within national law and the possibility of citing the provisions of the CRC by private parties in a court or administrative proceeding, even irrespective, of the existence – as in the case of Azerbaijan – of a constitutional court.

In practice, the direct application of the CRC has come up against specific problems that render enforcement of the Convention either difficult or impossible. These problems are of various kinds (generally relating to the absence of rules, or even to the formal characteristics of specific institutions). For this reason, it is worth mentioning them in general terms, then relating them, where appropriate, to the specific findings of the various national studies.

In most of the countries with a civil law tradition (all the Latin American countries are highly representative examples of this situation), ratification of the CRC has been followed and accompanied by a process known as 'promulgation', that is, the transformation and express approval of the Convention as national law by Parliament. The first problem arising, as mentioned earlier, is the pre-existence of specific laws regulating the same issues whose content and nature are, as a general rule, antagonistic to the content and nature of the Convention. This antagonism is due fundamentally to two different aspects: (a) the universality in the aims and scope of the Convention, which is set as a law protecting *all* children and not only certain categories of children, as was the case of the old child laws; and (b) the fact that *all* children are regarded as 'subjects of rights', as opposed to *some* children being regarded as mere 'objects of protection'. In the case of Latin America, such pre-existing child laws correspond to the period from 1919 to 1939. In the cases of Armenia and Azerbaijan, they correspond to the period of the former Soviet Union. And in the case of Burkina Faso, they correspond to the laws in force in the mother countries of the respective colonial powers (i.e., French laws). There are clearly certain peculiarities to be highlighted in the case of the Soviet Union, relating to two basic aspects: (a) the absence of divisions in power; and (b) the total confusion between government, the political party (there being a single party) and the State. Leaving these peculiarities aside, however, it is clear that the direct application of the CRC is hampered by the lack of political prominence of child-related issues rather than by an absence of specific constitutional provisions stipulating the application of human rights treaties.

The resistance to the CRC by children's judges or the administrative officials responsible for deciding conflicts involving children is highly representative. The reference to administrative officials is relevant to all countries where (as in the case of Mexico up until today) there is not even a judicial figure responsible for children's issues, such role being played by an administrative body. The resistance displayed is in almost all cases due to the reduction of judicial and administrative discretionary decision making resulting from legal reforms based on the CRC that thus regard children as subjects of rights.

It is clear that discretion has its part within the judicial function, but that such function is covered by the so-called principle of legality (i.e., under which the judge is required by law to bring a specific case into line with a general and abstract legal rule). The right of 'minors' prior to the CRC openly ignored the principle of legality that has prevailed, with respect to adults at least, since the modern juristic age following the French Resolution. The provisions within laws on minors prior to the CRC explicitly negate the principle of legality. All the laws preceding the CRC contain, in a more or less explicit way, a principle that negates, radically, the principle of legality. When listing the measures that can be ordered by the judge for the 'protection of the minor', something along the following lines is invariably included: "and any such measure as the judge considers appropriate" (the wording varies from country to country but the essence remains the same).

The attention raised toward the dangers of a total discretionary and thus potentially arbitrary interpretation of the best interests principle, and the increasingly restrictive interpretation of the principle, are heightening the problem of non-acceptance by the judiciary of the new processes of legal reform.

In this context, legal reform, that is, the explicit adaptation of national legislation to the provisions of the Convention, is a necessary condition yet not sufficient in itself if we are to take at all seriously the implementation of the CRC, and thus its effective validity.

Legislative reform, far from a 'luxury' to be dealt with only when other more pressing problems have been resolved, is essential if serious consideration is to be given to social policies relating to children. These policies can be thus sustainable and capable of reproducing on a broad scale the most successful results achieved through small-scale child-focused programs. This point will be elaborated in the following section.

The CRC and Its Specific Impact on Various Kinds of Social Policy
Aimed at the Child

What is the relation between laws and social policies aimed at children?
The first point to be made is that the expression 'social policy' encompasses such a varied range of concepts that certain major distinctions need to be drawn. The real and potential impact of the CRC has, moreover, varied significantly depending on the kind of social policy in question. The first and most obvious distinction refers to the governmental or non-governmental nature of social policy. Although theoretically the concept of social policy is linked to a far greater extent to government actions than to those of civil society, which is more an executor of state-conceived programmes, in reality we are seeing in certain countries an expanding process of privatization of social policy. This may be linked to the processes of state reduction and dismantling undertaken primarily during the 1990s. We should recall, by way of example, that such structural adjustment processes took place (irrespective of the geographical areas) with greater or lesser levels of intensity in each of the four countries studied in this chapter. In some countries, especially those least developed, the volume of international cooperation can exceed by far the volume of resources invested by the State in social policy. Yet this is not true in the case of the Latin American countries – with the exception of Haiti – but it is true in some African countries.

Although very little attention has been paid to this specific issue, there can be no doubt that these structural adjustment processes have contributed decisively to the fragmentation of social policy and to its reduced impact and role as an instrument of social cohesion. Similarly, and as a result of the empowerment resulting from the incorporation of the CRC into the national arena, we are now beginning to hear about a significant distinction between governmental social policy, on the one hand, and public social policy, on the other. In this context, the adjective 'public' is understood not merely as a synonym of 'governmental' but as the result of coordination   obviously not devoid of conflict – between government and civil society. One of the best examples of specific institutionalization of child-related public policy is that of the Councils for the Rights of the Child envisaged in the Child and Adolescent Statute in Brazil.[26] These councils, which are made up 50 per cent of governmental representatives and 50 per cent of non-governmental representatives, also have the merit of having included the so-called private sector, along with other civil society organizations. The Municipal Councils for the Rights of the Child in Brazil, envisaged in a national child law, are thus the best example of a legal framework allowing the design of public

---

[26] Estatuto da Criança e do Adolescente, Law N° 8.069, 13 July 1990, Diário Oficial da União, 16 July 1990 (Br.) [Child and Adolescent Statute].

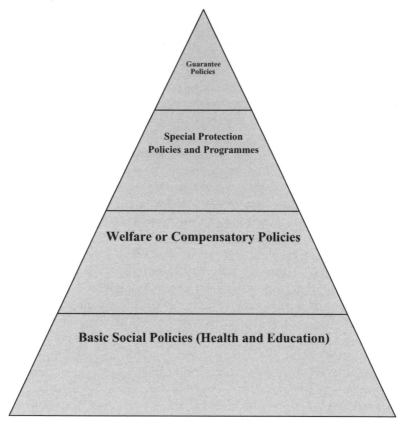

FIGURE 2.1. The Social Policy Pyramid.

policies specifically for children, the term 'public' being understood as the meaning indicated above. However, the most significant distinction to be drawn in relation to the concept of social policy relates to the number of children and adolescents targeted by these policies and to the areas they cover. As we will see later, there is no better way of representing this than in the form of a pyramid (see Figure 2.1). At the base of the pyramid we find the 'basic' social policies, also referred to as 'universal' policies, which relate to health and education and which in almost all countries enjoy constitutional backing. In this connection, we find the unresolved problem of the regulatory or de facto restrictions that some countries apply to persons who are not their nationals. These restrictions, very often related to mass migration movements because of economic conditions or armed conflict, tend to take on an explicitly discriminatory nature. In Latin America, where such discrimination rarely acquires formal or institutional status, the best examples of children thus excluded are Nicaraguan children in Costa Rica or Colombian children in Venezuela.

In the case, for example, of the new Eastern European constitutions, our attention is drawn to their broad scope and the total absence of legal discrimination, especially based on children's nationality. It is also worth mentioning a decision by the Russian Constitutional Court of 23 May 1995. This judgement, handed down on an appeal for legal protection, declared partially unconstitutional a 1991 law targeting the victims of political repression because the law excluded children under the age of 16 from its benefits.[27] The fundamental claim on which the appeal was based was that the prohibition of discrimination on the basis of sex, race or religion should be extended to include the prohibition of discrimination on the basis of age.

Returning to the issue of the basic social policies that lie at the base of the pyramid, national constitutions stipulate, as a general rule, that these policies are 'the duty of the State and rights of all persons'.

One level above these policies, we find the so-called welfare or compensatory policies. Generally speaking, these policies also have constitutional backing, although the legal provisions relating to them differ slightly from the provisions relating to basic or universal policies. Once again, it is established that these policies are the duty of the State. Access to compensation or welfare benefits constitutes a right, however, only of those persons who need them.

These welfare or compensatory policies have been designed for two major distinct hypotheses: (a) for disabled persons who have so-called handicaps or (b) as a means of coping with exceptional situations of public emergency or natural disasters (e.g., floods, droughts and earthquakes).

At the next level up in the pyramid (note that the number of children benefiting from these policies decreases as we move up), we find the so-called 'special protection' policies. There is generally no constitutional backing for these policies and they tend to refer to entire categories of children at risk or in especially difficult situations but who, at the same time, are not in conflict with the law (such as child workers, child victims of sexual exploitation, children involved in armed conflict, etc.).

At the top of the pyramid, we find the so-called 'guarantee' policies. These policies, for which there may or may not be constitutional backing, relate to children who are generally in risk situations (although this need not be the case) and who are also in active conflict with the law. They relate to children and adolescents who are perpetrators of acts of violence and who breach the criminal law.

Moving on from a static to a dynamic description of the way in which social policies function, as a general rule, and particularly in the cases of the four countries studied, we see that the deterioration referred to in the living conditions of the child may be related to a qualitative and quantitative

---

[27] Ruling No. 6-P of 23 May 1995, Constitutional Court of the RF (Russ.).

reduction of 'basic' or 'universal' policies and an increase – in absence of the two conditions required for legitimization – of so-called 'welfare' or 'compensatory' policies. The general explanation for this is that the latter are easier to manipulate on a discretionary basis out of political self-interest than the universally institutionalized basic social polices.

With regard to the two kinds of policies at the top of the pyramid, we see that the lack of national legal adaptation to the basic content of the CRC or the absence of specific implementation mechanisms gives rise to a profound confusion reflected in social policies lacking a distinction between the children targeted. The confusion lies between those situations in which children are the victims of violence and those situations in which children – generally adolescents – are the perpetrators of acts of violence.

It should be pointed out that for certain complex reasons that are very hard to grasp, the impact of the CRC varies a great deal depending on the kind of social policy in question. However, most countries invariably report a range of difficulties that can generally be referred to with two interrelated aspects: (a) inadequate financing of social policies specifically targeting children, and (b) limited political prominence of child-related issues. Whereas the Convention has had a major impact on 'special protection' and 'guarantee' policies, it has had very little or no impact in the area of 'basic' social policies and on 'welfare' policies. In general terms it can be said – and this is reflected in the four countries studied – that the rationale of the CRC, that is, the recognition of basic needs as rights, has not yet permeated sufficiently the area of basic social policy.

The most important link between the various child laws and basic social policies lies in the creation of mechanisms that prevent these policies from functioning in a discriminatory way and, at the same time, in their envisaging juridical and institutional mechanisms capable of addressing the frequent inadequate availability of services, which thus deny children's right to access basic services.

Concrete experience has shown that translating international legal provisions into national laws and policies does not always go through the same route, even in countries that share a common legal tradition. Whereas in the Dominican Republic and Azerbaijan the most immediate translation of the CRC took place in the form of a law,[28] in the cases of Burkina Faso and Armenia, the most important translation of the provisions of the Convention took place in the form of National Plans of Action.[29]

---

[28] Code for the Protection of Children and Adolescents, Law 14-94 (1994) (Dom. Rep.), reformed by Law 136-03 (2003); Law on the Rights of the Child (1998) (Azer.); Civil Code (1999) (Arm.).

[29] In Burkina Faso, the first plan was adopted in 1996 and the second in 2003. In Armenia, the National Plan of Action on the Rights of the Child was adopted by decree on 18 December 2003.

The different impact of incorporating the CRC provisions either through laws or through national plans of action is worth analyzing, at least in terms of its most important implications.

It should be clarified first of all that these two forms of domestic incorporation of the content of the CRC are not necessarily exclusive. In many countries, legal reform and the adoption of national plans of action are mutually complementary and provide mutual reinforcement. In cases such as those referred to here, however, it is important to establish certain distinctions between these two forms of incorporation:

a) Incorporation of the Convention through law. This form of incorporation generally involves a far more drawn-out process of approval because parliamentary consensus requires difficult and arduous negotiations during which it is often necessary to make compromises or concessions that are detrimental to the consistency and technical quality of the law. By contrast, however, it must be said that the consensus reached via this route generally enjoys far greater legitimacy. Moreover, in democratic contexts, the law is a privileged instrument allowing for the sustainability and reproduction on a broader scale of the best experiences of social policy initially implemented on a smaller scale. In this context, the impact of legal reform tends not to be immediate. For this reason, under any kind of emergency-based conception of social policy (which is invariably also fragmentary), the capacity of laws to achieve change tends to be underestimated.

Despite the amount of literature generated, particularly within UNICEF, on the 'rights-based approach', it is very difficult to define, in essence, what this approach really consists of. As proof of this, concrete practical examples have shown how practices that are in reality antagonistic all claimed to constitute a rights-based approach. When everything, or almost everything, is a rights-based approach, the situation that may arise is one in which there is no rights approach. An honest, truly profound interpretation of the 'rights-based approach' concept should perhaps begin with a negative definition; in other words, by defining what such approach does not consist of. In this sense, a 'rights-based approach' should probably be defined firstly by its non-immediate nature. There is possibly nothing that exemplifies this situation better than the varied and contradictory positions related to the child labour issue. In general terms, under the 'immediate' approach, the survival argument will allow for the relativization of what is clearly stipulated by the CRC (the eradication not only of all dangerous forms of work immediately and explicitly, but also the eradication of all forms of work that compromise the development of the child within the education system).[30] Under a non-immediatist approach to child labour, tolerance or underestimation of its

[30] CRC, op. cit., Art. 32.

evils is viewed in the medium term as a justification to legitimize the reduction of public spending on education for poor children. Under the imme-
diatist approach, by contrast, child labour is often perceived as a survival
strategy and therefore as a solution.

The detailed analysis of the different kinds of social policy and of the
varying impact of the CRC on them will probably prove fundamental to the
development of universal guiding principles in this area (i.e., guidelines).

b) The incorporation of the Convention through national plans of action.
Under this form of incorporation, which is invariably promoted by the Executive, the emphasis is placed on rapid adoption of measures. However, even
when such speed is achieved, analysis of the plan's actual impact is required
under a rights-based approach in the non-immediatist sense explained. Measures adopted in this manner often suffer from a lack of continuity, as their
implementation is related not only to changes in government but also to the
typical fragmentation of social policy.

VII. IMPLEMENTATION AND ENFORCEMENT:
THE ROLE OF CIVIL SOCIETY

Legislative Reform and Processes of Social Participation
in the CRC Age

Irrespective of all the difficulties encountered in the processes of legal reform,
it can be affirmed that the CRC has changed not only the content of new
laws but also, in general terms, the processes whereby they are elaborated. A
greater level of participation by civil society has made it possible to change
the traditional processes of legal reform, which were characterized by their
technocratic nature and by the exclusion of any kind of civil society participation, except by select groups of specialists.

Let us take Latin America as an example. In its first cycle of legal reforms
(1919–1939), there was no social participation of any kind beyond that of
small groups of 'specialists' or experts responsible for actually drafting the
laws. The situation as from the second cycle of reforms that followed the
adoption of the CRC has been very different. There have been three key
periods in this second cycle of reforms, which runs from 1990 through the
present day. The first of these key periods relates to a single, particular case
and corresponds to the first legal reform in this region subsequent to the
Convention: We refer to the case of Brazil. The case of Brazil was so singular
in nature that it cannot be regarded as forming part of any other process.
A second period that did involve the entire region spanned the years from
1992 through 1997. This period can be referred to as the period of 'juristic-
cultural expansion' of the rights of the child. A third period, also common to

the whole region, runs from 1997 to the present day and may be referred to as the period of 'authoritarian reversal'. For the sake of a clearer and easier understanding, a schematic approach of the above cycles is proposed.

In terms of what has been referred to in this study as the second cycle of reforms, the case of Brazil, as indicated earlier, is truly special and atypical, and it deserves closer examination.

The final drafting process of the CRC coincided with an interesting process of redemocratization in Brazil that started in 1985, following almost 25 years of military dictatorship. At this point in time a legal reform process started, unprecedented in terms of its high level of social participation in the elaboration of a new national constitution (finally approved towards the end of 1988). At the same time, a nearly definitive draft of what would later become the text of the CRC had already been in circulation in Latin America, and in Brazil in particular, for a while. During this process of constitutional reform, the Brazilian movement fighting for children's rights took advantage of the possibility of introducing a popular constitutional amendment. All these efforts eventually resulted in Article 227 of the Brazilian Federal Constitution, effectively a summary of the entire Convention, which at the time was still pending approval.[31] With this constitutional base established, a children's bill was drafted, which was then debated at great length by all relevant social movements and finally approved by Parliament on 13 July 1990 (by which time the Convention itself had also been adopted by the UN General Assembly). The Brazilian law was innovative not only from the point of view of the participatory process practiced for its elaboration but also in terms of its content. In this connection, reference will presently be made to certain innovative mechanisms it introduced for the institutionalization of community participation, particularly the so-called Municipal Rights Councils. However, before moving on to consider those periods corresponding to trends involving the entire region, it is important that we stress the unique and unprecedented regional impact of the Brazilian process.

Influenced by the events taking place in Brazil in 1990, the period 1990–1992 saw a rapid series, across the entire Latin American region, of ratifications of the CRC. This paved the way for the beginning of this second cycle of reforms, identified here as the period of 'juridical-cultural expansion' of the rights of the child. This occurred between 1992 and 1997. Practically all the significant legal reforms in Latin America (at least 80 per cent of them) took place during this period, a time when those countries that were going ahead with legal reforms repealed their old child laws in force since the beginning of the twentieth century and adopted norms that marked a substantial change in two central children's issues, namely: The rules under which a child could

---

[31] Constituição da República Federativa do Brasil (1988), Art. 227 (Br.).

be separated from his or her biological family on grounds of poverty were repealed and, in the area of criminal law, provisions were introduced that gave significant weight to the principles of legality and the guarantee of due process established under of the CRC.[32] Without overlooking the resistance to change and the difficulties that arose, the truth is that major changes were thus introduced in all areas relating to adolescents' problems and criminal law. We also should recall, however, that some key countries in the region have remained, to this day, entirely impervious to this process of reform: The child laws in force in Argentina, Chile, Mexico, and Colombia are still those dating from the early twentieth century.

From 1997, these positive developments tended not only to grind to a halt, but even to go into a process of reversal in several countries in the region. This marked the commencement of a third period involving the entire region, which we refer to here as the period of 'authoritarian reversal'. This reversal was seen both in the area of legislation and, on a more subtle plane, in judicial practice and case law. On the one hand, it is difficult to identify clearly the instances of regression in judicial practice, but it is very easy, on the other hand, to identify regressive changes of a strictly legal nature. The best examples are provided by Argentina, El Salvador, and Peru.

In the case of Argentina, the clearest manifestation of this authoritarian regression is the application of life imprisonment sentences to minors. Between 1997 and the present day, Argentinean courts have condemned 11 minors to life imprisonment. To date, at least, this situation has been repeated in no other country in the region. The legal grounds for these sentences was a decree – dating from 1980 and issued under the military dictatorship – that was unconstitutional, and whose repeal has still not been achieved after more than 20 years of democracy.

In the case of Peru, the Executive issued two decrees in 1998 that served to define new criminal law concepts so vague as to make them practically incompatible with the minimum requirements of democracy. We refer first to the Law against Aggravated Terrorism, which envisages minimum prison sentence of 30 years for minors.[33] In the case of the Law against Pernicious Youth Gang Membership, although the punishments are not as harsh as in the previously mentioned law, they apply to such vaguely described behaviours that, practically, their definitions are left to the subjective criteria and absolute discretion of the judges, who thus become legislators.[34]

The case of El Salvador is far better known (similar situations being encountered in Honduras and Guatemala). In these countries, the laws against the *maras* (the local name given to juvenile gangs) can be said to

---

[32] See CRC, op. cit., Arts. 37 and 40.
[33] Ley contra el terrorismo agravado, Decreto Legislativo N° 895, Art. 2(b), May 1998 (Peru).
[34] Ley contra el pandillaje pernicioso, Decreto Legislativo N° 899, May 1998 (Peru).

constitute a synthesis of the authoritarian tendencies described earlier. The untempered increase in the harshness of punishments, the vagueness in the description of the kinds of conduct to be punished and the failure to respect the most elementary guarantees are the most notable characteristics of this new reform process.

Judging from these and many other examples, it is no exaggeration to say that what we are seeing in Latin America is a vast and profound process of authoritarian reversal, which clearly also implies a process of regulatory and institutional reversal. We are seeing a movement of deep regression, reflected from the regulatory perspective in the examples mentioned above and, in the area of social policy, through a return from rights to needs, and from needs to charity. The transformation of universal policies into small-scale programmes marks the return to a situation that appeared to have been overcome. From here, however, it is impossible to make any accurate prediction with respect to the future of the rights of the child in Latin America.

Nevertheless, despite the general trends mentioned, the perspective in this area is not uniform and in each process of post-Convention legal reform we find a broad range of social participation levels.

Experience has shown that the different forms of children's and community participation in general in reform processes can be and are very varied. Participation processes tend to be spasmodic and fragmentary in nature insofar as they depend on political decisions and on the current prevailing socio-economic conditions. Although there is no hard-and-fast rule in this respect, laws cannot only be repealed or changed but can also fail to be carried into effect, yet the forms of participation established by law can be much further consolidated and amplified than the participation forms that are the product of political decisions based on prevailing conditions.

Participation by non-governmental organizations in the reform process
The participation of non-governmental organizations has played an increasingly significant role, which has not necessarily – although there are exceptions – resulted in the institutionalization (i.e., through legal rules) of community participation. Thus, the absence of real and effective mechanisms for institutionalized civil society participation has simultaneously weakened control mechanisms. In fact, experience has shown that there is no effective control without real participation.

In this regard, much attention should be paid to afford the concept of 'public' a different and larger scope than the notion of 'governmental'. By 'public', we are to understand the result of the coordinated efforts of both government and society.

One of the best examples of community participation established by law is that of the above-mentioned Municipal Councils for the Rights of the Child, established in the Child and Adolescent Statute in Brazil as a result of the legal reform of 1990. The law stipulates that these local councils are to be "equally represented and deliberative."[35] (The equal representation requirement means that 50 per cent of members must be representatives of municipal government and the other 50 per cent representatives of civil society. The deliberative nature of these councils refers to their capacity to make decisions in specific areas, rather than serving as a merely advisory body.) It should be stressed that the Brazilian national law (which is the equivalent of the Code for the Child and Adolescent in other countries) does not create these councils artificially. What it does, instead, is create the required conditions, envisaging the possibility that government and society at the local level may decide to create them.

The prime function of these councils is to begin by establishing an inventory of the resources available and the existing needs in the municipality. This function is essential, bearing in mind that one of the endemic weaknesses of social policy in general and in Latin America in particular is its hyper-centralization as well as the existence of a surplus offer of services in areas where demand is low, and a lack of such services in areas where the demand is high. These councils, in short, cannot work magic, but they are a powerful instrument to be used in the correction of the endemic deficiencies of social policy. Brazil is a country of continental dimensions with approximately 6,500 municipalities; almost 15 years after the start-up of these councils, however, they are in existence in almost 5,000 of these 6,500 municipalities.

The levels of their operational efficiency vary. It is important to note, however, that their efficacy invariably depends on governmental political will and on non-governmental will at the local level. These councils are unique instruments, to be used not only for the promotion but also for the institutionalization of community participation in the area of child policy. In other words, they serve to turn governmental and non-governmental policies into public policies (i.e., implying coordination between government and civil society).

It is hardly necessary to stress that this instrument of social policy is no magic wand, and it is certainly not irreversible. It has been shown by concrete experience, however, that in a continent characterized by an absolute lack of continuity in social policy, these councils are still operating 15 years after their creation and have survived in Brazil through four different national administrations with varied priorities and diverse political orientations.

The case of Guatemala demonstrates how law alone does not constitute a "magic bullet". Despite councils of the type above being envisaged in legislation they remain on the drawing board.

---

[35] Child and Adolescent Statute, op. cit. See supra note 26 and accompanying text.

Child participation in the reform process

The question of child participation is both more complex and more delicate. Considered from a historical perspective, there has been an extraordinary leap forward in qualitative terms in the area of child participation since adoption of the CRC. Articles 12 to 15 of the CRC have proved decisive for a new understanding of this concept and have formed the basis of certain child participation programmes, of varied levels of success. Of the four countries studied, only Burkina Faso has developed specific and formalized experience in the area of child participation, on a broad scale and with high visibility. We refer to the Children's Parliament, created in 1997. This body is composed of 100 members, and despite all the obstacles and difficulties imaginable, it is still in existence.[36]

The complex and delicate nature of the issue of child participation derives mainly from the major risks of manipulation in this area by adults. 'Decorative' or 'token' (and therefore manipulated) participation, involving young children in particular, had been present in practically all countries until just a few years ago.

A growing awareness of the risks of manipulation has nevertheless resulted in a visible decrease in the amount of 'decorative' or 'token' child participation. First – and in this respect Latin America has been the pioneering region – the distinction between children (generally considered as those up to 12 or 14 years old) and adolescents (those ranging from the end of childhood until the completion of 18 years of age) has been legally consolidated. This distinction has been fundamental to the design of concrete strategies of participation. The manipulation of children often can prove all too easy. Adolescents, however, are extremely difficult to manipulate.

To conclude this point, concrete experiences of participation may have allowed development of a practical method of verification to distinguish between non-legitimate and legitimate forms of participation. In the former case, children tend to speak as if they were adults and adults as if they were children. In the second, children speak as children and adults as adults. A considerable part of what must be achieved for the fulfilment of the rights of the child is closely related – as we see from this example – to the recovery of the capacity to perceive what is obvious.

In relation to the question of child participation, an issue deserving particular consideration is the involvement of children and adolescents in judicial processes relating to them. Children's right to participate in judicial proceedings derives directly from the CRC, which establishes the broad yet barely explored concept of 'evolving capacity' (whereby children's opinions are to

---

[36] M. C. Yabiyuré Konsimbo, 'Legislative Reform Initiative Country Study: Burkina Faso' (unpublished study for the Legislative Reform Initiative, UNICEF, 2004), pp. 25–6.

be taken seriously into account according to their age and level of maturity).[37] This fundamental principle of the evolving capacity of the child has had an important impact on legislation, insofar as it has resulted in the establishment of specific measures for the participation of children in judicial and administrative procedures.

It is particularly important to monitor case law developments in this area. The core of the issue is that the right to be heard should have (according to most advanced interpretations) a specific impact on the procedural status of the child. In this regard, the *ex parte* appointment of an attorney in litigation involving either one or both parents is currently being debated in relation to the scope of this right.

CONCLUSIONS

1. The four case studies commissioned by UNICEF appear to confirm, as a general trend, that the main obstacles encountered in the path of the legal reform processes are not primarily of a technical nature. On the contrary, these obstacles have a deep cultural origin, which may be traced back to the relationship established historically between adults and institutions and children. The most outstanding manifestation of this situation is the still prevailing lack of political prominence of child-related issues.

2. Legal reform constitutes an essential, yet not sufficient, condition for bringing about both a new kind of relationship with the child and for the full incorporation of the CRC in the social life of all countries. As the study on Azerbaijan concludes, "We cannot assume the adoption of new legislative as being an absolute insurance of CRC requirements in Azerbaijan."[38] Likewise, the Armenian case study concludes "the adoption of new laws and amendments and additions to existing laws is not sufficient for the creation of a friendly – protective – participatory environment for children."[39]

3. Legal reform is a permanent process. Despite the revocable nature of laws and the difficulties involved in their implementation, legal reform appears to be a more legitimate mechanism for the formulation of child-specific policies (i.e., for the reproduction on a large scale of the best experiences drawn from small-scale programmes), rather than administrative decisions taken in response to prevailing conditions. The same can be said of the relation between the law and the limited temporal sustainability of social policies.

[37] CRC, op. cit., Art. 12.
[38] E. Humay, 'Legislative Reform Initiative National Study of Azerbaijan' (unpublished study for the Legislative Reform Initiative, UNICEF, 2004), p. 32.
[39] H. Khemchyan, 'National Study, Civil Law Legal Tradition: Republic of Armenia' (unpublished study for the Legislative Reform Initiative, UNICEF, 2004), p. 24.

4. The existing gap between law and reality – particularly in those countries in which the so-called initial cycle of reforms for national adaptation to the CRC has already taken place – would appear to be explained far more by the refractory nature and lack of sensibility in relation to the rights of the child by certain institutions (the courts of justice in particular) than to the absence of child-specific legal regulations.

5. Advocacy and the training of key players constitute fundamental tools in legislative reform strategies. There is a need for greater support to independent pro-rights legal mechanisms (such as lawyers' groups, legal defence centres, etc.) in addition to the efforts already being undertaken to support and train the main players involved in the administration of justice for children.

6. If we are to take seriously the cultural obstacles that need to be overcome, we must attach the importance it deserves to the question of the political prominence of children's issues. Specifically, this means that a considerable part of the lobbying and awareness-raising tasks to be undertaken should be targeted also at persons or institutions not directly involved with child-related issues. Electoral processes and major legal and institutional reforms (e.g., processes for constitutional reform) offer key opportunities that should not be missed. The constitutional reforms already undertaken in Argentina and Ecuador, and the process currently under way in Angola, are good examples of this.

In these legal and institutional reform processes, the Concluding Observations of the UN Committee on the Rights of the Child can provide useful guidance as to areas of law and institutions where reform is needed, and serve as an advocacy tool to ensure that children's issues are prominent on the political agenda.

Legal Reform: Democracy and the Child

As in the case of any complex instrument, there is more than one possible way of defining the CRC. In this sense, in addition to establishing a minimum ethical framework that is practically universal, the CRC also constitutes a specific human rights treaty with respect to individuals whose only defining characteristic is the fact that they have not yet reached 18 years of age. It is therefore somewhat surprising that a treaty devoted to an issue that has traditionally been viewed as low-priority among national and international concerns (e.g., as the four case studies show, children's issues were afforded very poor or no prominence at all), has become the treaty that, in the entire history of humanity, has been most ratified, most accepted both socially and culturally and most broadly disseminated.

Despite all the difficulties – both relating to the scarce financing devoted to social policies and those deriving from the fact that child-related issues continue to be perceived as culturally inferior – the CRC has brought about an extraordinary leap forward, in qualitative terms, in the treatment of the legal and material situation of the child. We continue to see, however, a situation of asymmetry between the child and politics or, in other words, between the child and democracy. There is indeed an increasing number of people working seriously and from various angles on child-related issues who have overcome a stage of naivety and are convinced of the relevance to children of major political issues. The asymmetry arises precisely because of the persistently small number of such persons working seriously on politics and democratic issues, who at the same time attribute to children's issues the importance and prominence they deserve.

The fact that the CRC, the minimum ethical common denominator of a virtually universal nature, takes the form of a law is neither arbitrary nor coincidental. Its legal nature either presupposes the existence of a democracy or constitutes an instrument for democratic recovery.

The four case studies examined in this chapter clearly show that the implementation of the CRC is beset with problems. The scarce financing granted to children; the absence of child-specific, efficient institutions; the lack of political prominence attributed to children's issues; and the various forms of corruption are problems that are reproduced with surprising similarity in different political and cultural contexts as diverse as those of the four particular countries studied. One possible conclusion is that the difficulties in implementing the CRC are none other than the problems in implementing a fully democractic system. Accordingly, if we contribute to solving children's problems, we will be making a decisive contribution to the solution of the democracy's problems. And it is no less true that if we contribute to solving the problems pertaining to democracy, we will be making a fundamental contribution to the solution of the problems pertaining to the child.

Legal reform aimed at adapting national legislation to the CRC is an extraordinary tool to be used in bringing about these changes.

BIBLIOGRAPHY

Aries, P. *Centuries of Childhood: A Social History of Family Life*. London: Jonathan Cape Ltd., 1962.

Farto, L. M. *Códigos y Concordatos Napoleónicos*. Buenos Aires: Dunken, 1998.

García Méndez, E. *Adolescents and Penal Responsibility*. Buenos Aires: Ad-Hoc, 2001.

García Méndez, E. *Derecho de la Infancia Adolescencia en América Latina: De la situación irregular a la protección integral*. Ibagué: Forum Pacis, 1997.

García Méndez, E. and M. Beloff, eds. *Infancia, Ley y Democracia en América Latina*. Buenos Aires: Temis, Depalma, 1998.

Humay, E. 'Legislative Reform Initiative National Study of Azerbaijan'. Unpublished study for the Legislative Reform Initiative, UNICEF, 2004.

Khemchyan, H. 'National Study, Civil Law Legal Tradition: Republic of Armenia'. Unpublished study for the Legislative Reform Initiative, UNICEF, 2004.

Martínez, A. G. 'National Study: Civil Law Legal Tradition in the Dominican Republic'. Unpublished study for the Legislative Reform Initiative, UNICEF, 2004.

Ventura, M. and D. Zovatto. *La función consultiva de la Corte Interamericana de Derechos Humanos*. Madrid: Civitas, for Instituto Interamericano de Derechos Humanos, 1989.

Yabiyuré Konsimbo, M. C. 'Legislative Reform Initiative Country Study: Burkina Faso'. Unpublished study for the Legislative Reform Initiative, UNICEF, 2004.

CHAPTER THREE

A Comparative Perspective of the Convention on the Rights of the Child and the Principles of Islamic Law

LAW REFORM AND CHILDREN'S RIGHTS IN MUSLIM JURISDICTIONS

Shaheen Sardar Ali

INTRODUCTION

This chapter evaluates the impact of the United Nations Convention on Rights of the Child (CRC) in a selection of Muslim States parties. It will comment on legislative reform initiatives (in addition to existing legal frameworks, statutory provisions and institutional mechanisms) undertaken in Jordan, Mauritania and Morocco affecting child rights, highlighting compatibility or otherwise with substantive provisions of the CRC. Arguing from a socio-legal and law-in-context approach, the chapter will propose a framework for enhanced convergence of the Islamic legal tradition and the CRC to create an enabling environment for child rights in these jurisdictions.

I. THE CONTEXT FOR LEGAL REFORM ON CHILD RIGHTS IN MUSLIM JURISDICTIONS: PAST AND PRESENT

An overview of the status of human rights treaties, including the Convention on the Elimination of All Forms of Discrimination against Women (CEDAW) and the CRC, presents an interesting pattern of ratification and reservations. Although many countries have ratified with reservations, Muslim countries are unique in the fact that they have specifically identified the Islamic religion and Islamic law as justification for many of these reservations. It is therefore pertinent to initiate the discussion of implementation of the CRC in Muslim jurisdictions by presenting an overview of the conceptual foundations of human rights and child rights in Islam, which to a large extent informs the legal system in Muslim countries.

Conceptual Foundations of Human Rights in Islam: An Overview

The concept of human rights in the Islamic tradition is firmly grounded in its sources and accompanying juristic techniques, namely, the Quran, *Hadith*,

Ijma, Qiyas and *Ijtihad*. The Quran, believed by Muslims to be the word of God, is the primary source of Islamic law and the *Shari'a*. Any human rights regime must, therefore, conform to those rights and duties, privileges and obligations enjoined upon believers in the Quranic verses.[1] Out of the 6,666 verses of the Quran, approximately 500 have a legal element. The vast majority of these deal with worship rituals, leaving only about 80 verses of legal subject matter in the strict sense of the term.[2] Of particular interest in the context of our present inquiry is the principle of *naskh* (abrogation or repeal of the legal efficacy of certain verses of the Quran in favour of other verses). The content of some of the later verses appears contradictory to the earlier ones.[3] Because the Quran is the primary source of Islamic law, the question of legal validity of every verse therein is crucial. Questions facing Muslim jurists down the ages have been: Can one (later) Quranic verse abrogate another (earlier) verse? If the later verse abrogates the earlier one, then what of the principle that each and every verse of the Quran has absolute authority and validity? If the answer to the first question is 'no' and if both sets of verses as the words of God are equally valid, are Muslims at liberty to choose whichever verse they wish to use as the basis of a rule of law? There is a difference of opinion regarding the subject in the Islamic legal tradition, and it is particularly important in the context of the human rights of women and minorities since some Quranic verses tend to create gender hierarchies and legitimize discrimination against women and non-Muslims, whereas others enjoin complete equality of rights and treatment.[4] It appears

---

[1] A. R. I. Doi, *Shariah: The Islamic Law* (London: Ta Ha Publishers, 1984), pp. 21–2. The Quran, which is written in the Arabic language, was revealed piecemeal over a period of 22 years, 2 months, and 22 days, according to the needs of time and to provide solutions to the problems that came before the Prophet Mohammed. The Quran is divided into 114 chapters and contains 86,430 words and 323,760 letters of the alphabet. The total number of verses is 6,666. In order to facilitate its reading, the Quran is divided into 30 sections and 540 *ruku* and 7 *manazil*.

[2] S. C. Vesey-Fitzgerald, 'Nature and Sources of the Sharia', in *Law in the Middle East*, ed. M. Khadduri and H. J. Liesbeny (Washington, DC: The Middle East Institute, 1955), p. 87; H. J. Liebesny, *The Law of the Near and Middle East* (Albany: State University of New York Press, 1975), p. 12; F. Rahman, *Islam* (London: University of Chicago Press, 2nd edn., 1979), p. 69; N. J. Coulson, *History of Islamic Law* (Edinburgh: Edinburgh University Press, 1964), p. 12 (cited at n.35 in A. A. An-Naim, *Towards an Islamic Reformation: Civil Liberties, Human Rights, and International Law* (Syracuse: Syracuse University Press, 1990), p. 20).

[3] The Sudanese Muslim reformer Ustadh Mahmood Mohammad Taha has argued that the Quranic verses revealed during the Meccan era are more egalitarian and democratic in spirit, whereas the Medinese verses display a hierarchical trend. Abdullahi Ahmed An-Naim, who translated the book of Taha entitled *The Second Message of Islam*, has written extensively on the subject.

[4] See An-Naim, *Towards an Islamic Reformation*, op. cit.; A. A. An-Naim, 'A Modern Approach to Human Rights in Islam: Foundations and Implications for Africa' in *Human Rights and Development in Africa*, ed. C. E. Welch Jr. and R. Meltzer (Albany: State University of New York Press, 1984); A. A. An-Naim, 'Religious Minorities under Islamic

to be the opinion of the Hanafis[5] and most of the Shafei and Maliki jurists that one Quranic text may repeal another. At the same time it is also stated that even though the injunction of the Quranic verse may have been repealed, its words would still be regarded as part of the Quran.[6] The inference of this view would be to base a rule of law only on the later verse and not on the superseded one. Nonetheless, a small minority of Muslim writers contends that because each and every word of the Quran holds equal legal validity, it would be legitimate to base a rule of law upon a repealed verse if doing so advanced the interests of justice.[7]

The *Hadith*, that is, the custom or usage of the Prophet Mohammed, is known as *Sunna*; that is, his words and deeds. *Hadith* means the traditions of the Prophet Mohammed – the records of his actions and his sayings. Unlike the Quran, which was written and compiled during the lifetime of the Prophet Mohammed, the *Ahadith* (plural of *hadith*) were not so compiled. After the death of the Prophet the community realized that in addition to the Quran, the sayings and actions of the Prophet were guiding principles for Muslims. The *Hadith* constitutes the second source of Islamic law. The *Ahadith* were not compiled under state supervision. At first, a particular Companion (*Sahabi*) of the Prophet Mohammed had his own collection of the words and deeds of the Prophet in memory or in writing. These collections were then passed on to others, thus starting a chain of narrators of the Prophet's traditions. However, because narration of *Hadith* is an important act akin to giving testimony in court, it becomes imperative to have rules governing its transmission.[8]

Hadith literature, however, is surrounded by controversies, in particular regarding the question of their authenticity.[9] It is a historical fact that

Law and the Limits of Cultural Relativism', *Hum. Rts. Q.* 8 (1987): p. 1; A. A. An-Naim, 'The Islamic Law of Apostasy and Its Modern Applicabilty: A Case from Sudan', *Religion* 16 (1986): p. 197; A. A. An-Naim, 'The Rights of Women and International Law in the Muslim Context', *Whittier L Rev.* 9 (1987): p. 491.

5 Muslims are divided into *Sunni* and *Shia*. *Sunnis*, who form the predominant majority of Muslims, are further subdivided into *Hanafi*, *Shafei*, *Maliki*, and *Hanbali*, after the names of the founders of these schools of juristic thought. *Shia* are subdivided into *Athna Asharia*, *Zaidya*, and *Ismailya*.

6 A. Rahim, *Muhammadan Jurisprudence* (Lahore: Mansoor Book House, 1995), p. 94.

7 Taha and An-Naim subscribe to this view. Taha was the founder-leader of the Republican Brotherhood in the Sudan, which had little electoral success but under the leadership of Taha emphasized the need for Islamic reform and liberation. That their ideas are far from acceptable to the large majority of Muslims can be ascertained from the fact that Ustad Taha was hanged by the Sudanese government of Jafar Numairy in 1985, as an apostate from Islam.

8 A tradition or *Hadith* is composed of two essential parts: the text or *matn* of the tradition and the chain of transmitters or *isnad* "over whose lips it (*Hadith*) had passed." Due to the very nature of *Hadith* literature, there emerged principles of criticism of the *Hadith* relating to both the *matn* and *isnad*.

9 According to Muslim jurists, no doubt can reasonably be entertained as to the authenticity of any verse of the Quran. There are, however, only five or six *Ahadith* that can be said

numerous *Ahadith* were generated to reinforce societal norms and political expediency.[10] By narrating *Ahadith* favourable to its own group, political legitimacy could be acquired by the ruling elite.[11] Unfortunately for Muslim women, this policy of using *Hadith* for excluding political rivals was employed to introduce a misogynistic trend within the Islamic tradition by attributing to the Prophet sayings that were derogatory of women.[12]

In addition to the two primary sources of Islamic law given here, there are other juristic techniques accepted as its secondary sources; these include *ijma, qiyas* and *ijtihad.*

Ijma, or consensus of opinion, has been defined as agreement among the Muslim jurists in a particular age on a question of law.[13] Its authority as a source of laws rests on certain Quranic and *Hadith* texts.[14] The four Sunni schools of thought hold *ijma* to be a valid source of laws not only on the authority of the texts such as those mentioned above but also on the unanimity of the Companions of the Prophet Mohammed to that effect.[15] *Ijma* is an essential and characteristic principle of Sunni jurisprudence, one upon which the Muslim community acted as soon as they were left to solve the first and most important constitutional problem that arose on the death of the Prophet Mohammed, namely, the selection of the spiritual and executive head of the community. The election of Abu Bakr as the first among what

to be so proved. The reason for this is that, whereas the texts of the Quran were collected by authority of the State soon after the death of the Prophet, the traditions were not so collected.

[10] The *Hadith* implying the prohibition of a woman becoming Head of State is one such example.

[11] F. Mernissi, *Women and Islam*, trans. M. J. Lakeland (Oxford: Basil Blackwell Ltd., 1991), p. 46.

[12] Riffat Hassan, a Muslim woman theologian, has discussed this at length in her work, in which she takes up *Ahadith* that go against the spirit of Islam or against an express verse or injunction of the Quran. See R. Hassan, 'The Role and Responsibilities of Women in the Legal and Ritual Tradition of Islam' (paper presented at a biannual meeting of a Trialogue of Jewish–Christian–Muslim scholars at the Joseph and Rose Kennedy Institute of Ethics, Washington, DC, 1980).

[13] Rahim, *Muhammadan Jurisprudence*, op. cit., p. 97. Rahim cites the following authorities: 'Taudih', p. 498; 'Mukhtasar', Vol. II, p. 29; 'Jam'ul-Jawami', Vol. III, p. 288.

[14] The following Quranic verses (among others) are cited for *ijma* as a source of law:

"Today we have completed your religion."
"Obey God and obey the Prophet and those amongst you who have authority."
"If you yourself do not know, then question those who do."

Two *Ahadith* of the Prophet Mohammed are particularly used to establish the validity of *ijma*:

"My followers will never agree on what is wrong"; and
"It is incumbent upon you to follow the most numerous body."

[15] 'Bazdawi', p. 253; 'Taudih', p. 283; 'Mukhtasar', Vol. II, p. 30; 'Jam'ul-Jawami', Vol. III, p. 308.

are known as the 'Rightly Guided Caliphs' by the votes of the people was based on the principle of *ijma*.[16]

Qiyas, translated as 'analogical deduction', is the fourth source of Islamic law. As a source of law, it comes into operation in matters that have not been covered by a text of the Quran or tradition (the term tradition is used interchangeably with the *Hadith* of the Prophet Mohammed), nor determined by consensus of opinion. The law is thus deduced from what has been laid down by any of these authorities, by the use of *Qiyas*.[17]

An important source of *Shari'a*, but one which is usually known as a juristic technique in Islamic jurisprudential terms, is *ijtihad*. In the literal sense, the term implies striving hard or strenuously, but technically it means exercising independent juristic reasoning to provide answers when the Quran and *Sunna* are silent on a particular subject. *Ijtihad* was meant to occupy a central place in juristic deduction. A person qualified to carry out *ijtihad* is known as *mujtahid*. It is in the doctrine of *ijtihad* that the Islamic legal doctrine was meant to find its evolutionary path. Historically, however, with the emergence of the four schools of juristic thought, it was declared that 'the doors of *ijtihad* had closed forever' and that independent juristic reasoning, and hence legal development in keeping with the times, was precluded forever. This position has been challenged by many Muslim scholars who believe that *ijtihad* is an ongoing intellectual pursuit and cannot be discontinued.

Over the centuries, Islamic law developed by drawing upon these sources and juristic techniques. *Shari'a,* which is now used interchangeably with the phrase Islamic law, became rigid and less amenable to changing needs. Since the *Shari'a* drew heavily upon the two primary sources, the Quran and *Sunna,* for its formulations, in due course of time the entire corpus of the *Shari'a* was elevated to the status of divine law and thus immutable, beyond evolution and change. *Shari'a,* it may be argued, by its very definition has evolution built into its meaning and cannot be rigid. (The term *Shari'a* means a watering place, a flowing stream, where both animals and humans comes to drink water. Stagnant and standing water is *not Shari'a*.)[18] How is it, then, that a concept with mobility built into its meaning is perceived as being averse to developing new legal concepts such as human rights? It is submitted that Muslim scholars have failed to make sure of the inbuilt dynamism and flexibility in the *Shari'a*. Those juristic techniques in which principles

---

[16] This election of Abu Bakr as the first Caliph of Islam, however, laid the foundation of the deep and irrevocable schism within the Muslim community of the time as some of them felt that Ali, the cousin and son-in-law of the Prophet, should have succeeded to this office. The sect of Islam that arose out of this divide is known as *Shia*.

[17] Rahim, *Muhammadan Jurisprudence*, op. cit., p. 117.

[18] In the opinion of An-Naim, *Shari'a* was constructed by Muslim jurists and, although derived from the Quran and *Sunna*, is not divine because it is the product of human interpretations of those sources. An-Naim, *Towards an Islamic Reformation*, op. cit., p. 185.

of one school are applied to litigants who in theory belong to another school of Islamic thought have also not been employed.[19] In this context, responsibility for underutilization probably also stems from the lack of appreciation of how Islamic law and jurisprudence works and has evolved over the centuries. It also reveals the fact that writers professing a static view of *Shari'a* are unaware of the plurality of legal tradition in Islam or simply impatient with its complexities and desire to 'will them away' by refusing to engage in a discussion on the subject.[20] If Muslim scholars (and indeed this movement must come from within the Muslim community) succeed in overcoming this psychological barrier of not being able to work on reforming the *Shari'a*, which they perceive as being divine law, whole new vistas for evolving concepts such as human rights in cross-cultural discourse would open up.

The *Shari'a* and Transformative Processes in Islamic Family Law: From Divine Will to Human Agency

The social and legal position of a child and child rights are an integral component of Islamic family law, which, in turn, is based on the *Shari'a* or principles of Islamic law derived from the Quran, *Hadith* and secondary sources, *Ijma, Qiyas, Ijtihad* and other juristic techniques. "The term *Shari'a* refers to the general normative system of Islam as historically understood and developed by Muslim jurists, especially during the first three centuries of Islam – the eight to tenth centuries CE. In this commonly used sense, *Shari'a* includes a much broader set of principles and norms than legal subject matter as such."[21] Islamic law is generally used to refer to the legal aspects of *Shari'a*; many Muslims tend to believe that the legal quality of those principles and norms derives from their assumed religious authority. Yet, whenever enforced or applied by the State, *Shari'a* principles are legally binding by virtue of state action, through either enactment as law by the legislative organs of the State or enforcement by its courts. Islamic family law is that part of *Shari'a* that applies to family relations (such as marriage, divorce and custody of children), also called 'Muslim personal status law' (*Shari'at al-ahwal al-shakhsiyah* in Arabic), through the political will of the State.[22]

Child rights, for example, in relation to custody and guardianship, minimum age of marriage, inheritance rights of the girl child and so on, are part of a wider network of legal and social relations as perceived by jurists in that

---

[19] Such as the doctrines of *taqlid* and *talfik*.

[20] There is some evidence to suggest that this plurality irritated the colonial authorities in nineteenth-century India, for example, who wanted to 'apply' a cut and dried Islamic law in the courts. For an interesting discussion on the subject, see M. Anderson, 'Islamic Law and the Colonial Encounter in British India' in *Islamic Family Law*, ed. C. Mallat and J. Connors (London: Graham & Trotman, 1990), pp. 205–23.

[21] A. An-Naim, ed., *Islamic Family Law in a Changing World: A Global Resource Book* (London: Zed Books, 2003) [Global Resource Book].

[22] Ibid.

broader context and susceptible to the possibility of revision and reformu-
lation in light of significant changes in those legal and social relationships.
The reality, however, is that there is a lack of appreciation of the critical
role of human agency in the conception and development of Islamic family law. In the early days of Islam, numerous schools of juristic thought
erupted but soon died away. The early Abbasid era witnessed the emergence
of the main surviving schools of Islamic jurisprudence, especially the Sunni
schools of Abu Hanifah (d. 767), Malik (d. 795), al-Shafi'd (d. 820), Ibn
Hanbal (d. 855), and Ja'far al-Sadiq (d. 765 – the founder of the main school
of Shia jurisprudence). However, the subsequent development and spread
of these schools have been influenced by a variety of political, social, and
demographic factors. As openly secular state courts applying those colonial
codes began to take over civil and criminal matters, the domain of *Shari'a*
was progressively limited to the family law field. Whatever the reasons may
have been, family law remained the primary aspect of *Shari'a* that successfully resisted displacement by European codes during the colonial period,
and survived and outlasted various degrees or forms of secularization of the
State and its institutions in a number of Islamic countries. As such, Islamic
family law has become for most Muslims the symbol of their Islamic identity,
the hard, irreducible core of what it means to be a Muslim today.[23]

Recognition of the difficulty of transforming the religious text into contemporary statutes makes this task of realizing the CRC a formidable, if not
impossible, one. Lack of attention to the ethical and moral dimension of
Islamic law, picking up at random parts of the religious text, not giving legal
status to the justice element, and disregard for the representatives (as to who
decides which part of the text should go into the statute and legislation and
which should be excluded and be merely of persuasive nature) reflect lack of
a holistic interpretation and approach to Islamic legal tradition. Reservations
to the CRC and a general apathetic approach to child rights do not spring
from the religious text; socio-economic and political compulsions and a lack
of intellectual rigour in pursuit of applying the faculty of mind and thought
(*ijtihad*) to arrive at decisions have led to neglect of rights and entitlements
of people in the Muslim world. A brief overview of some of these issues is
presented here.

SOCIO-ECONOMIC RIGHTS AND ENTITLEMENTS IN THE
ISLAMIC LEGAL TRADITION: CHILD CARE AS
A SOCIAL RESPONSIBILITY?

A strong element of the Islamic tradition is the emphasis on child care as a
social responsibility and not simply that of the parents and immediate family.

---

[23] Ibid., pp. 4–15.

Laws in most Muslim jurisdictions originate, for the most part, in colonial times and hence are coloured by the value system of the colonizers and the times they lived in. The prevalent concept of that time established a clear dichotomy between the public and private spheres of life, and what people did within the home or private/familial sphere of life was considered entirely their own business with minimum interference from the State or community. This separation of the family unit as an autonomous patriarchal organization historically and traditionally resulted in categorizing women and children as groups without any independent legal and social status and therefore placed under the protective power of adult male authority within the family. This perception naturally led to perpetuation of male domination and cultivation of discrimination against women and children. Freedom from interference in the context of the public/private divides, on the one hand, and minimal commitment to human development and welfare on the other hand, contribute to diluting child rights to meaningless rhetoric.

Muslim jurisdictions do have a range of rights extended to 'all persons with the State', but low rates of literacy, lack of access to judicial forums to seek redress and weak implementation mechanisms render whatever laws are available meaningless because these cannot be translated into reality. Furthermore, in many societies, the rights of any member of the community pose a threat to existing power structures. Knowledge and awareness of rights threaten the culture of subservience, where abysmally low awareness makes it easier to perpetuate the status quo. A right is not acknowledged and recognized as the inherent right of every human being but conceded by persons in positions of power as a charitable handout withheld at will. Use of violence to subdue marginalized and disadvantaged sections of society is seen as a necessary corollary to the culture of subservience. Thus, the rights a child are most of all dependent upon where he or she is placed in the societal hierarchy, rather than because every child has certain basic, inalienable rights. If one were to place child rights on a continuum, the poor, orphan child would be the most disadvantaged, whereas the child of affluent living parents would be, in most cases, the one enjoying the most rights.[24] At the same time, the patriarchal social setup prescribes that children 'belong' to families, the undertones of ownership quite distinct. Obedience (to members of the family who are in control) is the desirable trait for children to have. When and if this obedience is not forthcoming, resort to violence is considered justifiable. It is crucial, therefore, to pose the question of why child rights as a social issue does not appear to have adequate grounding within the ideological

---

[24] For a detailed empirical analysis, see Democratic Commission for Human Development, *Report on Human Rights Situation in Rural Communities in Pakistan 1996* (Lahore: DCHD, 1996), pp. 97–114.

framework of society despite a strong 'child-friendly' religious tradition as well as statutory laws.[25]

The recognition and propagation of 'joint parenting' as well as involvement of the State in providing support, in other words, the concept of child care as a social responsibility, is a novel concept both for Western societies and international human rights instruments. For example, it suffices to look at the CRC and twentieth-century domestic law in some Western jurisdictions where the 'welfare state' participates in child rearing by offering child benefits and other facilities to parents. In the Islamic traditions, however, the concept has deep roots and many Quranic verses, *Ahadith* and writings of Muslim scholars clearly support child care as a joint parental and social responsibility. Although breastfeeding and its duration are recommended in the religious text, its modalities are to be decided by 'mutual consultation' of both parents. If the mother is unable to fulfil her duty, the father is under an obligation to make alternate arrangements, for example, by hiring a wet nurse, and so on. When the parents are divorced and the mother has custody, the father is duty-bound to feed, maintain and pay the mother as he would a wet nurse for performing this job.[26]

Similarly, involvement of the State in a supportive role is borne out by the practice of Islamic governments to pay a special allowance to the child upon weaning. This rule was misused by poor families who practiced early weaning to get the allowance. Omar Ibn Al Khittab[27] modified this rule and made its payment due on the birth of a child.[28] Little or no parallel state support for children is present in most Muslim jurisdictions today.

In contemporary Muslim jurisdictions, therefore, the balance between rights of the parents vis-à-vis those of their children assumes tremendous importance. What are the basic minimum rights that a child is entitled to

---

[25] S. S. Ali and B. Jamil, *A Comparative Study of The UN Convention on The Rights of The Child, Islamic Law and Pakistan Legislation* (Peshawar: Educational Computing Services for Radda Barnen (Save the Children, Sweden), 1994).

[26] Quranic verses:

> Nor should he (father) to whom the child is born
> (be made to suffer) because of his child.
> (An heir shall be chargeable in the same way
> if they both decide on weaning)
> If they desire to wean the child by mutual consent,
> And, (after) consultation, it is no sin for them,
> And if you wish to give your children out to
> Nurse, it is no sin for you provided ye pay
> (the nursing women as hired),
> What is due from you (i.e., money that has been either fixed or according
> to common practice)
> Observe your duty to Allah, and know that Allah
> Is Seer of what ye do.

[27] The second Caliph of Islam.

[28] Al Azhar Working Group, *Child Care in Islam* (Cairo: UNICEF, 1985), p. 38.

upon birth? Does every child have the inherent right to food, clothing, shelter, health, education and recreation? Who is responsible for the effective realization of these rights; is it the parent(s), society or the State? Do rights of the parents over their children take precedence over corresponding rights of children over their parent(s), society and the State? These questions have assumed great importance as they are central to any debate on children's rights. Child, family, society and the State are locked into an inextricable relationship, the dialectic of which is an interplay between claims, rights and obligations. This is a framework of human development that needs support mechanisms to facilitate the mutually reinforcing growth processes. Just as 'development' is the common denominator between the four participants, vulnerability or the degrees of 'vulnerability' also creates the need for the protection mechanism. In this scenario, the child stands at the apex of the vulnerability pyramid. It is precisely for this reason that almost all legal instruments and religion give 'special consideration' to children.

Legal frameworks are the institutionalizing mechanisms that can convert claims into rights and make actions obligatory for the survival, protection and development of its citizens. As conditions of poverty and deprivation escalate in third world countries, human and social norms come under stress. Muslim countries are no exception to this rule. Although, on the one hand, it is argued that, according to GNP indicators, most Muslim countries rank as middle-income countries, the Human Development Index (HDI) rank them as poor performers, especially when contrasted with countries having similar GNP per capita. For example, Vietnam has roughly similar income levels to Pakistan but is ranked 112 on the HDI, whereas Pakistan ranks 142 and is a low human development country.[29] This is because of higher life expectancy and literacy figures of Vietnam. The HDI is thus useful to illustrate the distinction between income and human well-being. By measuring average achievements in sectors such as health, education and income, the HDI is able to present a more complete picture of the state of human development in a country than measuring income levels alone.[30] The HDI also highlights the importance of policies that translate wealth into human development. According to the *Human Development Report 2004*, out of the 177 countries included in the list for the HDI, five Muslim countries – Brunei Darussalam, Bahrain, Kuwait, Qatar and the United Arab Emirates – fall into the high human development group at numbers 33, 40, 44, 47 and 49, respectively.[31] The majority of Muslim countries are placed in the medium or low human development categories despite higher GDP. The argument put forward is

---

[29] United Nations Development Programme, *Human Development Report 2004* (New York: UNDP, 2004), p. 154.
[30] Ibid., pp. 127–9. [31] Ibid., pp. 217–20.

that social sector or human development is not necessarily GNP driven but values of state systems can rearrange social priorities, so that the 'optimal' benefit can be accrued for people at a given level of GNP.

In middle- and low-income countries, the lagging of the national safety nets in social-sector development, juxtaposed against poverty levels, has set off a trend inducing parents to look at their children in terms of human capital, which must reap 'immediate returns' rather than be nurtured and invested in for the future. Children are thus induced into employment arrangements to supplement family incomes, often in the informal sector, by parents themselves and sanctioned by society but unprotected by law and the State. Child labour in this form denies the child the right to education, health, protection, leisure and expression, thus completely side-stepping the very basis of child care as a social responsibility. Moreover, given the very foundation of both Islamic law and the laws of Muslim jurisdictions, where the best interests of the child are of paramount importance and to be catered to, the question is: Who is the interpreter and provider of this most critical or 'elusive' provision? The child is not only side-stepped by the State and society but by the 'family' as well – the child's first layer of protection. How will the best interests of the child be articulated and by whom?

Although the right to privacy and family life are protected in Islamic law, acknowledging child bearing and child rearing as a social function affords States the ability to regulate the protection of human rights law in this previously 'out of bounds' field. Although it appears as an encroachment on the right to family life without interference, it is in keeping with the spirit of social responsibility that forms the cornerstone of an Islamic society. It means that there are limits to which parents can mould the lives of their children and although children are ordered to obey their parents, *wali*, or guardian and so on, this duty of obedience has been balanced by strict injunctions in the Quran of duties parents owe children.[32] In addition to

---

[32] Quran, Chapter 4, Al-Nisa, Verse 36, which reads thus:
   And serve Allah
   And ascribe nothing as
   Partner unto Him
   (Show) kindness
   Unto parents,
   And unto the near kindred,
   And unto orphans,
   And the needy,
   And unto the neighbour who is of kin,
   And the fellow-traveller,
   And the way-farer,
   And (the slaves) whom your
   Right hands possess.
   Lo! Allah loveth not such as are
   Proud and boastful.

the general verses on care and kindness to children, there is a special verse that advises taking care of disabled (whether mental or physical disability) children.[33] This discussion highlights the significance of the religious text in Islam in advancing child rights and possible strategies for using the Quran and *Hadith* to integrate the CRC into domestic law in Muslim countries.

Adoption

Another important but little-discussed issue with far-reaching bearing on the rights of children is that of adoption. The main argument put forward is that there is a clear prohibition in the Quran regarding this institution and, hence, the practice is illegal. At the same time, concepts such as fosterage and Quranic and *Hadith* injunctions regarding looking after *lakeets* or foundlings are also an integral part of the Islamic tradition. It is therefore proposed to enter into a discussion here as to whether Islam is opposed to adoption per se or do equivalent concepts exist within the Islamic tradition, perhaps with slightly different connotations.

The Quranic verses prohibiting adoption are stated in Surah Ahzab[34] (the clans) thus:

> Allah has not made
> For any man two hearts
> In his (one) body: Nor has
> He made your wives whom ye
> Divorce by Zihar your mothers.
> Nor has He made your
> Adopted sons your sons,
> Such is only your (manner of) speech
> By your mouths. But Allah
> Tells (you) the truth, and He
> Shows the (right) way.[35]
> Call them by (the names)
> Of their fathers: that is
> Juster in sight of Allah,
> But if ye know not
> Their father's (names, call them)
> Your brothers in faith,

---

[33] Quran, Chapter 4 Al-Nisa, Verse 5, which states:
> Give not unto the foolish (what is in)
> Your (keeping of their) wealth,
> Which Allah has given you to maintain,
> But feed and clothe them from it
> And speak kindly to them.

[34] Chapter 33, Verses 4 and 5.

[35] Quran, Surah Ahzab, Chapter 33, Verse 4.

> Or your Maulas,
> But there is no blame on you
> If ye make
> A mistake therein.[36]

First, it is submitted that a literal interpretation of this verse does not suffice and what is required here is an interpretation based on the Islamic principle of '*ad'l*' or social justice, which needs to be formulated and applied. Purposes behind prohibition of adoption were to contain and, in certain cases, to root out social evils. For example, the tribal Arab psyche of 'accumulation', if one may use the term, of male children provided extra hands during tribal warfare, and so on. This practice of adoption of male children also perpetuated and aggravated gender discrimination. Second, the issue of adopted children coming within prohibited degrees of relationship had to be considered. Before the coming of Islam, the degree of nearness of relationship within which a man or woman could lawfully intermarry was not clearly demarcated. Hence, it was possible for a son to marry the widow of his deceased father. Likewise, it was impossible for a man to marry the daughter of his adoptive father, and so on. By negating the idea of equating natural-born children with adopted children, the purpose may have been to allow greater space to people for intermarrying.

Third, the right of a child to be informed of and given the right to use his parents' identity was sought to be established. The context of the revelation of these verses is crucial. These were revealed when the Prophet Mohammed hesitated in marrying Zainab, the former wife of his adopted son, Zaid, because of a prohibition under Arab customary law that equated adopted with natural children and hence precluded marriage between a man and his (former) daughter-in-law. It is submitted that the focus of the verses is not prohibition of adoption as much as it is on the implications of equating relationships originating from different circumstances.

In analyzing this perceived prohibition, it is important to adopt a holistic approach towards the Quranic verses as well as *Ahadith* that exhort kindness to all human beings, particularly to those in difficult circumstances such as children deprived of family environment, the orphans, the needy and children with disabilities. Verse IV:36 of the Quran states:

> Serve Allah, and join not
> Any partners with Him;
> And do good –
> To parents, kinsfolk,
> Orphans, those in need,
> Neighbours who are near,
> Neighbours who are strangers

---

[36] Ibid., Verse 5.

> The Companion by your side,
> The way-farer (ye meet),
> And what your right hand possess;
> For Allah loveth not
> The arrogant, the vainglorious.

The above quoted verse clearly lays out the obligation of a Muslim towards his/her parents, near kindred, orphans and travellers. It is indeed rather strange to accept the notion that Islam disallows looking after children other than one's own. How can it be so when every Muslim is enjoined to look after the homeless and particularly where homeless and orphaned children need a home? I would therefore argue that the verses of the Quran cited here nowhere negate the idea of adoption as such; in fact, time and again Muslims have been exhorted to share the responsibility of rearing and supporting children, orphans, the needy and so on.[37]

Although all Muslim jurisdictions are unanimous in declaring adoption as un-Islamic,[38] the reality appears to be less categorical. Adoption does take place, mostly by issueless persons or by close relatives adopting the orphan child of a deceased sibling, and the practice seems to be accepted and acceptable in society under the conceptual framework of *kafalah*, which may be translated as 'looking after', 'caring for' or 'fulfiling the needs of'. In fact, bringing up orphans and other destitute children is considered laudable and encouraged, whereas those who neglect such vulnerable children are admonished. For instance, in Verse 107:107 of the Quran, it is stated:

> Do you know who really rejects the faith? That is the one who mistreats the orphans. And does not advocate the feeding of the poor.

Similarly, Verse 2:215 of the Quran states:

> They ask you about giving: say, "The charity you give shall go to the parents, the relatives, the orphans, the poor, and the travelling alien." Any good you do, God is fully aware thereof.

In the actual practice of adoption in Muslim jurisdictions, a range of mechanisms within the 'secular' legal system are invoked and, interestingly enough, mention of Islamic law is simply omitted. The most common 'method' employed is to arrange with doctors to insert the name of the adoptive mother at the time of discharge from hospital instead of the natural mother in the birth certificate.[39] The most common 'formal' method is for adoptive

---

[37] For instance, see Chapter 4, Verse 8 of the Quran.

[38] See reservations entered to CRC by Muslim States. Declarations and reservations to the Convention are available on the web site of the Office of United Nations High Commissioner for Human Rights, http://www.ohchr.org/english/countries/ratification/11.htm#reservations [CRC Reservations].

[39] Based on the author's personal communications and interviews with doctors and other hospital personnel in various cities in Pakistan.

parents to file affidavits stating that the child has been given into their care by the natural parents voluntarily and without any undue influence or coercion, and that they undertake to look after the child as their own and undertake all expenses in relation to the child's upbringing.[40] It may therefore be argued that despite the generally accepted notion of adoption as being contrary to Islamic law, the practice does exist within Muslim communities.

Fosterage as the Equivalent Concept to Adoption?

Although adoption (as a term implying looking after a child, giving him/her the adoptive family name, acknowledging his/her right to inheritance, etc.) has been prohibited by Islam, for the reasons stated earlier, equivalent concepts are definitely present within the Islamic tradition that engender and promote the spirit of caring and nurturing of children within a family environment. One such example is that of fosterage. It is the need of today that such positive ideas be disseminated and awareness of their existence created among the populace and government alike for use in legislation and policy making, and so on.

Fosterage, a relationship developed as a result of breastfeeding a child within the Islamic and Asian cultural tradition is, "next to that of blood, considered of the strongest and most lasting nature. Nursing is supposed to partake of the very nature of her from whose blood he receives his earliest nourishment. So strong and lasting an affinity is therefore supposed to be created by this circumstance, which operates to render marriage illegal in the same manner as actual consanguinity."[41] Hence the prohibitions occasioned by fosterage are analogous to those set forth in prohibited degrees of relationship on the basis of blood relationship. It is argued, then, that the spirit and purpose behind adoption and fosterage are similar as the rights and obligations of foster relations are at par with blood relations (inheritance being the sole exception). Even the issue of inheritance can be taken care of if one follows the Islamic injunction of biding by one's duty to one's (foster) relations. A conscious effort will then have to be made for foster children, in that property may be gifted to them by their foster parents, or a will could be made giving these children up to one-third of the foster parent/s' property. (Islamic law of wills allows a testator to give away by will, up to one-third of his/her property to a person who is not included in the table of inheritance as an heir.)

It is to be hoped that this question of developing fosterage as an equivalent concept to adoption will be taken up by researchers and scholars as it is felt that it has been relegated to the background and virtually ignored by researchers seeking to establish legitimacy for adoption within the Islamic

---

[40] Based on the author's personal communications with adoptive parents in Peshawar.
[41] C. Hamilton, *The Hedaya* (Lahore: Premier Book House, 1957), p. xiii.

tradition. Is it the fact that the practice of breastfeeding children has generally declined, particularly with the introduction of milk formulae developed in the West and then transferred to other parts of the world? Because in most third world countries the awareness, discussion and dissemination of crucial issues such as the welfare and rights of children are in the hands of that section of the people who have adopted Western notions, fosterage and its connotations have never been brought to the forefront.

Islamic Law Regarding *Lakeets* or Foundlings

That the child has certain inalienable and inherent rights irrespective of the marital status of his/her parents is borne out by two important principles of Islamic law: first, the laws respecting *lakeets* or foundlings, and, second, that welfare of the minor is of paramount consideration.

Lakeet in its primitive sense signifies anything lifted from the ground: The term is generally used to denote an infant abandoned by some person on the highway. In the language of the law, it signifies a child abandoned by those to whom it properly belongs, from a fear of poverty or in order to avoid detection in whoredom.[42] The child is termed *lakeet* for the reason that it is eventually lifted from the ground from where this term is figuratively applied, even to the property that may happen to be found on it. The person who takes up a foundling is termed the *mooltakit* or taker-up.[43]

The taking up of a foundling is deemed laudable in Islam, and where the taker-up sees reason to apprehend that it may otherwise perish, the taking-up of it is incumbent.[44] The maintenance of a foundling is to be defrayed from the public treasury. The *mooltakit* is not to exact any return from the foundling on account of his maintenance because in maintaining him he acts gratuitously, as he has no authority over him.[45] The law relating to *lakeets* or foundlings reinforces the principle of child rearing being an act of social responsibility and one that is obligatory upon the government and those in authority.

Concept of Father as Natural Guardian of the Child

There is a widely prevalent misconception among Muslims generally that the father is the sole 'natural' guardian of his children and the mother is only entitled to *hizanat* (custody) of a minor son up to seven years of age and a minor daughter up to puberty, provided she is of 'good' character and is not married to a person outside the prohibited degrees of relationship.[46]

---

[42] Ibid., p. 206.
[43] Ibid.
[44] Ibid.
[45] Ibid.
[46] S. S. Ali and M. N. Azam, 'Trends of the Superior Courts of Pakistan in Custody and Guardianship Cases (1947–92) – An Analysis' (Working Paper, Women And Law Project, Lahore, ShirkatGah, 1993).

The best interests of minors are usually qualified by religious arguments that welfare of minors alone, however, is to be the guiding factor in deciding matters of custody by the court, or that decisions as to who gets custody of a minor is to be determined by the personal law rules of the father of the minor.

One does not come across any verse of the Quran establishing the father as the sole legal guardian. However, there is a saying of the Prophet Mohammed (PBUH), which is an extract of his sermon on the occasion of the Last Pilgrimage (Hijjat-ul-Widah) to the effect that "The child belongs to him/her on whose bed it is born." Within the patriarchal setup of society, the man (in this case the husband) has to provide the household effects including the bed on which the child is born. It is therefore inferred that the child belongs to the father. This is in line with the earlier mentioned Islamic law argument of the father being made to pay for feeding and rearing his child even if it be by the child's own mother. But it may be argued here that these injunctions/ recommendations are always prefaced by the economic superiority of the man. The question that we would like to pose here is: What would be the position if one were to reverse situations and the woman/mother was the breadwinner/provider of the family? Another thought that surfaces here is that in the Quranic verses on joint parental obligations regarding child rearing, the emphasis is on consensus. If the father was sole 'owner' of the child, it would enable him to exercise arbitrary powers within these relationships and the best interests of the child would not be of primary consideration as it presently is.

That some Muslim jurisdictions have moved beyond the notions of classical Islamic law is evident in a study of 50 years of review of case law from the superior courts of Pakistan. A perusal of case law in the area of custody and guardianship reflects a divergence from the traditional notion of the father as the guardian of the child. In the vast majority of cases reviewed, it became evident that courts in Pakistan do not often distinguish between the terms, 'custody' (which both parents may hold), and 'guardianship' (which the father or other male relative has the right to). The result is that mothers have been granted what are effectively guardianship rights of their minor children, a trend that belies classical Islamic law.[47]

Children Born out of Wedlock

Although religious laws as well as constitutional provisions provide for complete equality to all children irrespective of status, birth, and so on, in actual fact religious, legal and cultural support for discrimination towards

---

[47] Ibid. For further details, see case studies of Jordan, Morocco, and Mauritania later in this chapter.

illegitimacy places an infant/child born out of wedlock at risk of both infanticide and abandonment. All major works on Islamic law draw a sharp distinction between the legal status of legitimate as opposed to children born out of wedlock. It is named after the mother, is debarred from inheritance from its father and is an outcast in society. The question arises: Is it in keeping with the principles of justice that a child is made to carry the burden of his/her parents' circumstances/actions? And what about a child born out of rape, where the mother was herself the victim of an offence? In the light of *Hudood* laws in some Muslim jurisdictions, can any woman claim that she is the mother of a child born out of wedlock and risk the severe penalty involved?

An analysis of some provisions of Islamic law, the CRC, and domestic legislation of some Muslim jurisdictions shows gaps between these legal regimes and the world view of the bulk of the population. Although compatibility within these may be worked out by developing a common legal value system in major areas if not in all, it is the social realities that are incompatible. A considerable percentage of the population of these countries operates in the informal sector; therefore, presence of formal legislation is of little or no use to them. Furthermore, enforceability of existing legislation is inadequate and in some cases, extremely poor. Gaining the confidence of the people at the grassroots level for any formal law-enforcing regime is an uphill task. Even progressive implementation of most rights will take an unknown number of years as a result of a lack of facilities/resources. Furthermore, for any measures undertaken for the protection, survival and development of the child to be successful, it is imperative to link it to the welfare of women. This includes: legislation ensuring survival and development of the child; maternity benefits to the mother; concept of child benefit provision of social security by compulsory social insurance; removal of illiteracy and provision for compulsory education.

At the level of the courts, it is fortunate that the concept of the best interests of the child is no doubt the dominant factor in judgements relating to custody and guardianship. But here, too, one encounters problems for children, especially minors in the custody of their mothers who have filed maintenance suits for themselves and the children. Although in the true patriarchal spirit, the father is conceived as the breadwinner and legally responsible for maintaining his minor children whether he has custody or not, it is often very difficult, despite a decree, to implement court orders. Evasion of responsibility by fathers deprives the child of the basic necessities of life.

The best interests of the child can only be met if each of the partners, family, society and State can fulfil their role in meeting their obligations to ensure that the 'due' rights are given to children. If a child-centred perspective is adopted at all levels, it is entirely possible that laws and values, be they secular or religious, can be harmonized and adjusted to put 'children first' as visible assets that need equitable, quality care and opportunities to maximize their potential.

II. THE CONTEXT FOR LEGAL REFORM – PAST AND PRESENT: AN OVERVIEW OF CONTEMPORARY 'MUSLIM' STATE PRACTICE AND RESPONSE TO INTERNATIONAL HUMAN RIGHTS LAW

Muslims today account for approximately 1 billion of the world population and are spread across continents, regions and countries of which 57 are members of the Organization of the Islamic Conference (OIC).[48] Not all OIC Member States are termed 'Muslim' jurisdictions, either because Islam is not the state religion or because less than 70 per cent of the population professes the Muslim faith.

A cursory glance at the membership of the OIC reflects a rich range and diversity of countries brought together on the basis of the Islamic religion. Simultaneously, these countries are independent sovereign States[49] with their own constitutions and legislative bodies as well as adjudicating forums that vary from each other to a greater or smaller extent.[50] Some commonalities, however, exist despite the variation. Thus, all Muslim jurisdictions subscribe to the Islamic law of personal status and jealously guard this area as the 'last bastion' of an Islamic identity.[51] Marriage, divorce, inheritance and

---

[48] The OIC is an international organization with headquarters in Jeddah, the Kingdom of Saudi Arabia. It was founded in September 1969, when Heads of States and governments of Islamic countries assembled in Rabat, Kingdom of Morocco, to deplore the act of arson in the Holy Al-Aqsa Mosque and to declare their firm resolve to close ranks and to consult together, with a view to promoting close cooperation among themselves in the economic, political, cultural, and spiritual fields. The number of member countries went up from the 25 founders to the present 57. These include Afghanistan, Albania, Algeria, Azerbaijan, Bahrain, Bangladesh, Benin, Brunei, Burkina Faso, Cameroon, Chad, Comoros, Djibouti, Egypt, Gabon, Gambia, Guinea, Guinea-Bissau, Guyana, Indonesia, Iran, Iraq, Libyan Arab Jamahiriya, Jordan, Kazakhstan, Kuwait, Kyrgyzstan, Lebanon, Malaysia, Maldives, Mali, Mauritania, Morocco, Mozambique, Niger, Nigeria, Oman, Pakistan, Palestine, Qatar, Saudi Arabia, Senegal, Sierra Leone, Somalia, Sudan, Surinam, Syria, Tajikistan, Togo, Tunisia, Turkey, Turkmenistan, Uganda, United Arab Emirates, Uzbekistan, Yemen, and Cote d'Ivoire. Organization of the Islamic Conference, http://www.oic-oci.org (accessed 26 Nov. 2004).

[49] Barring Palestine.

[50] Variations range from the mode to the ideology of the State. An Islamic State may be a monarchy, or a democracy (parliamentary or presidential, and so on); the constitution may declare Islam as a state religion or the country may term itself a republic. Colonial influences do colour the nature of the State. Thus, Francophone Islamic States have a different legal system to Anglophone ones. Ethnic and racial differences also bear upon the State and its institutions as well as the formula of power sharing.

[51] Turkey is seen as an exception in that it is an avowedly secular State, polygamy is banned, and marriage is a civil ceremony under the law. Yet the lived experiences of people are different from this 'official' approach. At the other end of the spectrum lie countries such as Saudi Arabia and Iran that may be singled out for strict adherence to Islamic tenets in

succession, custody and guardianship of children are governed by principles of Islamic law, in some cases without resort to formal legislation.[52] Simultaneously, Muslim jurisdictions subscribe to legal pluralism, in which principles of Islamic law coexist in a rather uneasy relationship with customary norms and what may be termed as 'secular' regulatory frameworks. Female genital mutilation, depriving women of inheritance, forcing girls into marriage against their will, boy preference and prohibiting female children from acquiring education are customary practices that are antithetical to the injunctions of Islam. Yet most countries calling themselves Muslim jurisdictions do acquiesce to some or all of these and other practices in the name of custom, culture and tradition. Adherence to these customary practices become serious violations of a child's right, especially of the girl child as she is deprived of her childhood and development rights.

A further common factor of Muslim countries is their common colonial[53] and post-colonial experiences that impact on the degree to which legal pluralism is embedded in their socio-legal culture and institutional practice. Finally, Islamic countries have an uneven relationship with Western democratic modes of governance and international conventions on human rights adopted by the United Nations, which is evidenced by the initial reluctance to become States parties and subsequently to qualify their accession with reservations in the name of Islam.[54]

In light of this reluctance, how might we interpret the attitude of Muslim States to international human rights instruments? Are reservations to these conventions indicative of a normative conflict defying engagement on the basis that Islamic law reigns supreme, or are there any core human rights values common to both sets of legal traditions?[55] The recent waves of 'revivalism' and political resurgence in the Islamic world raise some very fundamental questions about the attitude of Muslim States towards the present international legal order in general and international human rights law in

public and private affairs. Yet, the reality is that the governments of these countries have modern-day attributes of governance.

[52] Bahrain, Sultanate of Oman, the State of Qatar, and the Kingdom of Saudi Arabia are examples of unlegislated personal status norms derived from Islamic law. A few examples of Muslim personal status laws in Islamic countries include: The Muslim Personal Law Act (1991) (Sudan); The Family Law Act (1986) (Iran); The Code of Personal Status (1959) (Iraq) (which has now been modified); Jordanian Law of Personal Status (1976) (Jordan); The Syrian Law of Personal Status (1953); and The Muslim Family Laws Ordinance (1961) (Pak.).

[53] Other than Saudi Arabia and Afghanistan, which were never formally colonized.

[54] The majority of accessions by Muslim States to human rights instruments such as the CRC and CEDAW have come about in the decade of the 1990s and these, too, with sweeping reservations, entered in the name of 'Islamic tradition'.

[55] For a detailed analysis of this question, see 'Freedom of Religion versus Equality in International Human Rights Law: Conflicting Norms or Hierarchical Human Rights? (A Case Study of Pakistan)', *Nordic J. for Hum. Rts.* 21 (2003): pp. 404–29.

particular. For instance, does this resurgence imply and include an Islamic theory of external relations based on exclusivity? If so, then surely any collaboration in areas including subscribing to human rights norms emanating from the United Nations would be ruled out.

Moinuddin in his well-argued book[56] declares such an eventuality as untenable. He is of the opinion that, "... by agreeing to conduct their relations with other States on the basis of equality and reciprocity, Islamic States have abandoned a fundamental, theological, and legal doctrine."[57] In addition to the Quran and *Sunna*, Muslim jurists have employed several sources to construct the classical edifice of the *siyar*, or Islamic international law.[58] These include treaties and agreements made by Muslim rulers with non-Muslims,[59] official instructions of the Caliphs given to commanders in the field and other state officials,[60] writings of eminent Muslim jurists embodying legal opinion on matters of *siyar*,[61] arbitral awards,[62] internal legislation of Muslim States regulating matters of *siyar* and unilateral declarations of a Muslim State with regard to *siyar*[63] and custom and usage.[64] It has been contended that the sources of *siyar*, if interpreted in modern terms, conform generally to the same categories as defined by modern jurists and specified in Article 38(1) of the Statute of the International Court of Justice (ICJ).[65]

Current practice of Muslim States also lends credence to the emerging universality of principles of international law including human rights norms. It may be argued that a well-established trend among Muslim States today is the full acceptance of and participation in the UN system to contribute to the development of universally acceptable principles of international law. Muslim States have, since the inception of the United Nations, actively collaborated in drafting human rights instruments, including the

---

[56] H. Moinuddin, *The Charter of the Islamic Conference and Legal Framework of Economic Co-operation Among Its Member States* (Oxford: Clarendon Press, 1987).

[57] Ibid., p.14.

[58] See M. Khadduri, *The Islamic Law of Nations: Shaybani's Siyar* (Baltimore: Johns Hopkins University Press, 1966), p. 8.

[59] M. Hamidullah, *The Muslim Conduct of State* (Lahore: Sh. Muhammad Ashraf, 7th edn., 1987), pp. 18, 32; Khadduri, ibid., 142–57.

[60] Hamidullah, ibid., pp. 18, 299–311; Khadduri, ibid., pp. 75–94.

[61] Hamidullah, ibid., pp. 18, 23–8; Khadduri, ibid., pp. 8–9.

[62] Hamidullah, ibid., pp. 153–6.

[63] Ibid., p. 33.   [64] Ibid., pp. 34–7.

[65] Moinuddin, op. cit., p. 16. The Statute of the ICJ declares that the function of the Court is to decide disputes submitted to it in accordance with international law by applying: "(a) international conventions, whether general or particular, establishing rules expressly recognised by the contesting parties; (b) international custom, as evidence of a general practice accepted as law; (c) the general principles of law recognised by civilised nations; (d) subject to the provisions of article 59, judicial decisions and the teachings of the most highly qualified publicists of the various nations, as subsidiary means for the determination of rules of law." Statute of the International Court of Justice (1945), Art. 38(1).

UDHR,[66] ICESCR,[67] ICCPR,[68] the CRC[69] and CEDAW,[70] and ratified these important treaties. Whereas the International Bill of Rights (comprised of the UDHR, ICESCR and ICCPR) provides the foundation upon which the international system for the protection and promotion of human rights has been developed equally for men and women, CEDAW focuses on the discrimination aspect of the implementation of universal rights and highlights the concept of equality of rights for women. It was adopted to reinforce provisions of existing human rights instruments to combat the continuing discrimination against women. In fact, CEDAW represents the culmination of efforts to develop the international norm of non-discrimination on the basis of sex and has been ratified by many Muslim States. This treaty is seen as a major breakthrough in international human rights because it recognizes the need to go beyond legal documents to address factors that will help eradicate de facto inequality between men and women.[71]

The CRC is the 'children's treaty' focusing on the survival, protection, participation and development of all children, irrespective of their sex, origin, race and status of their parents, and all Muslim States are parties to it.[72] The linkages between the CRC and CEDAW lie in the fact that the girl child is a common beneficiary of both treaties and may act as the final catalyst in concretising women's human rights. The Vienna Conference of 1993 and the Beijing Conference of 1995 endorse this point of view, recognizing that "the

---

[66] GA Res. 217A (III), U.N. Doc. A/810 (1948), p. 71, *adopted* 10 Dec. 1948. Reprinted in *Am. J Int'l L* 43 (Supp. 1949): p. 127.

    For an interesting discussion on the subject, see generally J. Kelsay, 'Saudi Arabia, Pakistan, and the Universal Declaration of Human Rights' in *Human Rights and the Conflict of Cultures: Western and Islamic Perspectives on Religious Liberty*, ed. D. Little, J. Kelsay, and A. A. Sachedina (Columbia: University of South Carolina Press, 1988), pp. 33–52.

[67] G.A. res. 2200A (XXI), 21 U.N. GAOR Supp. (No. 16) at 49, U.N. Doc. A/6316 (1966), 993 U.N.T.S. 3, *adopted* 16 Dec. 1966 and *entered into force* 3 Jan. 1976. Reprinted in 6 *ILM* (1967): p. 360.

[68] G.A. res. 2200A (XXI), 21 U.N. GAOR Supp. (No. 16) at 52, U.N. Doc. A/6316 (1966), 999 UNTS 171, *adopted* 16 Dec. 1966 and *entered into force* 23 Mar. 1976. Reprinted in 6 *ILM* (1967): p. 368.

[69] Convention on the Rights of the Child, Convention on the Rights of the Child, G.A. res. 44/25, annex, *adopted* 20 Nov. 1989, 44 U.N. GAOR Supp. (No. 49) at 167, U.N. Doc. A/44/49 (1989), *entered into force* 2 Sept. 1990. Reprinted in 28 *ILM* (1989): p. 1448.

[70] G.A. res. 34/180, *adopted* 18 Dec. 1979, 34 U.N. GAOR Supp. (No. 46) at 193, U.N. Doc. A/34/46, *entered into force* 3 Sept. 1981. For a detailed analysis of the drafting process of CEDAW, see L. A. Rehof, *Guide to the Travaux Preparatoires of the United Nations Convention on the Elimination of All Forms of Discrimination against Women* (Dordrecht: Martinus Nijhoff, 1993); J. Connors, 'The Women's Convention in the Muslim World', in *Feminism and Islam. Legal and Literary Perspectives*, ed. M. Yamani (Reading: Ithaca Press, 1996), pp. 351–76.

[71] S. S. Ali, *Gender and Human Rights in Islam and International Law Equal before Allah, Unequal Before Man?* (The Hague: Kluwer Law International, 2000), p. 212 [*Unequal Before Man?*].

[72] Except Somalia.

full implementation of the human rights of women and the girl child (is) an inalienable, integral and indivisible part of all human rights and fundamental freedoms."[73] As Savitri Goonesekere states:

> This is a powerful development linking the Vienna and Beijing Declarations and commitments. Both sets of rights have their foundations in international human rights, and it is clear that gender equality cannot be realised without eliminating discrimination against the girl children.... A positive environment therefore has been created for developing strategies and plans of action which recognise that the realisation of children's rights and the human rights of women are intrinsically linked, both because the core agenda is one of human rights, and because gender inequality cannot be addressed without linking women's issues to the issue of equality of the girl child.[74]

Another dimension of vital importance in this discussion is that the CRC has developed a framework that recognizes the indivisibility of socio-economic and civil and political rights. This is crucial to affording women the full range of rights in all phases of their life cycle and in turn leads to the remarkable conclusion that were (girl) children afforded equal rights from birth to the first 18 years of their life, their rights as women would surely follow.[75]

In assessing the approach of Muslim States to the CRC, CEDAW and other human rights instruments, it is also important to recall that the principle of *pacta sunt servanda* is entrenched as a religiously sanctioned norm in the Quran – the primary source of Islamic law. Hence, if a Muslim State has given its consent to human rights treaties, it incurs the strict legal obligation to honour it both in international law as well as to ensure enforcement at home.[76]

Another dimension of this 'inclusionary' approach on human rights in Muslim state practice is the trend to present alternative human rights documents from a Muslim perspective. Since the adoption of the UDHR as the foundational human rights document emanating from the United Nations, Islamic scholars, politicians and official statements of governments of Muslim States have declared human rights as a basic norm of the Islamic tradition. Over the years, and in response to international human rights instruments, parallel documents offering the Islamic contribution and perspective to human rights have emerged. These include the Cairo Declaration on Human Rights in Islam (the Cairo Declaration),[77] the Tehran

---

[73] Vienna Declaration and Programme of Action, *adopted* by the World Conference on Human Rights on 25 June 1993, para. 18, U.N. Doc. A/CONF.157/23, 12 July 2003.

[74] S. Goonesekere, 'The Links between the Human Rights of Women and Children: Issues and Directions' (keynote address at the consultation meeting of UNICEF, IWRAW, Save the Children Alliance, New York, 21 Jan. 1998), p. 8.

[75] Ali, *Unequal Before Man?*, op. cit., p. 217.

[76] J. Schacht, 'Islamic Law in Contemporary States' *Am. Jf Comp.* L 8 (1959): p. 139.

[77] Adopted by Resolution No. 49/19-P, Doc. A/45/421. S/21797, by the Nineteenth Islamic Conference of Foreign Ministers (Session of Peace, Interdependence and Development),

Declaration on the Role of Women in Islamic Societies (the Tehran Declaration)[78] and the Islamabad Declaration on the Role of Muslim Women Parliamentarians in the Promotion of Peace, Progress and Development of Islamic Societies (the Islamabad Declaration),[79] adopted from the platform of OIC. The fourth document, entitled the Universal Islamic Declaration of Human Rights (UIDHR),[80] although not officially representing the views of Muslim States, is the result of the work of a group of eminent Muslim scholars and has been widely disseminated internationally.[81] Scholarly work on human rights by Muslim authors also will be discussed.

The UIDHR was adopted on 19 September 1981 by the Islamic Council. The foreword of this document states that it "is based on the Qur'an and Sunnah and has been compiled by eminent Muslim scholars, jurists and representatives of Islamic movements and thought."[82] The UIDHR does not take note of any international human rights document, treaty or convention recalling in its preambular statements, only the Islamic tradition. It consists of a preamble and 23 articles. It is proposed to discuss three of these articles, that is, Articles 3, 19 and 20, in an attempt to ascertain the degree of divergence between the UIDHR and similar documents adopted at the United Nations.

Article 3, entitled 'Right to Equality and Prohibition Against Impermissible Discrimination', has three subsections, stating the following:

a) All persons are equal before the Law and are entitled to equal opportunities and protection of the Law.
b) All persons shall be entitled to equal wage for equal work.
c) No person shall be denied the opportunity to work or be discriminated against in any manner or exposed to greater physical risk by reason of religious belief, colour, race, origin, sex or language.

held in Cairo, Egypt, 31 July–5 Aug. 1990). Full text can be found in the Annex of the Resolution.

[78] Adopted by the OIC Symposium of Experts on the Role of Women in the Development of Islamic Society, held in Tehran, Iran, 17–19 Apr. 1995 in accordance with resolution 10/7-C(IS) of the Seventh Islamic Summit Conference.

[79] Published in *Newsheet*, Vol. VII-3 (Shirkatgah, Pakistan, 1995), pp. 3–5.

[80] 21 *Dhul Qaidah* (1981): *1401, adopted* 19 Sept. 1981 by the Islamic Council in Paris [UIDHR]. The text of the UIDHR may be accessed at http://www.alhewar.com/ISLAMDECL.html.

[81] The Arab Charter of Human Rights is another document emanating from a group of Muslim States. Council of the League of Arab States, Res. 5437 (102nd regular session), 15 Sept. 1994. Reprinted in *Hum. Rts. LJ* 18 (1997): 151. This Charter has not yet come into force. The 22 Member States of the League of Arab States are Jordan, United Arab Emirates, Bahrain, Tunisia, Algeria, Djibouti, Saudi Arabia, Sudan, Syrian Arab Republic, Somalia, Iraq, Oman, Palestine, Qatar, Comoros, Kuwait, Lebanon, Libyan Arab Jamahiriya, Egypt, Morocco, Mauritania, and Yemen.

[82] UIDHR, op. cit., forward. Presented by Salem Azzam, Secretary General of the Islamic Council in Paris.

What appears to be problematic here is the phrase 'impermissible discrimination', giving the impression that, where permissible, discrimination will be permitted. The inference that may be drawn here is that on literal, traditional readings of the religious text in Islam, women may be discriminated against. The implications of Article 3, therefore, do not bode well for the norm of non-discrimination on the basis of sex.[83]

The next provision of the UIDHR affecting the status of women is Article 19 outlining the 'Right to Found a Family and Related Matters'. Divergence between current human rights documents is evident from the opening statement of this article, which declares that:

> every person is entitled to marry, to found a family and to bring up children in conformity with his religion, traditions and culture. Every spouse is entitled to such rights and privileges and carries such obligations as are stipulated by the Law.[84]

Within the Islamic legal tradition, a Muslim woman may only marry a Muslim male whereas a Muslim male may marry not only a Muslim woman but also a woman professing one of the revealed religions (*kitabia*).[85] Right to mutual consideration and respect in marriage is provided in Article 19(b), whereas Article 19(c) establishes the husband as head of the household by obligating him to maintain his wife and children.[86]

Article 19(h) of the UIDHR provides for sharing obligations and responsibilities within the family. This provision differs from Article 16(d) of CEDAW in that it stands qualified by the phrase " . . . to share . . . according to their sex, their natural endowments, talents and inclinations, bearing in mind their common responsibilities toward their progeny and their relatives."[87] Article 19(i) appears in line with UN human rights provisions in stating, "No person

---

[83] For a similar line of argument, see A. E. Mayer, *Islam and Human Rights Tradition and Politics* (Boulder, CO: Westview Press, 1998), pp. 102–9.

[84] UIDHR, op. cit., Art. 19(a). The explanatory note provided states that "the term 'Law' denotes the *Shariah*, i.e., the totality of ordinances derived from the *Quran* and *Sunna* and any other laws that are deduced from these two sources by methods considered valid in Islamic jurisprudence."

[85] Cf. article 16(1) of the UDHR, which provides that: "Men and women of full age, without any limitation due to race, nationality or religion, have the right to marry and found a family." Article 16 of CEDAW provides that: "States Parties shall take appropriate measures to eliminate discrimination against women in all matters relating to marriage and family relations and in particular shall ensure, on a basis of equality of men and women: a) the same rights to enter into marriage."

[86] Cf. discussion in the Quran, Verse 4:34, stating that men are providers and maintainers of women because they are obligated to provide for them out of their earnings.

[87] Cf. Article 16(d) of CEDAW provides for "The same rights and responsibilities as parents, irrespective of marital status, in matters relating to their children; in all cases the interest of the children shall be paramount."

may be married against his or her will, or lose or suffer diminution of legal personality on account of marriage."[88]

Article 29 of the Universal Declaration of Human Rights (UDHR) makes a detailed provision on rights of married women, including providing a wife the right to residence in her husband's house, to receive maintenance during the marriage and for the period of *iddat* following dissolution of the marriage, and the right to seek dissolution of the marriage and inheritance.[89]

The Cairo Declaration is an example of a human rights document formulated and adopted from an 'official' Islamic forum, namely the OIC on 5 August 1990. The Cairo Declaration consists of a preamble and 25 articles and is similar in tone and substance to the UIDHR. Article 1 lays down the principle of equality and non-discrimination by stating:

> All human beings are equal in terms of basic human dignity and basic obligations and responsibilities, without any discrimination on the grounds of race, colour, language, sex, religion, belief, political affiliation, social status or other considerations.[90]

Article 6 declares:

> woman is the equal to man in human dignity; and has rights to enjoy as well as duties to perform; she has her own civil entity and financial independence, and the right to retain her name and lineage.[91]

Article 6(b) is similar in formulation as Article 19(c) of the UIDHR making the husband responsible for the support and welfare of the family.

The Tehran Declaration and the Islamabad Declaration, among others, may be used as evidence of the emerging trend of women's and children's human rights instruments in Muslim States. These documents are distinctive in that the issues relating to the rights of Muslim women (impacting on the girl child) were debated, drafted and adopted by women – in conferences where rights of Muslim women were the focus of discussion. These Declarations are also important statements on Muslim women's perspectives regarding their human rights prior to the Beijing Conference held in September 1995.

The first of these conferences was the OIC Symposium of Experts on the Role of Women in the Development of Islamic Society, held in Tehran, Islamic

---

[88] Cf. Article 16(2) of the UDHR, which provides that "Marriage shall be entered into only with the free and full consent of the intending spouses." Article 16(b) of CEDAW makes a similar statement: "The same right freely to choose a spouse and to enter into marriage only with their free and full consent."

[89] The rights outlined in Article 20 are in keeping with traditional principles of Islamic law. See M. A. Mannan, *Mulla's Principles of Muhammadan Law* (Lahore: PLD Publishers, 1995); J. Nasir, *The Islamic Law of Personal Status* (London: Graham & Trotman, 1986).

[90] Cairo Declaration, op. cit., Art. 1(a).   [91] Ibid., Art. 6.

Republic of Iran from 17–19 April 1995.[92] Recommendations of the Symposium to the Twenty-third Conference of Islamic Foreign Ministers present a number of interesting points of departure from other documents coming from Muslim forums, including the UIDHR and the Cairo Declaration. The most prominent of these is reiterating the commitment of Member States of the OIC to the principles and objectives of the UN Charter.[93] Moreover, the interdependence and indivisibility between civil and political, and economic, social and cultural rights are clearly acknowledged and upheld.[94] The recognition of the element of 'cultural' Islam and the manner in which it has adversely affected the rights and status of women in Muslim countries also has been underscored, coupled with the need to reject adverse cultural encroachments detrimental to the identity and personality of Muslim women.[95] This commitment is further elucidated by demanding the:

> eradication of all forms of violence and exploitation of women, including domestic violence, sexual exploitation, pornography, prostitution, trafficking in women, sexual harassment, genital mutilation and other negative traditional and cultural practices.[96]

'Genital mutilation', a stronger term than female circumcision that has been used to describe the practices so often ascribed to the Islamic tradition, is sought to be discontinued. Special protection for pregnant and nursing mothers is also demanded, but the fact that women's roles are not confined to motherhood is also made clear by the need for:

> facilities to effectively meet the requirements of women and encourage their participation in public life thus enabling them to reconcile their family and professional responsibilities with their political rights and participation in decision making.[97]

A particularly groundbreaking provision of the recommendations is one that accepts the fact that women may be heads of households, thus moving away from the traditional statement of men alone are, or can be, providers

---

[92] This Symposium was organized in accordance with Resolution 10/7-C (IS), adopted by the seventh Islamic Summit Conference. Delegates from 34 Islamic countries participated in the deliberations. Three documents were submitted to the Seminar: 'Recommendations of the Seminar to the Twenty-third Islamic Conference of Foreign Ministers'; 'Principles presented as Guidelines to the Fourth World Conference on Women in Beijing'; and the 'Tehran Declaration on the Role of Women in the Development of Islamic Society'. The author led the Pakistan delegation and was elected Rapporteur for the conference.

[93] See 'Recommendations of the Symposium of Experts on the Role of Women in the Development of Islamic Society to the Twenty-Third Islamic Conference of Foreign Ministers' (1995), preamble.

[94] Ibid.   [95] Ibid., para. 1.4.

[96] Ibid., para. 1.6.   [97] Ibid., para. 1.8.

and maintainers of households.[98] Another important demand articulated in the recommendations is for "facilitating and enhancing women's full access to appropriate, readily available and free quality health care and related services and facilities, including family planning, reproductive and maternal and infant health in the context of Islamic principle," thus ruling out the position by some that Islam prohibits family planning.[99] The importance of education as an effective tool of empowerment is underscored as is the recognition of women's roles as *Mujtahid*.[100] The 23 points in the recommendations are condensed in the Tehran Declaration for consideration of the Twenty-third Conference of Foreign Ministers of the OIC.

The Islamabad Declaration was adopted at the first Muslim Women Parliamentarians' Conference in Islamabad on 1–3 August 1995.[101] The main objective of the conference was to allow women parliamentarians from Muslim countries to meet to forge closer links and develop deeper understanding of the problems facing Muslim women. This conference, too, like the Tehran Symposium, was significant in its timing, coming just before the Beijing Conference.[102] It adopted the Islamabad Declaration.

Similar to the Tehran Declaration, the striking feature of the Islamabad Declaration is the reiteration of recognition of, and commitment to, international human rights instruments affecting women. It resolves to "promote the implementation, as appropriate, of the provisions of international conventions on the rights of women and urge all countries to adhere to these conventions."[103] It may be argued that by specifically taking note of human rights conventions affecting women's rights, the Islamabad Declaration appears to be formulating an 'operative' Islamic international law norm of non-discrimination on the basis of sex, evidence of which was barely visible in either the UIDHR or the Cairo Declaration.

A further outstanding feature of the Islamabad Declaration lies in its recognition of Muslim women's rights to participation in public and political life and decision making, including the right to become Head of State and

---

[98] "Provision of necessary financial and social support and protection and empowerment of women heads of household ... " Ibid., para. 1.15.

[99] Ibid., para. 1.18.

[100] A person with the capacity to engage in independent legal reasoning. This process is known as *ijtihad*. Tehran Declaration, op. cit., para. 1.3.

[101] Thirty-five high-level delegations from Muslim countries participated. These included representatives from among others: Pakistan, Libya, Chad, Malaysia, Oman, Azerbaijan, Morocco, Syria, Yemen, Albania, Algeria, Kyrgyzstan, Iraq, Bangladesh, Egypt, Palestine, Jordan, Senegal, Iran, Indonesia, Sudan, Turkish Republic of Northern Cyprus, Turkey, and a representative of the International Parliamentary Union. The author was a member of the Pakistan delegation to this conference.

[102] Official report prepared by the Conference Secretariat, reprinted in *Newsheet*, op. cit., p. 1.

[103] Ibid., at p. 4.

government.[104] This pronouncement, it is submitted, may also be employed as evidence of an emerging 'operative' Islamic law regarding women's right to public life.

Building upon the Tehran Declaration (although the connection between the two documents was not made officially), the Islamabad Declaration seeks to establish the interdependence and indivisibility of all three generations of rights. The Islamabad Declaration also sought to echo the linkage and interdependence now being sought within the UN system between the CRC and CEDAW. To this end, the Islamabad Declaration seeks: "To promote and protect the human rights of women at all stages of their life cycle in the true spirit of Islam."[105] A further commonality between the provisions of the Tehran and Islamabad Declarations, and those of human rights documents adopted at the United Nations, is the emphasis on women's central role within the family and the family itself as the basic unit of society.[106]

Both the Tehran and Islamabad Declarations acknowledge the fact that presently laws in Muslim countries do not accord equal rights to women and call for working to promulgate laws supportive of women's positive role and rights in society: "We will make special efforts to abrogate discriminatory laws, as well as cultural and customary practices so that our society can advance on an egalitarian and just basis."[107] To this end, current human rights issues arising out of adverse cultural practices towards women also have been addressed, for example, violence against women.[108]

As compared to the UIDHR and the Cairo Declaration, the Islamabad and Tehran Declarations present a tone and terminology that is closer to the women's rights language of the United Nations. A number of articles of the latter Declarations present similarity with human rights instruments emanating from the United Nations. But, alongside these similarities, some differences are also discernible, the most pronounced being the fact that interdependence of rights and obligations is both brought into prominence in the human rights documents presented from Muslim forums. That is not to argue, however, that UN human rights documents lack the

---

[104] Cf. Tabandeh's view that women are not allowed in public life. Also note the *Hadith*, where it is stated "Those who entrust their affairs to a woman will never know prosperity."

[105] Islamabad Declaration, op. cit., p. 3. para. (a).

[106] See Preamble of the Islamabad Declaration stating that "Recognising that woman, as enshrined in the *Quran* and *Sunnah*, is the centre of the family which is the basic unit of society and hence the cornerstone of the edifice of a stable, peaceful and prosperous polity." UN human rights instruments articulate similar formulations. See, for example, ICCPPR, op. cit., Art. 23; ICESCR, op. cit., Art. 10.

[107] Islamabad Declaration, op. cit., p. 3; Tehran Declaration, op. cit., paras. 1.4 and 1.6.

[108] Islamabad Declaration, op. cit., p. 4 "sustained efforts to end suppression, discrimination and violence against women in all forms especially domestic violence, women in armed conflict and crisis situations." Tehran Declaration, op. cit., para. 1.6.

element of corresponding obligations; the distinction appears one of where the emphasis lies.

Furthermore, obligations of States parties as opposed to individuals as key participants in the fulfilment of rights appears the norm presented in UN human rights instruments. This lack of emphasis on private actors has been critiqued on the basis that beyond state institutions, it is in the private sphere and at the level of society and community that human rights are denied to women. By contrast, 'Islamic' human rights documents place responsibility squarely on the shoulders of recipients of these rights, that is, individuals within the State, as well as state structures and institutions.

Among contemporary Muslim scholars, Syed Abu'l A'la Mawdudi, a Pakistani and founder of the right-wing Islamic party, the Jamaat-i-Islami, has written and spoken prolifically on the subject. In his much publicized pamphlet, *Human Rights in Islam*,[109] Mawdudi takes as his point of departure the human rights documents of the 'West' and, more specifically, the United Nations. He criticizes them as inadequate and late entrants in the field where Islam had already granted human rights since seventh-century Arabia.[110] Mawdudi's list of fundamental human rights includes the right to life, right to the safety of life, respect for the chastity of women, right to a basic standard of life, the individual's right to freedom, right to justice, equality of all human beings, right to cooperate and right not to cooperate.[111] Mawdudi also devotes Chapter 4 of his pamphlet to rights of citizens in an Islamic State. He enumerates a list of 15 rights of citizens in an Islamic State using gender-neutral language implying the application of these rights to both men and women.[112]

Another document to mention here and evidence of the multiplicity of interpretative positions adopted by Muslim scholars, States and institutions is a critique of the UDHR. Authored by Sultanhussein Tabandeh,[113] the document, *A Muslim Commentary on the Universal Declaration of Human Rights*,[114] was presented to representatives of Muslim countries

---

[109] A. A. Mawdudi, trans. K. Ahmed, *Human Rights in Islam* (Leicester: Islamic Foundation, 1980).

[110] Ibid., p. 15; this point is also emphasized by K. Ahmed in the foreword at p. 9.

[111] Ibid., chapter 3, entitled, 'Basic Human Rights', pp. 17–22.

[112] These rights are as follows: security of life and property, protection of honour, sanctity and sanctity of private life, security of personal freedom, right to protest against tyranny, freedom of expression, freedom of association, freedom of conscience and conviction, protection of religious sentiments, protection from arbitrary imprisonment, right to the basic necessities of life, equality before the law, rulers are not above the law, right to avoid sin, right to participate in affairs of the State. (Ibid., pp. 23–34.)

[113] A *Shia* scholar who inherited the leadership of the Nimatullahi Sufi order, a mystical brotherhood affiliated with the *Athna Asharyia* sect of *Shia* Islam.

[114] S. Tabandeh, trans. F. J. Goulding, *A Muslim Commentary on the Universal Declaration of Human Rights* (Guildford: Goulding, 1970).

attending the International Conference on Human Rights held in Tehran in 1968. Tabandeh, like Mawdudi, focuses on the prior claim to human rights by the Islamic religion. In his words, "Most of its (UDHR) provisions were already inherent in Islam, and were proclaimed by Islam's lawgivers and preceptors."[115] What sets Tabandeh's views apart from Mawdudi, in the words of Mayer, is that, "Tabandeh is exceptional in his forthright assertion that Islam opposed the idea of male-female equality."[116] Although Mawdudi does not call for rejecting human rights instruments formulated at the United Nations, Tabandeh is adamant that the Islamic sources of human rights are the only authoritative ones, and, where any discrepancies exist, the UDHR should be rewritten to make it conform to Islam.[117] He (Tabandeh) also castigates representatives of Muslim countries who were involved in drafting of the UDHR for not rejecting in particular Article 16, which provides for equal rights for men and women in matters of marriage and divorce and guarantees the right to marry without limitations due to race, nationality and religion.[118] In Tabandeh's opinion, a wife must obey her husband, consult his wishes, not go out of the house without his permission, take due care of the property, look after the household equipment, invite a guest only with her husband's agreement, uphold the family's good name and maintain her husband's good standing when he is present or absent.[119] In short, Tabandeh's exposition of women's rights and her status in Islam is, to a certain extent, representative of traditional and conservative Muslim writers and (male) Muslims alike.

Surveying the writings of Mawdudi, Tabandeh, UIDHR, Cairo, Tehran and Islamabad Declarations, the question arises: How representative of Muslim thought, belief and views are these forums and writings? This question does not lend itself to an easy response as it is a very complex problem indeed. What is evident, however, is the fact that male interpretations of the Islamic tradition with regard to women's rights are invariably more restrictive than women's forums in their formulations of similar issues. For instance, the Tehran Symposium, despite being hosted by Iran, a regime known worldwide for its strong religious conviction, sought to present the more positive side of rights for Muslim women.

At the same time, it has to be conceded that the documents reviewed fail to adequately spell out and address the problematic areas relating to women's rights in Islam. These areas awaiting deliberation include evidence rights of women, polygamy, divorce, inheritance rights, custody and guardianship of children and so on. What the Tehran and Islamabad Declarations have, however, achieved is to draw attention to these difficult areas by subsuming these

---

[115] Ibid., p. 1.   [116] Mayer, op. cit., p. 98.
[117] Tabandeh, op. cit., pp. 41–5 (commenting on Article 16 of the UDHR).
[118] Ibid., pp. 41–5.   [119] Ibid., p. 58.

under the heading of 'problems' sought to be resolved by Muslim women, or through progressive 'women-friendly' interpretations of religious texts considered as legitimate grounds for the human rights of Muslim women.

Outside these 'official' deliberations and documentation on women's human rights and status, recent years have witnessed a spurt of literature concerning women in Muslim societies from a philosophical, sociological, historical and (very few) from a legal perspective.[120] These works argue that the Islamic tradition is not a monolithic entity. On the basis of its main sources, namely, the Quran, *Hadith, Ijma* and *Qiyas*, Islamic law lends itself to a variety of interpretations that have far-reaching implications for women's human rights in Islam and rights of the girl child. The thesis of these studies is that the egalitarian aspect of Islam has been silenced by patriarchy, a task achieved by adopting a literalist as opposed to a progressive interpretation of the sources of Islamic law. Contrary to common perception, the *Shari'a* does not consist of an immutable, unchanging set of norms but has an inbuilt dynamism that is sensitive and susceptible to changing needs of time. A final factor affecting rights of women and the girl child is the disparity between the theoretical perspectives and its application in Muslim societies determined by elements of cultural practices, socio-economic realities and political expediencies on the part of governments.

The context for legal reform in the area of child rights therefore varies from one Muslim country to another but is essentially informed by the Islamic legal tradition. This fact is borne out by reservations of Muslim

---

[120] Some works on Muslim women include: L. Beck & N. Keddie, eds., *Women in the Muslim World* (Cambridge, MA: Harvard University Press, 1978); J. L. Esposito, *Women in Muslim Family Law* (Syracuse: Syracuse University Press, 1982); A. al-Hibri, 'A Study of Islamic Herstory: Or How Did We Ever Get into This Mess?' *Women's Stud. Int'l F.* 5 (1982): p. 207; B. Utas, ed., *Women in Islamic Societies* (London: Curzon Press, 1983); F. Hussain, ed., *Muslim Women* (New York: St. Martin's Press, 1984); F. Mernissi, *Beyond the Veil* (Bloomington: Indiana University Press, 1987); D. Kandiyoti, ed., *Women, Islam and the State* (London: Macmillan Academic and Professional Ltd., 1991); F. Mernissi, *Women and Islam*, trans. M. J. Lakeland (Oxford: Basil Blackwell, 1991); L. Ahmed, *Women and Gender in Islam: Historical Roots of a Modern Debate* (New Haven: Yale University Press, 1992); C. F. El-Solh and J. Mabro, eds., *Muslim Women's Choices* (Oxford: Berg Publishers, 1994). For a comprehensive list of research on Muslim women, see E. Fernea, 'Ways of Seeing Middle Eastern Women', *Women: A Cultural Review* 6(1) (1995): pp. 60–6; M. Yamani, ed., *Feminism and Islam. Legal and Literary Perspectives* (Reading: Ithaca Press, (1996); A. El Sonbol, *Women, the Family, and Divorce Laws in Islamic History* (Syracuse: Syracuse University Press, 1996). For a legal analysis of the Islamic legal tradition, see S. S. Ali, *Unequal Before Man?*, op. cit.; Riffat Hassan and Amina Wadud Mohsin approach the discourse on Muslim women from a theological perspective. Some of their works include: R. Hassan, 'The Role and Responsibilities of Women in the Legal and Ritual Tradition of Islam' (paper presented at a bi-annual meeting of a Trialogue of Jewish-Christian-Muslim scholars at the Joseph and Rose Kennedy Institute of Ethics, Washington, DC, 1980); A. Wadud-Muhsin, *Quran and Woman Re-Reading the Sacred Text from a Woman's Perspective* (Oxford: Oxford University Press, 1999).

States to the CRC and CEDAW where norms of *Shari'a* are cited as reasons for entering reservations. (See later discussion.)

The Legislative Reform Initiatives for Implementation of the CRC in Muslim Jurisdictions: A Historical Perspective

Of human rights treaties emanating from the United Nations, the CRC comes closest to universal ratification with 191 States parties (the United States and Somalia are the two countries that have not acceded to the CRC). This development has been described as remarkable especially in view of the relative novelty of the concept as well as a comprehensive documentation of the three generation of indivisible human rights.[121] What is equally noteworthy is the fact that countries that have not ratified the two Covenants (ICCPR and ICESCR) have nevertheless become parties to the CRC.

But does this near-universal acclamation denote universality of norms represented in the substantive provisions of the CRC? Some of the contentious issues debated during the drafting process and evident from a study of the *travaux preparatoires* reflect divergence in opinion among representatives of various States parties. Indeed, it is those very issues, translated as 'difficult' provisions, that emerged as reservations in the post-CRC period and remain contested terrain.

In the early stages of the drafting process, the 'North' was overrepresented, leading to the fear that the treaty would be a "heavily Northern-oriented text,"[122] but this was attenuated by active participation from a number of countries from the South, including many Muslim jurisdictions. Treaty formulations entail protracted debate and controversy, and the CRC was no exception. What is relevant for purposes of our discussion is the fact that those controversial provisions became the subject of reservations and impinge on the universality of child rights norms espoused in the CRC.

The first issue in question was definition of the minimum age of the child (whether childhood started at conception or at birth). The existing formulation of Article 1 was a compromise to get over this difficulty. The second problem area was the extent and scope of Article 14 regarding freedom of religion. Initially modelled on Article 18 of the ICCPR, which includes "the freedom to have or to adopt a religion... of his choice," this article was reworded to address the strong objections articulated by representatives of Muslim jurisdictions. They pointed out that in the Islamic tradition, a child who is born to Muslim parents does not have the right to change his or her religion. Another area where Muslim States parties raised objections was the

---

[121] H. J. Steiner and P. Alston, *International Human Rights in Context* (Oxford: Oxford University Press, 2nd edn., 2000), pp. 511–12.

[122] Cited in ibid., p. 513.

institution of adoption as conceptualized in the 'Western' legal tradition. The final example of controversial issues was the age at which children should be permitted to take part in armed conflict.

Reservations of OIC Member States to the CRC: An Analytical Overview

An overview of OIC States parties to the CRC shows an interesting pattern of positions adopted towards the substantive provisions of this treaty. Not all Member States have entered reservations and, of those that have, not all cite conflicting norms with Islamic law and *Shari'a* as reasons for reserving. This reflects the multiplicity of norms informing the Islamic legal tradition and lack of a unified interpretation of what constitutes 'Islamic'. Afghanistan, Algeria, Brunei Darussalam, Djibouti, Egypt, Iran, Iraq, Jordan, Kuwait, Mauritania, Morocco, Oman, Pakistan, Qatar, Saudi Arabia, Syrian Arab Republic and the United Arab Emirates have entered reservations in the name of Islam. Of these countries, Egypt[123] and Pakistan[124] withdrew their reservations on 31 July 2003 and 23 July 1997, respectively. Bangladesh, Indonesia, Malaysia, Mali, Tunisia and Turkey have not mentioned Islamic principles as the cause of their reservations but state constitutional and national laws, traditional values and custom as the motivation behind entering reservations. A third category of States have ratified the CRC without entering any reservations. These include Albania, Azerbaijan, Bahrain, Benin, Burkina Faso, Cameroon, Chad, Comoros, Gabon, Gambia, Guinea, Guinea-Bissau, Guyana, Kazakhstan, Kyrghyz Republic, Lebanon, Libyan Arab Jamahiriya, Mozambique, Niger, Nigeria, Senegal, Sierra Leone, Sudan, Suriname, Tajikistan, Togo, Turkmenistan, Uganda, Uzbekistan, Yemen and Cote d'Ivoire.

Are these reservations indicative of a wider ideological conflict between child rights as enunciated in the Islamic tradition and those articulated in the CRC, and, if so, are these differences irreconcilable? Furthermore, and more important, how does one account for weak commitment of many Muslim jurisdictions in areas of rights and entitlements where no incompatibility exists between the CRC and Islamic law particularly in the areas of health, education, clean drinking water and so on? Finally, what motivated Egypt and Pakistan to withdraw reservations entered in the name of Islam?

As indicated earlier, Jordan, Morocco and Mauritania have entered reservations to some or all of the provisions of the CRC.

---

[123] Egypt had reserved Articles 20 and 21 (relating to adoption) in the name of *Shari'a*. See CRC Reservations, op. cit.

[124] Pakistan had indicated in its reservation that it would interpret the provisions of the CRC in light of principles of Islamic law and values. Ibid.

Jordan clearly declares its position that it is reserving certain articles in the name of the Islamic religion by stating that: "The Hashemite Kingdom of Jordan expresses its reservation and does not consider itself bound by articles 14, 20 and 21 of the Convention, which grant the child the right to freedom of choice of religion and concern the question of adoption, since they are at variance with the precepts of the tolerant Islamic Shariah."[125]

Morocco, too, cites Islam as the motivating force behind its reservation: "The Kingdom of Morocco, whose Constitution guarantees to all the freedom to pursue his religious affairs, makes a reservation to the provisions of Article 14, which accords children freedom of religion, in view of the fact that Islam is the State religion."[126]

The reservation entered by Mauritania is a general reservation to the effect that: "In signing this important Convention, the Islamic Republic of Mauritania is making reservations to articles or provisions which may be contrary to the beliefs and values of Islam, the religion of the Mauritania People and State."[127]

One inference from this analysis of reservations to the CRC among OIC countries is very clear: that interpretation of what constitutes Islamic varies among jurisdictions. Therefore, measures towards effective implementation of the CRC, whether legislative, policy-oriented or among civil society, also vary as will be seen in the discussion of the legislative reform initiatives in these countries.

Legislative Reform Initiatives in Selected OIC Countries

This section draws upon a desk review of legislative reform undertaken by the United Nations' Children's Fund (UNICEF) Innocenti Research Centre, Florence, in January 2004; country studies by UNICEF as well as reports of States parties to the CRC; and Concluding Observations of the Committee on the Rights of the Child. In most OIC countries, a number of initiatives have been adopted to bring national legislation in conformity with the CRC. These range from adopting comprehensive children's codes to modifying existing legislation and ushering in child-friendly policies and are presented here.

Burkina Faso has not yet adopted a comprehensive child rights law but has taken some legislative measures in relation to social sector laws. Thus, under the 1996 Education Act (No. 13/96) education is compulsory from age six to sixteen; the Penal Code (No. 43/96) brings within its ambit offences such as crime against humanity, physical abuse of women and infringement

---

[125] Ibid.   [126] Ibid.
[127] Ibid.

of the right to marry. Forced marriages have been banned and stand penalized under article 234 of the Code on the Individual and Family and the Labour Code. In Egypt, a major legislative initiative towards implementing the CRC has been to adopt a Children's Code in 1996 under the auspices of the National Council for Children and Motherhood, which acts as an Ombudsman for children's complaints.[128]

The Libyan Arab Jamahiriya promulgated Act No. 2 of 1992 ratifying various conventions including the CRC, now an integral part of its national law. Two laws merit particular mention here as these legislative initiatives were adopted to bring national laws in conformity with the CRC: the 1991 Child Protection and Welfare Ordinance and the Child Protection Act 5 of 1997. The Libyan position is that, except for Article 21 of the CRC regarding adoption, there is no inconsistency between its laws and that of the CRC.

The Sudan, too, promulgated the Third Constitutional Decree of the revolution Command Council in 1989 to enable it to ratify the CRC and incorporate it into the national law upon ratification in 1990. In 1993, the Ministry of Justice underwent a review of all relevant laws to determine the consistency with the CRC and claimed its compatibility with national laws. Although Sudan is said to be considering enacting a children's code, that has not yet materialized. The 1997 Labour Act, however, is an important piece of legislation impacting on child rights.

Tunisia has passed a Child Protection Code in 1995, a major legislative measure to bring its national laws in conformity with the CRC. This is a comprehensive law covering a wide range of rights and protective services for children. Tunisia has, however, entered a general declaration that:

> The Government of the Republic of Tunisia declares that it shall not, in implementation of this Convention, adopt any legislative or statutory decision that conflicts with the Tunisian Constitution.

The reservation, too, reinforces the position that Tunisia considers its national legislation to have precedence over the CRC by stating that:

> The Government of the Republic of Tunisia enters a reservation with regard to the provisions of article 2 of the convention, which may not impede implementation of the provisions of its national legislation concerning personal status, particularly in relation to marriage and inheritance rights.

---

[128] Child Law 12, published in *Official Gazette* No. 13 (1996) (Egypt). The Code covers the following areas: definition of a child, respect for the opinions of the child, access to health, culture, education, provisions for foster mothers, access to care for handicapped children, child labour, juvenile justice, social security, and the creation of the National Council for Childhood and Motherhood.

In the case of Bangladesh, the CRC cannot override national law; the Constitution is the supreme law and takes precedence over national and international law. The CRC, however, does have persuasive value in courts and has been cited in child custody cases.[129] Bangladesh has not adopted a comprehensive child rights law, but a major legislative initiative has been the Suppression of Violence Against Women and Children Act 2000.

Legislative Reform Initiatives in Jordan, Morocco and Mauritania

This section draws upon UNICEF-commissioned studies of Jordan, Morocco and Mauritania under its Legislative Reform Initiative (LRI). All three countries identified have a predominant Muslim population and Islamic law has a preeminence in the legal system alongside civil and common law elements; hence, the need to dedicate a distinct chapter to *Shari'a*-based legal systems. Simultaneously, these 'Islamic' legal systems also fall within plural legal jurisdictions; hence the reference in this chapter to Jordan, Morocco and Mauritania as *Shari'a*-based and plural legal systems. The reviews of Jordan, Morocco and Mauritania provide valuable insights into issues of legislative reform for application and implementation of child rights emanating from the UN human rights treaty regime. They highlight commonalities and differences of approach of States parties sharing the Islamic legal tradition as well as secular traditions based upon colonial European legal systems and customary norms. The research reflects the complexities and difficulty inherent in the interplay of secular and religious normative traditions. It also brings to the fore the variation between sects and sub-sects of Islam. Jordan follows the Hanafi Sunni tradition, whereas Morocco and Mauritania are influenced by the Maliki school of juristic thought in Sunni Islam. Receded and confined to family law and issues of personal status, Islamic law is still the bedrock and *grundnorm* of regulation. So pervasive is the influence of Islamic law that even areas of legislation that appear independent of religion are nevertheless informed by it (in varying degrees and depth in the three countries under review, as will be indicated later). Any legislative reform initiative is therefore 'filtered' through the lens of the Islamic legal tradition but in the spirit of what I have described elsewhere as the 'operative Islamic law'.[130]

As indicated in the section on sources of Islamic law, Muslims are divided into two main sects: Sunni and Shia. Sunnis in turn are followers of

---

[129] Committee on the Rights of the Child, 'Second periodic reports of States parties due in 1997: Bangladesh', U.N. Doc. CRC/C/65/Add.22, 14 Mar. 2003.

[130] I develop and present this concept in my monograph, S. S. Ali, *Gender and Human Rights in Islam and International Law Equal before Allah, Unequal Before Man?* (The Hague: Kluwer Law International, 2000).

various juristic schools of thought, that is, Hanafi,[131] Maliki,[132] Shafei,[133] and Hanbali.[134] Shias are subdivided into Athna Asharia, Ismailis, and Zaidyas. From the perspective of evolving a child-friendly jurisprudence within the Islamic legal tradition, a point of significance is the fact that whereas there appear disparities among these schools of juristic thought on children's rights, legal status and similar issues, it has historically been possible to achieve the 'best possible combination' of legal rules by a process of cross-fertilization. The best known among these techniques are known as *talfiq*' or 'patchwork' whereby Muslim jurists pick rules of what they perceive to advance the interest of justice from among the various schools and create a patchwork of rules. Codes of personal status adopted in the nineteenth and twentieth centuries by a number of Muslim States are examples of this method. For instance, the Hanafi and Hanbali schools allow an adult Muslim woman to marry of her own accord without requiring the consent and presence of her male guardian (*wali*), whereas Maliki and Shafei schools require it. Modifications in the Moroccan personal status law have 'imported' this Hanafi rule. Likewise, the Hanafi school does not require adherence to the principle of *kafa'a* or doctrine of equality in status between two spouses, whereas Shafei and Maliki schools subscribe to it. All schools of thought (*Sunni* and *Shia* alike) agree that the mother has the first claim to custody of her infant. Difference of opinion exists between the schools as to when the period of a child's custody comes to an end. Thus, Hanafis declare that a mother keeps custody of a girl until she is nine years and of a boy until he is seven. The Malikis state that a mother loses custody upon the boy attaining puberty and upon a girl when she marries. The Hanbali school of thought fixes seven years for both girl and boy, and thereafter the child is given a choice between both parents. Finally, Shafeis do not hold out a fixed age limit for when a mother loses custody of her children. On attaining the 'age of discretion', the child is given an opportunity to decide which parent to live with.

---

[131] This school is named after its founder, Imama Abu Hanifa (d. 767). The school originated in Iraq and is also known as the Kufa school. The oldest and, in the opinion of many scholars, the most liberal, it has as its special characteristic its reliance on the principles of *Qiyas*. Abu Hanifa is known as the 'upholder of private judgement' or *ahl al rai'y*.

[132] The founder of this school is Imam malik ibn Anas (d. 795). This school is also called the 'Medina' school. Malik was inclined towards jurisprudence based on the Quran and *Hadith* rather than independent exercise of reason in interpretation.

[133] The founder of this school is Imam Shafei (d. 820), who was a pupil of Imam Malik. Shafei is regarded as the founder of the science of the classical theory of Islamic jurisprudence. He developed the doctrine of *ijma*.

[134] Named after Imam Ahmed ibn Hanbal. He strictly adhered to the principle of following the hadith literally and reacted strongly to *ahl al rai'y* or people of independent legal opinion.

These examples of diversity between the various schools of juristic thought in Islam reflect the potential for rich cross-fertilization and evolving norms on child rights that are in their best interest.

The Hashemite Kingdom of Jordan[135]

Jordan remained part of the Ottoman Empire until World War I and was then placed under an indirect form of British Mandate rule. The Ottoman legal system was retained. In 1927 many Ottoman laws were re-enacted with some modifications including the Ottoman Law of Family Rights 1917. The Hashemite Kingdom of Jordan was established as an independent State in 1947, with Islam as the state religion and Islamic law and *Shari'a* as the foundational sources of the legal system. The first constitution of Jordan was adopted in 1948, and a process of developing a national legal system to replace remnants of Ottoman rule was initiated. Both the 1948 and 1952 constitutions of Jordan declare Islam to be the state religion.

A provisional Law of Family Rights was adopted in 1947 and remained in force until it was replaced by the Law of Family Rights 1951.[136] The Jordanian Law of Family Rights 1951 was one of the first laws of personal status adopted in a number of newly independent Arab States. A new constitution was adopted in 1952 that retained the jurisdiction of Islamic law in the area of personal status. The Jordanian Law of Personal Status also was enacted in 1952 revising the earlier law and providing for a comprehensive code while retaining reference to the classical Hanafi rules in the absence of a specific reference in the text.

All Muslim jurisdictions have plural legal systems, and Jordan is no exception. In relation to the impact and effective implementation of the CRC, it appears that in the hierarchy of laws, principles of Islamic law, the Constitution, international agreements and national laws and customary practices is the 'pecking' order.[137] This hierarchy of regulatory norms is visible in various comments in the report and provides an insight into why the CRC has not impacted as deeply as it has the potential for. In the UNICEF commissioned report on the impact of the CRC in Jordan (the Jordanian study), it is stated that:

---

[135] This section draws upon the following: M. Al-Qudah, 'Legislative Reform Review: The Case of Jordan' (unpublished study for the Legislative Reform Initiative, UNICEF, 2004); Committee on the Rights of the Child, 'Initial Report to the Committee on the Rights of the Child' (Jordan), U.N. Doc. CRC/C/8/Add. 4, 27 Nov. 1993; Committee on the Rights of the Child, 'Second Periodic Report to Committee on the Rights of the Child' (Jordan), U.N. Doc. CRC/C/70/Add. 4, 13 September 1999; and An-Naim, *Global Resource Book*, op. cit.

[136] This new law followed the Ottoman Law of Family Rights.

[137] Al-Qudah, op. cit., p. 6.

However the global interest and all efforts exerted to protect and care for children, are no more important than the interest Islamic legislation pays to the protection of children, especially since the issue was raised before any and all other legislation, namely that Islam gave children rights that even current laws have yet to grant.[138]

In its Core Report to the United Nations, however, the Jordanian government states that:

The international conventions which Jordan has ratified have the force of law and take precedence over all local legislation, with the exception of the Constitution. The national courts accord precedence to international conventions, except in cases which pose a threat to public order. This affirmation is confirmed by judgment 32/82 of 6 February 1982 in which the Court of Cassation ruled that international covenants and treaties take precedence over national legislation.[139]

Jordan is a monarchy with the king as the executive Head of State. Laws are promulgated after being adopted by Parliament, ratified by the cabinet of ministers and approved by the king. Thereafter these laws are published in the Official Gazette. Courts are divided into three categories: civil courts, religious courts and special courts. In terms of child rights, all categories of courts play a vital role. Religious courts are divided into *Shari'a* courts, church tribunals and tribunals for other religious sects. *Shari'a* courts deal with family law impacting on child rights as they deal with custody and guardianship matters, inheritance and so on. Among special courts, juvenile courts have a bearing on children at variance with the law.

Legislative reform enabling Jordan to withdraw its reservations to Articles 14, 20 and 21 of the CRC and Articles 9, 15 and 16 of CEDAW does not seem to have made much headway. The Jordanian study has engaged in an in-depth analysis of reservations entered by Jordan and made good linkages between the CRC and CEDAW in the discussion of Jordan's reservations to these treaties and why the government is not agreeable to consider withdrawal of reservations.[140]

Reservations to Article 14 regarding freedom of religion is one that is clearly at variance with the generally held belief that children born of Muslim parents will be brought up as Muslims. The problem and contradiction lie within human rights law itself. On the one hand, children are persons under 18 and require various degrees of protection; on the other hand, they are to be accorded freedom of religion. Along with rights in the field of education, this right brings to the fore tensions within human rights

---

[138] Ibid. p. 4.

[139] 'Core document forming part of the reports of the States Parties: Jordan', para 40(c). U.N. Doc. HRI/CORE/1/Add.18/Rev.1, 3 Jan. 1994 [Core Document].

[140] Al-Qudah, op. cit., pp. 11–16.

conceptualization of child rights and the tension between rights of the child and rights of parents/guardians. Change of religion implies (in most cases), repudiation of family and social ties since relationships between members of the family and community are influenced by religion; any member who changes/repudiates his/her religion also removes him/herself from the community and runs the risk of being uprooted from his/her environment. Thus, it is indeed a heavy burden to expect of a child who is also at a highly impressionable stage of life and different from a discussion of a right to choose one's religion as an adult.

Furthermore, the law in Jordan allows for a non-Muslim foundling to be brought up in his/her religion of birth. Should that information not be available or possible to access, then does that child have a right to choose after he or she attains the age of 18 a particular religion to which he or she is accustomed to? Does the child – who is a foundling and is by virtue of being found in Jordan and given the state religion – have the right to change his or her religion after he or she attains majority?

With regard to Article 21, adoption per se is not allowed in Jordan along with many other Islamic countries. However, concern in the *Shari'a* for the dignity of an individual, which calls for the protection of child in a family environment and provision for the basic economic, social, psychological and emotional needs of the children, does raise questions of the extent to which the country seeks to employ alternative mechanisms for child care as enunciated within the Islamic legal tradition mentioned earlier.[141]

With regard to reservations to Article 9 of CEDAW, the Jordanian government is considering changing the law enabling Jordanian women married to non-Jordanian men to pass their nationality to their husband and children. It is pertinent to state here that Article 9 of the CRC and Islamic law are in complete unanimity, and therefore child rights advocates could use the Islamic argument to make the case for retracting the reservation.[142]

Jordan has also reserved Article 15(4) regarding the same rights to personal movement and 15(2) regarding matrimonial residence. Jordan's reservation is not based on an unequivocal and uniform interpretation of Islamic law. Dr. A. Al-Khayyat is of the view that Islamic law affords an element of flexibility in terms of choosing the matrimonial home and residence. He states that:

> A Muslim woman has the right initially to object to residing in a particular place she considers not suitable or harmful in any way to her well-being. A Muslim woman is entitled to specify this condition in her marriage contract, and it will become her lawful right.[143]

---

[141] Cf. discussion on adoption in this chapter.

[142] M. Al-Qudah, op. cit., pp. 13–14.

[143] See L. Nasser, *Implementation of CRC and CEDAW in the Arab Countries: An Analysis of Reservation. A Case Study of 6 Project Countries: Egypt, Jordan, Lebanon, Sudan, Morocco, Tunisia* (Amman: UNICEF, 1997), p. 15.

Reservations to Article 16 of CEDAW may be addressed by canvassing the contractual nature of marriage within the Islamic legal tradition to argue for equality and non-discrimination within marriage, during its subsistence, and at its dissolution. A progressive interpretation of both CEDAW and Islamic family law renders a number of elements of compatibility. Sameness and equality are two different concepts, and a simplistic interpretation and reading of CEDAW lends itself to problems in the Islamic tradition.

After acceding to the CRC in 1991, a national conference was held in Jordan in 1992 under royal patronage. This conference made several recommendations, the most important of which was to formulate a National Plan for Childhood by 2000, drafting a children's rights law and establishment of the National Council for Childhood, whose tasks are currently being undertaken by the national Council for Family Affairs (NCFA) headed by Her Majesty Queen Rania Al Abdullah. One of the projects initiated by the NCFA, entitled 'Project for Analysis of Legislation related to Family including Childhood Sector', has within its purview a comparative analysis of national law with the CRC and highlights disparities and areas for legislative reform.

Over the years, a number of disparities have come to light and legal reforms to address these have continued, some of which are presented here.

The definition of 'child' in the CRC and various Jordanian statutes was not in unison. To this end, the draft children's rights law defines a child as a person not yet 18 years old. The Law of Civil Status was amended by the Interim Civil Status Law in 2001, whereby the legal age for marriage was increased for both sexes to 18 years. The House of Representatives has not yet accorded its consent to this amendment. This proposed amendment portrays a significant shift in the official position of Jordan vis-à-vis this provision. When submitting its Reply to the List of Issues in connection with its initial report to the Committee on the Rights of the Child, the official Jordanian position with regard to the minimum age of marriage was:

> The difference in minimum marriage ages for boys and girls in Jordanian legislation is based on the age of maturity which in Jordan is usually regarded as occurring earlier among girls than among boys. This is in keeping with local custom, traditions and cultural particularities. Accordingly, the age of maturity is legally set at 15 years in the case of girls and 16 years in the case of boys.[144]

This statement reflects the reason for reluctance on the part of the legislature to amend the law of same minimum age of marriage for boys and girls and

---

[144] Reply to the 'List of issues to be taken up in connection with the consideration of the initial report of Jordan' (U.N. Doc. CRC/C/6/WP.4), 7 Apr. 1994. The initial report of Jordan to the Committee on the Rights of the Child (U.N. Doc. CRC/C/8/Add.4) was submitted on 27 Nov. 1993.

is indicative of the difficulty of attempting to bring about change in societal attitudes through formal law-making.

A further attempt at legislative reform is in the area of labour law. The Jordanian labour law prohibited a child below the age of 10 to work and a child below 17 to undertake dangerous work. Consequent to ratification of the CRC and ILO convention, this law was amended in 2002 to ban children below the age of 18 years from dangerous work and work hazardous to their health.

In the area of family law, the civil status law was amended in 2001 giving both parents equal visitation rights for their children. This amended law also stipulates that any birth should be registered within a specific period including provisions for providing an identity to children born out of wedlock. The juvenile law was amended in 2002 and is part of a wider project, the Family Protection Project (FPP) supported by DFID, which is also assisting in placing structures for special interviewing techniques for abused children, and developing an inter-agency approach to child rights and women's rights under the umbrella of family protection measures.

The government is also working on amending the passport law, which presently requires approval of the husband if the wife and children apply for separate passports. The legal reform initiatives, however, have suffered a setback due to the refusal of the House of Representatives to adopt some of the interim laws and amendments to legislation related to children's rights. These amendments include the Interim Civil Status Law and the penal law. Despite the passage of two years, the House of Representatives has not reviewed these laws. The children's rights draft law is in its final phases of formulation.

There has been discussion regarding Article 340 of the Penal Code that before its amendment gave men lesser sentences and justification for killing or injuring his wife or close female relative on the basis of 'honour'. The subject of killing in the name of honour has raised passionate debates and arguments, but the way to effectively address this is to make the Islamic code of honour and sanctity of life as having more legitimacy and priority than the tribal code of honour. This article was amended by an Interim Penal Law in 2001 giving both spouses the same right to a reduced sentence in case they caught their spouse committing adultery. The amendment, it is submitted, is hardly a satisfactory solution and requires further and intensive research, advocacy, and lobbying at all levels of the population.

An important reform initiative in the area of child rights is providing obligatory bequest *al-wasiya al-wajiba* to orphaned grandchildren but restricting this to the grandchildren through predeceased sons, not daughters. This is a departure from classical Islamic law but one that has, through juristic techniques within the Islamic legal tradition, been adopted in other Muslim countries as well. The Muslim Family Laws Ordinance of 1961 (of Pakistan) in Section 4 provides for a similar 'safety net' for the orphaned grandchild but extends it to children of predeceased daughters as well as sons. This provision of the MFLO, however, has come under fire in the superior courts of Pakistan, and rulings of the Federal Shariat Court (FSC) have struck it down as un-Islamic.[145]

The Jordanian report also shares instances in which positive action has been taken by Jordan in light of the CRC. These areas include minimum age to enter armed conflict, selling and trading of children and child pornography. These issues are dealt with at great length in the Quran and *Hadith* and can be highlighted. The study presents the example of how a holistic approach towards child rights can be employed by showing the interplay of CEDAW, ILO, and other human rights instruments as essential for the implementation of the CRC. For example, where nationality of the child stems only from the father, children of estranged or divorced fathers of other nationalities are left without citizenship in Jordan. Women's right to pass on their citizenship to their children is essential for the welfare for the children as well.

Kingdom of Morocco

Morocco was acknowledged as part of the French sphere of influence by the early part of the twentieth century when it was divided between Spain and France in 1904. A French protectorate was established in 1912; Spanish Morocco faced a revolt in 1920, which nearly succeeded in driving the Spanish out. A French and Spanish alliance, however, re-established Spanish authority in 1926. Morocco gained independence in 1956 and Spain relinquished its authority over most of its Moroccan territory. An-Naim states that:

> Under French and Spanish rule, the colonial legal systems influenced local developments outside of the sphere of family law. *Shari'a* courts continued to apply Maliki *fiqh* during the first half of the century (in addition to local tribunals applying customary law). Following independence in 1956, a Law reform Commission was established in order to draft a Code of Personal Status. A Code was passed into law within the next year, based on dominant Maliki doctrines as well as *takhayyur*, *maslaha* and legislation from other Muslim countries.[146]

Like Jordan, the Moroccan legal system is pluralist in nature with a variety of foundational sources; Islamic law governs family law and other areas are influenced by (French) colonial law. Morocco is one of the Muslim jurisdictions where Islamic family law underwent reform and codification in the mid-twentieth century and has continued to do so. The overarching guiding

---

[145] See, for instance, the case of *Mst. Farishta v The Federation of Pakistan PLD* (1980) Pesh. 47; *Federation of Pakistan v Mst. Farishta PLD* (1981) SC 120.

[146] An-Naim, *Global Resource Book*, op. cit., p. 179.

principles of any family law reform, however, remain entrenched in Islamic law (in this case, the Maliki school of Sunni Islam).

According to its Constitution, Morocco subscribes to the Convention's values and objectives. However, it is not clear whether the Convention forms part of the national legal system. In the early 1990s, just after ratification of the Convention, Morocco amended legislation relating to personal status. Many of these amendments concerned the status of children in general or certain categories of young persons, including young offenders and disabled young persons. Amendments relating to the care of children, guardianship and the obligation to provide maintenance have been made to the Code on Personal Status, the Code of Obligations, and the Code of Civil Procedure.

In 1992, a law on the social protection of the blind and partially sighted was enacted. It requires the parents or guardians of a partially sighted child to inform the public authorities. Two further laws were adopted in the following year. One relates to the protection abandoned children (i.e., the Abandoned Children Act 1993) and the other to disabled Children (i.e., the Social Protection of the Disabled children Act 1993). Article 1 of the latter provides that "the prevention, diagnosis and treatment of disabilities and the education, instruction, training, qualification and social integration of disabled persons are a national responsibility and duty."

In 1998, a ministerial committee was established to bring Moroccan law into line with ratified international human rights conventions. The ministry in charge of human rights serves as secretary of this committee. The harmonization of Moroccan laws with the CRC was a focal concern for various events, including the 1998 and 1999 sessions of the National Congress on the CRC. As a result, various departments and ministries have initiated a process to reform relevant legislation. Reportedly, at the initiative of the National Observatory, a draft text has been tabled for priority laws, being the Code on Personal Status, the Nationality Code, the Civil Status Laws, the Criminal Code and the Royal Decree on Abandoned Children. In 2002, this resulted in the amendment of the law on the Protection and Abandoned Children, according greater protection to abandoned children. The Ministry of the Interior has undertaken a comprehensive review of legal texts governing civil status. The Ministry of State for Disabled Persons has been engaged in a process of harmonizing legislation relating to the disabled with relevant international standards in order to provide better protection for disabled children.

In 1999, a new law on the functioning of the penitentiaries was enacted. It contains several key provisions for the protection of juvenile delinquents. For example, the Code provides that minors are to be separated from other inmates and to be placed in separate quarters or wings. Penal institutions are divided into four categories, one of which includes reform and re-education centres reserved for convicted minors and persons under the age of 20. Also, new legislation on birth registration was enacted. In 2003, the Criminal Procedure Law was enacted containing a special chapter concerning juveniles in conflict with law.

The UNICEF Annual Report 2002 stated that a new law on juvenile justice was adopted in 2002, which increased the legal protection of children in conflict with the law.[147] The Penal Code is being reviewed and will include several articles that concern penal sanctions for adults engaging in sexual activities with children. This new law will be in conformity with the additional protocol on the sale of Children, pornography and so on, which was ratified by the country in 2002.

The Committee on the Rights of the Child has welcomed the various adopted legislative measures.[148] It nevertheless expressed concern over the remaining discrepancies between domestic legislation and the Convention. Legislative measures were particularly encouraged as regards the prevention and elimination of discrimination on the grounds of sex and birth; prohibiting all forms of physical and mental violence, including corporal punishment and sexual abuse of children in the family, in schools and in institutions; bringing existing labour laws into full compliance with ILO Convention No. 138 and 182 by enacting a new Labour Code; and extending protection against sexual exploitation in all relevant legislation to all boys and girls below the age of 18 years.

In Morocco today, there appears a conscious move towards codification of rules, including those based on Islamic law. Although this approach provides space for reform and clarity within the legal system, it also raises a problem of fossilization of Islamic jurisprudence stagnating at the point of reform and arresting an ongoing process of systematic intellectual discourse and evolution of norms.

The author of a UNICEF-commissioned report on implementation of the CRC in Morocco[149] makes an important comment regarding obstacles inhibiting use of international treaties in domestic jurisprudence. Lack of access to treaties and international agreements by the judiciary might be overcome to make legislative reform initiatives, especially in the international human rights arena, more effective.

The Moroccan report, in the section on the position of international law vis-à-vis domestic law, engages in a very incisive analysis of the hierarchy of legal systems. It does afford space for arguing that international treaties

---

[147] UNICEF, *Annual Report 2002* (2003).

[148] See, e.g., Committee on the Rights of the Child, 'Concluding Observations: Morocco', U.N. Doc. CRC/C/15/Add.211, 10 July 2003 [CRC, 'Concluding Observations: Morocco].

[149] M. Zerrari, 'Initiative for Legislative Reform in Morocco' (unpublished study for the Legislative Reform Initiative, UNICEF, 2004).

override domestic law unless otherwise expressly indicated.[150] Another very important and interesting point for discussion raised in the report is the fact that Morocco is signatory to The Hague Convention of 19 October 1996 on Jurisdiction, Applicable Law, Recognition, Enforcement and Co-operation in Respect of Parental Responsibility and Measures for the Protection of Children – one of the few Muslim jurisdictions that have ratified the treaty. It would be important to share the preparatory documentation and discussions with other Muslim countries with a view to encouraging their engagement with this important treaty in the area of children's rights.

In reform undertaken in the area of family law, initiative and support of the king himself are evidence of political will. Modifications in provisions of family law relating to polygamy, joint parenting, divorce and so on appear more in consonance with the spirit of the religious text and something that other Muslim jurisdictions may wish to consider. Since the adoption of the new Family Code in 2003, there is uniformity in the age of marriage fixed at 18 for boys and girls.[151] Further reform calls for special effort to grant name and legal personality to children born out of wedlock, which is important to cross-reference and use in other Muslim jurisdictions.

The Moroccan report makes a very pertinent point, that is, the inextricable links between civil law and Islamic law of personal status. The particularly apt example is of law of personal identity linked to the mode of filiation. Legal pluralism with its attendant ambiguities is obvious.[152]

It is interesting to see how classical Islamic law notions of the father as the sole guardian are being challenged by legislative reform;[153] likewise, that the concept of *kafalah* is being employed to provide a home and a family environment through statutory formulation. But what will make the reform a reality is to provide effective enforcement mechanisms to support the legal initiative. There is strong evidence from the report that the Moroccan State has taken its international obligations seriously and made efforts to bring its laws in consonance with international human rights treaties (e.g., those undertaken in various treaties and protocols protecting child rights). Before the legislative reform, criminal law influenced by secular (French) law was discriminatory to women and children. Nationality rights remain unequal, as do guardianship rights. The report raises concern and dissatisfaction at the pace of reform in the area of child labour (especially labour in traditional

---

[150] Cf. "Muslim must follow their contractual obligations" does seem to provide religious grounds for this course of action (wider and more public dissemination to be proposed).

[151] Moudawana (Family Code) (2003) (Mor.).

[152] Where the national plan of women's human rights had to be abandoned in the face of stiff opposition in the name of religion.

[153] In other Muslim jurisdictions, for example in Pakistan, it is the superior judiciary that has engaged in stretching the boundaries of classical Islamic jurisprudence. See S. S. Ali, *Shaping Women's Lives* (1996).

handicraft and domestic servants and child-maids). It is evident how customary practices and socio-economic compulsions have crept in to perpetuate class and economic disparities, highlighting the limits of black-letter law for reforming practices and improving lives of people.

Islamic Republic of Mauritania

The Islamic Republic of Mauritania was founded in 1960; its official language is Arabic but, due to its French colonial 'encounter', French is widely spoken and understood.[154] The predominant percentage of the Mauritanian population is Muslim and subscribes to the Maliki Sunni sect of Islam.

The legislative reform report commissioned by UNICEF on Mauritania (Mauritanian report) provides a concise introduction to the legal pluralism at play and contextualizes the discussion of implementation of the CRC and CEDAW.[155] In keeping with the trends of most post-colonial jurisdictions of the South, the Mauritanian Constitution refers to the UDHR as well as the African Charter for establishing its linkage with international human rights norms and documents. The Mauritanian legal system is described as 'inspired' by *Shari'a* but not subordinate to it. In other words, although hierarchies do not exist, the author suggests the supremacy of *Shari'a* in family law and reservations to international human rights instruments.[156] Because Islam is the state religion, to what extent may we argue that it is only a source of inspiration and not one of the main sources for the legal system?

As in the legal reform initiatives in Jordan and Morocco, in Mauritania, too, the impetus for reform in the area of child rights was to bring national legislation in conformity with the CRC. To this end, a number of laws impacting on child rights have been adopted or, in some cases, existing laws revised. These include the Code of Personal Status, the Law on Compulsory Schooling, a labour code, a law for prohibition of human trafficking, a project to draft a code for the protection of minors, and the reform in the juvenile justice system.

The Mauritanian report states that the reform embarked upon in recent years has had a comprehensive and holistic approach touching upon health, education, labour, justice, and so on, yet it lacks an intrinsic logic as it has been approached in a fragmented manner. The report is of the view that the

---

[154] The capital is Nouakchott. The population is 2.5 million and land area is 1,025 thousand square kilometres. Mauritania is situated on the Atlantic Ocean shores of Western Africa and shares borders with Algeria to the northeast, Mali to the east, and Senegal to the south.

[155] A. Yessa, 'Implementation of the Child Rights Convention in Mauritania: Constraints and Prospects' (unpublished study for the Legislative Reform Initiative, UNICEF, 2004).

[156] Ibid.

reform initiative has been activated and is centred on adaptation of various provisions of the CRC but it has an ad hoc mannerism to its overall impact and design.

III. IMPLEMENTATION AND ENFORCEMENT: THE ROLE OF STATE ORGANS AND CIVIL SOCIETY AND CONSTRAINTS IN IMPLEMENTATION MEASURES

In most OIC countries including the three countries under review, legislative reform has received impetus due to ratification of the CRC, mushrooming of non-governmental organizations (NGOs) including human rights and development organizations, regional and international movements and discussion on human rights. With the support and assistance from UNICEF and other international agencies, valuable input into policy, research and law-making has taken place. But this movement has largely been a top-down process and approach and driven by international developments and pressure of the international community. Hence, the simultaneous drive towards placing institutional frameworks and implementation mechanisms is either absent or weak and inadequate. The individuals responsible for framing of policy and legislation to bring national laws in conformity with the CRC have a cursory awareness (at best) of the CRC or indeed its ethos, language and concepts.

Another factor in weak implementation of legislative reform initiatives to implement the CRC at the national and local levels lies in the emergence of competing discourse of 'indigenous' (in this case, 'Islamic') human rights norms. A significant proportion of the population, government officials as well as members of NGOs and civil society organizations consider human rights treaties of the United Nations as a foreign Western imposition and at variance either with Islamic values or Islamic culture, custom and tradition. Invariably, the discourse within the countries becomes one of outdoing the UN human rights regime by declaring precedence (chronological and historical) of the Islamic human rights tradition rather than of convergence between the two traditions. This atmosphere of competition, sometimes apologetic, at others dismissive of 'Western' human rights, undermines the CRC and CEDAW, and thus inhibits ownership of legislative reform initiatives based upon these treaties.

Policy pronouncements from the top political leadership reflect political will in most Muslim countries, and these result in initiating the movement towards institutional development and implementation mechanisms. Some examples are discussed later. In Jordan, royal patronage for the CRC was present and this resulted in establishment of the National Council for Family Affairs (NFCA), a body headed by Her Majesty Queen Rania Al Abdullah. As such, it is well placed to undertake the task of facilitating implementation of the CRC. But what has to be borne in mind is the fact that the NCFA is a relatively new and young organization and needs consistent and continuous support to evolve and acquire the expertise to handle such an important and huge task, including monitoring legislative reform.

Another institution is the National Centre for Children's Rights, a body set up to monitor human rights violations and receive complaints of such violations. An elaborate list of tasks has been assigned to the Centre to implement human rights in the field of children's rights.[157] The difficult question, however, that we must confront is the issue of where the 'natural home' of implementing human treaties appears within the governmental structure and formation. Surely bodies such as the NCFA or the NCCR are formed to monitor, advocate and suggest measures of implementation but are not implementing bodies in and of themselves. In all countries under review, it falls to the Ministry of Social Development (or an equivalent name and nomenclature), which also have as their remit youth affairs, 'special education' for children with disabilities, orphanages, women's crisis centres and so on. As soon as the country ratifies the CRC, the Ministry of Social Development becomes the focal point and recipient of tasks to implement the CRC.

This practice brings with it many disadvantages. First is the harsh yet real question of the hierarchy within governmental ministries, the status, clout and leverage that each ministry enjoys within the overall structure of the government. All too often, the finance and planning ministry is the most influential as it controls the pursestrings, followed by the ministries of the interior, industry and commerce, education and health. Social development or social welfare ministries and women's development ministries and human rights (where they do exist) come very low down the ministerial ladder, both in the size of their budgetary allocation as well as the human resources assigned to them. Thus, child rights and women's rights are reduced to an issue of welfare, and not rights, and relegated to the lowest priority ranking within government spending and importance.

A further factor is the lack of interagency and interdepartmental or ministerial collaboration on child rights. The CRC embraces cross-cutting issues of children's lives that require inter-sectoral dialogue and understanding. Links among ministries of health, education and social development are just as crucial in the chain of service providers to children and their families as are the legislature and judiciary to enforce them. None of the countries reviewed reflect a satisfactory holistic approach towards implementing legislative reform within their jurisdiction.

The Jordanian report also raises the issue of legitimacy of the black-letter law and how far it reaches out to the population. See, for instance, the Family Protection Project (FPP) funded by DFID to address issues of child

---

[157] See Al-Qudah, op. cit., p. 17.

abuse, juvenile justice and violence against women. Almost five years and many million British pounds down the line, this report has about one paragraph to devote to such a large project. What does it say for the efficacy of reform initiatives? Where are donors, bilateral and multilateral organizations going wrong? Legislative reform without placing mechanisms and supporting structures creates pressure on existing resources and weakens implementation chances. This is especially true of donor-driven agendas and projects. Project approach to reform is particularly problematic as it tends to create parallel and vertical structures that weaken and sometimes even disintegrate when the funding ends. It would be interesting to know the extent to which the ethos and working of the FPP have extended into the governorates. Some useful lessons may be learned from the project that adopted a human rights based approach and introduced the interagency approach, which could be employed in child rights (since in most countries there is no single body looking after children's affairs).

As an example of the advocacy for adopting a non-discriminatory passport law, it is interesting to remember that, under Islamic law, everyone is a legal person; as such there is no bar on persons, whether women or children, to holding individual passports. Yet despite no prohibition, governmental efforts have not borne fruit. It is evident that officials, parliamentarians and decision makers are not used to giving priority to children's rights. Winning over key players in the government at all levels of the bureaucracy and creating awareness of human rights instruments among members of government departments are a prerequisite for the success of any legal or policy initiative.[158]

Likewise, the judiciary has a central role to break the barrier of exclusion of female children from inheritance rights, by handing down rights-friendly judgements. This is a problem faced by most Muslim jurisdictions despite being contrary to the Islamic legal tradition.

Concluding Observations on Jordan's Second Periodic Report to the Committee on the Rights of the Child[159] highlight the gaps and issues in implementation of legal reforms on child rights. Addressing legislative initiatives, the Committee raises its concern over reservations entered to Articles 20 and 21 when the CRC does provide for *kafalah* as an alternative institution to adoption.[160] Furthermore, it recommends that Jordan study its reservation to Article 14 with a view to narrowing it because, as it stands currently, "potentially gives rise to infringements of the freedoms of thought,

---

[158] Al-Qudah, op. cit., p. 28.
[159] Committee on the Rights of the Child, 'Consideration of Reports Submitted by States under Article 44 of the Convention, Concluding Observations of the Committee on the Rights of the Child: Jordan', U.N. Doc. CRC/C/15/Add.125, 28 June 2000.
[160] Ibid., paras. 10–11.

conscience and religion, and raises questions of its compatibility with the object and purpose of the Convention."[161]

The Committee also notes that despite the fact that 10 years have elapsed since Jordan ratified the CRC, it has yet to be published in the Official Gazette.[162] The need for independent monitoring bodies for child rights is also recognized and their establishment recommended; measures such as these require funds and skilled human resources, which are not readily available.

Definitional issues of childhood, discrimination between the female and male child, early marriage, and lack of access to basic entitlements such as education and health are some of the main areas of concern and action. The Concluding Observations are particularly useful in this regard as they present a broader overview of the State party's human rights obligation beyond the CRC. Thus, references are made to findings of the Human Rights Committee and CEDAW Committee to Jordan in its endeavour to eliminate all forms of discrimination by implementing Article 6 of its Constitution.[163] The Committee on the Rights of the Child also encourages the State party to "consider the practice of other states that have been successful in reconciling fundamental rights with Islamic texts."[164] This observation is made in the backdrop of the Committee's view that "Noting the universal values of equality and tolerance in Islam, the Committee observes that narrow interpretation of Islamic texts by authorities, particularly in areas of family law, are impeding the enjoyment of some human rights protected under the Convention."[165]

In Morocco, no special organization has been set up to assist in implementation of the CRC, but a Ministry for Human Rights was set up in 1993 that included a cell dedicated to child rights. This ministry, however, was closed down in 2004. Organizations under royal patronage for promotion and protection of child rights have been set up to give a high profile to the subject area and ensure political and economic support. Like the NCFA in Jordan, the National Observatory for the Rights of the Child aspires to lead the way and become the focal institution in this field. This approach has its advantages in being able to attract resources, both human and material, to undertake and achieve its goals but also is prone to ambiguities of legal status, and so on. It is also pertinent to mention here that strategies employed by the organization must be such that these are accessible to the largest number of children. Thus, whether a toll-free phone number for registering complaints or seeking help is a realistic strategy is a question that must be broached. The institution of Al Madhalim is another important institution, recently

---

[161] Ibid., paras. 12–13.
[163] Ibid., para. 30.
[165] Ibid., para. 9.

[162] Ibid., para. 15.
[164] Ibid.

established, which has the potential to be used to register and address child rights, whereas the Secretary of State, set up in 1998, was created for the social protection of women and children. Morocco also has a Ministry for Youth, a department for youth, childhood and women's affairs.

A gap that is visible in Jordan and in the Moroccan context is that although legislative reform initiatives are being successfully brought to fruition, institutional structures required by these initiatives are either absent or extremely weak. One reason for this lapse lies in the lack of, or inadequate, human and material resources to operationalize implementation mechanism. But a further reason for ineffective law reform implementation lies in the continued gap between the written law as a colonial and alien imposition and the internalized regulatory norms upheld by society.[166] The Moroccan court has a major disadvantage in terms of its contribution to promote child rights. Judicial decisions are not published regularly, and therefore it is not possible to trace any pattern or trend of the position adopted by courts to human rights cases and issues. An exception to this lack of judicial decisions is a recent study supported by the UN Population Fund. This study compiled decisions of the courts relating to violence against women, and categorized them by age, nature of the violence, social class and so on.

The Moroccan report raises the question of why the ICCPR was ratified without reservations while reservations were entered to similar provisions of the CRC and CEDAW. This is a very incisive observation indeed and one that does not lend itself to any easy resolution, and highlights the politicization of human rights ratification, which is neither uniform nor consistent even within a country.

The role of NGOs is emerging as a matter requiring serious discussion in Muslim jurisdictions. Although all societies have an element of civil society support organizations and the Islamic tradition is no exception, the nature, scope and parameters of work of contemporary NGOs are different, both in ethos and functioning. Most NGOs are seen as foreign-funded, donor-driven entities lacking roots within the communities they serve or aspire to serve. This is a point for discussion across jurisdictions and requires in-depth analysis.

Support to establish a regular reporting mechanism of judicial decisions is imperative to optimize and streamline positive and progressive judgements of courts in promotion and protection of child rights and setting rights-friendly precedents for others to emulate and cite.

Law reform, especially in the area of personal status, is very fragile as family law is considered the 'last bastion of Islam and Islamic identity'. Using

---

[166] This is the crux of the problem in Muslim jurisdictions where law reform is perceived as a 'foreign imposition' lacking legitimacy.

religious arguments and persistent internal discussion and debate invoking a rights-based approach to family law reform is one of the few strategies that stand any chance of success. But the most resilient inner core of norms that are difficult to displace consist of cultural practices, especially ones that have the perceived support of the religious tradition (cultural Islam).

Some innovative and interesting supporting initiatives have been adopted to support legislative reform that if sustained, would provide a basis for institutionalizing a rights-based reform in the difficult area of family law and child rights. In attempting to address the question of what policies and steps can bring about meaningful social change that is a rights-friendly and rights-supportive base for realizing legislative reform, the most crucial and difficult decisions are those of resource allocation and access to basic rights and services. The child's right to education is meaningless if unaccompanied by access to a school that is within reach of the child, has basic facilities of a desk and bench, books and stationery, toilet and playground and a safe and healthy environment. Without linking child rights to a child's needs and entitlements, the very best laws have little chances of success.

An important measure of implementation of child rights includes Concluding Observations of the Committee on the Rights of the Child.[167] The Committee, after consideration of the second periodic report of Morocco, highlighted achievements and constraints and made useful suggestions. Some of these will be shared in this section.

The Committee noted the positive developments in the area of human rights including ratification by Morocco of the two Optional Protocols to the CRC on the sale of children, child prostitution and child pornography (October 2001), and on involvement of children in armed conflict (May 2002) and ILO Conventions No. 138 concerning Minimum Age for Admission to Employment (January 2000) and No. 182 concerning the Prohibition and Immediate Action for Elimination of the Worst Forms of Child Labour (January 2001).[168] The Committee, however, expressed concern at reservations entered upon Article 14 of the CRC, as well as issues of non-discrimination against girls and child labour. The most crucial observation, however, is regarding inadequate budgetary allocations to assist implementation of basic human rights of children (health, education). Political commitment to legal reform is articulated through matching resources, both human and material, and this indicator is weak. Furthermore, the Committee suggests to the State party to "Develop ways to establish a systematic assessment of the impact of budgetary allocations on the implementation of children's rights and to collect and disseminate information in this regard."[169] Such efforts on the part

---

[167] CRC, 'Concluding Observations: Morocco', op. cit.

[168] Ibid., para. 3(a).   [169] Ibid., para. 12(b).

of the State party will require a nationwide mechanism to collect and analyze data, which presently is not in a satisfactory state.

The Committee also has raised the issue of children belonging to ethnic and linguistic minorities, including translation of appropriate material on child rights, facilities and available resources into the Tamazight and Moroccan dialects.[170] It further observed that "children belonging to the Amazigh community cannot always exercize their rights to their own culture, the use of their own language and the preservation of their own identity. In particular, the Committee is concerned that parents are not allowed to give Amazigh names to their children."[171] The Committee also remained concerned at the practice of children working as domestic servants (*petites bonnes*).[172]

In Mauritania, the Secretariat of State for the Status of Women (SECF), created in 1992, is an important department with the mandate for implementing child rights. As such, this institution has the potential of advancing child rights but requires human resources to fulfil its mandate. In addition to education, health and skill development, legal aid is a crucial prerequisite of any meaningful policy for implementation of legal reform initiatives. Children and their family members may well be aware of their rights, but without access to judicial and quasi-judicial forums, these rights and entitlements do not mean much. Therefore, government institutions must evolve a strong working relationship with non-state and non-governmental organizations to reach out to the people to make child rights a reality. To this end, support of civil society is considered important. The Mauritanian study comments on the embryonic stage of civil society in that country that lay dormant and inactive but, according to the author, is now active. How is the concept of civil society used in the context of this inter-country study? Who are members of civil society and what is its role? Is civil society the new name of non-state actors, individual and collective, who actively engage with the State and international organizations and institutions? How does a definition of civil society impact on legal reform initiatives in general and in the area of child rights in particular? These issues are not very clear from the study.

Under the Mauritanian legal system, the CRC is incorporated into national law and the treaty, once ratified, forms part of the national laws and may be invoked directly in a court. Furthermore, in case of a conflict between internal law or custom, Article 80 of the Constitution declares supremacy of international law. The role of courts in implementation of the CRC is, therefore, crucial.

---

[170] Ibid., para 22(a).

[171] Ibid. para. 69. The Committee made recommendations in line with those made by the Committee on the Elimination of Racial Discrimination ('Concluding Observations: Morocco', U.N. Doc. CERD/C/304/Add.57, 10 Feb. 1999).

[172] CRC, 'Concluding Observations: Morocco' op. cit., para 61(d).

The Mauritanian study states that until recently there was no juvenile justice system; a criminal court and code for children are being envisaged. In the meantime, this problem has now been addressed by the establishment of a special court within the regional administrative setup with special consultation rooms and court officials to deal with children at variance with the law. Alternative mechanisms, such as conciliation during the pre-litigation phase, result in very few children being given prison sentences. There is room for vast improvements in the role of the judiciary towards promotion and protection of child rights in Mauritania, and using the CRC may be one of the best ways forward.

Legal reform is one of the first steps in a wide range of actions required to breathe life into child rights. Thus, access to basic needs, for example, education, health, nutrition and so on, ought to be linked to the legislative reform initiatives. Across Muslim jurisdictions, social sector allocations are inadequate, thus leading to weak human development rankings compared to income levels. One of the factors appears to be the structural and organizational weaknesses of governance in Muslim countries, both in human and material terms. Bearing in mind the limited resources at their disposal, there is a need for reform initiatives to suggest structures that are 'light' on structure and heavy with expertise, skills and ability to deliver. In other words, legislative reform initiatives need to address the challenge of optimising existing resources by prioritizing measures to be adopted.

A further factor visible in the Mauritanian study, as well as the ones from Jordan and Morocco, is the limited ability to absorb and utilize available resources. Thus, funds allocated to certain initiatives lapse as a result of non-utilization.

Social sector development, such as education and health, form the backbone of child rights implementation. But to be effective, there is a need to move beyond simply putting legislation into place without matching implementation mechanisms. Education must seek to ensure skill development and chances of economic improvement. In the countries under review (as well as others not mentioned here), there are huge problems with ethos of general education, as it is tantamount to 'tearing' away the child from its soil and environment, giving some half-baked ideas of a better life without actually empowering the child or giving him or her some sense of direction. This predicament is also a result of the lack of a holistic approach towards child rights; all three studies 'cry out' for an interagency approach and contemplation of what it means to adopt child rights. What is visible is accession to human rights treaties under pressure of the international community but often not matched by appropriate action within the States parties. As in the study of Jordan and Morocco, the Mauritanian country report alludes to the 'suspicion' aroused in the minds of people of these countries towards human rights instruments, which they perceive as foreign impositions. Need for cross-cultural dialogue and understanding of comparable human rights traditions across the various religious and cultural divide are imperative, and innovative measures such as *fatwas* in favour of child rights by religious leaders may be an example of the way forward.

The Mauritanian study also raises the issue of the largely symbolic participation of Members of Parliament in the legal reform initiatives. What does the lukewarm and uneven response and commitment say about the agendas of these public representatives? Members of the executive branch of government appear to be more deeply involved in legal reform initiatives than parliamentarians, leading to the question whether the role of Parliament has faded away by comparison.

The author mentions laws abolishing slavery being ineffective and requiring further measures.[173] It appears that similar concerns were raised by a member of the Committee on the Elimination of Racial Discrimination in the Concluding Observations but had not been affirmed.[174] During consideration of the initial report of Mauritania by the Committee on the Rights of the Child, in response to a question on slavery, the representative of Mauritania stated that "Slavery had long been abolished in the State party. To her knowledge there were no cases of unremunerated work in Mauritania."[175] However, economically vulnerable and disadvantaged groups do exist within the country, which, in the opinion of the Mauritanian delegate, may be the reason for this particular concern. Is it a definitional issue (what constitutes slavery?)? Which forms of slavery are most prevalent, to what extent does society approve of this practice and, if so, from where does this approval seek its legitimacy? These questions need to be addressed and require further research and investigation.

IV. MAKING THE CRC A LIVING DOCUMENT: SOME REFLECTIONS ON THE WAY FORWARD

The purpose of this chapter was to evaluate the impact of the CRC in a selection of Muslim States parties with a view to present a framework for enhanced convergence of the Islamic legal tradition and the CRC and create an enabling environment for child rights in these and other jurisdictions. It placed the debate of child rights in Islam and international human rights law in context by assessing the reservations to the CRC and CEDAW, on the one hand, and actual legislative frameworks, policies, and implementation within the States parties on the other. This analysis has led to a number of important inferences, recommendations, and suggestions for policy and legal reform.

---

[173] Yessa, op. cit., p. 17, n. 8.

[174] Committee on the Rights of the Child, 'Summary record of the 724th meeting: Mauritania', U.N. Doc. CRC/C/SR.724, 4 Oct. 2001, para. 22.

[175] Ibid., para. 17.

Muslim jurisdictions are essentially pluralist in their legal systems; principles of Islamic law or *Shari'a* coexists with secular laws, customary practices and international human rights norms. Although its formulation differs in different countries, all Muslim countries operate under a hierarchical legal system as much as a pluralist one. Overtly, and for purposes of national and international consumption, *Shari'a* is the driving force behind any regulatory norm or legal system. The constitution, civil and criminal laws derive legitimacy from Islamic law, whatever the degree of 'inspiration' acknowledged. At an implicit level, customary practices and tradition are the most potent force and 'law' is, in most cases, unwritten and informal. A general rule, however, that is an overarching principle in all Muslim jurisdictions is the fact that family law is strictly governed by religious injunctions and whether codified or in precedent, form the hard, irreducible core.

The deeply entrenched Muslim identity of these countries is evidenced in a number of ways. At the national level, names of countries signify 'Muslimness'; family laws derive from the Islamic tradition. Internationally, a common platform of countries where the predominant percentage of the population is Muslim are members of the OIC, where they attempt to create strong ties between Muslim countries and respond to political and other actions required in support of another Muslim country. A further signifier of an Islamic identity is by entering reservations to human rights treaties emanating from the United Nations in the name of Islam, thus maintaining the hierarchy of laws (with supremacy of the *Shari'a* as paramount). In light of the research on implementation of the CRC in countries where Islamic law is dominant, the following concluding comments may be explored for policy, advocacy and legislative reform:

1. There exists a huge gap between the rhetoric and reality of the extent to which Islamic law and principles are adhered to by governments and people alike. At the political level it is often stated that all actions are being taken in light of Islamic injunctions. However, actions such as allocation of resources for health, education, clean drinking water, employment, access to justice and so on do not match this rhetoric. This is evident from the poor allocation to these sectors among most Muslim countries and their poor rankings in the HDI. An effective programme of child rights in Muslim countries must therefore adopt a strategy of highlighting the child-friendly and rights-friendly tradition of Islam and challenge poor resource allocation and service delivery by governments, in the name of Islam. A useful strategy, following the above, is to seek out examples of provisions of child rights that are child friendly but also those traditions that are more conducive than the CRC. For example, Islamic law of inheritance provides for a child to inherit even before it is born; hence protection of the rights of the unborn child are secured. Likewise, laying out the norm that the girl child

should be breastfed for a longer duration than a male child is a strong ground for cancelling out discrimination against the girl child. The Islamic tradition lays emphasis on healthy children, and breastfeeding is one important aspect of achieving that objective. If governments and international organizations such as UNICEF were to lend support to encourage breastfeeding using the religious argument, proponents of milk formula would find it difficult to respond. Encouraging such practice implies a struggle against the politics of global consumerism, especially in countries with few resources and caught in the web of global corporate culture.

2. Furthermore, extending the right to nationality to every child is a basic principle of Islamic international law; the Muslim *Ummah* is oblivious to geographical boundaries. Thus, Muslim countries that have entered reservations on equal rights to nationality for men and women are guilty of disobeying the principle of universal brotherhood, so valued in the Islamic tradition. In most non-Western jurisdictions (Muslim and non-Muslim), it is a widely held view that the definition of 'child', perspectives and expectations woven around the concept of childhood in the CRC reflect a Western, individualist and formal structure- or institution-led model. This position does not arise as a result of an in-built divergence in the normative base of the CRC and Islamic law but as a result of the complicated and resource-intensive legal and other institutional framework required of a modern nation-State. Developing countries that lack such institutional setup similar to the Western democratic polities are unable to cope with the obligations set forth in documents such as the CRC. A strategy therefore might be not to encourage coercive practices such as structural adjustment programmes that are technical, cumbersome, and unfair to the vast majority of people in these countries living below the poverty line. Instead, alternatives in the traditional practices of governing structure should be sought.

3. Most Muslim jurisdictions are in a transitional state of social organization. Old support structures have weakened and dissipated; new ones are not in place, resulting in a hazardous and fragile reality. The most effective way forward to actualize child rights is to project obligations of family, society and State as the triangle of the safety net for the child. Adequate food, clothing, shelter, health and education are entitlements that are well within the most entrenched traditions in Islam. Institutions of *zakat, ushr, sadaqa, khairat* and so on at one level appear welfarist in approach but, looked at more closely, they are entitlement and rights based. Thus, the money that must be given out to the entitled in *zakat* is not welfarist or a handout because that money does not belong to the person handing it out. It was never his/hers but belonged to God and his people.

4. Another important area for the enhancement of the rights of child in which Islam could come to the rescue of better implementation is education. Under Islamic tradition, it is the right and obligation of every Muslim to seek knowledge or the notion of '*Iqra*'. An emphasis on this concept from the point of view of a religious obligation would be a stepping stone to a better implementation of not just the provisions concerning a child's right to education, but it has the potential of increasing the minimum age of marriage. Because it is a religious obligation to acquire knowledge and get married only when one has the material and other means to do so, it stands to reason that in an invisible competition between the two obligations, education if supported rigorously by the State would lead to a higher age of marriage for girls and boys. This strategy also would preclude a controversial debate on the Islamic minimum age of marriage. Furthermore, a generation of educated females, socially and economically empowered through education and employment, will be able to sidestep the controversial issue of whether an adult Muslim woman requires a male guardian (*wali*) to enter into marriage.

5. The right to life is a basic entitlement and one from which no derogation is permitted within the Islamic tradition (as in the CRC and other human rights instruments). The Quran states:

> And do not kill your children out of fear of poverty; We shall provide for them and for you. Truly, the killing of them is a great sin.[176]

Female infanticide in particular was declared a grave sin. The Prophet Mohammed, when asked what he considered the most serious sin, responded thus:

> To ascribe divinity to someone other than Allah when He is the One who Created you.

The next? To which he is reported to have stated:

> To kill your child out of fear it will share your food.[177]

Equal access to resources and basic necessities including sustenance, education, health and care for children is another strong tradition in Islam. Al-Bukhari and Muslim report that parents are not permitted to neglect children in their care or abuse them. The Prophet is reported to have said: "Each of you is a caretaker (*ra'iy*) and is responsible for those under his care." Another *Hadith* reports: "Wasting the sustenance of dependents is sufficient

---

[176] Quran, Verse 17:31.   [177] Reported by al-Bukhari and Muslim.

sin for a man." Ahmed, al-Nisai and Abu Daoud report the Prophet as having said: "Allah will ask every caretaker (*ra'iy*) about the people under his care, and the man will be asked concerning the people of his household." Discrimination between children is prohibited. According to one report (by al-Bukhari and Muslim), the Prophet stated: "Do not ask me to be a witness to injustice. Your children have the right of receiving equal treatment, as you have the right that they should honour you." Another similar *Hadith* states: "Fear Allah and treat your children with equal justice."

This *Ahadith* may be used in articulating the principle of non-discrimination within the Islamic tradition and its convergent normative base. If the Prophet Mohammed, as the authoritative interpreter of the Quran, declared abhorrence to unequal treatment of children, can we not use this principle as creating a norm of non-discrimination?

6. Many Muslim jurisdictions have entered reservations to Articles 2 and 16 of CEDAW (among others) as well as Articles 14, 20 and 21 of the CRC, as being contrary to Islam. These are the most difficult and complex areas where convergence does not come easily. The earlier part of this chapter has tried to present the context of adoption within Islam and how it is not at variance with the CRC. What is more difficult to reconcile is the status of children born out of wedlock. Because of the negative implications for a child born out of wedlock, the Islamic legal tradition strives towards providing legitimacy to the child. A child born within six months of the marriage of the parents and up to two to three years after the dissolution of the marriage of the parents is considered a legitimate child and ascribed to the father. A child born out of wedlock is ascribed to the mother and may inherit from her and not the father. To this extent, Islamic law attempts to give the child an identity and a name; the father cannot give the child his name. The reality, however, is very difficult and painful. Sexual intercourse outside of marriage is a grave criminal offence in Islam and one that attracts very heavy penalties.[178] Therefore, how would an unmarried mother declare her child publicly in the absence of a father to whom she is married? If she makes such a declaration, she runs the risk of being arrested and flogged, stoned to death or imprisoned. This situation calls for further research in the area.

7. A major problem in Islamic jurisdictions is the dogmatic, inflexible and selective use of Islam devoid of its spirit, rationale and objective. Fossilization of the dynamic strains within the Islamic legal tradition of *Shari'a* as flowing water can take advocacy efforts a long way ahead.

8. Transformation of law and legal frameworks through internal initiatives are the most effective, lasting and resilient. Any researcher on Islamic/*Shari'a*

---

[178] Flogging or stoning to death.

law will be immediately struck by the lack of uniformity in interpretation and application of Islamic law across Muslim jurisdictions. There are significant divergences. The first step is to review jurisprudence relating to children in Muslim jurisdictions to highlight use of child-friendly approaches and interpretation of the religious text. Studies focusing on a comparative perspective of the CRC, domestic legislation, Quran and *Hadith* must be initiated.[179] The findings of these comparative studies may be shared in various forms bearing in mind the readership and users. Thus, handbooks and manuals as well as academic publications may be equally achievable as the experience of research on women and law in the Muslim world indicates. Such studies highlight the need for using a progressive interpretation of Islam as a tool for advocacy and the need for linkages between the CRC and CEDAW in policy and legal frameworks. Adopting a developmental- and progress-oriented approach ties up very well with the Islamic tradition. The CRC and CEDAW are examples of the indivisibility of the three generations of rights as is provided in the Islamic tradition.

9. Recognizing the potential of judicial decisions in one Islamic jurisdiction on the development of jurisprudence in other Islamic territories, it is important to conduct research to determine trends of courts and judicial forums in Muslim jurisdictions regarding using CRC provisions to advance child rights.[180]

10. Comparative research of Muslim jurisdictions also brings to the fore customary practices that are not Islamic but continue to be presented as such. The most glaring example is female circumcision, which is virtually unknown in Asia and, where known, has strong African origins predating Islam.

11. In many developing countries and particularly in Islamic jurisdictions, NGOs and their role are perceived to be donor-driven, Western, alien and politically motivated. Emphasizing the role of community-based organization within the Islamic tradition and synthesizing the efforts of the NGOs

---

[179] See S. S. Ali and B. Jamil, *A Comparative Study of The UN Convention on The Rights of The Child, Islamic Law and Pakistan Legislation* (Peshawar: Educational Computing Services for Radda Barnen (Save the Children, Sweden), 1994), p. 198; S. S. Ali, *The United Nations Convention on the Elimination of All Forms of Discrimination Against Women, Islamic Law and the Laws of Pakistan: A Comparative Study* (Peshawar: Norwegian Development Agency (NORAD), 1995), p. 168.

[180] S. S. Ali and R. Naz, 'Marriage, Dower and Divorce: Superior Courts and Case Law in Pakistan' in *Shaping Women's Lives Laws, Practices and Strategies in Pakistan*, F. Shaheed et al., ed. (Lahore, Pakistan: Shirkatgah, 1998), pp. 107–42; S. S. Ali and M. N. Azam, 'Custody and Guardianship: Case Law 1947–97' in ibid., pp. 143–62; S. S. Ali and K. Arif, 'The Law of Inheritance and Reported Case Law Relating to Women' in *Shaping Women's Lives Laws, Practices and Strategies in Pakistan*, F. Shaheed et al., ed. (Lahore, Pakistan: Shirkatgah, 1998), pp. 163–80.

with that of the government through programmes devised through participatory modes may minimize the antagonism between the State and the NGOs and will strengthen the efforts in the direction of the objectives of both the agencies. Another concern is the need for the civil society groups to focus on policy implementation alongside the advocacy for change.

12. Interpretation by jurists had always been a powerful source of Islamic law. It is thus crucial for the members of the judiciary, the Bar, and the academia to be trained in the interpretation of the Islamic texts and norms in the light of the CRC and other human rights instruments. Ensuring a rights-based approach to governance calls for specified skills and changes in the attitudes of the individuals playing important roles in the governance structure. Judicial activism, for instance, can play a major role in this direction. In order to internalize human rights documents such as the CRC and CEDAW, it is worth contemplating how a rights-based approach needs to be grounded and presented as an entitlement as well as obligation-based approach.

13. To complement legislative processes and initiatives, indicators that are grounded, tangible and quantifiable need to be developed. The questions that one needs to ask are: What is required to make this law implementable? What breathes life into the CRC? To cite an example, autonomy and respect for the body and privacy of the girl child need a tangible programmatic outcome of toilets subscribing to the needs of the girl child in every school.

14. Rules/laws governing rights/status of a child can be categorized into international law, Islamic law, constitutional law and statute law. Ideally, all four categories should reinforce each other for achieving the best interests of the child. But, unfortunately, substantive provisions of all these laws share neither the same degree of justiciability in a judicial forum nor a common normative base or value system, and, hence, are incapable of implementation. For instance, fundamental rights given under the constitution are justiciable, but rights afforded under the principles of policy of the same document are not. They simply are standard-setting norms conveying the aspirations of the people but not enforceable in a court of law. Next come the statutory laws, such as the various labour laws and others, that arguably undermine the equality provisions in the constitution. The manner in which Islamic law denies complete equality to the female child as well as the adverse effect of customary practices on the adequate protection, survival and development rights of the child, whether male or female, have been discussed earlier in this chapter.

15. By and large, it is the most inflexible fossilized form of the religious text and interpretation that finds expression in Muslim jurisdictions today. 'Unpacking', 'reminding' States parties, institutions and people of the

alternative interpretations of (varying) juristic techniques, is an important and crucial input that UNICEF can make. Statist agendas find it easier to hide behind custom and culture and religion to evade obligations. In the absence of a coherent, integrated policy and approach, donor-driven policies and ad hoc measures for child rights are a matter of grave concern. Donors are predominantly funding small, short-term projects for children in the labour market, rather than instituting long-term measures to address child labour. A scientific assessment of the need for such programmes, issues of owner-ship by the community of a certain programme, and, thus, sustainability are hardly built into the project-oriented programming of donor-driven activ-ities. Sustainable measures need to be thought through and an indigenous position on child rights arrived at, only if the community believes and is con-vinced of its philosophy of child rights; half-hearted measures are not likely to succeed.

BIBLIOGRAPHY

Primary Sources

The Quran, English translation by Abdullah Yousaf Ali

Reports/Documents

Democratic Commission for Human Development. *Report on Human Rights Situa-tion in Rural Communities in Pakistan 1996*. Lahore: DCHD, 1996.

Nasser, L. *Implementation of CRC and CEDAW in the Arab Countries: An Analysis of Reservations. A Case Study of 6 Project Countries: Egypt, Jordan, Lebanon, Sudan, Morocco, Tunisia*. Amman: UNICEF, 1997.

United Nations Development Programme. *Human Development Report 2004*. New York. UNDP, 2004.

Secondary Sources

Afshar, H. *Islam and Feminism: An Iranian Case-Study*. Basingstoke: Macmillan, 1998.

Ahmed, K. N. *Muslim Law of Divorce*. New Delhi: Kitab Bhavan, 1978.

Ahmed, L. *Women and Gender in Islam*. New Haven: Yale University Press, 1992.

Al-Azami, M. *On Schacht's Origins of Muhammadan Jurisprudence*. Oxford: Centre for Islamic Studies and Islamic Texts Society, 1996. (First published 1985.)

Al Azhar Working Group. *Child Care in Islam*. Cairo: UNICEF, 1985.

Alami, D. *The Marriage Contract in Islamic Law*. London: Graham & Trotman, 1992.

Alami, D. and D. Hinchcliffe. *Islamic Marriage and Divorce Laws of the Arab World*. London: CIMEL and Kluwer Law International, 1998.

Ali, S. S. *Gender and Human Rights in Islam and International Law Equal Before Allah, Unequal Before Man?* The Hague: Kluwer Law International, 2000.

Ali, S. S. *The United Nations Convention on the Elimination of All Forms of Discrimination Against Women, Islamic Law and Laws of Pakistan: A Comparative Study*. Peshawar: Norwegian Development Agency (NORAD), 1995.

Ali, S. S. and B. Jamil. *A Comparative Study of the UN Convention on Rights of the Child, Islamic Law and Pakistan Legislation*. Peshawar: Educational Computing Services for Radda Barnen (Save the Children Sweden), 1994.

An-Naim, A. A., ed. *Islamic Family Law in a Changing World: A Global Resource Book*. London: Zed Books, 2002.

An-Naim, A. A. *Towards an Islamic Reformation: Civil Liberties, Human Rights and International Law*. Syracuse: Syracuse University Press, 1990.

Anderson, J. *Law Reform in the Muslim World*. London: Athlone Press, 1976.

Arabi, O. *Studies in Modern Islamic Law and Jurisprudence*. The Hague: Kluwer Law International, 2001.

Burton, J. *The Collection of the Qur'an*. Cambridge: Cambridge University Press, 1977.

Burton, J. *An Introduction to the Hadith*. Edinburgh: Edinburgh University Press, 1994.

Burton, J. *The Sources of Islamic Law*. Edinburgh: Edinburgh University Press, 1990.

Calder, N. *Studies in Early Muslim Jurisprudence*. Oxford: Oxford University Press, 1993.

Coulson, N. *A History of Islamic Law*. Edinburgh: Edinburgh University Press, 1964.

Coulson, N. *Conflicts and Tensions in Islamic Jurisprudence*. Chicago: University of Chicago Press, 1969.

Crone, P. *Roman, Provincial and Islamic Law*. Cambridge: Cambridge University Press, 1987.

Doi, A. R. I. *Shariah: The Islamic Law*. London: Ta Ha Publishers, 1984.

Dupret, B. et al., eds. *Legal Pluralism in the Arab World*. The Hague: Kluwer Law International, 1999.

Edge, I., ed. *Islamic Law and Legal Theory*. Dartmouth: Aldershot, 1996.

Esposito, J. *Women in Muslim Family Law*. Syracuse: Syracuse University Press, 1992.

Fyzee, M. *A Handbook of Muhammadan Law*. New Delhi: Oxford University Press, 4th edn., 1974.

Haeri, S. *The Law of Desire: Temporary Marriage in Islam*. London: I.B. Tauris, 1990.

Hamilton, C. *The Hedaya*. Lahore: Premier Book House, 1957.

Hamidullah, M. *The Muslim Conduct of State*. Lahore: Sh. Muhammad Ashraf, 7th edn., 1987.

Iqbal, M. *Reconstruction of Religious Thought in Islam*. Oxford: Oxford University Press, 1884. (subsequent editions available).

Khadduri, M. and H. J. Leisbensy, eds. *Law in the Middle East*. Washington, DC: The Middle East Institute, 1955.

Khadduri, M. *The Islamic Law of Nations: Shaybani's Siyar*. Baltimore: Johns Hopkins University Press, 1966.

Little, D., J. Kersley and A. A. Sachedina, eds. *Human Rights and the Conflict of Cultures: Western and Islamic Perspectives on Religious Liberty*. Columbia: University of South Carolina Press, 1988.

Mahmood, T. *Family Law Reform in the Muslim World*. Bombay: N. M. Tripathi, 1972.

Mallat, C. and J. Connors, eds. *Islamic Family Law*. London: Graham & Trotman, 1990.

Mannan, M. A., ed. *Mulla's Principles of Muhammadan Law*. Lahore: PLD Publishers, 1995.

Maudoodi, M. A. A. 'Islamic and Western Laws on Divorce – A Comparative Historical Perspective'. *Islamic and Comp. Law Q.* 1 (1981): 17–23.

Mawdudi, A. A. *Human Rights in Islam*. Translated by K. Ahmed. Leicester: Islamic Foundation, 1980.

Mayer, A. E. *Islam and Human Rights Tradition and Politics*. Boulder, CO: Westview Press, 1998.

Meriwether, M. L. and J. Tucker. *A Social History of Women and Gender in the Modern Middle East*. Boulder CO: Westview Press, 1999.

Mernissi, F. *Beyond the Veil*. Bloomington: Indiana University Press, 1987.

Mernissi, F. *Women and Islam*. Translated by Mary Jo Lakeland. Oxford: Basil Blackwell, 1991.

Mir-Hosseini, Z. *Marriage on Trial*. London: I.B. Tauris, 1993.

Moinuddin, H. *The Charter of the Islamic Conference and Legal Framework of Economic Cooperation Among Its Member States*. Oxford: Clarendon Press, 1987.

Moors, A. *Women, Property and Islam, Palestinian Experiences 1920–1990*. Cambridge: Cambridge University Press, 1995.

Nasir, J. *The Islamic Law of Personal Status*. London: Graham & Trotman, 1986.

Nasir, J. *The Status of Women under Islamic Law*. London: Graham & Trotman, 1994.

Pearl, D. and W. Menski. *Muslim Family Law*. London: Sweet & Maxwell, 3rd edn., 1998.

Rahim, A. *Muhammadan Jurisprudence*. Lahore: Mansoor Book House, 1995.

Rahim, A. *The Principles of Muhammadan Jurisprudence*. Lahore: Mansoor Book House, 1995.

Rehman, F. *Islam*. London: University of Chicago Press, 2nd edn., 1979.

Rehman, F. *Islam and Modernity Transformation of an Intellectual Tradition*. Chicago: University of Chicago Press, 1982.

Rehof, L. A. *Guide to the Travaux Preparatoires of the United Nations Convention on the Elimination of All Forms of Discrimination Against Women*. Dordrecht: Martinus Nijhoff, 1993.

Roald, A. S. *Women in Islam: The Western Experience*. London: Routledge, 2001.

Schacht, J. *An Introduction to Islamic Law*. Oxford: Oxford University Press, 1964.

Schacht, J. 'Islamic Law in Contemporary States'. *American Journal of Comparative Law* 8 (1959): 133–47.

Schacht, J. *Origins of Muhammadan Jurisprudence*. Oxford: Oxford University Press, 1950.

Shaheed, F. et al., eds. *Shaping Women's Lives: Laws, Practices and Strategies in Pakistan*. Lahore: Shirkatgah, 1996.

Siddiqui, M. Z. *Hadith Literature*. Cambridge: Islamic Texts Society, rev. edn., 1993.

Sonbol A., ed. *Women, the Family and Divorce Laws in Islamic History*. Syracuse: Syracuse University Press, 1996.

Tabandeh, S. *A Muslim Commentary on the Universal Declaration of Human Rights.* Translated by F. J. Goulding. Guildford: Goulding, 1970.

Taha, M. M. *The Second Message of Islam.* Translated by A. A. Naim. Syracuse: Syracuse University Press, 1987.

Tucker, J. *In the House of the Law: Gender and Islamic Law in Syria and Palestine, 17th–18th Centuries.* Berkeley: University of California Press, 1997.

Weiss, B. *The Spirit of Islamic Law.* Athens, GA: University of Georgia Press, 1998.

Welch Jr., C. E. & R Meltzer, eds. *Human Rights and Development in Africa.* Albany: State University of New York Press, 1984.

Welchman, L. *Beyond the Code: Muslim Family Law and Shari Judiciary in the Palestinian West Bank.* The Hague: Kluwer Law International, 2000.

Yamani, M., ed. *Feminism and Islam: Legal and Literary Perspectives.* Reading: Ithaca Press, 1996.

Yamani, M., ed. *Feminism and Islam.* London: Ithaca Press, 1996.

CHAPTER FOUR

Law Reform and Children's Rights in Plural Legal Systems

SOME EXPERIENCES IN SUB-SAHARAN AFRICA

Savitri Goonesekere

INTRODUCTION

The ratification of an international human rights treaty by a State is meant to confer rights on people within that State. It also creates an obligation on successive governments to realize those rights within the country, and at the national level. The UN Convention on the Rights of the Child (CRC),[1] as one of the most recent international treaties, introduces a different dimension by adopting some new approaches to the content of rights, as well as obligations created under it. This has posed both challenges and opportunities in regard to using the legal system to implement the rights guaranteed under the Convention.

The CRC sometimes uses language that is familiar to many legal systems by imposing the obligation to realize rights on different agencies of the State. For instance, Article 3 refers to the obligation of public social welfare institutions, courts of law, administrative authorities or legislative bodies to make the best interests of the child a primary consideration in their actions concerning children. Similarly, Article 4 requires States parties to undertake "legislative administrative and other measures" for the implementation of the rights of the child.[2] The emphasis on the State and its agencies as the key duty bearers, as well as the role of legislation in realizing rights, conforms to the traditional view that adopting a law or legal reform is an isolated act of the State. However, the approach of the Convention in defining rights as well as the role of other actors and institutions introduces a new concept of legislative reform that is inter-sectoral in approach, and involves agencies and individuals who are non-state actors.

---

[1] Convention on the Rights of the Child, Convention on the Rights of the Child, G.A. res. 44/25, annex, *adopted* 20 Nov. 1989, 44 U.N. GAOR Supp. (No. 49) at 167, U.N. Doc. A/44/49 (1989), *entered into force* 2 Sept. 1990. Reprinted in 28 *ILM* (1989): p. 1448.

[2] Ibid., Arts. 3 and 4.

Article 3 of the Convention makes private social welfare institutions duty bearers under the Convention; Articles 5 and 18 place clear responsibilities on parents and family members. Several articles such as Article 4, Article 24 on the right to health and Article 28 on the right to education refer to the duty of international cooperation placed on all States. The concept of international cooperation and solidarity in realizing children's rights and implementing them at the national level is carried through in Article 45. This Article also envisages that civil society organizations will become partners in this effort.[3]

The CRC, like the UN Convention on the Elimination of All Forms of Discrimination against Women (CEDAW),[4] does not adopt a hierarchy of rights. It does not distinguish between civil and political human rights and social and economic rights. Consequently, the rights to health and education are considered as important as the right to freedom from violence and abuse, or the right to freedoms of expression, thought, conscience and religion. In many legal systems, especially in South Asia with its legal heritage of Anglo-American jurisprudence, civil and political rights that can be enforced in courts of law are differentiated from social policies on health and education that cannot be so enforced. Legislative reform therefore was not called upon to take into account or plan for the social policies and resource allocation that were critical to effective law enforcement. Because the CRC has recognized the indivisibility of rights and gives status to both sets of rights, it requires legislative reform to be considered a holistic process that will reinforce *all* rights. More important, the process of law reform and legislation becomes intrinsically connected to sustainable development or economic growth combined with equity and human development. Although enforcement of rights through laws and legal processes that protect against violations is important, implementation of rights requires other connected strategies. The State now acquires negative obligations to protect from infringements, as well as positive obligations to respect, promote and fulfil rights.

The concept of the indivisibility of rights, reflected in the CRC and CEDAW, requires States parties to address issues of poverty and disparity reduction as an urgent and necessary aspect of economic growth and development. It reinforces the idea that sustainable economic growth cannot be achieved without the development of the human resources in a country. The rights-based approach to development envisages that initiatives on economic growth will be balanced with human development and the implementation of human rights. Law reform, legal processes and institutional reform are considered important in achieving this goal. Regulatory frameworks and

---

[3] Ibid., Arts. 3, 4, 5, 18, 24 and 28.

[4] Convention on the Elimination of All Forms of Discrimination against Women, G.A. res. 34/180, *adopted* 18 Dec. 1979, 34 U.N. GAOR Supp. (No. 46) at 193, U.N. Doc. A/34/46, *entered into force* 3 Sept. 1981.

procedures for enforcement can vary, and are not limited to traditional litigation in courts. The rights-based approach involves the creation of a variety of administrative procedures and institutions to ensure that human rights are in fact implemented. The focus on balancing economic growth with human development and the realization of rights is especially important for women and children. Their interests are often marginalized when there is an exclusive focus on economic growth around a dialogue that is often non-participatory.

The need to protect personal security and provide access to basic needs such as health and education cannot therefore be postponed until a later stage of economic growth and improved financial resources. This is why the rights-based approach requires countries to address urgent social problems affecting women and children, such as early marriage, child labour, exploitation in prostitution and trafficking, through a holistic range of interventions that go beyond abolitionist provisions in legislation. The review process has to be participatory and resources must be committed for institution building, effective law enforcement and service delivery on basic needs. This has to be a mandatory aspect of legislative reform. The close interconnectedness between personal security, protection from exploitation and access to basic services makes it essential that legislative reform should not focus only on the prohibition of social practices that impact negatively on women and children.

Because the concept of partnership between state and non-state actors is intrinsic to the rights-based approach, resources cannot be dependent exclusively on state budgets. The State must engage with non-state partners, including families, communities, local civil society, the corporate sector and the international and regional agencies (including the financial institutions) in realizing rights. Human rights commitments can and must be used in negotiating with the donor community and international and regional financial institutions. The CRC in particular places accountability on this wide range of partners. The State cannot transfer its own responsibilities to the private sector, civil society, donors or the family and community. It must play a catalytic role in using both law and legal procedures, and negotiations and agreements by consensus, so as to promote accountability and partnerships between these groups in realizing human rights. Initiatives that are not purely legal, such as alternative mechanisms for cooperation and dispute resolution, self-regulatory codes of practice, and internal monitoring systems, can promote responsibility and strengthen the traditional enforcement procedures introduced by laws.

The Convention thus links human rights and law reform with the broad goal of development and mandates using law reform as an intrinsic dimension of a rights-based approach to development. The idea of rights incorporated in both the CRC and CEDAW goes beyond the liberal individualism associated with civil and political rights and a contract between the State and the individual. It incorporates what has been aptly called the concept of a social trust,[5] or a fiduciary responsibility on the part of the duty bearers to manage development so as to realize human rights. This new meaning given to human rights and development requires a much more participatory and inter-sectoral approach to legislative reform that focuses on the laws' actual impact in achieving children's rights and improving their situation within countries.

The concept of 'social trust' and partnership in realizing rights and the connection between individual and community rights is not a new dimension of human rights law. It is found in the values on intergenerational rights in indigenous communities and customary traditions in Asia and Africa, and has been incorporated into the jurisprudence of environmental law in many countries. The concept of basic needs as socio-economic rights has been introduced into the South African Constitution and has been reinforced in the African Protocol on Women's Rights to the African Charter on Human and People's Rights. Court cases in the Philippines and Sri Lanka on rights have recognized that the State has an obligation to protect the interests of children and future generations in the management of the environment.[6] The concept of social trust in State-citizen relations has been reinforced through the Declaration of the World Conferences on Development in Copenhagen and Johannesburg, and in the Millennium Development Goals. The meaningfulness of the CRC's Article 4 and the concept of partnership in realizing human rights have been poignantly demonstrated in the response of families, communities, civil society and the international community, including the international financial agencies in committing 'maximum available resources' for rehabilitation and reconstruction, in countries affected by the 2004 Asian tsunami. Ironically, if the concepts in the CRC on child rights had promoted partnerships in regard to early warning systems, poverty reduction and eco-sensitive coastal development in these countries, the massive loss of life and internal displacement of children and people could have been avoided. The experience shows what can be done, and what must be done, to realize child rights in developing countries and prevent the human and material costs of such humanitarian crises.

The Committee on the Rights of the Child, which monitors progress on States parties' obligations under the CRC, has issued a General Comment No. 5 of 2003 on 'General Measures of Implementation', which reiterates the indivisibility of rights, holistic implementation and the concept

---

[5] G. S. Kamchedzera, 'Economic Liberal Individualism and the Rights of the Poor Child', in *Understanding Children's Rights*, ed. E. Verhellen (Ghent, Belgium: University of Ghent, 1998), p. 302.

[6] *Minors Oposa v Secretary of the Department of Environment and Natural Resources DENR*, (1994) 38 I.I.M 178 (Phil. S. Ct.), cited in G.S. Kamchedzera, ibid.; *Banda Bulankulama v Secretary, Ministry of Industrial Development* (Eppawela Case), (2000) 3 Sri LR 243 (Sri Lanka, S. Ct.); Constitution of South Africa, Arts. 24, 26, 27, 28 (Children's Rights), and 29; Protocol to the African Charter on Human and People's Rights on the Rights of Women in Africa, *adopted* 11 July 2003.

of partnership and cooperation in realizing rights.[7] The Committee on the Rights of the Child also has clarified this approach in their 1996 'General guidelines for periodic reports'.[8] Consequently, any suggestions that legislation and legislative reforms should be delinked from 'other measures' to effectively implement children's rights are not supported by the tenor of the General Comment and the Guidelines. General measures of implementation are perceived in these documents as an inherent dimension of a project to use law to realize the human rights of children under the CRC. General Comment No. 5 declares that "States parties need to ensure, by all appropriate means, that the provisions of the Convention are given legal effect within their domestic legal systems."[9] The obligation to 'respect, promote, protect and fulfil' rights by both refraining from infringing rights and acting positively to implement rights thus becomes a basic obligation of the State, acting in partnership with a range of other actors. It is this ideology that must inform a legislative reform process that is meant to incorporate the CRC and realize children's rights within countries.

The chapter will use this conceptual framework with regard to legislative reform and human rights to examine the implications of the ratification of the CRC, and its impact on law reforms in a plural or mixed legal tradition. A mixed or plural legal tradition is usually derived from diverse systems of law such as civil and Anglo-American common law, and customary or religious laws. The diversity of these legal traditions adds another dimension to the process of integrating international human rights standards in law reform at the national level. The chapter will focus on the plural or mixed legal systems of three selected countries in Africa – Benin, Ghana and Zimbabwe – and also use comparative experiences from other countries in Asia and Africa with similar mixed legal traditions. The ratification of international human rights treaties, including the CRC and CEDAW, has made comparative case law and law reform especially relevant to the development of domestic legal systems when there is a shared legal heritage. This has been reiterated in several statements of Commonwealth judicial colloquia held in Bangalore in 1988 and 1998, and in Bloemfontein and Victoria Falls in 1993 and 1994.[10]

---

[7] Committee on the Rights of the Child, General Comment No. 5: 'General measures of implementation for the Convention on the Rights of the Child', U.N. Doc. CRC/GC/2003/5, 3 Oct. 2003 [General Comment No. 5].

[8] Committee on the Rights of the Child, 'General guidelines for periodic reports', U.N. Doc. CRC/C/58, 20 Nov. 1996.

[9] General Comment No. 5, op. cit., para. 19.

[10] See, e.g., 'The Bangalore Principles (1988)' in *Developing Human Rights Jurisprudence: Conclusions of Judicial Colloquia and other meetings on the Domestic Application of International Human Rights Norms on Government under the Law 1988–92* (London: Commonwealth Secretariat, 1992), p. 1; Commonwealth Secretariat, 'Victoria Falls Declaration on the Promotion of Human Rights of Women', in *Report of the Commonwealth Judicial Colloquium on Promoting the Human Rights of Women, Victoria Falls, Zimbabwe, August 1994* (London: Commonwealth Secretariat, 1994), p. 8.

I. THE CONTEXT FOR LAW REFORM IN BENIN, ZIMBABWE, AND GHANA: A HISTORICAL PERSPECTIVE[11]

Political organization and systems of governance, as well as the social organization and economic situation of countries, have a bearing on their capacity and efforts to fulfil treaty obligations and realize the human rights of children. The countries focused on in this chapter have witnessed significant changes in their political, social, and economic systems, through a long period of colonization, and decolonization, which commenced with the achievement of political independence. Their post-independence history has often been synonymous with political instability, internal conflict and violence. Globalization and transition to market economic policies also have posed new challenges to social and economic arrangements that have a bearing on children's lives.

Political Organizations

All three countries belong to sub-Saharan Africa and were organized on the basis of interaction between tribes that belonged to different ethnic groups, rather than through a centralized system of governance. They attracted the interest of successive Western regimes such as the Portuguese, Dutch, French and British, from the beginning of the sixteenth century.

The Republic of Benin was colonized by the French in 1894 and was originally known as Dahomey. The country was administered by the government of French West Africa and became a self-governing republic within the French community in 1958, gaining full independence in 1960. Benin experienced 12 years of political instability after independence, with a series of military coups. Following a coup on 26 October 1972, single-party rule was established, with adoption of a fundamental law in 1979 and single-party elections. Multiparty elections were held under a new Constitution adopted in 1990, and elections for presidential office and the National Assembly have been held regularly since then. Some election malpractices and manipulation of results is alleged but, in general, the right to elect governments has been respected. The political system therefore appears to be based on the concept of civilian rule and parliamentary democracy.

---

[11] Europa, *Regional Survey of the World: Africa South of the Sahara* (London and New York: Europa Publications, 33rd ed., 2004). See Bibliography, particularly: F. Dako, 'Study Report on the Initiatives of Reforms Related to the CRC in Benin' (unpublished study for Legislative Reform Initiative, UNICEF, 2004); N. Khan, 'National Study of Zimbabwe' (unpublished study for the Legislative Reform Initiative, UNICEF, 2004); K. Quashigah, 'Legislative Reform Initiatives, Institutional Development and Policy Changes in Favour of Children: A Ghana National Study' (unpublished study for Legislative Reform Initiative, UNICEF, 2004).

Although there have been complaints of torture and abuse of power against state authorities in general, the government has not been considered responsible for state-sponsored violations of civil and political rights. Government is a centralized system, although there are provinces and districts, and Benin has a system of local government. There is a current discussion on reforming the system of local administration to increase citizens' participation in the management of their communities.

Ghana is a country that has experienced a similar historical evolution from colonial to military and civilian democratic governance. Ghana's wealth in gold and minerals attracted various European powers from the late fifteenth century. The interests of these European powers also were further entrenched through a flourishing slave trade that they established. In 1902, Britain gained control of Ghana, which became a colony of the British Empire. Independence was achieved in 1957, and presidential elections were held under a new Constitution of 1960, when the country became a republic within the British Commonwealth. A period of political instability followed, with centralized one-party rule, a series of military coups and brief periods of democratic civilian governance. In 1993, a new republican Constitution was adopted. The country has had regular elections since then, under a multiparty system, with parliamentary democracy and an elected executive president. Although fundamentally central in character, the system of governance is supported by an elaborate local governance structure, through which most development programmes are planned and implemented.

Recent civilian governments have been commended by treaty bodies for their efforts to strengthen human rights. The establishment of an independent Commission on Human Rights and Administrative Justice has been a major initiative to promote accountability in regard to the promotion and protection of human rights. In 2001, this Commission received an award from the international human rights organization Human Rights Watch, as one of the three best human rights institutions in Africa.

Zimbabwe's political history is somewhat different from Benin and Ghana. Whereas both Benin and Ghana experienced colonial rule under a single European country, France and England, respectively, Zimbabwe came under the influence of both the Dutch and the British. The Dutch were the first settlers who came to the country in the seventeenth century. They were followed by the British, who initially administered the region through the British South African Trading Company. Subsequently, in 1922, the white population opted to become the British colony of Southern Rhodesia. The white minority population led by Ian Smith pronounced a Unilateral Declaration of Independence, when Britain refused to grant independence to the State of Southern Rhodesia within the constitutional framework suggested by the white-dominated regime. Internal conflict and a people's war to overthrow the Ian Smith regime eventually led to independence in 1980. The country was then established as the independent State of Zimbabwe, within the British Commonwealth of Nations. Elections were held in 1980, under a multiparty system. A prolonged period of political unrest and instability followed independence. Internal political conflict, the establishment of an executive presidency and a one-party political system have led to deterioration in the human rights situation within the country. Independent monitors also have alleged electoral malpractices, in 2000 and in 2002. Critics of the current regime have alleged intimidation and interference with the judiciary. A former Chief Justice, Anthony Gubbay, is said to have been forced to resign for delivering judgements that invalidated or challenged elections. Several other Supreme Court judges also have resigned, allegedly on grounds of political pressure. Suppression of dissent and torture of political opponents and journalists have received wide publicity in the international press and other documents. University reforms have introduced control over academic freedom. The government has had to face youth and student unrest, and there are allegations of torture of student leaders. Forcible eviction and violence against white farmers through politically motivated land policies also have placed Zimbabwe in a situation in which the government is faced with constant allegations of human rights abuses in international fora and the media.

Zimbabwe was temporarily suspended from the membership of the Commonwealth after the presidential election of 2002, which was widely criticized as rigged by the government. The deteriorating human rights situation in regard to political dissent and opposition led to the suspension of membership being extended in 2003. Since then, the country has withdrawn from membership of the Commonwealth. The recent acquittal of the main opposition leader by the High Court in a treason trial that has received international publicity is considered by some as a reassertion of the independence of the judiciary that can pave the way to an improved environment for democratic governance.

Some Relevant Social and Economic Factors[12]

The three countries have different social and economic profiles with some areas of commonality. Benin is the economically poorest country, with a low Human Development Index (HDI) ranking of 161. Benin's problem of widespread poverty has frequently surfaced before treaty bodies monitoring progress on treaty commitments.

---

[12] Statistical information taken from the Human Development Index, found in United Nations Development Programme, *Human Development Report 2004* (New York: UNDP, 2004), pp. 139–42.

The population of 6.6 million is multiethnic and mainly young and female. Traditionally, Benin's values emphasize the importance of family and community, and this has sometimes contributed to unequal life chances for women and children. Social indicators for these sectors of the population have improved in the decade from 1990 to 2000, based on 2002 figures. Yet life expectancy, although higher for females, is only 51 in this country. Adult literacy rates are also as low as 39.8 percent, with female literacy at 25.5 percent. Primary enrolment rates were high at 71 percent in 2000, but participation rates for girls are much lower. Infant and under-five mortality rates are still high at 93 and 151, respectively, per 1,000 live births. Although high participation of women in politics has been noted, women are in general under-represented in professions and decision-making posts in the public and private sectors. There is also widespread gender-based discrimination particularly in rural areas, and domestic violence is a problem that is now attracting concern. Customary practices such as female genital mutilation (FGM), forced marriage and abduction and rape of a child bride also continue to infringe the rights of bodily integrity of girls and women. A traditional practice of a poor family placing children and especially girls in the care of the wealthy (*vidomégon*) now operates as a form of bonded labour.[13] This and other practices such as infanticide and abandonment of children as a result of birth defects also have been highlighted in recent years as infringements of children's rights.

The country's economy was influenced by Marxist–Leninist ideologies in the 1970s, but a national conference held in 1990 settled a multiparty system, abolished the socialist system and decided to encourage a free-market economy and foreign investment. Faced with a large foreign debt and pressure from international financial institutions, governments since 1989 have adopted structural adjustment policies. Economic liberalization has been encouraged, and several state enterprises have been handed over to the private sector. The government's aim of introducing balanced economic liberalization does not seem to be operationalized effectively. Significant job losses have increased unemployment, especially among the young and female population. This has increased the burden of poverty on large sectors of the population. Health and education services also have been affected by these economic policies of structural adjustment. Fee levying, for instance, has had a negative impact on access to primary and secondary education. The

---

[13] This practice was historically a means of ensuring that children in rural areas with poor infrastructure had access to schooling by being placed with an urban family, where they would exchange work for their room and board. Customs and links between parents and recipient households provided some safeguards for the children involved. Today, however, this traditional practice is perverted and has become a lucrative trade in which economic gain is considered over and above the rights or well-being of the child.

economy remains largely undiversified, and based on subsistence agriculture and small-scale oil production.

Ghana also has a multiethnic population of approximately 19 million, which is largely rural. As in Benin, youth and women constitute the bulk of the population. At independence, Ghana's economy was very strong. There was a dramatic decline in a period of 25 years, culminating in a situation in which Ghana's foreign debt has placed it in the category of one of the highly indebted poor countries of Africa. Structural adjustment policies have been introduced as in Benin, but investment in the social sector has continued, and Ghana is categorized today as within medium human development nations with an HDI ranking of 131. Education is compulsory and is free from primary to secondary school. Ghana's illiteracy rate is one of the lowest in Africa, and its social indicators for women and children are better than in many other developing countries with similar levels of income poverty. Adult literacy improved from 1990 to 2000, and is 73.8 per cent, although female literacy is still much lower at 47 per cent. Infant and under-five mortality rates are 60 and 97, respectively, for 1,000 live births. Life expectancy is similar to that in Benin and is as low as 54.8.

Ghana has been commended by the international financial institutions for its economic recovery in the period from 1990 to 2000. As in Benin, the extended family is important in Ghana, and traditional social relationships focus on family and community rather than the individual. Traditional practices such as child fosterage between families encourage exploitation of child labour today, especially in the informal sector. Forced and early marriage and discrimination against women are also deeply inherent within customs and traditions of many communities. Traditionally, girls are more prone than boys to drop out of school in situations of poverty, and there is a lower level of participation in education at all levels by females. Despite legislative intervention, the custom of *trokosi*, which is a type of sexual slavery perpetrated against girls, continues to prevail. The problem of domestic violence that affects women and children also has been highlighted over many years as endemic across all communities within the country. The government has not been successful in eradicating the practice of FGM, which is practiced in some rural communities. Stereotypical attitudes in the community also lead to discrimination against women in access to employment and decision-making positions in the private and public sector.

Zimbabwe had a population of 10 million in 1992, which is now estimated to be about 12 million. The country has suffered an HIV/AIDS pandemic. A dramatic drop in life expectancy has occurred, and life expectancy, which stood at 61 in 1991, dropped to 38.9 in 2002. The HIV/AIDS pandemic has altered the demographic profile, and resulted in a significantly young population. As in the other countries, social organization focuses on the extended family and the community. However, the extended family has been put under pressure in recent years, coping as caregivers with the large number of orphans.

Zimbabwe's external debt is high. The transition from a regulated to a market economy and the introduction of structural adjustment policies has led to a cutback in budgetary resources for the social sector. Education was compulsory and free and the country had high literacy rates of 90 per cent in 2002, with a female literacy rate of 86.3 per cent. Fees are now charged for primary and secondary education. There is also concern that the drop-out rates of girls in education is higher than boys, particularly in secondary school, in part because of a social problem of teenage pregnancies, and in part because of a government policy of expelling pregnant girls from school. Health services also have been affected as a result of budget cuts, fee levying, retrenchment of workers, and pressure of the HIV burden on health services. In 2002, infant and under-five child mortality rates were, respectively, 76 and 123 per 1,000 live births. The economy, which is dependent mainly on agriculture, mining, eco-tourism and manufacturing, has suffered due mostly to the drought, the unstable political situation, current land policies, and the HIV/AIDS pandemic. The country's HDI ranking has fallen to 147.

Discrimination against women and girl children in the family has been commented upon by treaty bodies and in other documents. Women are under-represented in government employment and politics, in access to land, and in informal sector employment, which attracts a majority of women. Many traditional practices also encourage domestic and community violence against women and children. Exploitative child labour, forced marriage, ritual murders and sexual and widow abuse, in particular, are supported by traditional custom and practice. In 2006, the Domestic Violence Bill, providing protection and relief to victims of domestic violence, was adopted to address issues of violence.[14]

Legal Systems: The Implications of a Mixed Legal Tradition

The CRC, CEDAW, and other human rights instruments require a holistic approach to the integration of international human rights standards within countries. Initiating reform and effectively implementing and enforcing rights through law-based initiatives become even more complex when the legal system is based on several legal traditions that apply within one country. Harmonizing domestic law with treaty commitments and creating the necessary institutions and policies to support implementation must take account of the interaction between the various systems, as well as the opportunities and challenges posed by this diversity.

---

[14] Domestic Violence Bill, 2006 (Zimb.), H.B. 9, 2006. Published in the Government *Gazette*, 30 June 2006.

Benin, Ghana and Zimbabwe are countries where the legal system is derived from the major legal traditions of the world, as well as their own legislation and indigenous customary laws. These customary laws themselves are complex in their diversity, with differences based on ethnic, religious and regional influences. Benin's legal system is therefore based on its own legislation, as well as Roman law–inspired colonial French civil law and customary laws. Ghana, by contrast, has a system derived from local legislation, judge-made law, colonial English common law and customary law. Zimbabwe has the most complex of these plural legal traditions. The Zimbabwe legal system is derived from local legislation, Roman Dutch law derived from a civil law tradition as modified by English common law and customary law. The customary law survived all these influences and remained the 'living law' for most of the people. Islamic law operates in all three countries as a dimension of customary law, rather than as a separate or distinct system of law, connected with religious belief.

The status, scope and application of these diverse legal traditions within one domestic legal system mean that a dissimilar range of laws determines the rights of persons who belong to different communities within the country. State law applies as a generally applicable law, but these plural systems are also recognized. This diversity is linked to the pluralism and multiethnic and multireligious character of countries of sub-Saharan Africa. However, the legal pluralism also has been significantly influenced by their history and experience of colonization by Western powers.

The colonizing Western powers reinforced the pluralism in the legal system through their own approach to law-making. The new legal culture of the colonizing powers sought to introduce a centralized political and economic order within their colonies. However, colonial law and policy recognized the wisdom of not intervening with local laws and domestic relations that had no special relevance to their political and economic project. Customs and traditions that were in conflict with European ideas and behaviour were in general recognized by the local system, unless they were considered totally unacceptable to the colonizing power's own concept of justice and morality. For instance, British colonial law based on an eighteenth-century case[15] recognized that local laws existing in a colonized country should continue. This is why the Roman Dutch law introduced in the Cape of Good Hope by the Dutch and applicable in 1891 came to be recognized as a generally applicable system of law in Rhodesia, and subsequently in Zimbabwe. The French, following a civil law tradition, compiled some customary laws in Benin and adopted the Coutumier du Dahomey in 1931.[16]

---

[15] *Campbell v Hall*, 20 State Trials 239, 98 Eng. Rep. 1045 (K.B. 1774).
[16] Circular letter (1931) (Benin) (referred to in some sources as the Dahomey Code of Customary Law).

British colonial law and policy, consistent with this approach, developed two strategies in Zimbabwe, Ghana and Botswana as well as in other parts of their empire, for achieving some uniformity in legal norms within the accepted scenario of legal pluralism. Customary law to be enforced had to be proven in the courts by 'expert' witnesses. When customs could not be proven according to the standards or norms imposed by the colonial courts, they were rejected. British colonial legislation and colonial courts also adopted a 'repugnancy principle', which enabled courts to reject customary laws. In Botswana, for instance, the Customary Courts Act states that customary law is recognized only if it is not inconsistent with the provision of any enactment or contrary to morality, humanity and natural justice.[17] Customary laws and practices that were deemed to violate the English law concept of 'equity and good conscience and public morality' would be declared invalid by the colonial courts and would not be recognized by the legal system. Colonial courts of the French regime adopted a similar selective approach to customary law in Benin.

The British and French colonial powers also introduced the concept of choice – the right of all persons to opt out of their indigenous customary laws by deciding to have their legal relations governed by the colonial state laws. The latter regime was sometimes described as the 'civil law' or 'common law'. The state law in Benin, for instance, was based on French civil law. In Ghana, English common law and principles of equity and some general statutes applicable in England in 1874 when the first local legislative body was established, became a major source of state law. Roman Dutch civil law became the basis of state law in Rhodesia (now Zimbabwe).

The French colonial authorities adopted the concept of direct rule. However, the British adopted a concept of indirect rule in Africa that recognized the power and authority of local chiefs in administration. Both powers permitted local tribunals to resolve customary law matters. The British colonial power officially recognized a distinct system of customary courts. This recognition was more informal in Benin during the French colonial regime.

These developments created an environment for mutual influence and interaction between the colonial legal tradition and the customary or indigenous tradition.[18] Conflicts in legal norms were often resolved either through

---

[17] Customary Courts Act, CAP 16:01, No. 51 of 1969 (Botswana), cited in G. Kamchedzera, 'A report of the Multisectoral Reference Group on the Legislative Reform Initiative and the Children's Reference Group' (unpublished study for the Legislative Reform Initiative, UNICEF, 2004), p. 6.

[18] E. Cotron, 'The Changing Nature of African Marriage', in *Family Law in Asia and Africa*, ed. J. N. D. Anderson (London: Allen & Unwin, 1968), p. 11; B. Rwezaura, 'The Concept of the Child's Best Interests in the Changing Social and Economic Context of Sub Saharan Africa', in *The Best Interests of the Child: Reconciling Culture and Human Rights*, ed. P. Alston (Oxford: Clarendon Press, 1994) [Alston, *The Best Interests of the Child*], p. 82; F. Banda, 'Inheritance and Marital Rape in Zimbabwe', in *The International Survey of*

the 'repugnancy' principle used by courts or by the adoption of state laws that had conferred the right of choice to opt out of the indigenous system. The expansion of state laws and mutual influence of diverse indigenous systems created in time a core of laws that applied to all people in the country. For instance, some principles of private ownership in land law, and laws regarding guardianship, custody and contracts reflected a similar legal base. State law introduced a concept of private ownership, which differed from the concept of communal access to and use of land. State law also recognized the nuclear family for purposes such as labour law in place of the extended family relationships in the clan recognized by customary law. The British and French colonial powers anticipated that the 'repugnancy' principle, colonial legislation on various matters of importance to the State, and the choice concept would in time diminish the scope and application of the diverse customary laws.

Choice to opt out of customary law was more often recognized in the case of economic transactions such as contracts, whereas statute law significantly modified land transactions and economic activities in the colonial period. A common base of criminal law, land law and labour law restricted the application of customary laws. However, the choice to contract marriages under state law was recognized, only to a limited extent, and the main law applicable on family became the customary or indigenous laws. These customary laws applied on the basis of various ethnic and religious or regional identities and also differed accordingly. In time, they came to be known as 'personal family laws', which were distinct from the system generally applicable to all citizens. These customary family laws were of special importance for their impact on women and children. They had evolved within an essentially patriarchal extended family and social organization, and reflected a male-centred value system. Nevertheless, women and children also were assured of some security in access to communal resources through the concept of family duty and obligation.

The status of the colonial regime's courts as superior courts, which could hear appeals from customary courts, and the status of the customary courts as a separate system, and the lowest in the judicial hierarchy in these three countries and other African countries, such as Botswana, contributed to the transformation of customary law. Judges trained in a Western legal tradition used the technique of judicial interpretation to transform the principles of family law in areas such as marriage and parental rights. The concept of

Family Law, ed. A. Bainham (London: Jordan Publishing Ltd., 2001), p. 475; A. Belembago, 'The Best Interests of the Child: The Case of Burkina Faso', in Alston, ibid., p. 202; Savitri Goonesekere, 'Colonial Legislation and Sri Lankan Family Law: The Legacy of History', in *Asian Panorama*, ed. K. M. de Silva et al. (New Delhi: Vikas, 1990), p. 193; P. Kameri Mbote, 'Gender Dimensions of Law, Colonialism and Inheritance' (monograph) (Geneva: East Africa International Environment Law Research Centre, 2002).

the single male head of household and breadwinner in the colonial laws, and private ownership, gradually transformed the customary laws on inheritance, marriage and guardianship. The changes reinforced the patriarchy in customary law and undermined those aspects of communal access to resources and family obligation that impacted positively on women and children. The ensuing marginalization of women and children in the legal system has been recorded in other jurisdictions, too, with a similar experience of colonization and transformation of customary law.

British courts thus used the repugnancy principle, or the concept that there were no applicable principles in customary law, to introduce principles of state law. For instance, the concept of the biological fathers' preferential status as natural guardian and his sole responsibility for family support, which had no place in the African family tradition of extended family and community, was introduced into customary law. The concept of access of women to land, and its user, was undermined through the state law focus on a cash economy and private ownership. British and French colonial law introduced concepts of illegitimacy that were contrary to the approval customary law gave to the child of a non-marital family. By contrast, concepts such as the 'best interests' of the child were interpreted so as to modify norms of customary law that negatively impacted on children. Norms on family inheritance and land ownership also changed because of the interaction with colonial law and the new context. At the time of independence, the indigenous laws had thus become a 'subordinate system' in relation to the 'dominant' colonial law.

Efforts to restore or codify customary law also contributed to the process of transformation and subordination of customary law in the legal system. Customary laws were in essence flexible, and responded to the situation and context. Codification as a process undermined this flexibility. Gaps surfaced in the customary codes, and these were filled by the norms of state law. The Coutumier du Dahomey 1931 in Benin is an example of an attempt to codify some aspects of customary law. The compilation has a positive approach to the status of non-marital children. Yet the concept of filiation based on the colonial French civil law modified the legal position of the non-marital child in Benin. By contrast, the concept of the best interests of the child modified positively the approach to child custody in the Dahomey compilation. The gaps and limitations in the compilation provided opportunities for colonial courts to use concepts of French civil law in dispute settlement.

The English law–based common law of Ghana, as well as the Roman Dutch law applicable in Zimbabwe as state law, often incorporated gender discriminatory legal values derived from a European legal regime of the seventeenth to nineteenth centuries. Local legislation and jurisprudence developed in the state courts modified the content to some extent, but the core remained unchanged. Thus gender-biased legal values in regard to sexual offences such as rape, the husband's marital power, prostitution and vagrancy, citizenship, guardianship, and child maintenance in the state law in all three countries were located in a particular time frame of legal developments in Britain, Holland, and France. The law on juvenile justice also reflected the essentially protective approaches of the period, which failed to recognize the child as a person.

This plural legal tradition could have been changed at the time of independence, as all systems now acquired status as equally important legal traditions. We shall see how the failure to review both state law and customary law in a comprehensive sense has entrenched the diversity in legal systems within these countries. The 'imposed' legal tradition of the colonial period, especially with regard to state law, has become the received law of these countries and continues to be the major source of formal law. Thus, the French Civil Code continues to provide the basis for non-customary state law in Benin. Similarly, the Roman Dutch law and the English common law in Zimbabwe and Ghana, respectively, are the foundation of their state law. In Botswana, the presumption in regard to application of law is with the English common law and Roman Dutch law, and customary law continues as the inferior law.

In the post-independence period, legislative power in all three countries and in Botswana has been conferred on Parliament or national state assemblies. National parliaments and legislative assemblies are required to exercise the task of legislative reform because these countries have unitary systems of governance. We shall observe later that their efforts at reform have, in the main, been ad hoc. The marginalization of women and children that occurred through the social and economic changes of the colonial period and the transformation of customary law has not been addressed in comprehensive law reform. There also has been no effort to introduce comprehensive generally applicable laws to replace the diversity that exists between state law and customary law, and between different types of customary law, including Islamic law. This is still perceived as 'customary' rather than a religious law in these countries. The choice concept continues to be recognized in all three countries. Indeed, the Outline Law of Benin recognized the right of choice when the country became a self-governing colony, even before independence in 1960. In Benin, Zimbabwe and Ghana, the right of choice to marry under civil state law or customary law has been sustained in the legal systems in the post-independence period, although a majority continue to marry under customary law.

A common hierarchy of trial and appellate courts has been established in all three countries, and the concept of separation of powers and the independence of the judiciary has been recognized in post-independence constitutions. In the Roman Dutch legal tradition of Zimbabwe, the civil courts are 'Upper Guardians' of all minors, with a special role and responsibility in safeguarding their interests. The customary law continues to be administered in all three countries and in Botswana, by inferior state courts in the common judicial hierarchy. However, customary law is important for the majority of the population. The customary tribunals of traditional chiefs function in local languages that people understand. They resolve disputes through mediation, conciliation and compensation in an environment very different from the adversarial procedures conducted in English in the superior courts.

There is some concern with regard to the independence of the judiciary, as well as the training and capacity of lower court judges to address the complex issues of application of customary law. The issues of fact and law become more difficult to determine in an evolving social and economic context, in which the legal system gives the option to move out of customary law. Systems of judicial precedent exist, but research has highlighted inadequacies in the process of decision making and the anomalies perpetrated by the judiciary through their conflicting decisions on customary law, especially in the area of family law. Women and children are prejudiced by the diversity and complexity of the law, which provides the opportunity for wide judicial discretion and inconsistency and uncertainty in the law. Judicial discretion can benefit women and children sometimes, when it is exercised with sensitivity to the situation of women and children. Women and children are, in fact, often confronted with a denial of access to justice in matters relating to guardianship, land rights and inheritance and family support.[19] This aspect will be considered later with reference to law enforcement through the courts.

The English common law legal tradition does not recognize the concept of incorporating rights in a written constitution. However, Ghana and Zimbabwe, like many other countries with a mixed legal tradition, have adopted post-independence constitutions with bills of rights that can be enforced. Benin, a country influenced by the French civil law legal tradition, also has adopted a post-independence constitution with an enforceable bill of rights. These constitutional developments have provided space and opportunity to address the negative impacts of diversity and conflict in the legal norms of customary law and state law. The superior courts now have an opportunity to develop a body of jurisprudence that can forge positive human rights–based

---

[19] Rwezaura, op. cit.; Banda, 'Inheritance and Marital Rape in Zimbabwe', op. cit.; A. Armstrong, 'School and Sadza, Custody and the Best Interests of the Child in Zimbabwe', in Alston, *The Best Interests of the Child*, op. cit., p. 150; F. Banda, 'Custody and the Best Interests of the Child: Another View from Zimbabwe', in Alston, *The Best Interests of the Child*, op. cit., p. 191; E. Gwaunza, 'Inheritance Rights of Women under Customary Law of Zimbabwe', in *Bringing International Human Rights Law Home* (New York: United Nations, 2000), p. 125; C. Owinson, 'Customary Law of Benin', in *Bringing International Human Rights Law Home* (New York: United Nations, 2000), p. 129.

uniformity in legal systems, and also catalyse legislative reform in harmony with international human rights standards. The judicial activism becomes especially important when the constitution and the legal system adopt a dualist approach to international law, where ratification of a treaty by the State does not automatically give rights within the legal system. Treaties, according to the dualist approach, confer rights on citizens in a country only when these norms have been incorporated into domestic law by legislative policy or judicial interpretation. Both the Committee on the Rights of the Child and the Committee on Racial Discrimination have commented on the need to ensure that legal pluralism does not undermine human rights protected by treaty law.

Post-independence Constitutional Reform: Legal Pluralism and Human Rights

All three countries have ratified the major human rights instruments: the International Covenants, the Convention on Racial Discrimination, the CRC and CEDAW. The latter Conventions have been ratified without reservations. All these countries have submitted initial reports on several of these conventions including the CRC and CEDAW, although they have not been regular in their submission of subsequent periodic reports on the CRC and CEDAW. This is despite the fact that Zimbabwe established an inter-ministerial Committee on Human Rights and Humanitarian Law chaired by the Minister of Justice in 1993, which is expected to monitor treaty ratification and reporting. Ghana has a well-established Commission on Human Rights and Administrative Justice, which has received international recognition, but its reporting record has not been consistent. All countries seem to have given priority to reporting in recent years to the treaty bodies monitoring the International Covenants and the Convention on Racial Discrimination.

Benin, which is a country with a received civil law tradition, adopts a monist approach to treaties in Article 147 of its Constitution (1990). Treaties, and therefore the CRC, supersede national legislation from the time of ratification and publication. When a woman tried to invoke the CRC, the Constitutional Court in a decision of 2003 decided that this treaty had not been published in the official gazette and was therefore not applicable.[20] If the omission is rectified, the CRC will be part of Benin law. Ghana, which has a received English common law tradition, could have been expected to adopt a strictly dualist approach to treaties. Article 75 of the Ghana Constitution of 1992 requires Parliament to incorporate all ratified treaties into the

---

[20] 2003 Const. Ct. Decision DCC 03-009 of 19 February (Benin), cited in Dako, op. cit., p. 7.

legal system through an Act of Parliament. Article 27 also clarifies that treaty standards take precedence over national legislation. This suggests that Ghana has endorsed an approach that is more monist in regard to application of treaty law. Zimbabwe is a country with a received Roman Dutch civil law tradition. The influence of English law is seen in the approach of the post-independence Constitution (1980) and the legal system to treaties. The Constitution of 1980 and subsequent amendments do not provide for automatic reception of treaties in the legal system. They must be incorporated into domestic law by Parliament.

Whether a monist or dualist approach to treaties is adopted in these mixed legal systems, the role of the courts can be important in ensuring that domestic law is harmonized with treaty standards. A bill of rights in constitutions can be, and has been, used in many countries to integrate treaty standards into domestic law. This process often helps to forge uniformity in legal values in place of the diversity and conflict of laws prevalent in plural legal systems. The importance of judicial activism in integrating international treaties through interpretation has on occasion been referred to in the Zimbabwe Supreme Court.[21] In his decision upholding the High Court's judgement in *Unity Dow v Attorney General,* Court of Appeal Judge President Amissah stressed that international treaties must be used in the interpretation of the law. In his words: "Botswana is a member of the community of civilised States which has undertaken to abide by certain standards of conduct and, unless it is impossible to do otherwise, it would be wrong for its Courts to interpret its legislation in a manner which conflicts with the international obligations Botswana has undertaken."[22]

The bills of rights in all three countries recognize civil and political rights and provide for an enforcement procedure through applications to an apex court. Constitutional cases can be brought for and on behalf of children or adults in the Supreme Courts of Ghana and Zimbabwe, or the Constitutional Court in Benin. Approaches to recognition of specific child rights, including socio-economic rights, and the status of customary law, however, vary significantly.

Benin's Constitution in Articles 7 to 40 (which are dedicated to rights and responsibilities of human beings generally) does not specifically recognize child rights. However, Article 26 does affirm that the State protects the family, and particularly children and mothers, and there are some references

---

[21] *A Juvenile v State,* (1989) 2 ZLR 61, p. 67, per Dumbutsena CJ, cited in Khan, op. cit., p. 11.

[22] *Attorney General of Botswana v Unity Dow,* (1992) Botswana LRC Const. 623 (C.A.) [*Unity Dow* case], *included in* R. Merton et. al., *International Women's Rights Cases* (London: Cavendish Publishing Ltd., 2005), p. 592.

to economic and social rights. For instance, the Constitution guarantees an equal right of access to health and education, and obliges the State to provide access to primary education and progressively ensure free public education. The earlier discussion on the social indicators and education policies in Benin indicates how the government has undermined and even rejected the constitutional guarantees, through its economic policies on structural adjustment. The Committee on Economic, Social and Cultural Rights has expressed its concern in regard to these developments, and their negative impact on children's access to primary and secondary education. The government has not been able to use its commitments under international conventions in its negotiations with international financial institutions to resist pressure to introduce macroeconomic policies that call for a cutback in public spending in the social sector.

Zimbabwe's Constitution does not contain any reference to child rights or economic and social rights. The Ghanaian Constitution, by contrast, has a specific provision, Article 28, on the rights of children. This Article is not drafted like an analogous provision in the South African Constitution, so as to confer special rights on children over and above the general constitutional guarantees on fundamental rights. Parliament is merely *required* to enact laws to ensure certain defined children's rights. These 'rights' deal with maintenance and support, parental care, protection from abuse and torture and hazardous work. The only specific reference to health and education is the right not to be deprived of medical treatment, education or social and economic benefits by reason of religious beliefs of others.[23] Directive Principles of State Policy, which set out guidelines for governance as opposed to rights, require the State to be guided by "international human rights instruments which are relevant to the development process."[24] Article 38 requests the State to provide free compulsory and universal basic education. Article 34(1) gives the judiciary the right to use these provisions in the interpretation of laws and the Constitution.

Recent constitutional jurisprudence in South Africa has interpreted rights guaranteed by that Constitution to give access to shelter, emergency health care and access to drugs to prevent mother-to-child transmission of HIV/AIDS.[25] Case law in the Indian Supreme Court interpreted the civil and political right to life by reference to similar Directive Principles of State Policy and recognized a child's fundamental right of access to education. A child's right to economic resources so as not to be exploited in child labour

---

[23] Constitution of the Republic of Ghana (1992), Art. 28.

[24] Ibid., Art. 37.

[25] *Soobramany v Minister of Health*, (1997) CC 4 32/97 (emergency health care); *Minister of Health v Treatment Action Campaign*, (2002) 10 BCLR 1033 (CC) (HIV/AIDS drugs) *Govt. of RSA v Grootboom*, (2000) 11 BC LR1169 CC (Shelter); see also *Khosa v Minister of Social Development*, (2004) 6 BCLR 569 (CC).

that is prejudicial to health and education also has been accepted in a leading constitutional case, in India. The Indian Constitution was recently amended, recognizing a child's right to education, to reflect this jurisprudence.[26] Case law in the Philippines and Sri Lanka has recognized the intergenerational rights of children in the environment, through an interpretation of constitutionally guaranteed fundamental rights.[27]

We shall observe that Zimbabwe's Supreme Court has developed some jurisprudence on fundamental rights relating to women and children. However, this type of jurisprudence on socio-economic rights has not been used to promote accountability in formulating national policies on health and education. We therefore see an undermining of constitutional guarantees on socio-economic rights through macroeconomic policies, even when they have been recognized in national constitutions. The opportunity to develop generally applicable norms on children's rights in this area also has not been fully utilized.

The post-independence experience on customary law in Ghana, Botswana, and Benin has, however, been somewhat different from the experience of some other countries in Asia and Africa. In these countries, post-independence ideologies of nationalism and ethnic and religious identity have renewed commitment to religious, indigenous, or customary law. These customary and religious laws are perceived as immutable and unchanging. Courts have found it difficult to use even constitutional guarantees on rights to prevent discrimination in customary family laws in areas such as inheritance, marriage and divorce.[28] There have been rare occasions in which judicial decisions have interpreted constitutional guarantees on equality to undermine negative aspects of customary or religious-based law that discriminate against children or women. International treaty standards have sometimes been cited to support these interpretations.[29]

---

[26] *Unni Krishnan v State of Andhra Pradesh*, JT (1993) 474; *Mohini Jain v State of Karnataka*, (1992) 3 SCC 666; *M C Mehta v State of Tamil*, (1996) Nadu Writ Pet. 465/ 1986; Constitution of India (Constitution (Eighty-sixth Amendment) Act, 2002), Art. 21 A.

[27] See *Minors Oposa* case, op. cit.; *Eppawela* case, op. cit., and discussion accompanying *supra* note 6.

[28] A. Belembaogo 'The Best Interests of the Child: The Case of Burkina Faso', in Alston, *The Best Interests of the Child*, op. cit., p. 202; *Mohammad Ahmed Khan v Shah Bano Begum and Others* (*Shah Bano* case), AIR (1987) SC 943 (India); *Madhu Kishwar v State of Bihar* (1996) 5 SCC 125 (India); *Ahmedabad Women's Action Group v Union of India*, (1997) 3 SCC 573 ; *Meera Dhungana v Ministry of Law and Justice et al.*, Nepal Law Journal (1994): 462.

[29] See *Comparative International Law Journal of Southern Africa*, Vol. 1998 onwards; *Gita Hariharan v Reserve Bank of India* (1999) 2 SCC 238; *John Noel and Others v Obed Toto*, (1995) Supreme Court Luganville, Santo. Case 18/1994 (Vanuatu) (cited in G. Phillips, 'Application of Customary Law in Fiji and Pacific Region', in *Bringing International Human Rights Law Home*, op. cit., p. 121); *Humaira Mehmood v State* PLD (1999) Lahore 494 (Pakistan); Belembaogo, op. cit. (on Burkina Faso).

We have seen how the repugnancy principle, the choice concept, and the interaction with state law modified customary law in all countries. The approach of independence constitutions to fundamental rights and customary law can be a catalyst for further transformation. Constitutional provisions can contribute to the development of uniformly applicable legal norms in an environment of legal pluralism.

In Benin, the Constitution's provisions on fundamental rights and Article 147 on the impact of international treaty law have been used by the Constitutional Court in 1996 to question the enforceability of customary law. Article 26 of the Constitution emphasizes the right to equality and non-discrimination, and this has been reinforced by the Personal and Family Code of 2004. The law also states that customs will not have legal force in regard to all areas covered by the Code. This development has increased opportunity for judicial activism in reducing and eliminating pluralism, and developing uniformly applicable norms, especially in the area of family law and the legal status of women and children. In Botswana, the Customary Law Act prohibits the application of principles that are contrary to morality, humanity and natural justice. The 1987 Chieftaincy Act states that customary law must not be injurious to the welfare of the people or repugnant to the Constitution or any other enactment. There is some jurisprudence indicating willingness of the courts to occasionally recognize that customary law is not static and can be developed in a contemporary context. The chiefs also play an advisory role in the development and interpretation of customary law.

At independence, Ghana recognized the important status of customary law in the legal system by the Courts Act of 1960. Instead of being required to be proven in the courts, customary law acquired the status of enforceable law. The Constitution recognizes Parliament as the supreme legislative authority, and defines the sources of law as legislation and existing written and unwritten law prior to the Constitution. Customary law has therefore been specifically recognized in the Constitution as a source of law. However, Ghana's Constitution declares the supremacy of the Constitution and states that all laws must conform to it. Customary law is therefore subject to modification by legislation; it needs to be harmonized with the Constitution and the norms on fundamental rights guaranteed by the Constitution. This is made very clear in Article 26, which adds that "all customary practices which dehumanize or are injurious to the physical and mental well being of a people are prohibited."[30] Two further articles, 270 and 272, are important. These recognize the institution of chieftaincy, although traditional rulers no longer have legislative, judicial or executive authority under customary law. The National House of Chiefs is mandated to undertake a progressive study of customs with a view to creating a unified system, and eliminating those

---

[30] Ghana Constitution, op. cit., Art. 26.

customs and usages that are outmoded and harmful. The right to equality and non-discrimination in Ghana's Constitution and other rights can therefore be interpreted so as to challenge norms of customary law that infringe the CRC and CEDAW.

Ghana's constitutional approach to customary law clearly recognizes the concept of transformation of customary law, providing an opportunity to develop a jurisprudence on rights that harmonizes with both the Constitution and international human rights standards. The catalyst for reform can be the legislature, the courts and the internal system of chieftaincy. However, the fact that the balance between customary law and state law in the legal system is not clear today has been highlighted by the Committee on the Convention on Elimination of Racial Discrimination in its Concluding Observations on Ghana's report in 2003. The National House of Chiefs does not seem to have made progress in working on the task of reform and revision of the diverse systems of customary law, with a view to both reducing diversity and developing common norms that harmonize with the Constitution and treaty standards.

Zimbabwe's approach to customary law in the post-independence period has been quite different. Perhaps because of the nature of its struggle for independence, the Constitution and the legal system reflect a policy of giving precedence to customary law. Article 11 of the Constitution also declares that all persons are entitled to fundamental rights without discrimination on the ground of race, sex and so on, and certain other aspects that are defined. However, customary laws in conflict with these rights also can be enforced. Article 23(1), which contains the equality provision, confers a right to equality and non-discrimination that can be enforced in relation to state acts. It excludes the important area of the private sector, and thus may not impact on acts of private persons that are legitimized by customary law. Article 23(2) also specifies gender rather than sex and age in reference to the grounds of discrimination. Thus, discrimination against children where it occurs in state law and especially customary law is not covered by the provision. This can undermine the constitutionally guaranteed rights of children, and especially girls. In addition, Article 23(3) permits derogation from the constitutionally guaranteed rights of equality, if a law relates to certain specified aspects of family law, and all matters of 'personal law'. Application of customary law can also derogate from rights in cases involving persons governed by customary law and those not governed by customary law, where they have consented to the application of customary law. A Customary Law and Courts Act (1990) has now recognized traditional chiefs as lower court judges.

The obligation to protect, respect and fulfil constitutional rights and treaty standards of the CRC and CEDAW on equality and non-discrimination by local laws, including customary law, is weakened by the conflict of laws between customary and received laws. These particular provisions that qualify the right of equality and non-discrimination under the constitution are a significant barrier to law reform in harmony with the fundamental rights guaranteed by the constitution, and international treaties. They also can impact negatively on the enforcement of fundamental rights.

The practical negative impact of these norms in Zimbabwe is observed in the well-known case of *Magaya v Magaya* (1999).[31] Zimbabwe customary law on inheritance in general discriminates against female heirs. The Administration of Estates Act of 1997 attempted to remove this discrimination. In a case filed before the Act came into operation, the Supreme Court of Zimbabwe relied on the constitutional provisions giving significance to customary law, and rejected the claim of the female heir from an African customary marriage to the intestate estate of her father. The Court preferred the claim of the eldest male child of the deceased on arguments based on customary law. The Supreme Court held that the discriminatory aspects of "customary law were shielded from the non-discrimination clause" of the Constitution.[32] The Court went on to decide that the commitments of Zimbabwe under international human rights treaties on gender equality could not in any way undermine the validity and enforceability of customary law.

Zimbabwe's constitutional provisions thus restrict the capacity to use the international standards and constitutional rights to realize the rights of women and children. In other jurisdictions, including some in Africa, superior courts have, as mentioned earlier, interpreted customary law in harmony with constitutional norms on non-discrimination and equality, and the standards of CEDAW or the CRC. The 1991 *Unity Dow* citizenship case in Botswana, the 1990 *Ephrahim v Pastory* case in Tanzania, decisions of the Nigerian Court of Appeal on inheritance rights, and the *Fitzpatrick* case in South Africa[33] are instances in which the superior courts used the national constitutions and international standards to reinforce the right of equality and non-discrimination, despite customary law provisions or religious beliefs that seemed to endorse discrimination. In Unity Dow's case, the Botswana Citizenship Act of 1984, which denied a woman who married a foreigner the right to pass her citizenship to her children while permitting a man married to a foreigner to do so, was challenged as an infringement of the constitutional guarantee of equality. Unity Dow argued that she should have the same right to pass her Botswana citizenship to her children. Although the Citizenship

---

[31] (1999) I ZLR 100, discussed in F. Banda, 'Inheritance and Marital Rape in Zimbabwe', op. cit.

[32] Ibid., p. 477.

[33] *Unity Dow* case, op. cit.; *Ephrahim v Pastory*, 87 ILR 106 (1990); *Minister of Welfare and Population Development v Fitzpatrick*, (2001) 1 LRC CC; *Mojekwu v Mojekwu*, (1997) 7 Nig. Weekly L Rep. 238; *Muojekwu v Ejikme*, (2000) 5 Nig. Weekly L Rep. 402.

Act reflected the values of colonial law on citizenship, the counter-arguments in this case were based on the interpretation that the Act reflected the patrilineal social fabric of customary law, and must be interpreted according to the customary or personal law rather than the Constitution. The Court of Appeal in Botswana relied on CEDAW, the CRC and the African Charter on Human and People's Rights in interpreting the constitutional provision on equality. It refused to accept that the Citizenship Act could be applied according to customary law without reference to the Constitution, CRC and CEDAW, and regional human rights standards on women and children's rights. In *Ephrahim v Pastory,* the High Court of Tanzania upheld the right of a woman to sell clan land, although this was contrary to customary law, on the ground that Tanzania's Constitution, CEDAW and other international instruments ratified by the country prohibited discrimination against women. The Court concluded that Tanzanian women now had the same right as men to inherit and sell clan land. Customary laws on inheritance were declared unconstitutional in the Nigerian cases as contrary to justice and equity, and international human rights standards.

A similar approach was adopted by the Constitutional Court of South Africa in the *Fitzpatrick* case, when it refused to permit a challenge to a state law that prohibited corporal punishment in schools, by a group who argued that the law infringed the right of Christians to freedom of religion. The Court relied on the constitutional guarantee protecting a child's right to dignity and personal security, and the State's obligation to promote respect for those rights and protect the child's best interests.

The idea that custom is not static and is evolving is supported by the reality in many African and Asian societies, where traditional values have been undermined by colonialism and post-independence economic and social processes. The breakdown of the extended family and kinship relations, private ownership and a cash economy are known to have transformed customary norms on bride price, widowhood, maintenance and family support linked to land inheritance and user. The transformation has invariably impacted negatively on women and children and marginalized their interests.[34]

In this context, judicial activism can help to interpret, develop and harmonize customary law with the human rights protected by the Constitution and human rights treaties, especially the CRC and CEDAW. As Justice Albie Sachs of the Supreme Court of South Africa said in *State v Makuwenyaye,* "aspects and values of traditional African law have to be developed to ensure compatibility with the Constitution."[35] Whereas the provisions in the Benin and Ghana Constitutions have made that task possible, the language of Article 23(3) in Zimbabwe restricts the scope for this type of interpretation. The

[34] See discussion, *supra* note 17 and accompanying text.
[35] *State v Makuwenyane* (1995) 6 BC LR 665 (CC), para. 383.

continued reference to customary law in the post-independence period, both in the formal legal system and at the non-formal community level, has made it critically important to ensure that it evolves in harmony with human rights standards.

The promise of post-independence constitutions in forging uniform legal values in harmony with human rights treaty standards in place of diversity and conflict of legal values cannot be realized, when the constitution itself recognizes that customary law can derogate from constitutional norms. Shielding customary law from fertilization with other systems also can further entrench the conflict in values with state law. In the 1999 Zimbabwe case of *H v H*, for instance,[36] the court interpreted Roman Dutch 'common law' or received state law in line with developments on marital rape in England. The court decided that the concept that a married man could not rape his wife was not part of the Roman Dutch law–based civil law on marriage, and was contrary to norms of a civilized society. The difference in judicial approaches in interpreting state civil law and customary law has a significant impact on women's and children's access to justice through the legal system.

The proposed African court and the regional standards[37] on human rights accepted in Africa can be an important influence in integrating human rights standards. However, they have not had that impact. Indeed, they are in conflict with the current approach of the Zimbabwean legal system. The African Charter on Human Rights and People's Rights declares in Article 18(3) that States must eliminate discrimination against women and protect their rights under international law. This standard has been elaborated in the comprehensive document, the Protocol on the Rights of Women in Africa (2003). The Protocol incorporates the idea of infringement of women's rights in the public and private spheres and the right to live in a positive cultural context without discrimination. The African Charter on the Rights and Welfare of the Child (on Children's Rights), adopted after the CRC, recognizes that customary law is not static but is modified in changing conditions and through interaction with other systems. It incorporates the non-discrimination

---

[36] (1999) 2 ZLR 358.
[37] G. S. Kamchejzra, 'The Complementarity of the Convention on the Rights of the Child and the African Charter on the Rights of and Welfare of the Child' in *Understanding Children's Rights*, ed. E. Verhallen, op. cit., p. 549; C. Beyani, 'Towards a More Effective Guarantee of Women's Rights in the African Human Rights System' in *Human Rights of Women*, ed. R. Cook (Philadelphia: University of Pennsylvania Press, 1994), p. 307; African Charter on Human and People's Rights, *adopted* 27 June 1981, OAU Doc. CAB/LEG/67/3 rev. 5, 21 I.L.M. 58 (1982), *entered into force* 21 Oct. 1986; and the Protocol to the African Charter on Human and Peoples' Rights on the Establishment of an African Court on Human and Peoples' Rights, *adopted* 10 June 1998 and *entered into force* 2004; Protocol to the African Charter on Human and Peoples' Rights on the Rights of Women in Africa, *adopted* 11 July 2003, Art. 17(1).

principle and makes it enforceable against state and non-state or private actors, thus including any person or authority.[38] The African Charter on Children's Rights also requires States to discourage those customs and practices that are inconsistent with the Charter. It specifies some customs such as child marriage that must be prohibited. The Charter has a general provision that States must discourage customs that are prejudicial to the child's health and life, or when they discriminate on the grounds of sex or other status. The Charter uses the term 'discourage' and 'prohibition' in reference to customary law,[39] and endorses the perspectives on customary law in the plural legal systems of both Ghana and Benin. The African Charters thus reinforce the need to harmonize customary law with international and regional human rights standards through law, policy and judicial activism. They reflect an approach that should fertilize constitutional provisions and constitutional jurisprudence on customary law.

Fundamental rights jurisprudence is developed when constitutions give a right to challenge state actions or inaction in administration through the courts. Private sector actions may be challenged, either through judicial interpretation or because the constitutional guarantees cover non-state action. National legislation also can be challenged for violation of fundamental rights if the power of judicial review of legislation is given by the constitution. Fundamental rights jurisprudence that is based on the constitution can help to ensure that a bill of rights and treaty ratification are not merely aspirational or a declaration of intent.

It would appear that the general norm of the supremacy of the constitution and or treaty law has not been used by the courts in these countries to strike down legislation that is in conflict with these standards. Where the courts have pronounced such decisions in Zimbabwe, the legislature has intervened to negate the decision. It will be seen later how Zimbabwe's Corporal Punishment Act 1990, permitting juveniles to be whipped, conflicts with the Constitution and undermines a case decided by the Supreme Court. Other fundamental rights have been modified by legislation in Zimbabwe by amending the Constitution with a two-thirds majority. Rights are not perceived as 'entrenched' guarantees when legislation contrary to rights can be passed without challenge by parliaments.

There is no evidence that constitutional provisions on the supremacy of the constitution have been used to challenge legislation or actions affecting children in either Ghana or Benin.

This important dimension of fundamental rights law and judicial review to determine the constitutionality of laws has been used in other countries

---

[38] African Charter on the Rights and Welfare of the Child, OAU Doc. CAB/LEG/24.9/49, *adopted* July 1990, *entered into force* Nov. 29, 1999.

[39] Ibid., Arts. 1(3) and 21.

with written constitutions to challenge various pieces of legislation, either
before or after they are enacted, and even rules of evidence and court procedure. In Egypt, legislation to lower the age of majority to 15 years has
been successfully challenged in the Supreme Court for inconsistency with
the CRC. In Kenya, a recent case has interpreted the constitutional guarantee on equality in a rape case to reject a gender-biased rule of evidence
based on English law. The *Unity Dow* case in Botswana successfully challenged gender discriminatory legislation on citizenship, which prohibited a
married woman passing her citizenship to her children, as a violation of the
constitutional guarantees on equality.[40]

The capacity to challenge legislation or court practice, and judicial review
of the constitutionality of a law as a bill before it is adopted by Parliament,
is an important strategy for realizing rights, including children's rights, in
domestic law. Judicial review can help to create consistency or uniformity
in legal values. Widened *locus standi* that gives non-governmental and civil
society organizations the right to bring such cases in the courts has proven
to be useful in monitoring legislation for conflict with the constitution. The
Class Action Act 1999 in Zimbabwe allows legal proceedings to be brought
on behalf of a group of persons, but there is a limitation. The consent of the
Attorney General or the High Court must be obtained. This may account
for this failure to use this procedure to challenge legislation that is contrary
to the Constitution.

II. THE LEGISLATIVE REFORM INITIATIVE

The Reform Process

The period after the ratification of the CRC indicates that all three countries
have tried to introduce law reform and policy change to improve the situation
of children. Their initiatives have not always been consistent with the CRC
or effective in impact, but the consistency in political will to introduce reform
is striking. In the case of Benin and Ghana, the post-CRC period in these
countries coincided with a political shift from military rule towards civilian
government and parliamentary democracy. This provided an opportunity
for national and international non-governmental organizations and agencies, concerned with children's issues, to articulate their views. They have
been able to freely engage in advocacy lobbying and law review projects on
behalf of children's rights and CRC implementation. These efforts seem to

---

[40] *Daniel Latifi v Union of. India* (2001) 7 SCC 740; Shenaz Shaik Case 10 Jan. 2001
(India); Broadcasting Corporation Case (1996) 1 SLR 157 (Sri Lanka); UNICEF, 'Law
Reform to Implement the Convention on the Rights of the Child'. Innocenti Research
Centre Background Paper (Jan. 2004); *Mukungu v Republic* (2003) EA. 30 Jan. 2003
(C.A. Kenya), *Unity Dow* case, op. cit.

have strengthened and supported the government's law reform initiatives. By contrast, the period after 1990 has been a difficult and unstable time in the new nation-State of Zimbabwe that was established in 1980 after a long period of internal political violence and armed conflict. One-party rule has been established and the government has been under constant criticism in international fora and the media for human rights violations. Nevertheless, international agencies and non-governmental civil society organizations have been able to continue working on a CRC-related child rights agenda. The government has continued to demonstrate political will in regard to children's issues. We shall observe that the political environment has impacted negatively on the human rights of other sections of society, including women. Not surprisingly the situation of children and law reform initiatives on children's rights, in particular, also has been negatively affected by the political environment and context.

Legislative reform to realize child rights in harmony with the CRC raises general problems and issues that are of concern to all States parties. However, the issues of diversity and non-discrimination, and using the legal system to develop generally applicable laws and introduce common norms, become critical in a mixed plural legal tradition. The interface with women's human rights issues, and the need for consistency in realizing the rights of both women and children through law reform, are even more important because of the customary and received colonial law in the legal system. The problems of initiating law reform and achieving effective implementation thus become more complex.

Legislative reform in harmony with the CRC is important in countries with a mixed or plural legal tradition because it gives an opportunity to reject those areas of received colonial and customary law that conflict with human rights standards accepted under international law. It is critical when the legal system adopts a dualist approach, and requires domestic incorporation of treaty standards for their application at the national level. Legislative reform can help to eliminate contradictions in the local legal system, between the different internal systems and also the distinct areas of law such as family law, criminal law and juvenile justice laws. The process of harmonization with the CRC thus becomes an opportunity to introduce general laws applicable to the whole population and eliminate internal inconsistencies in legal values. Harmonizing international treaty law through legislative reform also can contribute to reinforcing constitutional guarantees on equality, non-discrimination, and important fundamental rights. This is especially important in a situation in which the procedure for enforcement of fundamental rights is not effective, and the power of judicial review by the courts is limited. We have seen how Parliament, as the supreme law-making and legislative body, can undermine, and even negate, fundamental rights guaranteed in the constitution.

Ratification of the CRC in Benin, Ghana and Zimbabwe has catalysed this important process of legislative reform. A vigorous reform process is also evident in Botswana. In Zimbabwe, the obligation to present the initial report to the CRC treaty body led to a government initiative on a desk review of children's laws in 1994–1996. A high-level Inter-Ministerial Committee on Human Rights and Humanitarian Law was established in 1993, and is mandated to review progress on treaty commitments and reporting, including the CRC and CEDAW. This Committee facilitates the collection of data and inter-sectoral networking by the major ministries concerned with children in carrying the rights agenda forward and monitoring progress. National committees to review children's laws such as the National Victim Friendly Courts Committee have been appointed. They have examined priority areas for law reform through a consultative process. A few ad hoc child-friendly law reforms, which will be discussed later, have emerged from this national legislative review process. The current political situation has perhaps contributed to the failure to sustain these initiatives. Periodic reporting to the Committee on the Rights of the Child has been delayed, and the Committee has been unable to sustain the momentum for change through a review of progress.

In Ghana and Benin, too, CRC reporting has been a catalyst for law reform. In Benin, the constitutional reform process, the move towards civilian rule and the submission of the initial report to the Committee on the Rights of the Child all combined to give momentum to a legislative reform process. Specific legislation has been introduced. A National Commission on the Rights of the Child was established after Benin reported to the Committee on the Rights of the Child in 1999, and the Committee's Concluding Observations were communicated. The African Union's reform initiative on family law in 2003 also strengthened the national process on review of family law. A comprehensive Personal and Family Code that sought to harmonize laws with the CRC and CEDAW was adopted in 2004.

Ghana's National Commission on Children conducted a review of laws in preparation for the submission of the initial report to the Committee on the Rights of the Child. An inter-sectoral governmental Child Law Reform Advisory Committee, which included judges, professionals and the police, and the Commission on Human Rights and Administration Justice were appointed to harmonize the domestic law with international law. This initiative resulted in a more comprehensive legal reform process than in either Zimbabwe or Benin. The Ghana Law Commission proposed the adoption of a uniformly applicable Children's Act that also would set out basic principles. It also selected some priority areas like criminal law and juvenile justice as areas for general reforms, which would be relevant to all children. These reforms are important because they undermine the diversity in legal norms found in the colonial legislation and in customary law.

In Botswana, a review of the Children's Act was initiated in 1999. This type of law reform tried to make the law more compliant with international human rights conventions, CEDAW and the CRC in particular. The approach in these reviews was to compare international standards with national laws and make recommendations for amendments. The same approach was used to review legislation impacting on the status of women. This legal review made recommendations affecting many statutes and the Constitution.[41] Vision 2016, launched in 1997, underlined the importance of legal reviews in the light of constitutional and international standards, arguing that "the challenge in the next twenty years will be to review those laws and practices that are inconsistent with the full enjoyment of constitutional rights, to ensure their conformity with constitutional and international standards."[42] Dissatisfaction with the reform process led to a fresh review in 2004, with a new focus on integrating a rights-based approach into law reform.

This process has led to a comprehensive review of the whole of Botswana's legislative framework impacting on children. It is during this process that customary law issues and their impact on children's rights were discussed seriously. Contradictions with the written law were highlighted. Failure to comply with the CRC tenets, as well as harmful practices that should be abolished, were raised in the discussions.

The findings have been handed over to the Ministry of Local Government for drafting the amended Children's Act, as well as reforms in other sectors. A dialogue has been initiated with the House of Chiefs on customary law. A broad-based Reference Group, with children to lead the process as well as community discussions, is being planned with the support of chiefs.

The issues that have been prioritized for specific law reform reveal the influence of CRC standards and the children's rights issues that have been recognized as important internationally. It will be observed later that all countries referred to above have taken some initiative to introduce reforms in specific areas such as family law, trafficking, child labour, sexual abuse and domestic violence. Law reform on HIV/AIDS has been a priority in Zimbabwe and Botswana because of both national and international concern with the issue. These general areas surface the centrality of gender issues in realizing the human rights of children in these countries.

The human rights treaty bodies such as Committees for CEDAW, CERD, CRC, ICCPR and ICESCR have addressed these general areas of concern. They have, on occasion, referred to specific customary practices such as FGM, *trokosi* in Ghana, *videmogan* and the Coutumier du Dahomey in

---

[41] Department of Women's Affairs, Ministry of Labour and Home Affairs, 'Report on a Review of All Laws Affecting the Status of Women in Botswana' (Gaborone: Government of Botswana, 1998).

[42] Presidential Task Force Group for a Long Term Vision for Botswana, 'Long Term Vision for Botswana' (Gaborone: Government of Botswana, 1997), p. 26.

Benin. Specific recommendations have proven to be important in motivating legislative reform at the national level.

The internationalization of some of these issues also has enabled UN agencies, international, regional and national NGOs and other civil society groups to be active in promoting constitutional and legislative reform. It has given some legitimacy to concerns that can be otherwise dismissed as the promotion of alien values or an interference with state sovereignty.

Local NGOs appear to be active and vibrant in Zimbabwe, Ghana and Benin, and there seems to be government recognition of their interest in both children's and women's rights issues. Local NGOs and especially regional women's organizations have been active in monitoring the situation, and in research advocacy, lobbying and awareness-raising. International child rights NGOs such as Redd Barna (Save the Children Norway) also have supported law review in Zimbabwe.

UN agencies have been active on children's issues such as child labour and FGM, which also connect with gender. UNDP has been involved in the review of customary law and CEDAW in Zimbabwe. UNDP and UNIFEM also have supported the constitutional reform process and focused on issues of good governance. UNIFEM has supported work by NGOs on constitutional reform, whereas UNDP has worked with the government on this issue. UNICEF has been active on all areas of concern to children and women, and also supported the government on constitutional reform and the legislative reform process relating to children in all four countries. Although the UNDAF process allows for coordination and collaboration, most agencies have pursued their mandate, although they have on occasion collaborated with each other.

Indeed, UNICEF's contribution has been an important influence in catalysing reforms in all four countries. Their support has taken a variety of forms, such as supporting research and review of laws by a range of personnel, capacity building among government institutions and awareness-raising on rights. UNICEF in Zimbabwe also has supported sharing of experiences from other countries in the region as a first step in the review of domestic law for compatibility with the CRC and CEDAW. Gender equality and law reform on women's human rights have been considered a central issue in UNICEF's activities in all countries, reinforcing the importance of this link for the children's rights agenda.[43]

Although NGOs and professionals have been active on law reform initiatives, the interest of parliamentarians and judges has been harnessed in both Benin and Zimbabwe on selected issues with the support of international

---

[43] Details on law reform – see section *infra* on The Legislative Reform Project. For details on the other interventions referred to, see Dako, op. cit.; Khan, op. cit.; Quashigah, op. cit.

UN agencies. Traditional rulers have been given a specific role in regard to reform of customary law in Ghana. However, their interest has not been catalysed for reform. In Botswana, however, a dialogue with the community and traditional leaders who are considered custodians of customary law has been an important aspect of the legislative reform process.

The limitations in the work that has been undertaken will be considered in examining the type of law reform that has taken place in these countries. A general observation is that civil society groups and UN agencies have not been successful in sustaining the regularity of the reporting process to treaty bodies, to monitor and also activate progress.

The Legislative Reform Project

We have observed that diversity poses a special challenge in integrating the CRC concept of rights applicable to all children. We also have noted that discrimination against women and girls is embedded in the diverse domestic legal traditions derived from both colonial law and customary law. Consequently, legislative reform in line with the CRC has to comprehensively review laws to eliminate this diversity, and reinforce constitutional and CRC values on non-discrimination and equality.

The Scope of Legislative Reform

The legislative reform project has not addressed either of these important priorities with consistency in most countries. The discussion on the Constitution and customary law indicates how the constitutional values that link to the CRC have been contradicted by the Corporal Punishment Act 1990 in Zimbabwe. Similarly, the Administration of Estates Amendment Act 1997, strengthening women's rights to inheritance, is undermined by constitutional provisions protecting customary law. The latter provisions significantly entrench discrimination against women in customary law and are in conflict with the non-discriminatory approach to women's rights in the Legal Age of Majority Act and the Matrimonial Causes Act. Some provisions of the Sexual Offences Act are in conflict with other laws on marital rape. Ghana's Children's Act 1998 and Benin's Family Law Code 2004 try to introduce some uniform values linked to the constitutions, CRC and CEDAW. These laws can help to increase areas of uniformity in the legal system. They set out some general principles but are also selective and limited in scope.

Ghana's Criminal Law Amendment Law 1998 and Zimbabwe's Sexual Offences Act (2002), accompanied by the Criminal Procedure and Evidence Amendment Act (1997), eliminate some of the gender discriminatory and negative features of received colonial law. The Roman Dutch law in Zimbabwe, the French Civil Code applicable in Benin and the English law applicable in Ghana reflect the gender discriminatory legal values entrenched in the jurisprudence of these countries from the seventeenth to the nineteenth centuries. This jurisprudence invariably did not recognize children as persons who could be rights holders. These colonial received laws reinforce discrimination against women and conflict with CEDAW, and undermine children's rights concepts under the CRC, although some concepts such as 'the best interests of the child' have a creative impact on domestic law. Post-independence general legislation in the areas of marriage, guardianship, custody and maintenance has repealed some negative aspects of the colonial law. A residue remains, however, even in the area of family law. The negative discriminatory aspects of colonial law also are seen in some areas of criminal law, prostitution, domestic violence against women and children and citizenship laws.

The discrepancies and contradictions inherited from the colonial period in regard to the definition of childhood also can be seen in Zimbabwe. These differences are based on arbitrary classifications in post-independence legislation and colonial law, rather than the concept of 'evolving capacity' in childhood adopted in the CRC. Ghana's Children's Act and the Family Code in Benin have attempted to introduce some consistency and uniformity in regard to the definition of childhood in harmony with the CRC and CEDAW, especially in relation to the age of marriage, child labour and criminal responsibility. The general legislation on children, the Child Protection and Adoption Act in Zimbabwe, however, covers specific aspects of protection rights and entrenches rather than eliminates the discrepancies in the approach to the definition of childhood, and especially with the Legal Age of Majority Act. The work of the Victim Friendly Courts Committee resulted in the adoption of a package of law reforms that promoted consistency in the law on sexual abuse as well as evidence and procedure in child abuse litigation. This approach has not been followed in other areas of law.

All countries have prioritized law reform in specific areas such as birth registration, sexual offences and child abuse, child labour and family law that impact on women and children. Zimbabwe has enacted legislation in 1995 on international child abduction in harmony with The Hague Convention. The family law reform has been ad hoc in all countries and does not address the conflicts with customary law in a comprehensive manner. The criminal and family laws in Ghana and Benin, however, prohibit specific customary practices such as FGM, *trokosi* and *vidomégon*. These reform initiatives were a response to the repeated concluding observations of treaty bodies examining country reports, and the national and international campaigns against FGM, slavery, trafficking, sexual exploitation and child labour. Benin enacted a composite specific trafficking law in 2004. This law is essentially a revision of the Law 61-20 on Trafficking in Children, meant to remedy the insufficiencies of the 1961 law and conform it to the Palermo Protocol on transnational organized crime and the Optional Protocol to the CRC on the sale of children, child prostitution and child pornography. Aspects of juvenile justice also have been reformed in Zimbabwe and Benin, whereas Ghana has introduced a broad-based Juvenile Justice Act.[44]

The ratification of the CRC and CEDAW has promoted law reform to eliminate discrimination in citizenship/nationality laws in Maldives and Sri Lanka in South Asia. The *Unity Dow* case in Botswana, which also cited international standards, promoted a reform of the Citizenship Act and eliminated discrimination against women and children. Several decisions of the Zimbabwe courts on resident visas for foreign spouses adopt an approach that undermines the discriminatory aspects of the law, and consider the interests of female spouses and children. However, citizenship law has not been harmonized with CRC and CEDAW standards.[45]

The CRC envisages child rights as an indivisible and universal group of survival, development, protection and participation rights. The protection rights emphasis in law reform is apparent in all these countries and Botswana, and development and participation rights have received less priority.

The concept of child parliaments and giving children throughout the country an opportunity to articulate their views has been accepted in Benin and Zimbabwe in the post-CRC period. Ghana's National Commission has organized a system of child advocates to discuss children's issues at the community level. Although child participation is recognized in these initiatives, it is contradicted by other legal provisions or the failure to enforce laws that can reinforce a child's right to participation within the CRC framework of evolving capacity. Customary laws in Benin, Botswana, and Ghana, for instance, authorize corporal punishment. The Committee on the Rights of the Child has drawn attention to the fact that this is not prohibited by law, in Concluding Observations on Ghana's initial report. The Committee also has commented on the failure to enforce laws against corporal punishment in Benin. The Zimbabwe Act of 1990 has institutionalized this form of punishment for juveniles in conflict with the law. The Law and Order Maintenance Act restricts freedom of expression and can impact on education. Forced marriage is prohibited but there is no commitment to prosecute, and the legislation has not incorporated other strategies such as strong compulsory education regulations to support enforcement. Indeed, Zimbabwe law permits expulsion of girls who become pregnant from school – a legal provision

---

[44] Juvenile Justice Act (2003) (Ghana).

[45] *Rattigan and Others v Chief Immigration Officer*, (1994) 2 ZLR 54; *Salem v Chief Immigration Officer*, (1994) 2 ZLR 28; Constitution of Zimbabwe Amendment (No. 14) Act, (1996). Published in *Official Gazette*, Acts, pp. 143–9; *Kohilhas v Chief Immigration Officer*, (1997) 2 RLR 441.

that violates both the development and participation rights of girls. Forced marriage according to customary tradition is a problem in all countries, and early marriage contributes to the higher dropout rates for girls. A human rights–based approach to law reform seems necessary to ensure that law reforms are truly comprehensive and based on the objective of maximizing the child's well-being.

Access to Health and Education and Legislative Reform

The indivisibility of rights is key to a human rights–based approach to programming. The idea that indivisibility is a reflection of the concept of social trust and responsible management of national resources, and is inherent in good governance relating to child rights, is reflected in Article 4 of the CRC. The indivisibility of rights is especially important in a mixed plural legal tradition because it can help to create and reinforce a supportive environment for the introduction of uniform laws applicable to all children. Access to education and health is key to disparity reduction and the elimination of discrimination. We have observed that, except in Ghana, law reform has not prioritized giving access to health and education as legal rights. Indeed, constitutional guarantees in this regard have been undermined by structural adjustment macroeconomic policies. Because resource allocation for a public education and health system is perceived as a matter of policy rather than law and legal rights, it has been easy to cut back financial allocation in budgets, and so undermine provisions in constitutions and educational statutes. Consequently, the post-CRC National Plans of Action on children in Ghana, Benin and Zimbabwe, and more recent poverty reduction plans, do not refer to legislative reform in these key areas. These plans seek to combat poverty without addressing the need for disparity reduction and equality of access to life chances. They therefore do not reflect the CRC and CEDAW approach to the critical issue of poverty. Ghana has taken some policy initiatives such as establishing a girls' education unit, and universities have affirmative action policies on female education. Benin has put in place a policy of not charging school fees for girls in rural areas. Zimbabwe's Poverty Alleviation Plan exempts low-income children from some categories of school fees. Nevertheless, the concept of affirmative action is not reflected in legislation or the constitution as a dimension of realizing the right to equality and non-discrimination. In Botswana, by contrast, a chapter on policy and legislation has been included in the most recent National Plan of Action for Children in an attempt to ensure the recognition and realization of all children's rights.

The concept of an individual child's positive social and economic rights, especially in health and education, has not been integrated into the legal system in the post-CRC period and continues to be perceived as relevant to non-enforceable social and economic policies. This area is a self-regulating one, where the State has a minimal or neutral rather than proactive role. In Zimbabwe and Benin, as in many other African countries, NGOs and the private sector rather than the State play a significant role in service delivery in these areas.[46]

Constitutional jurisprudence discussed earlier clarifies how enforcement strategies, public law and legislative intervention by the State are critical in implementing the CRC standards of children's rights to health and education. Non-governmental organizations can be a catalyst for monitoring state responsibility in this regard, and in cooperating with the State to ensure service delivery and effective planning. However, the CRC and CEDAW impose the primary responsibility in this regard on the State.

The policy-based approach is a provision of basic needs strategy, which is contrary to the perception of legal rights and obligations reflected in international human rights law. The UNDAF and NEPAD process does not appear to have integrated this rights approach in their work, and this has reinforced the social policy approach to children's development rights under the CRC. Treaty bodies for the CRC and ICESCR have commented on the need to adopt the rights perspective in their Concluding Observations on the reports of Benin and Zimbabwe. The failure to adopt a rights approach also has meant that legislation prohibiting child labour, child trafficking, child abuse and customary practices has not impacted as significantly as it could have, if it were supported by interconnected legislative reforms on socio-economic rights of access to health and education.

Method of CRC Incorporation

When legislative reform is introduced to harmonize with the CRC, countries have a choice with regard to either wholesale incorporation of the CRC or selective law reform. The Committee on the Rights of the Child, in its Concluding Observations and its General Comment No. 5 of 2003 on implementation, recommends a general incorporation strategy. Benin, Ghana and Zimbabwe have all adopted a selective approach, prioritizing the areas already discussed for the incorporation of CRC standards. The legislative process has usually resulted in the enactment of some state laws applicable to all children, so as to introduce uniform legal values and procedures and eliminate the choice to opt out.

However, the uniformity is limited to specific matters covered by the legislation. Contradictions and discrepancies in various areas of law remain untouched. Benin's Family Code and Zimbabwe's Children's Act introduce some principles that have a bearing on the general area of child law in the

---

[46] N. Van de Walle et al., eds., *Beyond Structural Adjustments: The Institutional Context of African Development* (New York: Palgrave Macmillan, 2003), Ch. V and p. 18.

country. Only Ghana has adopted the model of a uniformly applicable comprehensive basic Children's Act with general principles harmonizing with the CRC, supplemented by legislation in specific areas of priority and concern for children. Egypt also has introduced a general Children's Act, which incorporates many of the principles of the CRC.

The model of a core Children's Act, supplemented by specific legislation relating to defined areas, seems more appropriate than the wholesale incorporation of the CRC. The treaty is comprehensive and wide in scope. It seems unrealistic to incorporate it totally as a single enactment enforceable in domestic law. It seems more practical to have specific and strong constitutional guarantees as in South Africa, and a uniformly applicable Children's Act, specifying the core principles of the CRC on definition, the best interests of the child, non-discrimination, and the indivisibility of rights. The Ghana Children's Act presents such a model and also refers to the right to education though it does not comprehensively address the indivisibility of rights. Specific laws on matters such as child abuse and child labour must also be enacted. When such select areas are chosen for law reform, it is also useful to amend and reform connected laws. This has been done in Zimbabwe, where the Sexual Offences Act was combined with amendments to the law on evidence and procedure.

Access to legislation also can be facilitated by having a system of consolidating and compiling all laws pertaining to children in one chapter of the legislative enactments of the country. Consolidation means that all existing legislation pertaining to a particular matter is declared in a single statute. Consolidated laws are then compiled as one enactment. This procedure has been adopted in Burkina Faso and in several Asian countries. Codification of laws is a process that goes beyond consolidation. Codification involves a restatement of the law in a particular area, subject to revisions. This process has been used in enacting Benin's Code of Family Law and Ghana's Children's Act. Codification provides an opportunity to harmonize constitutional and treaty standards such as the CRC and CEDAW, retaining positive features in existing law.

The process of codification is especially important in countries with a plural mixed tradition, with received colonial law and customary or religion-based law. Some aspects of these laws can have creative and positive concepts that are especially relevant for the country's economic development. Codification presents an opportunity to eliminate negative features of customary and religion-based law and incorporate them into forward-looking new legislation that harmonizes constitutional and treaty standards. The earlier alternative of giving choice to opt out of customary law becomes irrelevant when uniformly applicable codes can acquire legitimacy by incorporating some positive dimensions of customary law. We have noted that Zimbabwe has adopted a conservative approach to customary law, whereas Benin and

Ghana have, in general, adopted an abolitionist approach, and also introduced a range of uniformly applicable specific laws in the post-CRC period that eliminate choice. This approach is correct when customary practices are harmful and infringe survival development and protection rights. However, customary practices that do not do so, and incorporate positive dimensions such as extended family obligations and the rights of non-marital children, can strengthen the legislative reform project. Burkina Faso's Family Code and Sri Lanka's Maintenance Ordinance (1999) are composite codes that draw on diverse sources of law and also incorporate CRC standards. The codification of Islamic law in Maldives and Egypt has provided similar opportunities to harmonize with CRC and CEDAW standards. When Islamic law is not perceived as a distinct religious law, and is considered another system of customary law, codification and revision becomes a much easier process. The right to freedom of religion can operate as a constraint to reform of Islamic law, through a process of codification in a multireligious country in Asia or Africa.

III. ENFORCEMENT OF THE LAW, POLICIES, INSTITUTIONS, AND BUDGETS

Because the CRC contemplates the indivisibility of social and economic and other human rights, we have noted that the rights relating to education and health should be incorporated into the domestic legal system, through constitutional provisions and legislation.

In all three countries, these important areas are considered discretionary state policies, which are dependent on discretionary budget allocation and resources. The Millennium Development Goals also reflect this approach. For instance, achievement of primary education is identified as one of the goals. The experience of Asia indicates that adequately resourced, compulsory education up to secondary level has increased literacy and life chances for low-income children, particularly girls. The focus on primary education as a social policy is therefore likely to further hamper the effective enforcement of laws that seek to realize the protection rights of children.

It is increasingly evident that the incorporation of institutional arrangements connected with social support programmes and budgetary allocation into laws or as part of the legislation process are critical to ensure effective enforcement. For instance, domestic violence legislation in South Africa and other countries incorporates provisions on access to support facilities such as counselling, legal aid and shelters, and resource allocation. This approach has not been followed. Ghana has incorporated education rights into its laws and also allocated budgetary resources. But, in general, cutbacks on social investment because of conflicting macroeconomic policies have meant that social policies and institutions set up by legislation are inadequately resourced to achieve their objectives. This has meant that the legislation that has been put in place has not had the impact envisaged on the problems it seeks to address.

We have observed that affirmative action policies have been introduced in Benin to foster enrolment of girls from rural areas in schools. Special education measures to prevent girls dropping out of schools have been adopted in Ghana. The Poverty Alleviation Programme in Zimbabwe now gives some relief in payment of school fees to very low-income families. Nevertheless, there is continuing concern with the exploitation of children in child labour, and girls are dropping out of school. Zimbabwe has responded with a National AIDS Action Policy, and it has introduced family support policies that focus on the community's contribution to home-based care and the care of orphans. These policies, however, do not appear to address the need for accessible health care in state medical services. Even though it is known that Botswana is allocating more than 30 per cent of its yearly budget to social services, this has not been reflected in indicators for children, suggesting the need for focused child rights budgeting. This matter was commented on as a major weakness in the monitoring of budget allocation when Botswana reported to the Committee on the Rights of the Child in 2004.[47]

All three countries and Botswana have a diverse range of institutions. The political will in regard to legislative reform on children's rights is also reflected in the creation of these institutions to strengthen the implementation of the laws. However, inadequate allocation of resources, the lack of a broad cadre of professionals with capacity to give leadership and duplication of functions seem to be common problems faced by these institutions.

There are several institutions, such as ombudspersons, human rights commissions and special police units, the impact of which is directly relevant to law enforcement through prosecution and dispute resolution. There are, in addition, a variety of state/government departments and directorates that deal with sectors such as child welfare and social services, child protection, health and education at the national and decentralized provincial or municipal levels. Benin and Ghana have several institutions to deal with juvenile justice and children in conflict with the law. National Commissions on Children have been established in Ghana and Benin and operate as national policy formulation bodies that also deal with law revision and reform. They also coordinate the treaty reporting process. Ghana has, in addition, a Law Reform Commission that also deals with law reform on children's rights. Ad hoc committees deal with specific issues. Benin's ILO/IPEC Programme National Committee is an example. Botswana has an ombudsman who, even though not especially mandated, can deal with children's issues. A National

---

[47] Committee on the Rights of the Child, 'Concluding Observations: Botswana', U.N. Doc. CRC/C/15/Add.242, 3 November 2004, paras. 18–19.

Child Welfare Committee exists, although presently it is dysfunctional. However, the main recommendation of the Committee on the Rights of the Child was the creation of a National Children Council to promote legal reform. Parliament now selects a Committee on Law Reform to carry out the process.

It is not clear how these various institutions connect with state initiatives undertaken under national plans of action and, more recently, poverty alleviation or reduction plans. It is apparent that there is an overload of institutions in an environment of scarce resources. The critical issues of disparity reduction and promoting uniform legal values do not seem to receive attention, although they are critical in mixed legal systems.

Some institutional mechanisms in all three countries and Botswana focus on children's participation and community-based advocacy and monitoring of child rights. Zimbabwe has organized a Children's Parliament and the Committee on the Rights of the Child has commended this initiative in its Concluding Observations of 1996. Yet we have noted that the government also enacted a Corporal Punishment Act and the State Law and Order Maintenance Act, which restricts freedom of speech and expression. Benin has institutionalized Children's Parliaments into its action plan for promoting children's rights. District Assemblies in Ghana are required to foster networking between government agencies. They are required to establish Child Panels, which have a wide mandate to advocate and promote child rights, monitor infringements and offer services for dispute resolution and counselling. Some of these Panels have been established in a few areas. UNICEF and Save the Children have supported informal community groups, known as Child Protection Teams, in identified communities.

There appears to be an informal parallel system that also tries to advocate for children's rights and monitor infringements at community level. These efforts at children's participation and community-based intervention can be an opportunity to promote uniform values and interventions on children, based on the CRC, in place of the diversity that is entrenched in these countries in the approach to children's rights.

Civil or public service reform was prioritized as part of structural adjustment macroeconomic policies. The 'downsizing' that occurred was met with protest, but these reforms have been implemented. It is not clear that this has 'promoted internal efficiency' in Benin. Ghana, Botswana and Zimbabwe introduced systems of performance assessment and contract appointments that are said to have impacted on senior executive positions in the public service.[48] However, there has been no focus on human rights or child rights training for senior bureaucrats.

None of these countries have put in place special budget planning processes that ensure or even encourage adequate budgetary allocation to

---

[48] Van de Walle, op. cit., Ch. IV, p. 125.

support the legislative reforms and institutional change that have been introduced to achieve progress on children's rights. Ghana and Benin have parliamentary committees to monitor budgets, but this has not been used to
focus in particular on children or women, although allocation for both categories would invariably be connected in key areas such as health, education,
justice and protection from exploitation and violence. Budget planning is
also invariably centralized in ministries of finance, and even the decentralized bodies at the provincial and municipal levels have no control of their
budgets. Some laws, such as the compulsory education laws in Ghana and
the victim-friendly courts initiatives in the criminal procedure and evidence
amendment laws in Zimbabwe, should be accompanied by a costing exercise
on implementation. This has not been done. There is, in general, no transparency in regard to the resource allocations system, so there is no opportunity for public scrutiny or civil society participation. Bilaterals support the
national budgets in both Ghana and Benin. However, they do not appear to
use their status under the human rights treaties to promote a rights-based
and good governance approach to allocation and management of national
resources and donor funding.

The fact that budget allocation is critical to implementing laws has
been recognized in some new initiatives in several countries across different regions. These have been originated by the State, as well as national
NGOs, as budgets are considered an issue of national sovereignty.[49]

In South Africa, costing legislation was considered an important dimension of legislative reform on juvenile justice. The Children's Justice Act is a
uniformly applicable statute that, in that plural or mixed jurisdiction, regu-
lates this area in relation to all children. It incorporates various interventions
that require effective service delivery, prosecution in law enforcement, legal
aid, and diversion from courts and prisons. The bill was costed before it was
tabled in Parliament. An NGO, which is a think tank on development issues,
has engaged in analysis and evaluation of budgetary allocation for children
in poverty reduction plans, in relation to commitments in the National Plan
of Action. NGOs in India also have engaged in budget analysis in relation to
human rights commitments. This kind of initiative encourages the use of constitutional bills of rights to challenge policies and administrative decisions
that undermine resource allocation for the social sector. The constitutional
jurisprudence in this regard has been discussed earlier, in discussing constitutional and socio-economic rights.

UNICEF has played an important leadership role in promoting accountability in resource allocation for children's rights through its work in
Ecuador. UNICEF provided expertise to help the government analyze the

---

[49] See R. Gore, 'Influencing Budgets for Children's Rights'. Working Paper. New York:
UNICEF, 2004.

budget, in terms of commitments to children, and also strengthened the capacity of the government to use this information in macroeconomic policy negotiations with the World Bank. The Committee on the Rights of the Child has focused incidentally on budget allocation when making Concluding Observations on issues of access to health and education, or strengthening of child rights institutions within countries. However, the ICESCR Committee has made Concluding Observations that request States parties to use treaty obligations in developing macroeconomic policies in consultation with international financial institutions.

Prosecution and Dispute Resolution

This is an important area for the enforcement of rights. Access to justice and the implementation of laws is traditionally assessed in most legal systems by reference to the effectiveness of the court system and other methods of dispute resolution. Ghana, Zimbabwe and Benin have introduced a single court structure in the post-independence period so that state courts rather than customary courts have the legal status to resolve disputes. They have also introduced a common system of appeals in a judicial hierarchy that consists of low-level courts and superior trial and appellate courts. The apex court in this structure is a Supreme Court, which hears constitutional cases. Benin, however, has established a separate Constitutional Court. Judicial reform seems to have been prioritized in Zimbabwe. Zimbabwe is the only country that introduced amendments to criminal law and evidence to create a victim-friendly court environment to hear children's cases.

The Customary Law and Courts Act 1990 in Zimbabwe created a common system, which linked headmen's courts and chief's courts into the judicial structure. This is consistent with Zimbabwe's approach to customary law. Although Ghana's Constitution recognizes the role of traditional rulers, we have observed that they have no official or legal role in the dispute resolution process. Yet in both Ghana and Benin, traditional rulers, who are usually male, play an important role in dispute resolution in the community. In Ghana, community tribunals have some legal status in juvenile cases under the Court's Act 1993. Their approach to reconciliation and mediation is said to often operate against the interests of women and child victims of violence. For instance, the tradition of *labola* can be used to pressure a girl or woman who is raped to marry the rapist. This intervention is considered in the best interests of the child from a community perspective, but it undermines the legal value of the CRC and the Ghanaian Criminal Code provisions on rape. The traditional method of dispute settlement can thus operate informally but in conflict with state law and the CRC. Mob violence when communities resort to self-help and administer mob justice also has been considered a problem in Benin. This type of phenomenon is a reflection of impatience or a community belief that redress cannot be obtained through the formal state system of prosecution and trials in courts.

In Burkina Faso, a wide publicity campaign at the community-based level accompanied the law reform initiative on a family code. Egypt has similar experience in regard to human rights awareness-raising among Islamic religious leaders who act as judges and engage in dispute resolution. It is necessary to create awareness of human rights among traditional rulers to encourage customary law interpretations in conformity with constitutional guarantees and international human rights. It is important to prevent alternative systems of dispute resolution undermining women's and children's rights protected by state laws and international law. This type of awareness-raising can also help traditional rulers, particularly 'queen mothers' or women traditional rulers, to fulfil their constitutional mandate in Ghana to review customary law and harmonize it with constitutional standards.

The earlier discussion on constitutional jurisprudence and treaty law indicates that superior courts and other courts deciding cases adopt conflicting approaches in regard to the human rights of women and children. In Zimbabwe, positive Supreme Court decisions on juvenile justice and corporal punishment and resident visas for non-citizen male spouses have been undermined by subsequent legislation enacted by Parliament. Legislation on equal inheritance rights has not prevented judicial decision making that denies women equal rights of inheritance. Yet several leading cases in Zimbabwe have interpreted the law on resident visas of the foreign spouses of Zimbabweans on the basis of obligations of family support for children and spouses.[50]

In Ghana and Benin, the courts sometimes recognize the human rights of women and children and, at other times, pronounce negative judgements. The best interests concept is also sometimes interpreted in maintenance and custody cases in Zimbabwe in a culturally relativist manner to justify interpretations that conflict with CRC and constitutional standards.[51] The lack of consistency is not uncommon in legal systems in which judges do not interpret principles on judicial precedent, in harmony with core norms in the constitution or the law on children's rights. An understanding of human rights can impact to prevent conflicting approaches in the courts.

---

[50] Citizenship Act (2001) (Maldives); Citizenship Amendment Act (2003) (Sri Lanka); *Rattigan* case, op. cit.; *Salem* case, op. cit.; Corporal Punishment Act (1996) (Zimb.); *Kohilhas* case, op. cit.; *A Juvenile v State* (1989) 2 ZLR 61, per Gubbay J. A.; Constitution of Zimbabwe Amendment (No. 14) Act (1996).

[51] Owinson, op. cit.; B. Duncan, 'Cultural Practices Affecting Child Maintenance in Ghana' (New York: UNICEF, 2004); Rwezaura, op. cit.; Banda, 'Inheritance and Marital Rape in Zimbabwe', op. cit.; Armstrong, op. cit.; Banda, 'Custody and the Best Interests of the Child: Another View from Zimbabwe', op. cit.

Superior court judges in particular need to perceive themselves as responsible to safeguard human rights in an environment conducive to judicial independence. As the Bloemfontein Statement of Commonwealth judges declares "Fundamental rights and freedoms are more than paper aspirations. It is the province of judges to ensure that laws are realized in the daily lives of the people. The judges bear the particular responsibility to ensure that the legislature, the executive and the judiciary itself conform to the legal principles."[52] It is in this spirit that leading cases in Commonwealth jurisdictions have decided that the ratification of an international treaty creates legitimate expectations that administrative decisions, in the absence of legislative or executive indications to the contrary, will harmonize with the Convention.[53] The professionalism, capacity and independence of the judiciary is therefore critical to achieving progress on the human rights agenda, including the project on women and children's rights.

The state system in all countries is staffed by a cadre of judges who are usually lawyers or have legal training. Children's and women's cases are often heard by low-level magistrates' courts, family courts or juvenile courts. In Zimbabwe, these magistrates can even be civil servants who lack legal training. The inadequate training of these judges is sometimes said to make them more susceptible to political pressures. Allegations of interference with the judiciary have been highlighted in the cases of Zimbabwe and Benin. Judicial independence is also undermined when legislation is introduced, as in Zimbabwe, to undermine a Supreme Court decision in harmony with child rights. In Botswana, by contrast, the government eventually respected the decision of the Court in the *Unity Dow* case and amended its Citizenship Act to conform to the Constitution.

All three countries have an established state court system, and there are judges who exercise their responsibilities with commitment and professionalism. The jurisprudence that has emerged in constitutional cases, as well as the manner in which judges decide other cases, reinforces the commonly held view that judicial training on human rights and child rights is critical for effective law enforcement. In Benin, the Constitutional Court has been invited to events of the Children's Parliament, and there have been ad hoc workshops for judges. The Ghana Law Commission also conducts sensitization workshops for judges and lawyers. There is no evidence of consistent training for judges in any of these countries or the incorporation of child rights in legal education. This has impacted on the quality of judicial decision making, where conflicting decisions have been pronounced in court

---

[52] 'The Bloemfontein Statement' in *Developing Human Rights Jurisprudence, Vol. 6: Sixth Judicial Colloquium on the Domestic Application of International Human Rights Norms, Bloemfontein, South Africa, 3–5 Sept. 1993* (London: Commonwealth Secretariat, 1999).

[53] *Minister of State for Immigration v Teoh*, (1995) 183 CLR 273 (Austl.); *Travita v Minister of Immigration*, (1994) 2 NZLR 257 (N.Z.).

cases relevant to children's and women's rights. The political environment for judicial independence also must be strengthened and supported by the highest levels of national and international scrutiny.

The formal court system's role in dispute settlement and prosecution has been supplemented by other institutions connected to law enforcement, in all countries. Special units on women and juveniles in the Ghana Police Service, and victim-friendly units of the Zimbabwe police, have been established to strengthen the response to child abuse cases and juvenile justice problems. The Brigade for the Protection of Minors functions in a similar manner in Benin's Police Service. Special human rights instruments function in all four countries. Thus, Zimbabwe has adopted the institution of the ombudsman, whereas Ghana and Benin have established human rights commissions. Their work seems to duplicate the work of child rights commissions in these countries. However, there is a difference in that ombudsperson procedures and human rights commissions have a distinct responsibility to receive complaints, investigate violations, resolve disputes, or channel them to courts and relevant authorities for redress. They thus incorporate investigative powers and a complaints procedure. These commissions have to report to Parliament and interact with civil society, NGOs, and the public. This means that they also can be a catalyst for promoting law reform, institutional change, and resource allocation for strengthening the implementation of human rights. They can promote transparency and accountability in governance and public administration.[54]

The CERD Committee has observed in its Concluding Observations of 2002 that the Zimbabwe ombudsperson is empowered to deal with a limited range of cases in which infringements by public officials occur. The government in its report to the Committee on the Rights of the Child in 1996 said that children's cases would be included. It is not clear that women and children's complaints are addressed. Ghana's Commission on Human Rights and Administrative Justice, established in 1993 by Act of Parliament, has a mandate to deal with children's and women's rights violations. The Commission has decentralized its work to the regions. It is active in human rights awareness-raising programmes.

The Commission works with NGOs. It has been acknowledged as one of the best in Africa. It is not clear that the Commission has played a role in reaching traditional rulers with a view to catalysing them as a force to realize human rights in their committees. This Commission has up to now received most complaints in family-related 'private matters'. It can make an important contribution to transforming stereotypical attitudes that are negative to women and children's rights through its work.

---

[54] J. Hatchard, 'A New Brand of Institutions: Human Rights Commissions in Commonwealth Africa' in *Comparative and International Journal of Southern Africa* 32 (1999), p. 26.

Ghana also has established a National Civic Education Commission, which is mandated to raise awareness on the constitutional protection of human rights. The Commission has conducted awareness-raising programmes on harmful customary practices. The institutional linkages between these two bodies are not clear but are necessary to avoid duplication and inconsistencies. Benin has a Consultative Committee on Human Rights, which meets twice a year. It has NGO representation and is meant to promote a dialogue between government and these organizations on the implementation of human rights. It is similar to parliamentary consultative committees on human rights found in many countries. The Committee does not duplicate the work of the National Commission. It merely provides space for a focus on children's and women's rights issues of critical concern and raises the administration's and government's awareness on priorities for reform. Benin also has a committee that monitors the human rights treaties, coordinating preparation of all treaty body reports, including those to the Committee on the Rights of the Child.

The term 'civil society' is currently used in many countries to refer to organized national groups that are active in lobbying advocacy and service delivery in areas of concern to the community. More recently, individual activists who work professionally in their personal capacity without an organization base also are considered to reflect the views of 'civil society'. Because these individuals often have stature in their society as community leaders and support the work of established NGOs or community-based groups, the organizational link is invariably present.

Civil society in this sense has been active on human rights and children's rights issues in all these countries. We have noted in discussing the process of reform that they have been an important influence in promoting legislative reform in key areas of concern to children and women. They have worked with regional and international NGOs and international organizations to ensure that social and economic issues of concern have been addressed nationally by governments. Governments in all countries have provided a space for civil society activities, perceiving them as partners and often transferring to them the responsibilities for service delivery in important sectors. Despite the fact that the environment on civil and political rights seems to have deteriorated in recent years in Zimbabwe, civil society continues to function and appears to have been given the space to work on women's and children's rights concerns.

We have noted in discussions on the constitutions that civil society has not played the significant role that it has in come countries, that is, to challenge human rights infringements through the courts. This is unusual, given that the regional instruments, constitution and the human rights institutions provide space for this activism. Indeed, the African Charter on Children's Rights incorporated a complaints procedure and has widened standing to enable NGOs to address the African Committee monitoring the Charter. Only Zimbabwe's legal system seems familiar with the concept of class action suits, and public interest litigation on rights has not been developed in these countries. Civil society organizations have a role to play in this regard by filing test cases on infringements of women and children's rights on behalf of those affected, in the apex courts. At the moment, they focus on service delivery and awareness-raising, including legal literacy work. Legal aid facilities with limited coverage also are provided by some NGOs, including women's groups that operate in providing such programmes. The treaty bodies provide opportunities for dialogue with NGOs at their regular sessions. They also request States parties to distribute Concluding Observations to civil societies and ensure wide publicity. It is not clear whether NGOs in these countries participate in these meetings, or whether they use the Concluding Observations of the Committee on the Rights of the Child and the Committee on the Elimination of Discrimination against Women in their work.

CONCLUSIONS

The three countries concerned in this study have a population that is mainly young and female. In the country context, critical problems that affect children in general impact on women. There is an interface between realizing the human rights of women and children, and a link between constitutional and international human rights standards in CEDAW and the CRC. The interventions taken to realize children's rights thus have a bearing on women's human rights and national progress in regard to the general human rights situation within these countries. The ratification of the CRC has catalysed a process to integrate these standards in all three countries. Botswana is a country that has an especially important comparative experience on post-CRC reform. This process of reform also has reinforced interventions to integrate CEDAW, by addressing in particular issues of gender discrimination, protection against violence and sexual exploitation.

The CRC presents an ideology of indivisibility of rights and solidarity or partnership in realizing rights. The key duty holders are States, but there is also a responsibility imposed on parents, families, civil society including the corporate sector and the international community to realize rights. The State's obligation goes beyond the traditional negative role of protecting children from infringements. They are required to respect and promote rights, prevent infringements by their agencies and private non-state action and also to intervene positively to fulfil rights. This ideology creates a new approach to law-making. Laws become not just a declaratory statement of norms and standards but also one dimension of a range of measures to realize rights. This has special relevance for these and other developing countries, as law-making and legislative efforts must now be integrated with measures such as institutional development, social policy and budgetary and resource allocation.

Experience in all these countries suggests that implementation has been weak. Often this has been because legislation and standard-setting to harmonize the CRC have not been integrated with these 'other measures', which now must be an intrinsic part of the law-making process. The Committee on the Rights of the Child itself, in its Concluding Observations, sometimes makes a distinction between 'legislation' and 'other measures'. The country experience on ineffective implementation of legislation and poor impact of laws suggests a link between legislation and 'other measures'. This seems essential to achieving real progress on rights. The concept of partnership between state and non-state action and indivisibility of rights is also the core of the human rights–based approach to economic development and growth.

The experience in these countries reveals that the State and civil society have worked together on children's issues. Children and youth, however, have not been actively involved in this effort because there has been no real progress in addressing participation rights. Despite the diversity in the political environment of these countries, and a deterioration of the civil and political rights situation in Zimbabwe, all countries have afforded space for partnership with civil society. However, it is clear that an open democratic process gives a wider opportunity for transparency in policy formulation and resource allocation and public and judicial scrutiny of government and corporate sector performance. The independence of the judiciary needs to be fostered and strengthened in all countries. Civil society and the international community should use the ratification of international treaties, including the CRC and CEDAW, to legitimize public scrutiny of government, and obtain greater accountability from government on respecting judicial independence. Constitutional provisions on the independence of the judiciary must be revisited. Creating an open democratic environment with an independent judiciary is crucial for obtaining accountability from government in realizing the full range of development, protection and participation rights of children.

All three countries and others such as Botswana have initiated a reform process, reformed some laws and created new institutions after ratifying the CRC. The approach has not been holistic and often has not taken into account reforms in customary law. However, countries such as Botswana are now trying to review the earlier reform processes to initiate comprehensive reforms, including of customary law. Consultative and interactive processes to engage communities, families, children, traditional leaders and chiefs in the reform agenda have commenced.

All countries considered in this study have given priority to reform in the area of protection rights. This is so even in Zimbabwe, which currently has a difficult political and human rights environment. The fact that all three countries have adopted structural adjustment policies has meant that socio-economic rights of children and integrating these into national plans of action and poverty reduction efforts have not been addressed. Only Ghana has retained commitments to giving equitable access to health and education. National plans therefore do not refer to or connect with law reform efforts. None of these countries have adequately focused on participation rights. Although the concept of children's parliaments and child advocates on community issues have been integrated into state programmes, these emerge as a token involvement of children. The education system has not been used effectively to foster participation rights or to forge uniform CRC values that undermine negative customary and social practices. Child participation projects of other countries can be of comparative interest and generate rethinking how to foster participation rights within the CRC concept of a child's evolving capacity. Protection rights cannot be realized effectively without achieving progress in regard to realizing children's development and participation rights. This is clear from the difficulties experienced in enforcing laws on child labour, early marriage and trafficking.

Development and participation rights are particularly important in mixed jurisdictions, where governments must face the challenge of disparity reduction in a multi-ethnic and-religious environment. These rights, if realized, can help to create a uniform base of laws and social values. Achieving children's rights requires non-discrimination and equal life chances for children of all communities. Yet customary laws often give legitimacy to practices that infringe these rights. It often results in discrimination and the denial of life chances, for women and girls in particular. Colonialism has had the impact of creating separate courts for customary law cases and recognizing the choice to be governed by these laws rather than state laws. Laws enacted in the colonial period have often entrenched negative and discriminatory seventeenth- to nineteenth-century values in European law on the status of women and children in the community. These colonial laws undermine any positive attributes of customary law and reinforce the negative values on women and children in customary law. These laws are therefore sometimes based on norms that conflict with CRC standards. Although the concept of 'the best interests' of the child entered legal systems as part of received colonial law and has a positive impact in some court cases, it is sometimes interpreted in a culturally relativist manner so as to reinforce negative values that conflict with the CRC. Post-independence legislative reform has not adequately addressed the challenge of comprehensively reforming customary law or the received colonial law and introducing uniform laws in harmony with the CRC and CEDAW. Children's acts and specific acts have only introduced a few laws applicable to all children in conformity with the CRC.

Ghana's approach to adopting a general children's act, based on the CRC with basic concepts and special laws in specific areas, is a useful model for reform. This appears to be the approach that will be adopted in Botswana. Current reforms are important and must be sustained, while expanding uniform laws. Codification of laws in specific areas is a strategy for introducing uniformity and introducing a rights approach based on the CRC and CEDAW into the substantive law of a country. Codification also provides an opportunity to introduce connected reforms in areas of evidence and procedure, which are critical for effective prosecution and law enforcement. Zimbabwe's connected reforms on criminal procedure and evidence, for instance, accompanied the Sexual Offences Act. Bringing all the laws on children into one book of legislative enactments by compilation also facilitates access to information on these laws. Botswana's human rights–based approach to law reform adopted in revising the Children's Act is also a useful initiative. It has led to the inclusion of customary law issues in the legislative reform process and paved the way for collaboration with traditional leaders and institutions.

Judicial reforms have created a common courts structure and an appeals system. However, inconsistency and discrepancies in judicial decision making have prevented the courts from responding creatively to modifying customary law and expanding the scope of uniformly applicable laws. Jurisprudence on customary law also can contribute to the reform process as there are concepts that link with international human rights norms. There is an urgent need for judicial training and legal education integrating international human rights, including children's and women's rights. Judicial colloquia that bring judges in the region with a common legal tradition together can be an effective way of creating sensitivity, professionalism and independence in protecting human rights guaranteed in the constitution and treaties. The Victim Friendly Courts Committee in Zimbabwe is a useful initiative involving judges. This type of committee provides an opportunity to bring judges into the reform process and expose them to the new ideology of child rights.

Legislation has been enacted to change customary law, and Benin's legal system adopts an abolitionist approach. This facilitates such law-making. However, post-independence constitutions with bills of rights present a better opportunity to scrutinize government performance on human rights and promote uniformly applicable standard setting and law reform in regard to children's and women's rights. The argument that uniformly applicable legislation is 'Western' and 'colonial' can be countered when it is based on constitutions that incorporate bills of fundamental rights. Such bills of rights reinforce obligations in ratified human rights treaties including the CRC and CEDAW and the African Charters. Even when countries adopt a monist approach to international law and consider treaties such as the CRC and CEDAW that have been ratified a part of domestic law, there is usually no procedure for enforcement. Domestic constitutional guarantees, by contrast, provide opportunity for judicial activism in linking with international treaty standards, including the CRC and CEDAW, and realizing rights. Constitutional jurisprudence also linked to regional standards can help to challenge colonial laws and domestic legislation that infringes children's and women's rights. It can promote political will in introducing reform in controversial areas of customary law so as to eliminate negative customary practices. Regional standards in the African Charters on Human Rights have not yet been used in constitutional jurisprudence as they should be, to review and eliminate, which encourage the elimination of negative customary practices.

Public interest litigation has not been developed in these countries and is not used by NGOs that are active on child rights issues. They have engaged in legal literacy work, service delivery and advocacy, but have not used the litigation system. They should be able to bring test cases using the experience of other countries in Asia and Africa, such as South Africa. An engagement of interest in this area also could lead to more focused advocacy and activism on children's rights connected to reporting to the treaty bodies and their Concluding Observations. NGOs and civil society groups have been active and worked with the South African Human Rights Commission. However, advocacy has not been focused on areas such as resource allocation, disparity reduction and undermining pluralism in the laws. It seems important for NGOs and civil society groups to lobby for changes in constitutions to strengthen enforcement of the bill of rights and the power of judicial review. Such changes can give legitimacy to judicial activism and scrutiny of government commitment in promoting human rights. Governments will find it difficult to bring legislation to undermine or ignore court decisions, or undermine the integrity of the judiciary. A strong bill of rights also legitimizes public and international scrutiny of a government's performance in respecting, promoting, protecting and fulfiling rights.

Traditional rulers no longer have an official role and responsibility in dispute settlement in the three countries considered in the study. They do have an official role in Botswana. It is clear that in any case they are all in fact involved in dispute resolution at the community level. Ghana's Constitution gives them a role and responsibility in catalysing law reform, and similar provisions are found in Botswana legislation. Botswana's recent efforts to reform the Children's Act in 2003 have targeted chiefs, and the government has initiated a consultative process that is very important. Neither state institutions nor NGO groups have adequately targeted this sector in human rights awareness programmes. Some countries in Asia have legalized alternative dispute resolution and provide training for mediators. Introducing laws on alternative dispute resolution, and formalizing the process, offer an opportunity to ensure that human rights and CRC norms are integrated into traditional community-based dispute settlement. Formalizing the process also can help to prevent the operation of a de facto dispute resolution system that is in conflict with state laws integrating the CRC.

Constitutional guarantees with effective enforcement procedures are especially important in promoting transparency and accountability in resource allocation and macroeconomic policies so as not to sacrifice the social sector. They also can be used to scrutinize budgets and sustain resource allocation in this area, despite changes of government and global economic pressures. They can promote the accountability and partnership of the private sector and the international community that the CRC envisages. Equal opportunities and non-discrimination legislation also can strengthen constitutional guarantees and include the private sector, whose acts are sometimes not covered by the constitution. Constitutional guarantees and enforcement procedure are especially important because they provide governments with a rationale for negotiating with the international donors and financial institutions on the basis of treaty obligations and constitutional commitments. They can try to use these obligations to resist pressure to cut back on expenditure on the social sector and negotiate for debt relief, debt reduction or moratoriums or even debt cancellation. Article 4 of the CRC, in particular, calls for international cooperation in realizing children's rights. The recent tsunami disaster in Asian countries has promoted unprecedented consensus on the need for debt relief, debt moratoriums, and debt cancellation. The international community, including the international financial institutions, has pledged support for national programmes for rehabilitation and reconstruction. The corporate and private sectors have been persuaded to support this effort, including the sharing of scientific information and early warning systems on natural disasters. Ironically, these efforts have already been described as state, international community and private sector obligations in the CRC.

Although many laws have been passed to address critical child rights protection issues, adequate national budget resources have not been allocated to enable these institutions to function efficiently. A multiplicity of institutions have been created without adequate attention to the resulting duplication of functions and financial and human resources. Institutions such as national commissions, human rights commissions, national children councils and ombudspersons are important. But they need to be well resourced and they must not overlap with other institutions. The South African practice of incorporating resource analysis into legislation at the bill stage can strengthen institutional development. It also can ensure social investments that are critical to effectively enforce and implement legislation.

Both national poverty alleviation plans and national action plans for children must support the implementation of laws by integrating a rights approach to investment in the social sector. While the critical issue of poverty reduction has not been addressed, the enforcement of rights protected by law has also been prejudiced. Although countries have tried to initiate legislative reform to integrate the CRC, their achievements have been very limited partly because of the macroeconomic policies that they have often been required to follow because of their status as highly indebted poor countries (HIPCs) and the pressure from international financial institutions. These countries need to be supported in their endeavours to realize their commitments under international conventions, including the CRC and CEDAW. There is an urgent need to reassess these policies in harmony with human rights–based development and the concept of a 'social trust' placed upon government and its local and international partners to strengthen good governance and manage national resources in the public interest. As Julius Nyere once said, "Only as poverty is reduced, will existing political freedoms be properly meaningful, and the right to human dignity become a fact of human dignity."[55] Poverty reduction through recognition of basic needs as basic rights is essential to make a State's legislative reform project meaningful, and to realize the promise of Article 4 of the CRC.

BIBLIOGRAPHY

Zimbabwe

Committee on the Elimination of Discrimination against Women. 'Initial report of States Parties: Zimbabwe'. U.N. Doc. CEDAW/C/ZWE /1. 20 July 1996.

Committee on the Elimination of Racial Discrimination. 'Concluding Observations of the Committee on the Elimination of Racial Discrimination: Zimbabwe'. U.N. Doc. CERD/C/304/Add.92. 19 Apr. 2000.

Committee on the Elimination of Racial Discrimination. 'Fourth periodic reports of States parties due in 1998 (Addendum): Zimbabwe'. U.N. Doc. CERD/C/329/Add.1. 20 Oct. 1998.

Committee on the Rights of the Child. 'Initial reports of States parties due in 1992 (Addendum): Zimbabwe'. U.N. Doc. CRC/C/3/Add.35. 12 Sept. 1995.

Economic and Social Council. 'Implementation of the International Covenant on Economic, Social and Cultural Rights: Initial reports submitted by States parties under articles 16 and 17 of the Covenant (Addendum): Zimbabwe'. U.N. Doc. E/1990/5/Add.28. 25 Sept. 1995.

Human Rights Committee. 'Initial reports of States parties due in 1992 (Addendum): Zimbabwe'. U.N. Doc. CCPR/C/74/Add.3. 29 Sept. 1997.

Isanga, A. et al. *Children's and Women's Rights in Zimbabwe: Theory and Practice.* Harare: UNICEF Zimbabwe, 2002.

Khan, N. 'National Study of Zimbabwe'. Unpublished study for the Legislative Reform Initiative, UNICEF, 2004.

New York Times International. 16 Oct. 2004.

'Student Leader Battles for Life'. *Zimbabwe Standard.* 17 Oct. 2004 (Zim Online (S.A), 19 Oct. 2004, www.zwnews.com/issuefull.cfm?ArticleID=10399).

Sunday Mirror Zimbabwe. 17 Oct. 2004.

U.S. Department of Labor, Bureau of International Affairs. 'Child Labour Report: Zimbabwe'. 8 Oct. 2004.

U.S. Department of State. *Country Reports on Human Rights Practices – 1999: Zimbabwe.* 23 Feb. 2000. www.state.gov/g/drl/rls/hrrpt/1999/279.htm.

---

[55] As cited, Kamchedzera, op. cit., p. 556.

Benin

Committee on Economic, Social and Cultural Rights. 'Concluding Observations of the Committee on Economic, Social and Cultural Rights: Benin'. U.N. Doc. E/C12/1Add.78. 5 June 2002.

Committee on the Rights of the Child. 'Concluding Observations of the Committee on the Rights of the Child: Benin'. U.N. Doc. CRC/C/15/Add.106. 24 Aug. 1999.

Committee on the Rights of the Child. 'Initial reports of States parties due in 1992 (Addendum): Benin'. U.N. Doc. CRC/C/3/Add.52. 4 July 1997.

Dako, F. 'Study Report on the Initiatives of Reforms Related to the CRC in Benin'. Unpublished study for Legislative Reform Initiative, UNICEF, 2004.

Economic and Social Council. 'Implementation of the International Covenant on Economic, Social and Cultural Rights: Initial Reports Submitted by States Parties under Articles 16 and 17 of the Covenant (Addendum): Benin'. U.N. Doc. E/1990/5/Add.48. 5 Sept. 2001.

Human Rights Committee. 'Consideration of reports submitted by States parties under Article 40 of the Covenant, Initial report: Benin'. U.N. Doc. CCPR/C/BEN/2004/1. 16 Feb. 2004.

U.S. Department of State, *Country Reports on Human Rights Practices – 2002: Benin*. 31 Mar. 2003. www.state.gov/g/drl/rls/hrrpt/2002/18168.htm.

Ghana

Committee on the Elimination of Discrimination against Women. 'Concluding Observations of the Committee on the Elimination of Discrimination against Women: Ghana'. CEDAW/C/GHA/1-2, 1992.

Committee on the Elimination of Racial Discrimination. 'Concluding Observations of the Committee on the Elimination of Racial Discrimination: Ghana'. U.N. Doc. CERD/C/62/CO/4. 2 June 2003.

Committee on the Elimination of Racial Discrimination. 'Seventeenth periodic reports of States parties due in 2002 (Addendum): Ghana'. U.N. Doc. CERD/C/431/Add.3. 1 Oct. 2002.

Committee on the Rights of the Child. 'Concluding Observations of the Committee on the Rights of the Child: Ghana'. U.N. Doc. CRC/C/15/Add.73. 18 June 1997.

Committee on the Rights of the Child. 'Initial reports of States parties due in 1992 (Addendum): Ghana'. U.N. Doc. CRC/C/3/Add.39. 19 Dec. 1995.

Duncan, B. 'Presentation on Cultural Practices Affecting Child Maintenance in Ghana'. Accra: UNICEF Ghana, 2004.

Quashigah, K. 'Legislative Reform Initiatives, Institutional Development and Policy Changes in Favour of Children: A Ghana National Study'. Unpublished study for Legislative Reform Initiative, UNICEF, 2004.

Botswana

Committee on the Rights of the Child. 'Concluding Observations: Botswana', U.N. Doc. CRC/C/15/Add.242. 3 Nov. 2004.

Kamchedzera, G. 'A report of the Multisectoral Reference Group on the Legislative Reform Initiative and the Children's Reference Group' (Botswana). Unpublished study for the Legislative Reform Initiative, UNICEF, 2004.

General Resources

Imam F. Abdul Rauf. *What's Right with Islam*. San Francisco: Harper Collins, 2004.

Alston, P. ed. *The Best Interests of the Child: Reconciling Culture and Human Rights*. Oxford: Clarendon Press, 1994.

Anderson, J. N. D., ed. *Family Law in Asia and Africa*. London: Allen & Unwin, 1968.

Bainham, A., ed. *The International Survey of Family Law 2001*. London: Jordon Publishing Ltd., 2001.

Comparative and International Law Journal of Southern Africa, Vols. 1998–2002.

Cook, P. 'The Role of Culture in Implementing and Monitoring Children's Rights' in *Understanding Children's Rights*, edited by E. Verhellen, p. 67. Ghent, Belgium: University of Ghent, 1998.

Elias, T. O. *Law in a Developing Society*. Ibadan, Nigeria: Ibadan University Press, 1973.

Europa. *Regional Survey of the World: Africa South of the Sahara*. London and New York: Europa Publications, 33rd edn. 2004.

Gore, R. 'Influencing Budgets for Children's Rights'. Working Paper. New York: UNICEF, 2004.

Merton, R. et. al. *International Women's Rights Cases*. London: Cavendish Publishing Ltd., 2005: pp. 572+.

Nundy, K. 'The Global Status of Legislative Reform related to Convention on the Rights of the Child'. Unpublished paper for Legislative Reform Initiative, UNICEF, 2004.

United Nations. *Bringing International Human Rights Law Home*. New York: United Nations, 2000.

United Nations Children's Fund. *Law Reform to Implement the Convention on the Rights of the Child: Background Paper*. Florence: UNICEF Innocenti Research Centre, 2004.

United Nations Children's Fund. *Legislative Measures in 50 States Parties to the CRC: Preliminary Overview*. Florence: UNICEF Innocenti Research Centre, 2004.

United Nations Children's Fund. *The State of the World's Children 2004*. New York: UNICEF, 2003.

United Nations Development Programme. *Human Development Report 2004*. New York: UNDP, 2004.

Van de Walle, N. et al., eds. *Beyond Structural Adjustment*. New York: Palgrave Macmillan, 2003.

van Genguglen, W. and C. Perez-Bustello. *The Poverty of Rights*. London and New York: Zed Books, 2001.

Verhellen, E., ed. *Understanding Children's Rights*. Ghent, Belgium: University of Ghent, 1998.

Index